GL - 331-32
read 247 →

Ruth Rosborough-Larocca
April 28, 1994

# GARY NULL

# HEALING YOUR BODY NATURALLY

**Alternative Treatments
to Illness**

# GARY NULL
# HEALING YOUR BODY NATURALLY

## Alternative Treatments
## to Illness

WINGS BOOKS

New York • Avenel, New Jersey

This book is not intended to replace the services of a physician. Any application of the recommendations set forth in the following pages is at the reader's discretion. The reader should consult with his or her own physician concerning the recommendations made in this book.

This 1994 edition is published by Wings Books,
distributed by Outlet Book Company, Inc., a Random House Company,
40 Engelhard Avenue, Avenel, New Jersey 07001,
by arrangement with the author.

Random House
New York • Toronto • London • Sydney • Auckland

Book design by Kathryn Wolgast


Printed and bound in the United States of America

**Library of Congress Cataloging-in-Publication Data**

Null, Gary.
    Healing your body naturally : alternative treatments to illness /
Gary Null.
      p.   cm.
    Updated and rev. ed. of: Gary Null's complete guide to healing
your body naturally. 1992.
    Includes bibliographical references.
    ISBN 0-517-09301-4
    1. Alternative medicine—Popular works.  I. Null, Gary.  Gary
Null's complete guide to healing your body naturally.  II. Title.
R733.N85  1994
615.5′3—dc20                    93-21315
                                    CIP


8  7  6  5  4  3  2  1

# CONTENTS

# Acknowledgments

This book represents 25 years of accumulating important data on alternative healing systems. During this time I have interviewed more than 6,000 individuals and reviewed tens of thousands of pages of transcripts containing essential information on the subject of this book.

Most of the leading preventive medicine physicians in the United States and Europe have been interviewed for background material. These include Drs. James Anderson, Lawrence Burton, Stanislaw R. Burzynski, Alan Cott, William Crook, Claude Frazier, Charlotte Gerson, Ross Gordon, Abram Hoffer, Josef Issels, Morton Jacobs, Richard Kunin, Ira Laufer, Alan Levin, Virginia Livingston, Marshall Mandell, John McDougall, Janice Phelps, William Philpott, Richard Podell, Alan Pressman, Theron Randolph, Doris Rapp, Emanuel Revici, William Rhea, Michael Schacter, Priscilla Slagle, Julian Whitaker, and Ray Wunderlich.

In addition, I would like to give special thanks to David Merrill, whose research and journalistic and editorial assistance were invaluable in the course of reviewing and synopsizing dozens of hours of taped interviews, hundreds of research papers, and at least 600 pages of manuscript.

The original production was helped immeasurably by the publisher of *Omni* and *Penthouse* magazines, Bob Guccione, with whom I have had a rewarding working relationship for the past 15 years.

I am also grateful to Trudi Golobic, Esq., whose writing, editing, research, and synopsizing assisted me greatly.

Finally, I wish to thank Dr. Martin Feldman, whose critical review as medical overseer allowed for a more objective and balanced presentation.

Needless to say, no book is complete without the gifted hand of a caring, knowledgeable, and professional editor. This I had in the persons of Leslie Meredith and Elisabeth Jakab.

# CHAPTER ONE

# Mental Illness

## Traditional and Alternative Approaches to Mental Health

Mental illness is a serious problem in the United States. Schizophrenia, depression, anxiety, and other mental problems affect children and adults alike. Traditional treatments of these disorders since Sigmund Freud invented his "talking cure" have included psychoanalysis, various other psychotherapies, and more recently, drug-induced behavior modification.

In *psychoanalysis,* the therapist helps the patient retrace his or her past in order to attain an understanding of the cause of the patient's irrational behavior. Whether this insight actually helps patients overcome such behavior, however, remains controversial, and a wide variety of psychotherapies have developed that claim greater effectiveness than traditional psychoanalysis. *Psychiatry* is concerned not so much with having patients explore the roots of their behavior as with directly intervening with pharmaceutical aids to render the behavior more socially acceptable. While psychotropic drugs can be dramatically effective in some cases of depression, psychosis, and anxiety, some patients are not helped, some require long-term treatment with drugs that have serious side effects, and others become addicted to antianxiety medications.

In this chapter we will explore alternatives to the traditional therapies. Our primary focus will be on *orthomolecular psychiatry,* a form of mental health care based on restoring the patient's psychological balance and biochemical harmony. It views mental illness in a new way, treating mental disorders as outgrowths of nutritional or other metabolic deficiencies or imbalances. Orthomolecular psychiatrists are not limited to trying to uncover the past to determine why specific behavioral patterns and abnormalities have evolved. They are forward-looking, taking active and constructive dietary and nutritional steps to help patients behave more rationally. For instance, Dr. Richard Kunin, a psychiatrist in private practice in San Francisco, supplements this treatment with behavioral approaches to help patients who have been sick most of their lives learn how to interact in socially appropriate ways.

The orthomolecular psychiatrist is also concerned with uncovering sensitivities to foods, chemicals, or environmental pollutants that may affect the patient's behavior adversely. Since this treatment is based essentially on nutritional rebalancing, it is nontoxic and safe and usually does not entail adjunctive drug therapies.

If you are suffering from mental or emotional disorders, you should certainly explore this approach before starting years of unduly expensive and often fruitless psychoanalysis or psychotherapy or subjecting yourself to the potentially harmful mind-altering drugs employed by psychiatrists that can exacerbate rather than alleviate your problems. It makes sense to find out whether your "emotional" problems have a physical cause before proceeding with a minute analysis of your history or psyche!

### Orthomolecular Psychiatry

The psychiatric profession's control over the manner in which mental disorders are treated in this country is undeniably very strong but by no means goes unchallenged. Discouraged by the results and

2

opposed to the invasive and toxic nature of the treatments utilized by mainstream practitioners, certain physicians specializing in mental health began to look for alternatives to the excesses of the traditional approach. These physicians, many of whom were themselves psychiatrists, studied the effects of food allergies, nutrition, vitamins, minerals, and amino acids in the treatment of such conditions as schizophrenia, depression, anxiety, and hyperactivity and autism occurring especially in children.

One of these alternative approaches is orthomolecular psychiatry. The term "orthomolecular" was coined by Nobel Prize laureate Linus Pauling in an article written for *Science* magazine in 1968 and refers to the preservation of good health and the treatment of disease by supplying optimal concentrations of substances that are required for good health and are normally present in the body. The term stems from the Greek *ortho* meaning "to correct." As used by Dr. Pauling, it refers to the correction of imbalances within the body through the use of vitamins, minerals, amino acids, and other naturally occurring nutrients. Orthomolecular physicians believe that with these substances there is less of a chance of harmful side effects and a greater potential for cure.

Dr. Michael Lesser, an orthomolecular psychiatrist practicing in Berkeley, California, who is the founder and president of the Orthomolecular Society of America, feels that orthomolecular medicine is more in keeping with the type of therapeutic care associated with Hippocrates, the Greek physician whom many regard as "the father of medicine." He notes that Hippocrates believed in treating illnesses by using their opposites. In other words, if your affliction is caused by too much stress, you should be taught relaxation techniques. Your depression or memory loss may be caused by a copper excess, which can be offset by increasing your level of zinc. Orthomolecular medicine involves balancing the nutrients in the body.

If you are in need of professional care for mental health, keep in mind some of the main differences between orthomolecular and traditional medicine. Orthomolecular practitioners identify and treat the root cause of a disease. Their objective is to rebalance and rebuild the whole body, not merely to mask or suppress symptoms. To do this, they try to establish an equilibrium among the essential nutrients that may be lacking, may be present in excess, or are being poorly absorbed by the body. The imbalance of minerals, vitamins, or amino acids may be the cause of your psychiatric problems.

An example of orthomolecular care is provided by a patient treated by Dr. Yaryura Tobias, an orthomolecular psychiatrist. He describes one of his patients "who was very depressed, somnolent, and anxious and who had lost interest in life." His previous physician had put him on antidepressant medication, but it had not really helped. The patient had also been seen for psychological problems and had undergone talk therapy. The results were equivocal and did not make that person feel well and functional.

"When I examined the patient, I observed that he had poor dietary habits, skipped meals, did not sleep well at night, suffered from nocturnal sweats, and was often fidgety and restless around noontime. Given these symptoms, the first thing I did was have the patient take the 5-hour glucose tolerance test in order to see how glucose was being metabolized in his body. When the results came back, they confirmed that the patient was suffering from a functional hypoglycemia, meaning that he had important drops in blood sugar. These shifts in levels of blood sugar can easily interfere with the normal biochemical and electric activity of the brain, which in turn can cause not only physical but also mental problems. When I corrected this disturbance with proper diet, the patient improved dramatically. He reported that he was happier and feeling better and that life looked brighter. This is a case where depression was, in part at least, related to something as basic as sugar metabolism. Sugar may not be the only factor. Illness may, for instance, reflect an amino acid problem of some kind. The point is that by correcting the underlying cause or causes of an illness, it is possible to correct the illness. In this case, there was no need whatsoever for antidepressant medication."

## The Whole-Body Approach

The whole-body approach to treatment used by orthomolecular psychiatrists also makes their diagnostic techniques differ substantially from those of traditional psychiatry. Traditional psychiatry approaches diagnosis from a purely symptomatic point of view. If a "cause" is identified, this usually occurs not through an individualized analysis of the patient's biochemistry but rather by means of an implied causation. In other words, traditional psychiatry does recognize that certain biochemical imbalances or "organic" factors may be causative in certain mental conditions. For instance, the DSM-III-R (*Diagnostic and Statistical Manual of Mental Disorders*)—the official diagnostic guide for psychiatrists—contains a diagnostic category "Organic Mental Disorders" which includes "Alcohol Withdrawal Delirium" and other mental disorders which have an obvious physical connection.

Traditional psychiatrists also assume that a given mental illness involves a biochemical imbalance. Depression, for instance, is treated with antidepressants designed to operate on the supply or metabolism of neurotransmitters. However, the traditional psychiatrist usually will not conduct tests to confirm that a patient with a given illness has the specific biochemical imbalance which psychiatry deems causative in that illness. The treatment is usually more of a guessing game in which one neurotransmitter, say, serotonin, may be supplemented and then the doctor and patient wait to see whether an improvement results. Even if the patient is found to have that specific biochemical imbalance, the diagnosis ordinarily stops with this discovery and the doctor does not look into the factors which may have triggered the imbalance to begin with.

With the orthomolecular approach, while a patient may present the classic symptoms of schizophrenia or another mental disorder, this presentation forms only a minor part of the diagnosis. The orthomolecular psychiatrist will look at diet, glandular functions, glucose metabolism, and a host of other biochemical factors which may play a role in the patient's mental disorder. Dr. Tobias points out that without such a thorough diagnosis, it is impossible to design a good treatment. A diagnosis which does not take the whole individual into account cannot provide long-term relief. It may lead to suppression of symptoms, but it is not curative.

### The Treatment of Schizophrenia

Another difference between traditional and orthomolecular psychiatry is the attitude of each toward the use of drugs. While traditional medicine uses drugs as the treatment of preference, in most cases the orthomolecular approach is to use drugs only as a last resort or in an emergency. Dr. Robert Atkins, author of *The Diet Revolution* (Bantam Books, New York, 1973) and a leading proponent of orthomolecular medicine, maintains that using harmless substances such as vitamins and nutrients first and having recourse to drugs only after safer and less toxic treatments have proved ineffectual is another way in which orthomolecular medicine is in keeping with the Hippocratic oath, which states, "First do no harm."

Dr. Bernard Rimland, a research psychologist and director of the Institute for Child Behavior Research in San Diego, California, explains orthomolecular medicine by contrasting it to what he calls toximolecular medicine. Dr. Rimland states:

"The two parts of the definition of orthomolecular medicine are not difficult to understand. Everyone can grasp the idea of obtaining optimal concentrations of nutrients. But the other part, the idea of trying to attain health by avoiding unnatural substances—chemicals that are not normally found in the body—is quite new to most people."

Dr. Rimland compares this approach with that of traditional medicine, which uses "sublethal doses of toxic substances" to try to restore health. He points out that if all the contraindications, side effects, and adverse reactions of drugs were deleted from the *Physicians' Desk Reference* (PDR), this comprehensive drug index which is about 3 inches thick would be reduced to about one-quarter inch.

Drugs used in the treatment of mental disorders are particularly good examples. The adverse reactions and contraindications for the major tranquilizer Thorazine (chlorpromazine) alone take up two pages of fine print in the PDR. This is one of the primary reasons why orthomolecular practitioners began to question the propriety of using these drugs before safer and less toxic avenues of treatment had been exhausted.

The use of drugs can be effective, of course. Antidepressant drugs, for instance, are helpful insofar as they raise serotonin levels in the brain. But nutrients can also do this, and since they are more compatible with the body's natural chemistry, they should be tried first. Why cure a malady with substances so foreign to the body that they may create new problems? This sort of chemical approach may be appropriate when nutrients have not been successful, but it should be seen as a last resort, not a first-line treatment.

Dr. Lesser talks about a patient who was suffering from apparent melancholy. "She was severely depressed to the point where she wanted to give up her affairs and her finances to her children. She was in the hospital and was put on lithium, which did not seem to help her. She came to see me, and I did something that a traditional psychiatrist would probably not do, which was simply to have her get a blood test. I do a comprehensive blood-testing procedure in cases of severe depression, and in her case I found that she was suffering from megaloblastic anemia, which is a form of pernicious anemia. This anemia can and often does cause mental illness as a side effect of the general anemia picture because it is due to a deficiency of certain important nutrients, in particular vitamin $B_{12}$ and perhaps folic acid.

"So, with a series of vitamin $B_{12}$ injections this woman is now up and about, no longer depressed at all, and perfectly capable of taking care of her financial affairs. There is a good chance that this would have been missed by traditional psychiatrists because they would not have thought to look at the body in this way. It is not part of the routine testing of traditional psychiatry."

Orthomolecular psychiatrists have found that some severely ill mental patients have marked deficiencies in certain nutrients. The pioneers in this field were Drs. Abram Hoffer and Humphrey Osmond, who as early as 1952 conducted a double-blind study on the effects of megadoses of vitamin B$_3$ (in the form of niacin or niacinamide) on schizophrenic patients. This was the first double-blind study performed in the field of psychiatry. They found that schizophrenia is not purely a behavioral or mental disorder but that it also has a basis in biochemical imbalance, particularly a deficiency of niacin. Schizophrenia is among the most difficult psychiatric conditions to treat, characterized by symptoms such as delusions, hallucinations, incoherent thought patterns and speech, and catatonic behavior. But Hoffer and Osmond had good results with the niacin treatment they offered to half a dozen schizophrenics in 1952. One patient—an overactive, delusional, and hallucinating 17-year-old boy—was nearly normal after just 10 days on this treatment and was reported well 10 years later. Encouraged by these results, they then set up a double-blind experiment with 30 schizophrenic patients. Those given niacin treatments did far better than those given only the placebo.

I spoke with Dr. Hoffer recently, and here are some examples of the results he has attained with vitamin B$_3$ therapy:

*Example 1:* "This was a patient I knew very well. She was admitted to a mental hospital in 1939 and was in that hospital continuously until 1952. During that time she received every treatment known to psychiatry. Eventually they had to give her a series of shock treatments every 6 months. In 1952, as part of our research program, I took her into my home, where she began to work for us. I started her on niacin, vitamin B$_3$. Since she had not left the hospital for so long, she had to be reeducated in terms of how to use the telephone, how to get into her car, and how to shake hands. She had to be completely resocialized. She was with us for about 2 years, during which time she improved dramatically. In 1955, she got a job at the university hospital on the cleaning staff, and recently she retired—she is now 65. After she left us, she would still come to visit every 2 to 3 years, and she was here just a couple of weeks ago.

"Now, this woman had spent 13 continuous years in a hospital without responding. With the niacin therapy, she was converted from a chronic, perpetually sick schizophrenic to a working, contributing member of society. Had she remained in the hospital, her medical care could have cost the government almost $1 million. Instead, over the past 30 years she has been working and paying taxes and has accumulated enough of a pension so that she can retire and live comfortably. I think this is a very striking case."

*Example 2:* "This is an especially good case because the patient was not even mine; I did not treat him. This was a young patient who, when he was 13, was examined in a West Coast university psychiatric department. There, he was declared to be a hopeless, chronically ill schizophrenic. His father was advised to send him to a mental hospital and forget him. The father, who was a professional person—a doctor—would not accept this advice. He read the literature, ran across our work, and called me in 1960. I advised him what to do—that is, to start the boy on vitamin $B_3$—and he did it.

"He began by feeding the vitamin $B_3$ to his son in jam sandwiches because the psychiatric department would not let him give the boy the vitamin. He would go to the hospital every day to take his son out for a walk, and while they were walking he would feed him jam sandwiches with $B_3$. After 6 weeks, the boy said, 'Daddy, I want to go home.' His father took him home. This boy remained well and finished in the fifth percentile in his twelfth-grade exams. After he had been on the vitamin for 18 months, in consultation with me, the father took him off to see if he still needed it. The boy had a relapse; he was put back on the therapy again and remained well. Since that time he has become a research psychiatrist and has recently published a very fine paper in the psychiatric literature."

The side effects of this megavitamin therapy are very minor compared with those of traditional treatment. Remember, the aim of this therapy is to supply optimal amounts of substances normally present in the body and required for good health. As little as 5 mg of vitamin $B_3$ a day is sufficient to prevent the disease pellagra, which only 70 years ago caused hundreds of thousands of people to suffer what was referred to as the four D's: diarrhea, dermatitis, dementia, and death. On the other hand, relatively massive doses of the vitamin can be administered with only minor side effects which disappear as soon as the dose is decreased or the vitamin is temporarily discontinued. The side effects include a tingling or numbness in the extremities and most commonly "flushing," in which parts of the body may become red and sensitive. Dr. Lesser reports that a buffered or time-release form of niacin taken with food and cold liquids has been shown to diminish this problem by helping the stomach handle large doses of niacin. The chemical niacinamide, by contrast, is potentially dangerous in high doses and can cause liver ailments.

Because the B vitamins appear as a complex in nature, a large dose of one of them can over time cause a deficiency to develop in the other members of the complex. Accordingly, during a megavitamin program involving the augmentation of a specific B vitamin, such as niacin, the other B vitamins should also be increased in the form of a B-complex supplement.

Dr. Lesser gives two examples of patients who were helped by niacin therapy:

*Example 1:* "A man I will call Ted was sort of a schizoaffective schizophrenic. He had fantasies and ideas that he was a very big man. He drove around in rented Cadillacs, which he charged on his credit cards, took all his friends to Las Vegas, heard voices, and did a lot of bizarre things—so bizarre, in fact, that one of his car-leasing schemes got him in trouble with the law. He was in legal trouble when I first saw him.

"We put him on niacin along with other nutrients and a high-protein diet, since the niacin seems to work better with a high-protein diet. He cleared up almost immediately and stopped

10

hallucinating. He went to prison because he had already committed a felony, but he became an honor prisoner, and the last I heard he was completely recovered."

*Example 2:* "This was another case I was lucky enough to get early. The earlier we can treat the illness, the better the chances of recovery. This man was a premed student. He broke up with his girlfriend and sort of fell apart—started eating a lot of junk food and soon started hearing voices, behaving bizarrely, and finding that he couldn't concentrate. He was a straight-A premed student, but his grades fell off severely in his last quarter because he was getting ill. That is the tragedy of schizophrenia—it can completely destroy the mental processes.

"He came to see me in desperation. I put him on a high-protein diet and on large amounts of niacin, and within a week he stopped hallucinating. He went on to medical school, and he called recently to let me know that he had graduated."

If these patients had been treated with traditional medicine, they probably would have been put on tranquilizers to make them more subdued and manageable. Perhaps psychotherapy sessions would have complemented the drug therapy. Nutrient deficiencies or malabsorption and allergies to common foods—notably wheat in the case of schizophrenia—would almost certainly be disregarded. In an attempt to mask the symptoms of the disorder, the traditional physician or psychiatrist would be likely to overmedicate the patient, leaving the patient calmer but virtually nonfunctional while completely ignoring the actual cause of the problem.

The orthomolecular psychiatrist, by directly addressing nutritional deficiencies and imbalances from the start, might find a simple biochemical cause for what a traditional psychiatrist would deem a complex and perplexing problem. Mental illness can indeed result from nutritional deficiency, but certainly, as Dr. Lesser points out, "no one has ever claimed that mental illness is caused by a deficiency in Thorazine." Moreover, even if no nutritional cause for the malady is found, such patients can only be made better off by improving their nutrient intake and absorption. Failure to do this can lead to further complications of the mental illness.

Dr. Tobias points out that some of the more severe cases of schizophrenia—those in which the patient manifests paranoid delusions—are very difficult to treat. While some patients may respond to the administration of certain vitamins or amino acids or to a correction of certain biochemical imbalances, others may not. However, he says, recent studies have indicated that patients who are given Haldol (haloperidol), an antipsychotic drug, appear to have better results when the drug is given in conjunction with vitamin C, which is an important coenzyme in some of the sophisticated functions of the brain. This is an example of how orthomolecular psychiatry can function as an adjunct to conventional treatment.

## The Treatment of Anxiety

Schizophrenia is not the only form of mental illness that is related to nutritional imbalance. Anxiety, a major health problem today, can be due to many different causes. Practically any nutritional deficiency that affects the mind (and almost all do in one way or another) can cause anxiety as a symptom. The most common type of anxiety today is called neurosis, or neurotic anxiety, or anxiety neurosis.

Orthomolecular treatment of this disorder involves things that would rarely be thought of in traditional psychiatry. A glucose tolerance test, for instance, is important in determining whether sugar is being properly metabolized. Anxiety attacks can occur when sugar levels get too low, as in hypoglycemics. Hypoglycemia can also cause a rebound effect when adrenaline is secreted to raise blood sugar levels. This adrenaline rush also causes anxiety. Dr. Lesser checks out sugar tolerance "rather than getting involved immediately in looking for . . . Oedipal or pre-Oedipal fantasies," because in a recent review of his cases he found that "92 percent of the neurotics had abnormalities in the glucose tolerance test."

12

Dietary recommendations based on the results of a glucose tolerance test may help the neurotic patient far more effectively, quickly, and safely than either psychotherapy or drug treatment. The main objective is to create stability so that sugar levels neither drop nor rise too sharply or rapidly. For the hypoglycemic, a high-protein diet is recommended by Dr. Lesser, because it digests very slowly, sending just a small trickle of sugar into the bloodstream, so that the blood sugar is kept stable for a long period of time. Then, when the patient eats frequently, he continues, the blood sugar remains stable. "I have these patients eat six or seven times a day, small snacks so as not to put on weight," he reports. "Actually, they can handle more calories than they could if they were eating one, two, or three large meals a day because the body is set up to metabolize the small meals frequently. When you have a large meal, you cannot metabolize all that nutrition, and the body turns a portion of that into fat."

Dr. Lesser stresses the fact that good nutrition is also important, since junk foods can spur anxiety. Simple, processed carbohydrates such as white sugar and white flour products may give a quick lift to the hypoglycemic, but this is followed by excessive insulin secretion that drives blood sugar down again, only to be pumped up once again by an adrenaline rush. This episode leaves a person with cold hands, jitters, anxiety, and panic. Special nutrients can help alleviate this problem, especially chromium—also called the glucose tolerance factor—which helps normalize blood sugar. Zinc and the B vitamins, especially thiamine and vitamin $B_1$, are also beneficial. Vitamin $B_3$, or niacin, has also been identified as an antistress factor. It lowers cholesterol and triglyceride levels, which are increased by anxiety, and affects the brain in ways that are similar to the effects of tranquilizers. Dr. Lesser is convinced of the efficacy of this nutritional approach, but emphasizes the need to be patient with looking for results. It may take months for the condition to begin to clear because "the body has been often run-down for a number of months or years, and you have to gradually repair all the cells in the body. The old cells have to die

13

off and be replaced by new ones that are better nourished. The natural life span of cells varies throughout the body. Some, such as blood cells, live 120 days, so you cannot really expect sudden dramatic improvement unless the condition has come on suddenly and you have caught it early."

Besides diet modifications and nutrient supplements, anxiety may be ameliorated by relaxation techniques, yoga, massage, exercise, and stress management. An orthomolecular psychiatrist will often suggest these approaches before turning to drugs. Drugs, unlike nutrients or stress-reduction techniques, often become addictive. If you suffer from anxiety and then develop an addiction to drugs that were intended to help that problem, you will only have augmented the agony you were trying to eliminate. In addition, the direct side effects that drugs often have may leave you less capable of living a normal, healthy life than you were when you first underwent treatment.

Orthomolecular psychiatry also puts psychotherapy on the back burner. The shortcoming of psychotherapy, according to Dr. Lesser, "is that most people who suffer from anxiety have only a limited capacity to deal with it through insight psychotherapy. There is a real risk and danger that an individual, by concentrating on his or her pathology—phobias and anxiety—and by delving deep into his or her childhood and looking for trauma, will become 'fixed' on the idea of his or her pathology. Rather than becoming more able and competent, that person will become fixed in his or her neurosis and in some cases will become even more anxious as a result of exploring the so-called unconscious. I have seen many cases—I am not saying this occurs in every case; perhaps I am seeing only the failed cases—of individuals who have been in psychotherapy for 4, 6, 8 or even 12 years with no apparent improvement. It seems to me that when a case goes on that long, someone should think about the possibility of using another approach."

### The Individualized Approach

Mental illness can be as diverse as the people who suffer from these disorders, and so the most appropriate treatment for any given person will depend entirely on that person's particular symptoms. If the person is treated orthomolecularly, the treatment will depend on any causative factors which may be discerned. Dr. Lesser gives an example of a patient suffering from a combination of anxiety and depression to illustrate the importance of an individualized approach to treatment:

"I saw a man who was quite upset. He was a very frightened and frightening man—sort of backwoods hippie type who was referred to me by another doctor who didn't know what to do with him because the patient was very angry and very upset. When I first saw him, he was on the lawn of my yard tearing up the grass, screaming in a very loud guttural voice. I was really frightened by him.

"I managed to talk to him long enough to get a history of a very severe depression and fearfulness approaching paranoia. When we did the blood tests, we found out that he had a low vitamin $B_{12}$ level. I always check the vitamin panel in severe cases like this. He also had a pernicious anemia picture in the bloodstream—the megaloblastic anemia where one gets abnormally large blood cells, which is generally due to a deficiency of vitamin $B_{12}$ and/or folic acid. We put him on vitamin $B_{12}$ injections. Because he lived some distance from my office, I trained him to give himself the shots. A person has to have a series of these injections; usually one or two won't cure the problem. With these injections, he became considerably better."

### The Treatment of Depression

Depression is a major health problem related to proper mental functioning. It can leave an otherwise healthy person unable to cope with the simplest everyday situations. Depression affects roughly 10 percent of the American population—perhaps 25 or 30 million people. This does not include the many people who function normally for the most part despite frequently finding themselves in low moods. Two-thirds of those who suffer from true depression are never treated and live their lives in misery without being recognized as victims of mental illness.

For the past 30 years psychiatry has been aware that certain biochemical changes which take place in the brain can both influence and reflect fluctuations in people's moods. A change in the delicate biochemistry of the brain is capable of governing how a person feels at any given moment. A physical deficiency in any of the chemicals responsible for maintaining "good moods" may lead to depression, just as a psychological stressing factor in a person's life may manifest itself in the body by altering the sensitive chemical balance in the brain, thereby also causing depression or low moods.

While psychiatry has recognized this mind-body connection in general terms for the last 30 years, it is only in the last 10 to 15 years that it has actually isolated some of the specific brain chemicals involved. Especially important among these chemicals are substances called *neurotransmitters,* which are released at the nerve endings in the brain and allow messages to be relayed throughout the rest of the brain and the body. Perhaps the most commonly known neurotransmitter is endorphin. It is responsible for pain relief within the body and is thought to be the chemical responsible for the "high" that runners experience after exercise.

Mood swings can be traced to a similar mind-body relationship. Scientists have found that a large number of depressed people have significant deficiencies of the neurotransmitters *norepinephrine* and *serotonin.* These neurotransmitters belong to a chemical group called the amines which are responsible for the control of emotions, sleep, pain, and many involuntary bodily functions such as digestion. Almost 90 percent of these amines are found deep in the brain; because of their importance, the normally functioning body has developed a recycling system, called reuptake, by which the nerve cell takes back 85 percent of the neurotransmitter for future use once the chemical reaction has been completed. Only the remaining 15 percent is destroyed by enzymes.

The metabolism of the neurotransmitters is intricate, and deficiencies can occur for many reasons. Dr. Priscilla Slagle, a board-certified psychiatrist practicing in southern California, states that age or genetics may cause a person to use up amines more rapidly than someone else might. She also points out that a defective receiving cell or reuptake mechanism or a deficiency of the amino acids, vitamins, and minerals that make up amines may be the culprit here. The nutrient deficiencies involved may result from excessive intake of caffeine, sugar, alcohol, or tobacco. Sugar and coffee can destroy the B vitamins and the minerals magnesium and iron, all of which figure significantly in neurotransmitter formation. Alcohol and tobacco also deplete almost all the B vitamins, vitamin C, zinc, magnesium, manganese, and tyrosine. These nutrients are essential to maintaining a good mood.

Stress is another factor which can contribute to depression. Most people tend to associate depression with what are called major stressors, such as the loss of a loved one, being fired from a job, or another circumstance which upsets one's life in a very significant way. However, even the stress associated with everyday living can directly deplete the vitamins, minerals, and amino acids that are so important in maintaining a good mood. Dr. Slagle explains:

"We have found very high levels of the hormone cortisol, which is secreted by the adrenal glands, in severely depressed patients. Indeed, scientists have devised a test which measures the levels of this hormone in the body to determine the degree of depression present. When people are depressed and highly stressed, their adrenal glands may secrete higher levels of cortisol, triggering certain enzymes in the body that destroy tyrosine and tryptophan. One would think that under extreme stress the body would compensate for this breakdown by facilitating the survival of these important amino acids. Instead, for whatever reason, these amino acids are used up. I believe that high cortisol levels induce depression in certain people."

Another thing Dr. Slagle has observed is the prevalence of depression as a side effect of many prescription medications. The list of these medications is quite extensive, including antibiotics, antiarthritis pills, blood pressure medication, birth control pills, tranquilizers, and even aspirin. When people are given these medications, they often are not warned that they may experience depression as a side effect. Dr. Slagle, together with most other orthomolecular psychiatrists, believes that rather than ignoring these side effects or waiting for them to appear, whenever a prescription drug is given that has a side effect such as depression listed in the PDR, a nutritional program should accompany the prescription in order to replenish the particular vitamins and amino acids which may be depleted by the medication.

When a traditional psychiatrist arrives at a diagnosis of depression, more likely than not the next step will be to put the patient on antidepressant medication. Some of the most common of these medications are Elavil (amitriptyline), Sinequan (doxepin), Tofranil (imipramine), and Nardil (phenelzine). They are all designed to increase in one way or another the concentration of the neurotransmitters, thereby prolonging their biochemical reaction. Although the manufacturers claim that there is no evidence of addiction to most of these drugs, they are not without serious side effects. The PDR entry for one of these, for instance, mentions many contraindications, warnings, precautions, and adverse reactions, including severe convulsions and possibly death if this drug is used improperly with other drugs, complications in patients with impaired liver function, hypertension, stroke, disorientation, delusions, hallucinations, excitement, tremors, seizures, blurred vision, dizziness, fatigue, baldness, and elevation and lowering of blood sugar levels. Because suicidal tendencies are a frequent characteristic of depression, perhaps one of the most serious problems associated with the antidepressants is the potential for drug overdose. The potential for suicide caused by the very medication prescribed to prevent it is further enhanced by the synergistic interaction of the antidepressives with alcohol, barbiturates, and other central nervous system depressants. A glance through the PDR indicates that the quantity and the magnitude of the dangers associated with Elavil are equally present with the other antidepressants.

Because norepinephrine and serotonin are formed from amino acids normally present in the body and in commonly eaten foods, orthomolecular psychiatrists believe that it makes more sense to try to treat depression by means of amino acid supplementation than to prescribe psychotropic drugs, which often have side effects worse than the depression for which they are prescribed.

Dr. Priscilla Slagle is an orthomolecular psychiatrist and a leading authority on the treatment of low moods and depression with amino acids and nutritional therapy. She became interested in the treatment of mood disorders as a result of her own depression, which lasted for many years and did not respond to traditional psychoanalysis or psychotherapeutic treatment. Disinclined to use antidepressant medications because of the adverse reactions which so commonly accompany them, Dr. Slagle discovered that "there are natural food substances that will create the same end effects, that is, elevate mood in the same way without causing side effects or toxicity. I started myself on [a program using certain single amino acids to control mood] and achieved very dramatic results. Although I have had tremendous stress over the past 10 years, particularly the past year, I have not had one day of a low mood. This has been a marvelous reprieve, since I have had and therefore understand the pain that low moods can create for many people."

In her book, *The Way Up from Down* (Random House, New York, 1987), Dr. Slagle outlines a safe and easily implemented program of treatment for depression using amino acids and other precursors required for the production of norepinephrine and serotonin. She is careful to emphasize that people should follow the program under the supervision of a physician. For those already on antidepressant medication, it is not advisable to stop abruptly since they may experience withdrawal symptoms.

Dr. Slagle explains the basis of the program:

"It consists of taking an amino acid called tyrosine, which in the presence of certain B-complex vitamins, minerals, and vitamin C will convert into norepinephrine in the brain. This neurotransmitter not only sustains positive moods but also helps our concentration, learning, memory, drive, ambition, motivation, and other equally important qualities. Additionally, it helps to regulate food and sexual appetite functions. Thus it is a very important chemical. The other amino acid used in the program is tryptophan, which forms serotonin in the brain, provided that the requisite cofactors—the B vitamins, minerals, and vitamin C—are present. In addition to sustaining mood, tryptophan also has other functions such as controlling sleep and levels of aggression. People who are quite aggressive, irritable, or angry are often suffering from a marked deficiency in serotonin. Indeed, very low levels of serotonin have been found in the brain of suicide victims at autopsy.

"With these two amino acids, a good multivitamin-mineral preparation is taken to provide all the nutrients necessary to catalyze or promote the conversion of the amino acids into neurotransmitters."

Dr. Slagle provides the following dosage for the two amino acids: around 500 mg of tyrosine taken twice daily and about 500 mg of tryptophan. She recommends that the tyrosine be taken first thing in the morning on an empty stomach and then also some time in the midafternoon. The tryptophan, because of its sleep-inducing effects, is taken before bed. Any amino acids used therapeutically must be taken separately from other protein foods, because protein interferes with their utilization. Dr. Slagle also specifies that the amino acids be taken in capsules (tablets can pass through the body undigested) and in the "free form," a form in which the amino acids are ready for absorption by the body, thus avoiding preexisting problems with digestion.

Diagnosis is another aspect of the orthomolecular psychiatrist's approach to depression which differs from that of the traditional psychiatrist. Traditional psychiatry diagnoses depression according to the criteria set forth in the DSM-III-R, which essentially defines it as a condition which includes at least five of the following symptoms during the same 2-week period:

1. Depressed mood
2. Markedly diminished interest or pleasure in all or almost all activities
3. Significant weight loss or gain (when not dieting)
4. Insomnia (a constant inability to sleep) or hypersomnia
5. Psychomotor agitation (a hyperanxious state) or retardation
6. Fatigue or loss of energy
7. Feelings of worthlessness or excessive or inappropriate guilt
8. Diminished ability to think or concentrate, or indecisiveness
9. Recurrent thoughts of death

While orthomolecular psychiatrists may use this definition as a starting point, they do not confine the diagnosis to these criteria. Orthomolecular psychiatry views depression or any other illness as a unique and individual condition. While there may be certain guidelines, such as those set forth in the DSM-III-R, a diagnosis which rigidly adheres to these criteria can arrive at a wrong conclusion either by missing the diagnosis altogether because the person's symptoms are not those normally associated with depression or by falsely diagnosing a person as being depressed simply because he or she has the textbook symptoms.

Often the depressed patient is not aware of the condition, especially when it is complicated by associated physical symptoms. If you suffered from chronic back pain, indigestion, or neck stiffness, would you immediately think that you might be manifesting symptoms of depression? Probably not. You might go to several doctors in search of relief, and there would be a very good chance that none of them would ever consider depression as the root of your problem. Even if someone were to ask whether you were depressed, you might quickly protest if, as Dr. Slagle puts it, you "have 'somatized,' that is, put [your] emotional feelings into the body, thereby inducing bodily symptoms." For this reason, Slagle explains, chronic pain clinics now are likely to evaluate patients for depression. Many will give antidepressant medication as a treatment for physical pain. Slagle proposes the use of the amino acid tryptophan, which has been found to play a significant role in pain control.

Sometimes a patient may develop responses to medication that are misinterpreted as purely physical. "For example," Dr. Slagle says, "an acquaintance of mine who lost her daughter through death a year ago became so anxious that her doctor started her on tranquilizers. Although she was on tranquilizers for 6 months, she became worse and worse. When I visited her, it was really apparent to me that she had severe depression. It was difficult to convince her of this because she could only relate to the anxiety and the insomnia she was having. I started her on the nutrient program, and she improved dramatically in 2 to 3 weeks. Of course, I tapered her off the tranquilizers, because if they are stopped abruptly, one can have withdrawal symptoms which can aggravate the anxiety."

Thus it is now understood how mental illness can be caused by imbalances in the body and how it can be rectified by reestablishing those balances. Drugs often disrupt biochemical harmony even more and therefore exacerbate mental distress rather than cure it. In some cases drugs have been so abused that they have transformed patients with relatively minor disturbances into people with a wide range of complicated physical and mental disorders. Nowhere is this clearer or more pitiful than in the treatment of children.

### The Treatment of Children

During the past 10 to 15 years there has been a significant increase in the number of American children who are diagnosed with mental disorders and who as a consequence are put on drugs to treat this "disease." To what is the increase attributable? Are our kids really crazier than they were 10 years ago? And if they are, is drug therapy the best way to treat mental disorders in children? The following example will address the first two of these questions, namely, how the treatment of childhood mental disorders came to be a major area of modern-day psychiatry. Later we will contrast the traditional approach to these disorders with that of orthomolecular psychiatrists and other health care practitioners in order to provide insights into the many different alternatives to drug therapy available in the treatment of children with mental problems.

Bobby is 6 years old and has just started the first grade. He is precocious and has been reading and writing for at least a year. He is an only child, has been somewhat spoiled at home, and is used to being the center of attention. He is extremely active and often plays from morning until night. Sometimes his activity gets on his mother's nerves, but on the whole, she and everyone else who knows Bobby find him to be a normal, healthy child who is usually well mannered and considerate.

From the very start, Bobby hits it off poorly with his first-grade teacher. Because he is used to being active, he usually starts to fidget 15 minutes into the class. Often when the teacher asks a question, Bobby blurts out the answer without being called on. The teacher, Ms. Thomas, has admonished him a number of times, and he does try to control himself. Since he already knows what Ms. Thomas is teaching and is not called upon to answer questions, Bobby often becomes bored and restless and is apt to become absorbed by things going on outside the classroom window to the point where he often does not hear what Ms. Thomas is saying.

Bobby's teacher finds him to be a disruptive influence and believes that he is hyperactive. She sends him to the school psychologist with a report stating that she suspects that Bobby is suffering from what is technically called attention-deficit hyperactivity disorder. A copy of the report is sent to Bobby's parents, who immediately become alarmed that something may be wrong with their son. The psychologist examines Bobby, notices nothing out of the ordinary, and sends him back to class with a note to both the teacher and Bobby's parents telling them about his conclusions and asking them to keep an eye on Bobby so that they can alert him if anything new occurs.

A month or so later the teacher files another report. This time, after the psychologist again examines Bobby and fails to notice any aberrant behavior, Bobby's parents are advised that he should be seen by a psychiatrist. After reading the teacher's report and examining Bobby, the psychiatrist concludes that Bobby is in fact suffering from attention-deficit hyperactivity disorder and prescribes Ritalin (methylphenidate).

Bobby's parents are somewhat bewildered by this and ask the doctor what the drug is and whether it is really necessary. The doctor explains that while he has not noticed any particular signs of the disorder, symptoms are not necessarily present when the child is having a one-on-one exchange or is in a new setting such as his office. "Typically," the doctor says, "symptoms worsen in situations requiring sustained attention, such as listening to a teacher in a classroom or doing class assignments." This is why Ms. Thomas has been in the best position to notice and report the disease. The doctor tells the parents that he suspects that Bobby is suffering from a chemical imbalance in his brain which, if uncorrected, could start to affect his performance at school and that bad grades could ruin the rest of Bobby's life. He adds that although scientists do not yet know how it works, Ritalin seems to stabilize children who have this disorder.

At first Bobby's parents are so confused by the diagnosis and so alarmed that their child is so ill as to require medication for an indefinite period of time that they simply go along with it. However, shortly after Bobby starts taking the medication, his parents notice that he has become very nervous and complains that he cannot sleep at night. He also shows a marked decrease in appetite and begins to lose weight. They decide to look into the drug more fully and discover that Ritalin is an addictive appetite-suppressing drug of the amphetamine family with numerous side effects, including those already experienced by Bobby: insomnia, loss of appetite, weight loss, and nervousness. When they discuss this with the psychiatrist, he tells them that the side effects are minimal compared with the damage that the boy could sustain if he stopped taking it and that furthermore, Ms. Thomas does not want him back in her class unless she is assured that he is taking the medication.

This example is hypothetical, but it is by no means exaggerated. Every year children like Bobby are diagnosed with nebulously defined "mental disorders" and receive treatment with Ritalin or other even more potent drugs such as Haldol and Thorazine. Since the "diseases" for which these drugs are prescribed first came into vogue in the 1960s, literally millions of American children, about three-quarters of whom are boys, have been labeled and drugged in order to tone down their conduct and make it more acceptable to those with whom their energy and activity may collide. But a bored and/or restless child does not deserve to be turned into a virtual zombie with sedating drugs that have numerous side effects.

During the 1960s and 1970s many of these "disorders" were lumped together under the rubric of minimal brain dysfunction (MBD). The history of MBD and how it suddenly became *the* childhood disorder provides a good insight into the nature and purpose of much of psychiatric diagnosis and treatment.

The term "minimal brain dysfunction" has been around in medical literature since the 1920s. In its original sense, the term was used to describe learning and behavioral problems that result from identifiable damage to the brain, such as those which sometimes occur at birth or through head injuries. The key is that actual physical brain damage existed which was impairing the child's or adult's ability to do certain things according to fairly objective standards. In 1963, however, all of this changed following a conference held by the U.S.

25

Public Health Service and the National Easter Seal Society for Crippled Children and Adults, which convened to discuss the issue of MBD. A report issued after the conference essentially claimed that the cause of the disease was organic (of a physical origin within the body) and redefined the term so broadly as to include almost any imaginable form of behavior. According to the head of the Public Health Service at that time, Dr. Richard Maseland (quoting from Richard Hughes and Robert Brewin, *The Tranquilizing of America*, Harcourt, Brace, Jovanovich, New York, 1979), the intent was to single out "that group of children whose dysfunction does not produce gross motor or sensory deficit or generalized impairment of intellect, but who exhibit *limited alterations of behavior or intellectual functioning*." (Emphasis added.)

The new definition of MBD was drafted by a special task force led by a psychologist at the University of Arkansas Medical School. It included a list of 99 criteria which were so vague and all-encompassing that the definition would have been laughable had it not become the basis for the psychiatric labeling and drugging of millions of American children. In *The Tranquilizing of America,* Brewin and Hughes synopsize some of the "symptoms" contained in the MBD definition and comment on its impact:

"It would be difficult to write a more all-inclusive definition for this new disorder subsequently used to label millions of children, but the task force didn't stop there, offering ninety-nine symptoms to help doctors and teachers spot these otherwise normal children. The symptoms include hyperkinesis (too active) and hypokinesis (not active enough); hyperactivity and hypoactivity (activity opposites of a milder nature); 'rage reactions and tantrums' and being 'sweet and even tempered, cooperative and friendly'; 'easy acceptance of others alternating with withdrawal and shyness'; being 'overly gullible and easily led' and being 'socially bold and aggressive'; being 'very sensitive to others' and having 'excessive need to touch, cling and hold on to others'; and sleeping abnormally lightly or abnormally deeply. . . .

"It's unlikely that any child, no matter how normal or healthy, could escape classification under such a hodgepodge of 'signs' pointing to an MBD child in need of treatment."

According to Brewin and Hughes, notwithstanding this basically meaningless cornucopia of definitions, the concept of MBD was enthusiastically welcomed by the psychiatric community, governmental health agencies, educators, and pharmaceutical companies.

Brewin and Hughes continue: "There is no way to get an accurate fix on the number of children drugged with Ritalin or other stimulants or tranquilizers since the MBD phenomenon began to flourish in the late 1960s, but it is safe to estimate conservatively that 3 to 4 million children have been chemically harnessed for MBD or various MBD symptoms, ranging from hyperkinesis to fidgeting, in the past decade. Ciba-Geigy continues to identify a substantial number of children as candidates for an MBD diagnosis and Ritalin therapy. The company estimates that '1 out of every 20 schoolchildren has MBD—three-quarters of them boys.' This means an MBD target population of 1.6 million children—some 1.2 million of them boys—between the ages of 5 and 13. With the federal government estimating the number of children with learning disabilities at 10 percent of the grammar school population of 32 million, there is an even greater potential for indiscriminate drugging of youngsters. . . ."

The drug companies have focused their promotional efforts not only on advertising their medications but also on convincing the public that MBD is a bona fide disease. Amphetamines became so highly esteemed in the educational community that many schools would not allow children diagnosed with MBD (often by their teachers) to continue in attendance unless they were on drugs. "By the early 1970s," Brewin and Hughes remark, "Ritalin had become so widely used that it was referred to as the 'smart pill' in playground talk, and some cynics referred to the three R's as 'reading, 'riting, and Ritalin.' "

While the term "MBD" is no longer used in the psychiatric

jargon, the concept has by no means been abandoned, nor has the use of amphetamines in its treatment. The DSM-III-R has an entire section devoted to "Disorders Usually First Evident in Infancy, Childhood, or Adolescence." This class includes "Developmental Disorders" such as mental retardation, autism, and particular learning disorders (e.g., writing, reading, and speech disorders), as well as the "Disruptive Behavior Disorders" such as attention-deficit hyperactivity disorder, conduct disorder, and oppositional defiant disorder. If your child is diagnosed with any of these disorders, Ritalin will most likely be an integral part of the treatment the child will receive from traditional psychiatrists.

Nowhere is the DSM-III-R more vague or subjective than in the sections concerning childhood disorders. While the "developmental disorders" do contain somewhat more objective criteria—for example, mental retardation requires that the diagnosed child have a "subaverage general intellectual functioning" as evidenced by a score of 70 or below on an IQ test—the diagnoses of the "behavior disorders" are almost entirely subjective and the symptoms are so broad-ranging that almost any healthy child could easily fall within their ambit. Consider the DSM-III-R definition of "Attention-deficit Hyperactivity Disorder." This disorder may be diagnosed if at least eight of the following signs are present:

1. Often fidgets with hands or feet or squirms in seat (in adolescents, may be limited to subjective feelings of restlessness)
2. Has difficulty remaining seated when required to do so
3. Is easily distracted by extraneous stimuli
4. Has difficulty awaiting turn in games or group situations
5. Often blurts out answers to questions before they have been completed
6. Has difficulty following through on instructions from others, e.g., fails to finish chores
7. Has difficulty sustaining attention in tasks or play activities

8. Often shifts from one uncompleted activity to another
9. Often talks excessively
10. Has difficulty playing quietly
11. Often interrupts or intrudes on others, e.g., butts into other children's games
12. Often does not seem to listen to what is being said to him or her
13. Often loses things necessary for tasks or activities at school or at home
14. Often engages in physically dangerous activities without considering the possible consequences (not for the purpose of thrill seeking), e.g., runs into street without looking

Children who are full of energy and not always cooperative may be annoying, but most people would not think of these traits as a sign of mental disease. In fact, to anyone who has spent time around children, it should be apparent from the definition of hyperactivity that a child such as Bobby, or *any* normal healthy child for that matter, could very easily fulfill eight if not all of the listed criteria at one time or another. Furthermore, depending on one's definition of "normal," this behavior may in many cases be a sign of mental health rather than mental disease. For instance, what normal person does not "fidget" or become "restless," have "difficulty remaining seated," or become "easily distracted" when a teacher or lecturer is giving a boring presentation?

Another major problem with definitions such as this is that they purport to establish a scientific basis for a medical diagnosis when in fact the diagnosis is totally subjective and has no scientific rationale whatsoever. The DSM-III-R does specify that a criterion should be considered satisfied "only if the behavior is considerably more frequent than that of most people of the same mental age," but rather than clarifying or objectifying the criteria, this condition only serves to introduce a further element of subjectivity into the definition.

What is "considerably more frequent?" Once a week? Once a day? Many times a day? What does "often" mean? How does a teacher know whether a child "has difficulty" playing quietly or following instructions? Does the teacher ask the child? Does the child tell the teacher? Most important, by whose standards are these things determined?

One of the most alarming things about this definition is that the determination of what constitutes normal behavior and what does not is often made by people who have an interest in labeling such things as restlessness and the blurting out of answers to questions as pathological. In other words, implicit in the definition is a belief that certain behavior should be controlled and suppressed simply because those in a position of authority may find it troublesome. Even a cursory examination of this definition reveals that it is primarily directed at a child's behavior at school. Ultimately, then, it is in the school rather than the doctor's office that learning and mental disabilities are first diagnosed.

The DSM-III-R does not just imply but rather explicitly states that "symptoms . . . may not be observed directly by the clinician" and that "when the reports of teachers and parents conflict, primary consideration should be given to the teacher reports because of greater familiarity with age-appropriate norms." What does this mean? The Citizen's Commission on Human Rights (CCHR), a nonprofit organization investigating psychiatric violations of human rights, comments:

"Presumably, there is a 'disease,' and teachers, practicing medicine without a license, and not the parents of the children, are the final and proper judges of which children have it."

According to a quote from a 1987 CCHR booklet, "How Psychiatry Is Making Drug Addicts Out of America's School Children," "It is the teacher's consideration of who is a 'normal' child which sets the standard for all other children. The psychiatrists (clinicians) don't have to *see* [the 'disease'] but can *treat* (cash in on) it, based on the *teacher's* 'diagnosis.' We're not to believe anyone who doesn't see the 'symptoms' of this mental disease because it's apparently invisible or at least disappears when the child is being seen by a new or perhaps impartial person in a 'one-to-one-situation,' including the parents when they disagree with the teacher."

It should be clear by now that the diagnosis of childhood mental disorders, particularly hyperactivity, is far from a scientific endeavor. Symptoms can inexplicably appear and disappear, teachers with no medical or psychiatric training are given the power to diagnose the disorder, and the definition of the disorder is based wholly on subjective criteria which depend more on the temperament of the person doing the diagnosing than on the actual mental health of the child being diagnosed.

This is not to say that children do not suffer from emotional and behavior problems which can dramatically affect the quality of their lives. Many doctors treating children for these problems report that such children are often aware of not acting like everyone else and are very disturbed and upset by this realization. Few would deny the importance to these children, and to society as a whole, of diagnosis and treatment aimed at getting at the root of their problems and designed to help them live a happy and fulfilling life. However, the treatment of legitimately ill children with safe, caring, and effective therapies is not what we have been talking about here.

There are a number of alternative approaches to childhood disorders which you may want to explore before letting a doctor put your child on drugs.

### Clinical Ecology and the Treatment of Allergies

One physician who has had considerable success in the treatment of children with emotional and behavior problems is Dr. Doris Rapp, an assistant professor of pediatrics at the State University of New York at Buffalo and author of *Allergies and the Hyperactive Child* (A Fireside Book, Simon & Schuster, New York, 1979). Dr. Rapp practices a branch of medicine called clinical ecology which looks at the role that the environment plays in people's overall health and well-being. In particular, clinical ecologists such as Dr. Rapp are concerned with *environmental allergies,* which they believe are responses a particular individual may have to substances in the environment that are tolerated by most people.

Dr. Rapp explains that most emotional disorders can be caused by allergies. Children can become moody, depressed, or even suicidal, hyperactive, agitated, or panicky—all for no apparent reason. They may suddenly cry, spit, or kick or hurt others or themselves. Dr. Rapp has observed that almost any emotional expression imaginable can occur as a result of an adverse reaction or sensitivity to substances in the environment. It sometimes happens in relation to ingesting certain foods or being exposed to certain chemical odors, lawn herbicides, chemicals (such as tobacco or perfume), or pollens and molds. Any of these can cause problems in some individuals at certain times."

Dr. Doris Rapp offered the following observation during a radio interview: "In my office I have seen and documented many patients, young children, who have acted in a very bizarre manner when they have been exposed to something that is unusual. For example, I had one little girl, about 5 or 6 years of age, who became very depressed and wished she was dead on days when it was damp and moldy. When she came into our office and we skin tested her for molds, she became very depressed, pulled her hair over her face, and became untouchable. When her mother walked toward her, she would pull away and scream; she wouldn't let anybody touch her. Then, when we gave her the correct dilution of mold allergy extract, on her own, she walked over to her mother, sat in her lap, gave her a hug and a kiss, and said, 'Mommy, I love you.'

"I had another little boy, about 4 years old, who never smiled. His mother brought in pictures of him at Easter, Christmas, at birthday parties and things like that, and he always looked very dour; he just didn't look happy at all. When we placed him on a diet that merely excluded highly allergenic foods, his mother said that she was really amazed because at the end of 1 week, he was smiling and happy for the first time in his life. When I talked to him, he said that he felt much better on the diet; he said that he didn't want to take Mikey's knife and put it right here, and he showed me where he thought his heart was. He was going to put a friend's knife right into his chest."

William Philpott, M.D., a leader in the field of clinical ecology and author of *Brain Allergies: The Psychonutrient Connection* (Keats Publishing, New Canaan, Connecticut, 1980), provides other examples of how allergic reactions can affect children:

"A 12-year-old boy diagnosed as hyperkinetic had the following symptoms on testing for spinach; he became overtalkative and physically violent, had excessive saliva, was very hot, developed a severe stomachache, and cried for a long time. Watermelon made him irritable and depressed; cantaloupe made him aggressively tease other patients. Once he avoided the incriminating substances in his diet, his hyperkinesis symptoms diminished dramatically.

"A 4-year-old boy diagnosed as hyperkinetic had a variety of reactions. String beans made him hyperactive, and he wanted to fight with everyone. Celery gave him a severe stomachache, after which he cried and became grouchy. Strawberries made him angry and hyperactive and caused a great deal of coughing. Unrefined cane sugar caused him to be irritable, after which he coughed and developed a stuffy nose.

"A 12-year-old boy became listless and depressed, and cried when tested for bananas. Then he became aggressive and picked up a stick as if to hit another patient. When he ate oranges, he sang at first but then became very tired, impatient, and eventually wild and aggressive. Rice caused him to experience a sensation of heat, followed by rebellious hyperactivity."

As can be seen from these examples, it is not necessarily unhealthy or "junk" foods which can be the worst offenders. Virtually any food can cause problems in a given individual. In fact, one of the major characteristics of allergy is that it is an individualized reaction to substances that ordinarily are well tolerated by other people.

Theron Randolph, M.D., considered by many the founder of clinical ecology, estimates that as many as 60 to 70 percent of symptoms commonly diagnosed as mental are actually caused by allergic-type reactions. Many emotionally disturbed people, especially those with psychoses, develop major symptoms when exposed to foods and chemicals that they frequently consume. Wheat, corn, milk, tobacco, and petrochemical hydrocarbons are some of the more common substances that trigger these allergic responses, which may include delusions and suicidal attempts.

There are a few tools that clinical ecologists use in treating children with allergy-related behavioral problems. The first is an elimination diet, which usually is recommended after the first visit with the physician. In certain severe cases the diet may take the form of a total fast for 4 to 5 days, but usually it eliminates only the specific foods the doctor suspects are a problem for the particular patient. The targeted foods are those which are common allergens (provoke allergies in many people), such as chocolate, dairy products, wheat, and cane and beet sugars, as well as foods which the patient has a tendency to "abuse." Clinical ecologists have found that people are often especially allergic to the foods which they eat most often. Sometimes the frequent consumption can even lead to a sort of addictive-allergic reaction where one craves the very food that is making one ill. As food residues can remain in the body up to 4 or 5 days, the object of the elimination diet is to clear the body completely of foods which may be causing problems. If allergy is at the root of the problem and the correct foods have been eliminated, the symptoms will clear at the end of the 5-day period. Dr. Philpott gives an example of how this can work.

"Henry, 17 years old, had been mentally ill for 3 years. Prior use of tranquilizers, psychotherapy, and electric shock had not succeeded in helping him appreciably. He believed that people were out to kill him, and he often had to be placed under restraint because of his attacks on innocent children and adults. He was placed on a fast from all foods and given spring water only. He remained mentally ill until the fourth day, at which time his symptoms cleared; he was released from his restraints. He telephoned his parents, saying, 'I love you. Please come and see me.' On the fifth day of the fast he was fed a meal of wheat only. Within an hour, he began to feel strange and unreal; within an hour and a half, he thought people were going to kill him. He telephoned his parents again, saying, 'I hate you. You caused my illness. I don't want to ever see you again.' Further testing confirmed the fact that when specific foods were withheld, his symptoms cleared, and when he was given wheat, the same paranoid reaction occurred consistently."

After the elimination diet, the body is particularly susceptible to allergens; consequently, even a small drop of an extract of the substance placed under the patient's tongue can reduplicate symptoms, sometimes very dramatically. This procedure of testing for allergies by placing a drop of extract under the tongue or injecting it subcutaneously is called provocative testing, and it is one of the major diagnostic techniques used by clinical ecologists.

Once the allergies are determined, a technique known as neutralization dose therapy is often used to eliminate the symptoms. In this procedure the physician uses increasingly diluted extracts of the particular substance until a dilution is found that reverses the patient's symptoms. This is the neutralizing dose. If you find this confusing don't worry. It is paradoxical, and science cannot explain how a diluted substance can have a more potent effect in relieving symptoms than a stronger solution of the same substance. Because neutralization therapy often is based on very weak dilutions of things such as wheat, milk, and corn, it is an extremely safe and nontoxic form of treatment. It is particularly useful for people who have a marked allergic reaction whenever they eat a particular food. For example, where chocolate invariably provokes hyperactivity in a child if the child eats birthday cake or inadvertently eats something containing chocolate, the symptoms can be "neutralized" by placing a few drops of the properly diluted extract under the child's tongue. The following example, provided by Dr. Rapp, shows how neutralization dose therapy worked on both a mother and her child:

"There is one woman I've tested three times for sugar allergies. She is about 40 years old, and when she is tested for sugar, she develops a catatonic state. She will be talking and kidding and joking, and you can give her an injection of a saline solution, and she stays fine; she doesn't know what you are testing her for. Then you can give her another injection of the saline, and she continues to write her name and act normally. But when you give her an injection of a weak allergy extract of sugar, within 10 minutes she is staring into space and unable to talk, her fists begin to clench, and she does not respond at all—she is totally unconscious. At that point, if she does write, she doesn't write her name as 'Catherine,' as she did before, but instead writes 'Cathy.' She seems to regress at that point and act much younger, more immature than she is. If you continue to give her weaker dilutions of the sugar allergy extract every 7 minutes, or faster if she doesn't look well, her hands will loosen up and her eyes will open. When you give her the right dilution of sugar, she comes back to normal completely and acts as if nothing had happened.

"We repeated the test three times on her and drew blood samples each time before the tests as well as during, when she was all tied up in a tight little knot and nonresponsive, and again when she was back to normal. We can show that there are changes in the neurotransmitter at the time when she is reacting. We also found something rather unusual in this patient: Her sedimentation rate changed. That is another study on the blood serum that usually is not altered by this kind of reaction, but it certainly was in this individual. If she eats sugar at home, the same thing happens to her that happened in the office.

"With this patient we were able to show that what we did is reproducible. We showed that she could not write her name when she was reacting, and then her handwriting went back to normal; we showed that there were changes in her blood each time we tested her; and we showed that we could treat her so that if she made a mistake and ate something with sugar in it, she did not have this kind of bizarre reaction.

"I might add that she has a son who became unconscious when he ate cherries from a cherry tree in the backyard, and when we gave him the correct dilution, he came back to normal. We also tested her for cherry, and she became unconscious again and had the tight fists."

Another treatment commonly used by clinical ecologists is the 4-day rotation diet. It is especially useful for patients who are not allergic per se to a given food but become "sensitized" to it when they abuse it or eat it frequently. In this diet almost all foods are rotated so that they are not eaten more than once every 4 days. This way the patient not only avoids the food to which he or she may be sensitive but also decreases the possibility of becoming sensitive to other foods which might have been overconsumed to compensate for the decreased consumption of the "abused" food.

According to Dr. Rapp, if a child is having behavioral or emotional problems, the parents should consider the potential role of allergies in these problems if the family has a history of allergies. She says:

"If your parents had hay fever and asthma or many of your children have these conditions, and you have one child who is having behavior and personality problems, you might consider the fact that the dust or the milk that is causing the asthma in one child may be causing bed-wetting or hyperactivity in the other. If a patient has an allergic history or typical allergies such as asthma or hives, this particular patient may also be having brain allergies—allergic reactions within the brain—that may be affecting his or her behavior or emotions."

Dr. Rapp also states that children who suffer from allergies often have a characteristic look. They frequently have bags or dark circles under their eyes, and many have bright red cheeks and earlobes when they are reacting. Many children with allergic reactions affecting the brain tend to cross their legs, fidget constantly, and have trouble remaining seated. Dr. Rapp has also noticed that very often the handwriting and drawings of children will vary significantly when they are reacting. She explains:

"The child who is exuberant and all over the place writes in a very large manner. However, the writing may be upside down or backward or in mirror image. But the child who is depressed and goes into the corner frequently writes in *extremely* small letters. The writing will be as small as it can be, or the child will just write his or her name as a dot. Then, when you treat the child with the correct dilution of the stock allergy extract, he or she can write in a normal fashion and act in a normal fashion.

"I recently saw one 8 year old, for example, who becomes depressed and suicidal each year during the tree pollen season. Last year when she came in, she drew pictures which were very unhappy with sad faces. Then, after we treated her for tree pollen, she drew a smiling face of a youngster who was very happy."

Dr. Rapp describes a 9-year-old boy who became very vulgar whenever he ate certain foods or was exposed to molds. His mother found that he was particularly offensive when he went to a particular school. Dr. Rapp explains: "We went to the school with an air pump, collected samples, and then bubbled this air through a saline solution. We took the youngster, who was sensible and normal at the time, and made him vulgar by placing a drop of his school air allergy extract under his tongue. He became vulgar in both his speech and his actions. We made him jump on the furniture and scribble on walls. He threatened to pee on his mother's leg and do very strange things. When we gave him the correct dilution of the school air, he came right back to normal."

Dr. Rapp says that before this boy is given the allergy extract, he is "a very nice intelligent youngster who draws very complicated pictures of fish, and if you just inject a drop of this in his arm, within a short period of time he is vulgar and abusive, writing on the walls and giving everyone the finger. If you ask him to draw at that time, he draws a note where he says somebody 'sucks royal.' He uses all the four-letter words, and he is just terrible.

"After he is given the correct dilution, within a few minutes he is drawing a fish again. On one occasion I said, 'C'mon, I'd like to hear you say some dirty words now.' He looked at me somewhat startled and said, 'Why do you want me to do that? I don't feel like it.' Finally, with a lot of prodding, he said a couple of dirty words, but he didn't say it as if he meant it, whereas before he was having a great time and was amused by his actions."

### Megadose Vitamin Therapy

Dr. Bernard Rimland, a research psychologist and the director of the Institute for Child Behavior Research in San Diego, California, has also done extensive work in childhood disorders. While recognizing the role that food allergies can play in many of these disorders, Dr. Rimland has also focused on the role that vitamins in "megadoses" can play in such conditions as autism and hyperactivity. Dr. Rimland focused his research particularly on autism, a condition that manifests before the age of three. Three-quarters of the victims are male. They look normal but are not responsive to the environment. They can hear perfectly well yet do not look at or appear to hear people when they are spoken to. It is as if they lived in a different world. While this was once thought to be purely a mental problem, it is now clear that autism has a basis in biological and neurological disorders.

Dr. Rimland's research, which has been confirmed by researchers in France and around the world, indicates that autistic children have deficiencies in certain nutrients, in particular vitamin $B_6$, and that for some unexplained reason their bodies require these nutrients in much larger amounts—up to 50 mg a day—than do ordinary individuals, who require only 10 to 15 mg daily. To maximize the effectiveness of this $B_6$ supplementation program, magnesium is also given. It is a very important mineral here because it can dramatically enhance the effectiveness of $B_6$. In addition, Dr. Rimland gives the rest of the B-complex, zinc, and other complementary minerals. "If that is done," he explains, "the individual's body has the maximum chance of using the vitamin effectively when it is given in large amounts to correct the metabolic error it is prescribed to correct."

Dr. Rimland's studies indicate that between 30 and 50 percent of children treated with vitamin $B_6$ and other nutrients show significant improvement. Not only do they improve behaviorally, his studies have shown that their objective tests improve as well. Urine tests run on autistic children indicate that they have much higher concentrations of a phenol called homovanillic acid (HVA). When autistic children are given vitamin $B_6$, their HVA levels often normalize along with their behavior. Additionally, certain abnormal brain waves which have been measured in autistic children also tend to normalize after the treatment. "So," says Dr. Rimland, "the $B_6$ and magnesium treatment has been shown to improve autism behaviorally, electrophysiologically, and biochemically."

A study published in 1979 by a doctor in Washington, D.C., showed that vitamin $B_6$ is at least as effective as Ritalin in ameliorating hyperactivity in children. The $B_6$ was found to be safer and cheaper, and its beneficial effects lasted longer. Even though this was a well-documented, carefully controlled double-blind study published in a reputable medical journal (*Biological Psychiatry*) it could not shake most medical professionals from their bias against nutritional approaches to mental and behavioral disorders. "Pediatricians, psychiatrists, and other physicians," observed Dr. Rimland during a radio interview, "continue to give kids Ritalin instead of $B_6$ to control their hyperactivity."

Currently, the medical literature displays heightened interest in the link between nutrition and mental illness. Schizophrenia has been associated with bowel disorders, as in Vojislav N. Perisic's "Celiac Disease and Schizophrenia: Family Occurrence," published in the *Journal of Pediatric Gastroenterology and Nutrition* (11:279, 1990). We know that in countries where wheat and rye intake are high, schizophrenia is more common. In some cases where psychiatric patients have been placed on a gluten-free diet, their mental states have shown significant improvement.

In "Involvement of Free Radicals in Dementia of the Alzheimer Type: A Hypothesis," by Volicer and Crino, published in *Neurobiology of Aging* (11:567-571, 1990), it is suggested that progressive nerve degeneration may result from free radical damage. Research into free radical pathology, once considered outlandish, is now an active area. Studies on the effectiveness of antioxidants, especially vitamins A, C, E, and Beta Carotene, show significant decrease in free radical damage.

Magnesium deficiency and aluminum toxicity, seen as possible causes of Alzheimer's and other types of mental illness, have also been the subjects of numerous recent articles, including one in the *Japanese Journal of Medicine* (July/August 1990) and one in *Medical Hypothesis* (31:211-225, 1990). High aluminum concentration in neurons has been associated with ALS (Lou Gehrig's Disease) and Parkinson's, as well as Alzheimer's. Low blood magnesium has been linked to depression and personality changes, and improvement has been noted with magnesium correction.

### Your Alternatives

While resistance to alternative mental health therapies persists in the medical profession, there is also a growing body of evidence, such as the Washington, D.C., study noted above, supporting nutritional approaches to dealing with mental and psychological maladies. As more and more physicians begin to adopt some of these methods and treatments, perhaps fewer mental health patients will be subjected to the dangerous and debilitating side effects of drugs.

Meanwhile, if you or a friend or family member suffers from mental or emotional distress, remember that the trouble may be rooted in biological and nutritional imbalances rather than brain damage or psychological trauma. You owe it to yourself to find a doctor capable of addressing these basic causes of your illness. Do not put your health in jeopardy by jumping into the quickest, most convenient form of therapy in which a doctor routinely offers you a toxic drug program simply to mask your symptoms and render your behavior more socially acceptable. If you do, you will pay a much higher price for such services than even the doctor's fee.

# CHAPTER TWO

# Heart Disease

Heart disease is a killer that claims the lives of more than 1 million Americans every year and may affect as many as 50 million more. Upwards of 1.5 million people in the United States will suffer a heart attack this year, and half a million will die. In addition, it costs over $70 billion a year in hospitalization, medication, outpatient services, surgery, and drug therapies to treat this ailment. This doesn't include loss of income to the individuals or to their employers. It is ironic that an affliction that accounts for half the national death toll is one of the most easily avoided diseases. Because people live with misconceptions about what being healthy means and with misinformation about how to maintain well-being on a daily basis, they adopt poor eating habits, fail to supplement their diets properly, and create lifestyle patterns that do not include a regular and diverse exercise program. Millions of Americans are unwittingly setting themselves up for various killer heart and cardiovascular diseases, yet these same people could avoid these diseases by making simple changes in their lifestyles.

This chapter outlines some of the classic initial signs of heart disease and the steps that can be taken to treat it. In addition, it features three separate therapies.

Dr. Julian Whitaker was on the medical staff at the Pritikin Center. Nathan Pritikin helped millions of people by prescribing a diet that eliminates refined carbohydrates and animal fats and putting patients on a strict but moderate exercise regimen. In 1979, Dr. Whitaker went on to found the Whitaker Wellness Center in Newport Beach, California. He has expanded the Pritikin Program, adding special vitamin supplements and eliminating most if not all animal protein from the prescribed diet.

Dr. John McDougall, unlike many physicians in the preventive health care field, practices what he preaches—vegetarianism. He feels that food is the best medicine; traditional therapies may be introduced in crisis situations, but the body benefits most from restoration of normal biochemical balance. The standard American diet, he feels, has lost its ability to maintain that balance. A natural diet, free of animal protein and consisting of small amounts of food eaten many times a day, can help restore it. His vegetarian diet helps not only people with heart disease but those who suffer from cancer, arthritis, and obesity.

Chelation therapy is an alternative therapy that has become especially popular since coronary bypass surgery has been pronounced ineffective for 75 percent of the people receiving it. Coronary bypass surgery and cardiovascular drugs and medications do offer slight though highly invasive relief of the acute complications of heart disease. However, chelation therapy, which is being administered to hundreds of thousands of heart disease patients, is proving quite successful, and it is considerably safer and substantially less expensive than bypass surgery. It is not new, having been in use for over 40 years.

Chelation therapy consists of intravenous treatment with a chemical drip solution called EDTA (ethylene diamine tetra-acetic acid), which slows or reverses some plaque formation in the arteries and thus retards the degenerative process. It does this by bonding with toxic metals such as mercury, lead, calcium, and aluminum and carrying them out of the bloodstream through the kidneys. EDTA enhances a freer flow of blood, thus permitting more essential oxygen and nutrients to circulate and be absorbed by the body.

As chelation therapy is more commonly used, chelation specialists feel that it will become the most important heart disease therapy offered in the future. Since 1990, Dr. Whitaker has been using chelation therapy in his practice.

## Dr. Julian Whitaker's Approach

In Newport Beach, California, Dr. Julian Whitaker runs an intensive 5-day nutritional and educational clinic designed to teach people dietary and exercise guidelines that can help them prevent or overcome heart disease. Many patients attend the clinic as an alternative to major surgical procedures and/or drug therapy. They are frequently able to avoid these invasive and toxic treatments, and, more important in the long run, they establish or regain a healthful lifestyle and vitality that they had assumed was beyond their grasp.

Dr. Whitaker's treatment is as much a matter of education as one of actual therapeutic intervention. Patients learn what they can do about their conditions so that the responsibility becomes theirs. Once patients understand how nutrition, vitamin supplementation, and exercise can help stop and even reverse most heart conditions and cardiovascular diseases they must be resolute in applying this knowledge to their own lifestyles. They make these changes a routine part of each day.

"Heart disease," Dr. Whitaker states, "is not really as much a disease of the heart as it is a disease of the artery." The arteries carry blood to the heart at a uniform rate of flow, and if this flow is interfered with—speeded up or slowed down—the heart must adjust its activity to compensate for the change. If the arteries become clogged, the blood supply to the heart may be insufficient to the point where "the heart muscle begins to die in sections. These are what we call heart attacks . . . when a section of the heart muscle does not receive enough oxygen and simply dies."

It is important to understand that the heart itself usually remains healthy until the arteries are damaged. The arteries, because they are too clogged or too rigid or become obstructed by clots and occlusions, are not able to get the blood supply to and from the heart at a steady, healthy rate. "Heart disease" patients must be taught first and foremost how to repair and maintain the cardiovascular system in general rather than the heart specifically.

## The Problem

Many people have been helped tremendously by the program at Newport Beach. It begins by conveying an understanding of the actual causes of various cardiovascular diseases. This is something many people are lacking, yet it is critical if they are to intelligently confront or avoid heart disease. Arteriosclerosis, for example, results from damage done to the inner walls (the endothelial layer) of the arteries. This damage can be caused and/or enhanced by the presence of elevated serum cholesterol levels and by high blood pressure. Knowing this, why would a person continue dietary and lifestyle habits that result in higher cholesterol?

High blood pressure in turn may be caused by a combination of too much salt and too little potassium. Too much salt increases fluid levels because sodium attracts water. People eating a lot of processed foods—as so many Americans do—will have low levels of potassium since processed foods usually have been stripped of their potassium. Moreover, processed foods often combine deficient potassium with excess sodium. Dr. Whitaker explains that, "A good example would be potato chips or French fries. The potato is very low in sodium. But when we chop it up, process it, and fry it, we take out the potassium and put in sodium. Many researchers have found that the ratio of sodium to potassium is probably more important in creating high blood pressure than is the increased sodium alone." Low calcium levels and the intake of meat products also contribute to high blood pressure, although the reasons for this are not clear, according to Dr. Whitaker.

*Angina*—severe chest pain—is caused by arterial blockage during exercise. This blockage is caused by the clumping together of blood platelets induced by excessive intake of fatty foods. "In the blood," Dr. Whitaker explains, "fat has a tendency to coat the red blood cells with a fatty layer. This causes a reduction in the electromagnetic charge of the blood cells. All our blood cells . . . have to carry oxygen through the capillaries. In order to get through the capillaries, these blood cells have to go single file, because the capillary is about 7 microns—about 1/10,000 of an inch—in diameter, and the red blood cell is about [the same size]. You cannot force four or five blood cells through the capillary at the same time; that would be like trying to get seven people to go through a single doorway. When you eat fat, it causes these blood cells to clump together at the same time. When they get to the doorway of the capillary system, they can't go through. Many researchers have measured the actual oxygen uptake of heart muscle before and after a fatty meal. They have documented that there is a 15 to 30 percent drop in oxygen utilization and oxygen availability to normal heart muscle [after] a fatty meal."

A 1955 study published by the AMA showed that an angina attack can be induced simply by giving test subjects a glass of cream just before they climb stairs and engage in minor physical exertion. Cream, a high-fat food, caused the subjects' red blood cells to clump together, making them unable to flow freely through the capillaries. Because of the resulting decreased oxygen supply to the heart, all 14 subjects suffered varying degrees of heart pain.

### The Program

Once patients understand these basic causes of their problems, the Newport Beach Program is geared to teach them how to deal constructively with the situation. Naturally, patients who smoke must

47

give up the habit. Then they learn how to structure a diet that will attack the root causes of the disease as well as the symptoms. While surgical and drug remedies may relieve symptoms temporarily, they do not deal directly with the underlying causes of the disease and rarely effect an actual cure or reversal of the dysfunction. Dr. Whitaker's approach focuses on showing patients how to deal with the actual disorders; this leads ultimately to the disappearance of symptoms when the disease itself is treated effectively. This can be very exciting if you are one of the millions of people who have long suffered from cardiovascular problems that traditional physicians consider insurmountable without radical and invasive intervention.

Heart disease patients working with Dr. Whitaker are educated while being treated. They are taught about reducing fats in their diet early on. Dairy products and processed meat are the chief culprits here. Eggs especially should be avoided by those suffering from heart and cardiovascular diseases. Just like meat, eggs are directly related to elevated cholesterol levels, leading to damage and corrosion of the epithelial tissue lining the arterial walls.

People who continue to consume meats, cheeses, eggs, and other animal proteins, says Dr. Whitaker, cannot seriously reduce their overall body fat. Strangely enough, even animal products such as yogurt that may have no fat or cholesterol trigger an internal reaction that treats them as if they did, simply because they are animal products. Dr. Whitaker describes a patient who could not lower his cholesterol level even though he had eliminated all meat and dairy products from his diet for 4 years. It was determined that his daily nonfat, cholesterol-free yogurt was the culprit. The reason for this phenomenon is unclear, but when you are suffering from heart disease, you are not as concerned about reasons as you are about results.

Dr. Whitaker notes that by getting away from animal proteins, it is estimated that "you shift from 49 percent fat down to around 15 percent fat, and you shift your carbohydrates from 40 percent on the American diet up to maybe 65 to 75 percent. This will dramatically lower the blood cholesterol if the shift is made accurately. The drop in the cholesterol level should be anywhere between 15 and 30 percent. It will also aid in weight loss, triglyceride control, and blood pressure control.

By adding more carbohydrates to the diet, one can effectively reduce the intake of animal proteins. Dr. Whitaker explains that with animal proteins, which have only two sources of calories—fats and proteins—it is still necessary to add carbohydrates for a balanced diet. However, carbohydrates contain all three caloric sources—fats, proteins, and carbohydrates—and therefore can replace animal proteins. Instead of bacon and eggs, you might have a whole-grain cereal or bread with fruit. Pasta and rice-and-bean dishes such as tacos or burritos along with vegetables and a high-fiber salad with plenty of calcium-rich dark greens constitute a fine substitute for the standard meat and potatoes. There's nothing wrong with potatoes in and of themselves but by the time they are smothered with butter, sour cream, and ketchup, they become fatty and high in cholesterol.

By turning away from meat and dairy products while increasing the proportion of fruits, vegetables, legumes, grains, breads, cereals, and pastas, the heart disease patient replaces high-fat, high-cholesterol foods with high-fiber, powerhouse-type foods. This switch will lower the patient's blood cholesterol levels, while the additional fiber will help clean out whatever fat and cholesterol is already clogging the system. Even foods containing significant amounts of fat, such as nuts and oils, can be used in moderation.

Olive oil, a monosaturated fat, "seems to be less deleterious to the system," Dr. Whitaker states, "than some of the polyunsaturated fats, such as corn oil and sunflower oil, which are common in our food processing. The Greeks and the Italians, who eat substantial amounts of olive oil, have been found to be in better [health] than, for example, the Israelis, who eat a substantial amount of corn oil and sunflower oil."

In the case of nuts, some are better to consume than others.

Walnuts, for example, have substantial amounts of omega-3 fatty acids, which are very beneficial for cardiovascular health. Peanuts, however, may contribute to sluggish blood flow related to serum cholesterol levels; they can be more harmful than even butter, a well-known villain in such instances. This information comes from rabbit studies conducted by Dr. Julian Whistler at the University of Chicago.

Some people are under the mistaken assumption that cholesterol can be burned off by exercise and activity and that as a result, people who engage in athletic and body-building pursuits can eat more meat and eggs without suffering ill effects. There is no scientific basis for this notion. To the contrary, studies have shown that good conditioning and muscle tone do not necessarily lead a person to be in good cardiovascular condition.

Dr. Whitaker refers to "studies done on marathon runners in South Africa in which five of them died of heart attacks. These were conditioned long-distance runners. . . . They all had cholesterol levels of 270, 290, etc. They were very fit but not very well."

Author Jim Fixx provides another case. Despite being a world-class runner and an authority on and champion of the benefits of aerobic conditioning, he died suddenly and prematurely of a massive heart attack. Many observers immediately blamed his exercise regimen, but an autopsy showed that he had vast arterial damage and blockage. This damage is not the result of too much exercise but of too much fat and cholesterol in the blood. In fact, Fixx had been advised several years earlier to lower his cholesterol count of 254. Unfortunately, he was convinced that it was of little concern to an athlete at his level of conditioning.

Besides the quality of the fats heart patients consume, it is crucial for them to reduce the quantity intake of all fats. Dr. Whitaker insists that "you need to reduce the fat intake by about 50 percent of what the American population is eating now to be at what I consider to be the upper limit of fat intake."

One reason why many people do not change their lifestyles sufficiently to establish good health is that they are encouraged by their doctors to maintain the *average* range of white blood cells, cholesterol, and triglycerides. Dr. Whitaker believes that his patients deserve better than this. He tries to get them to establish *healthy*, not just average, levels of these heart disease culprits. This is accomplished through exercise and socializing, proper vitamin and mineral regimens, and the reduction of animal fats in the diet, with their replacement by complex carbohydrates.

Carbohydrates are preferred to fats because they do not have the high cholesterol levels that fats do and do not sludge the arteries, interfere with normal blood flow, or damage the inner arterial walls. Carbohydrates are high in fiber, vitamins, and minerals, all of which promote overall cardiovascular health. They also do not convert into fat very readily, despite the fact that many people believe (partly because of misinformation from the scientific community) that carbohydrates are fattening.

Dr. Whitaker explains: "It is very difficult for carbohydrates to actually put fat weight into your system; some studies have shown that carbohydrates are not converted into fat nearly as rapidly or as efficiently as many scientists used to think. The conversion of carbohydrates into fat takes more energy than is actually present in the carbohydrate molecule trying to be converted, so the body just doesn't do it. The only thing that really deposits fat into fat is fat itself. Often, when people add carbohydrates to their diet, they add them to an already increased fat diet. Generally, when I put people on an increased carbohydrate diet, they will almost always lose weight, and they will call begging me to give them something to stop the weight loss if they are truly following a 70 to 75 percent carbohydrate diet. Believe it or not, the high-carbohydrate diet we use causes a weight loss that creates a problem."

It should be made very clear that Dr. Whitaker does not recommend increased intake of all carbohydrates. A lot of carbohydrates, particularly the simple and processed carbohydrates, are nothing but junk food. They are processed in such a way that their fibrous cellular structures have been broken down, and they have been robbed of much or most of their vitamin and mineral content. Cakes, jams, sugared fruit juices, baked goods, highly processed breads, and bleached flours and flour products are examples. Often the only thing left in these foods is sugar. The carbohydrates espoused in Dr. Whitaker's program are unprocessed, unrefined, and wholesome complex carbohydrates such as whole grains and fresh fruits.

Vitamin and mineral supplementation is another significant part of Dr. Whitaker's treatment program for cardiovascular patients. Vitamins A, $B_6$, C, and E are especially important, along with the minerals selenium, calcium, magnesium, and chromium.

Between 25 and 50 mg of $B_6$ may be used. Some B vitamins, such as niacin, are used in large doses much like a drug. "If there is an elevated cholesterol and triglyceride level which doesn't respond adequately to our diet," Dr. Whitaker explains, "we will use niacin at a rate of 500 to 700 mg per meal." This is strictly a therapeutic dose and should be used only in conjunction with a physician's prescribed treatment.

Vitamin C is of particular significance in maintaining the sound structure of the arterial walls since it promotes strong, healthy connective tissues. Dr. Whitaker cites a Canadian study in which guinea pigs were deprived of vitamin C. Their arteries began to corrode because the connective tissue inside the artery gave way, allowing cholesterol to go into the system."

This would probably not have happened if dogs or most other mammals had been used in the study, because these animals usually produce their own vitamin C and don't need to get it in a dietary or supplemental form. However, guinea pigs, like humans, do not manufacture their own vitamin C. When vitamin C was restored to the guinea pigs' diet, the process of arterial damage not only slowed but began to reverse. Evidence such as this has convinced Dr. Whitaker that vitamin C plays a critical role in cardiovascular health. "In my opinion " he says, "early on the most important vitamin, if there is a single one, would be vitamin C."

It is especially important that the patient's blood remain thin and free flowing, and this is where vitamin E plays a role in Dr. Whitaker's treatment. Vitamin E is an anticoagulant that keeps blood platelets from clumping together so that they can pass easily through narrow openings and small capillaries. It's also an antioxidant, protecting the arterial cells from damage which may be caused by free radicals.

Dr. Whitaker also uses Max EPA, a blood thinner and anticoagulant that acts somewhat like vitamin E. Max EPA, he says, "is beneficial to the patient who has an elevated level of triglycerides, plus elevated cholesterol. . . . We use large doses of it at that stage. We will use large amounts per meal to drop the triglyceride and cholesterol level." He goes on to note that Max EPA is ineffective in lowering cholesterol levels when very low levels of triglycerides are present. Dr. Whitaker warns that Max EPA alone is not a "panacea for lowering the cholesterol" as some sponsors have made it out to be, but is very effective when integrated with an overall treatment program.

Mineral supplementation is equally important in the therapy. Magnesium has been found to be deficient among heart patients, up to 50 percent lower than in other noncardiac patients studied recently at the University of California. To restore the mineral to acceptable levels, Dr. Whitaker uses injectable magnesium for angina patients. Diuretics, commonly prescribed to lower blood pressure in patients with cardiovascular disorders, deplete magnesium as well as potassium. While most physicians are careful to replace the potassium lost during diuretic treatment, few replace the magnesium. This can cause further complications, especially since the loss of magnesium affects serum calcium levels. This is part of the reason Dr. Whitaker believes that "diuretics, and the way they are currently used, are making a lot of people worse instead of better."

Dr. Whitaker believes that technology has been confused with science. Just because it is possible to do a coronary bypass or angioplasty does not necessarily mean that it always makes sense to undertake it. "It has been conclusively demonstrated," he states, "that bypass surgery fails to reduce mortality rates for 75 percent of heart patients who undergo the procedure." While failing to cure many heart disease victims, such surgery frequently puts the patient at needless risk, with 0.3 to 6.6 percent of such patients dying after the surgery. Still, Americans spend between $2 billion and $3 billion a year on coronary bypasses.

*Angioplasty*—a procedure in which a catheter is snaked through the arteries to open up blockages—has been hailed as a great technological feat. However, it has a death rate of 3.5 percent and a conversion to bypass rate of 15 percent, and the whole procedure must be repeated in more than one in three cases because it didn't work the first time. Even though angioplasty is still in the experimental stages, because it is a technologically innovative procedure, doctors strongly recommend it to their patients. There were 30,000 angioplasties in 1983 and 180,000 in 1985. Clearly, the medical establishment is giving quite a bit of support to angioplasty, even though Dr. Whitaker notes that "to date, there have been no studies that compare [its] effectiveness . . . to drug therapy, nor is its long-term effectiveness clear at this point."

Dr. Whitaker's treatment is not based on high technology or drastic surgical and/or drug intervention. He tries to determine what is causing the problem and decides how best to alter the patient's lifestyle to reduce the risk factors that determine whether a patient will recover. He considers the three major risk factors to be elevated cholesterol levels, elevated blood pressure, and cigarette smoking. After these factors, he looks for other high-risk factors such as obesity, diabetes, and lack of exercise. These too are important but "are not as strong or as predictive as . . . the other three."

Dr. Whitaker is most concerned with helping his patients modify their lifestyles. "We instruct them . . . how to eat, how to exercise, how to take vitamins and minerals, and about all the things they can do to stop the advance of cardiovascular disease and reverse the process." He notes that a condition such as arteriosclerosis "is a progressive disorder throughout life" unless patients change their lifestyle to slow it down or "become very serious about it and do what is necessary with diet and exercise to lower the cholesterol level and blood pressure. At this point . . . the arteries which have become clogged begin to open again."

Dr. Whitaker views most of the current therapies available to heart disease patients as needless and unjustified. Most are ineffective in terms of actually stopping and/or reversing the deterioration that has begun by the time the patient seeks treatment. Catheterization, for example, has no scientific basis whatsoever in Dr. Whitaker's opinion, yet thousands of catheterizations are done almost routinely. Catheterizations are used to detect arterial blockages and to open them up, often in conjunction with a balloon angioplasty or a bypass. The angioplasty technique, as has been explained in this chapter, is an invasive method of trying to force open blocked spots within the arteries, while bypass surgery involves severing the artery before the blockage and rerouting the blood flow through an unblocked vein taken from the leg.

An obvious problem with this routine approach to dealing with heart disease is that the catheterization itself—sticking a catheter inside the heart—can cause harm to the body. To perform this exploration without good reason is dangerous, yet it is commonly done to patients who do not have life-threatening conditions and frequently don't even suffer from chest pains.

Moreover, the results of catheterization are not dependable. Dr. Whitaker explains: "Studies were done comparing the blockages that were found in patients who had been recently catheterized and had died from some other cause, and they did an autopsy within 10 days of the catheterization. When they looked at the arteries at the

55

autopsy and looked at the angiogram picture of the way it was read, they found very little correlation. Even more alarming is that different doctors viewing the same catheterization had different opinions concerning the exact location of the blockage. Studies at the University of Iowa showed that blood flow measurements taken during surgery were quite different from what had been indicated by the angiogram.

Furthermore, catheterization usually leads to a series of other invasive techniques that frequently are not called for and are seldom successful in the long run. A patient may have only slight chest pain or other discomfort, symptoms that could well be stopped and reversed by means of appropriate lifestyle changes. Instead, the attending physician often finds it easier to ask that a catheterization be done "just to take a look." The dubious results may quickly lead to bypass and angioplasty. This whole chain of events, says Dr. Whitaker, "simply puts patients on a treadmill to further and further invasive techniques which then hurt the patient. We have heart disease and heart disease treatment. I'm not sure which is the worst problem. At least we know how to handle the heart disease with diet, exercise, and appropriate medication. But often, when you have patients who have been damaged by the treatment, there is no antidote."

The following case provides a good example of how traditional medical treatment of cardiovascular disorders can move a patient rapidly down the road of increasingly complicated interventions that would not have been necessary if the original problem had been understood.

The patient was a prominent businessman from Denver who had developed mildly high blood pressure about 5 years before he visited Dr. Whitaker's clinic. According to Dr. Whitaker, this condition can be remedied with a diet regimen. However, the patient's family physician had treated him with a potent diuretic called hydrochlorothiazide which causes a drop in serum potassium, which in turn leads to cardiac arrythmias. He was admitted to the hospital on two or three occasions because his potassium level had gone too low. He was extremely sensitive to the diuretic. Rather than stop the diuretic, his physicians prescribed another diuretic which was supposed to save potassium, and he was also given potassium supplements. For the arrythmia, he was given two other heart medications. The diuretic elevated his blood sugar level. Rather than stop the diuretic and treat the elevation in blood sugar level with a diet and exercise regimen, the family doctor started the patient on an oral medication for diabetes and then switched him to insulin, which he later increased to 130 units. All of this occurred over a 5-year period.

When he came to Dr. Whitaker, the patient was quite skeptical because he was seeing two prominent, board-certified internists and cardiologists. He did not believe that a diet and exercise regimen could improve on the kind of medical treatment he had been given.

Dr. Whitaker put him on a low-fat, high-carbohydrate diet which lowered his insulin requirements. On the first day his insulin medication was cut by half, and soon it was eliminated completely as his blood sugar remained very low. Gradually, the other medications were reduced as well, until at the end of 2 weeks the patient was taking no medication at all for high blood pressure, cardiac arrythmia, or diabetes. He was taken off his 130 units of insulin as well as 17 other prescription medications. A year and a half later the man is still taking no medication, his blood sugars are normal, his blood pressure is normal, and the only problem that has lingered is a tendency to have arrythmia, for which he is taking medication.

Several studies have indicated that physicians have a tendency to add drugs to drugs. If the diuretic, for instance, causes an elevation in uric acid, rather than stopping the diuretic, the doctor will introduce a medication to decrease the uric acid. This occurs frequently in the case of diabetes as well. A study done at Brook Army Hospital in Fort Sam Houston, Texas, found that diabetics taking insulin were also taking as many as four additional drugs for other problems, many of which altered the diabetic condition. Individuals on multiple-drug therapy must be given diet and exercise programs that address the problems for which they have been taking drugs. Only then can they begin to stop the drugs, because the lifestyle changes addresses all these problems.

The preceding example also illustrates the medical community's tendency to view diseases as totally unrelated to one another. Traditional physicians often fail to see any connection between diabetes, heart disease, and high blood pressure. Doctors like to label them separately when in fact they may be related. These are generalized problems that come from general defects in lifestyle, specifically, too much fat, too much animal protein, not enough exercise, too much salt, and not enough fiber. Where you address the causes of these illnesses, you can eliminate these medications quite rapidly. People should not start throwing away their medications; this should be done gradually *under medical supervision* of a physician who is schooled in, is interested in, and has respect for the power of diet and exercise as an alternative to these medications.

Dr. Whitaker treats patients within the framework of whole lifestyle change rather than through the isolation and invasive treatment of a single specified symptom. A 47-year-old attorney visited his office in December 1985. "He reported having severe chest pains while he was playing racquetball. At times the pain was so severe that he had to sit down for about 10 minutes before it went away. He saw a cardiologist who discovered severe blockages in three of his coronary arteries. An angiogram showed that he had 70 to 90 percent blockage in three of the major arteries. He was having pain and was taking three or four heart medication drugs. His cholesterol level at that time was around 247, and his blood pressure was moderately elevated. He was told by three of his physicians that he should have a bypass operation."

\*　　\*　　\*

Upon reviewing the patient's file, Dr. Whitaker suggested a program designed to stop the disease process and control the pain through diet and exercise in order to avoid surgery.

"The patient adapted to the program very well. His cholesterol level dropped from 247 to around 160. His blood pressure came down from around 160/110 to 140/85 and he lost about 25 pounds on the diet regimen. He enjoyed the regimen, and his pain went away in about 6 weeks. Pain that goes away this rapidly does so because the blood is thinned by the low-fat diet. Exercise also increases and conditions the heart in such a way that the heart is able to extract more oxygen from the blood passing through and therefore has a greater leeway or greater threshold before pain occurs. He has now been on the program more than 1 year and has not reported any pain in about 10 months. His blood pressure is under control, and he has avoided the bypass operation. The key to this person's treatment was the elimination of risk factors: high cholesterol level, high blood pressure, lack of exercise, and excessive weight. When we eliminated them, his symptoms and his pains from cardiovascular disease disappeared quit rapidly."

## Why It Works

Dr. Whitaker's program works because it takes into consideration the integration of various lifestyle factors contributing to the eradication of disease. People often think that good nutrition and exercise are advisable but do not constitute actual treatment, especially in the case of advanced heart disease. The success of Dr. Whitaker's lifestyle approach, however, indicates that the healing power that comes from rebalancing one's mind and body has been vastly underestimated. Surgery and medication cannot slow the progression of arteriosclerosis, for instance, but basic lifestyle changes can accomplish this very quickly and dramatically. Lifestyle changes address the cause of heart disease and allow the body to heal itself when given the proper tools and directed by a disciplined, discriminative, and essentially positive attitude.

### Dr. John McDougall's Approach

John McDougall was an assistant clinical professor of internal medicine at the University of Hawaii's John Burn School of Medicine and is now medical director of the innovative nutritional treatment program at St. Helena Hospital in California. He and others like him offer a theoretically sound and clinically proven therapy based on such lifestyle modifications as increased exercise and restructured diet. Their success has been so profound and undeniable that their opponents, mired in the traditional hierarchy, have finally begun to adopt much of what McDougall, among others, has been espousing for years.

### The Role of Diet

Today the American Heart Association, the National Institutes of Health, and other well-established organizations are recommending moderate changes in the way people eat. Unfortunately, this so-called prudent diet does not fully address the underlying issue. If people are consuming foods or engaging in lifestyles that cause disease, suggesting that moderation be exercised is like suggesting that they try to get moderately better. To achieve more than "moderate" health, people must do something more pronounced than make token gestures: They must make drastic changes in diet and lifestyle.

Dr. McDougall believes that the American public needs to be informed about the best diet available, not the moderate or prudent one. He recalls a woman who complained about the severe restrictions he had placed on her husband's diet. This patient had two bypass operations and a heart attack in 3 years, yet his wife thought his new diet should be more moderate. Dr. McDougall responded: "Madam, if you told me your husband had a terrible cough, was vulnerable to lung cancer, and was smoking cigarettes, what would you expect my advice to be: to cut down to half a pack of cigarettes a day, four cigarettes a day, or to quit altogether? She chose 'quit.' I told her that her husband was being poisoned by cholesterol.

All the health associations and every reasonable scientist say that cholesterol is the cause of this disease. Then I asked her how much cholesterol and animal fat we should feed him. But she couldn't give me an answer, and there is only one answer: Cut the fat out of your diet completely."

The reasons why many physicians suggest only minimal changes in the diets of heart disease patients is that they, like their patients, do not know what the best diet is. For too many years nutrition has been given little or no attention in medical school curricula, and so few doctors know how to prescribe diets appropriate for specific conditions. They tell their patients to cut down a little on fat, add a bit of fiber, and so forth, but patients with heart disease have their lives on the line and need much more informed direction.

Dr. McDougall, like most other physicians, went through 4 years of medical school without learning about nutrition. He never had a course in it and rarely heard the word mentioned. In his early practice he was content to follow the standard procedures he had learned as a student and intern and prescribe for his heart patients the medications that pharmaceutical representatives suggested he push. One day a 30-year-old patient with high blood pressure came to Dr. McDougall, who administered the traditionally accepted treatment consisting mainly of blood pressure medication. However, this drug therapy proved to be inadequate. Two weeks later the patient returned, complaining that his blood pressure was just as high and that in addition his normal sexual desire and function had ceased.

Here was a young man, newly married, his health and life in disarray, who was not getting any better by popping pills. It was Dr. McDougall's job to convince this patient that despite the way he felt, he was receiving the best possible treatment and that the blood pressure pills were really helping him. Dr. McDougall couldn't deny that he was powerless to help this patient.

Desperately groping for an effective way to deal with such cases, Dr. McDougall began taking dietary histories of his patients to see if he might get some clues. It was a strange experiment, since one of his greatest professional challenges had been trying to prescribe dietary regimens to his hospitalized patients. He took dietary histories of every one of his patients for the next 3 years and was amazed by what he found.

Practicing in rural Hawaii, he had a unique opportunity to study an isolated group through several generations. This group consisted of sugar cane plantation workers. The first, older generation was made up of Japanese, Chinese, and Filipinos who had come to Hawaii in their teens or early childhood. Their children, grandchildren, and great-grandchildren were natives of Hawaii and had a very different background in terms of lifestyle and diet.

The members of the older generation possessed far superior health to that of the second, third, and fourth generations despite the fact that they had been in the same location and the same industry for years. The members of the first generation were trim and hardy, still vital and vigorous even in old age. The younger generations, by contrast, were commonly obese or at least overweight, plagued with diseases that Dr. McDougall had been taught were primarily genetic: diabetes, colon cancer, heart disease, and high blood pressure.

Clearly, genetics was not the issue here. The only variable Dr. McDougall could clearly establish was dietary history. The members of the older generation were primarily vegetarians, consuming very few high-fat, high-cholesterol animal products such as eggs, cheese, and milk, instead eating mostly rice and vegetables. The younger generations, raised in Hawaii instead of Asia, had become accustomed to the American diet of animal products and meats, highly refined and processed food rather than whole foods, and sugar- and salt-laden snacks. Dr. McDougall came to realize that diet is a far greater factor in the incidence of degenerative disease than he and others in his field had been led to believe.

He also noted, in a broader perspective, that throughout history it was always those in the upper, rich, privileged classes who seemed to be plagued by the degenerative diseases. The royalty of past centuries were the people who had the means to enjoy rich diets replete with high fats, including dairy and meat products. The feast was a routine part of their privileged life, and gluttonous eating was a major source of socialization and entertainment. The poor peasants who tilled the earth from sunup to sunset could afford to eat only what they themselves grew—grains, vegetables and potatoes—a simple diet high in starch, complex carbohydrates, and fiber. This "poor man's diet" was largely responsible for the fact that the peasantry rarely suffered the degenerative diseases so common among the elite: heart disease, diabetes, gout, and the like. The diet rich in saturated fats, cholesterol, and salt might have been fit for a king, but it certainly did not keep the king fit.

Dr. McDougall also pondered the fact that for hundreds, even thousands, of years the general populace had not depended on high-protein foods such as meat and dairy products for their daily nutritional needs. In New Guinea and South America, whole civilizations revolved around sweet potatoes; the Indians of North America were hunters for whom meat was only an occasional treat, the main diet being primarily corn based; for Asians, to this day, rice has been central; Europeans originally ate high concentrations of grains, breads, and later, potatoes; Africans consumed mostly grains and beans; in Mexico and Central America, rice, corn, and beans provided the main sustenance; in the Middle East, wheat, sesame seeds, and chickpeas have been the traditional mainstays of the diet. Even today in many of these parts of the world meat is consumed infrequently.

We find almost invariably that among cultures and civilizations in which starch forms the basis of the diet, there is a very low incidence of obesity, high blood pressure, and heart disease. Dr. McDougall recalls that one of his professors could remember a time when heart failure—that is, a heart attack—was a "curious disease" in Hong

Kong. People would gather around the victim to witness this rare affliction. That was 35 years ago, and since the diet in Hong Kong has been westernized, the occurrence of heart attacks has risen sharply.

Wherever the traditional high-starch, high-carbohydrate diet is maintained, one finds stronger, trimmer, healthier people. On mainland China, for instance, where the traditional rice and soybean diet is still very much a part of the culture, there is very little degenerative disease. One seldom sees an overweight Chinese person. That same trim person with a strong heart and healthy cardiovascular system would quickly become obese, atherosclerotic, and hypertense if he or she came to the United States and adopted western ways of eating. Heart disease is not the only disorder resulting from the western diet. In Japan, following World War I, there were only 78 cases of prostate cancer among the entire population. In the United States today, there are thousands of prostate cancer cases every year. The incidence of breast cancer is far higher in the United States than it is in places such as China or Japan that still adhere to starch-based diets.

## The Correct Diet

Dr. McDougall, who had been taught nothing about nutrition in his years of medical training, came to realize how critical diet is to the likelihood of developing heart disease. He also came to comprehend that his patients would have to change their eating habits in order to control and reverse the arterial deterioration that was the root of their problems. In his search for the most effective dietary treatment, Dr. McDougall found that an abundance of supportive evidence had been accumulating for many years. He began to apply this knowledge to reshape the diets and lifestyles of his patients and has had tremendous success treating them in his clinic.

As Dr. McDougall discovered in his research, the best diet is one based on high-starch, complex-carbohydrate foods containing high fiber. This includes whole grains, legumes, fruits, and vegetables. The worst diet consists of high-fat "delicacies," or what Dr. McDougall calls the feast foods, basically foods of the animal protein variety: milk, eggs, cheese, beef, pork, poultry, and even chocolate. Americans' declining health is directly correlated with the rising consumption rates of these foods.

The goal of Dr. McDougall's dietary approach to coronary artery disease is to establish the best diet. He works at getting his patients off diets high in cholesterol, fat, and salt and onto diets high in fiber and starch. Dr. McDougall's complex carbohydrate diet is preferable for several reasons. For one thing, it fills the stomach with much less food more quickly. Although people eat partly to fill the stomach—to feel satisfied and relieve the pang of hunger—for many people this is the sole consideration in establishing eating patterns. However, it is important to realize that all foods are not equal in the way in which they fill people up.

Carbohydrates provide what are called low-density foods. Fats are high-density foods. The higher the density of a food, the less bulk it has. The less bulk, the more that must be consumed to fill the stomach. If you eat a small portion of low-density, high-bulk foods, you will feel just as satisfied as you would after consuming the same size portion of high-density, low-bulk foods, usually from the meat and dairy groups. Thus, you eat fewer calories to feel just as full as you would from eating far more eggs, meat, and cheese.

It is easy to see why people who eat primarily meat and dairy items are more likely to become obese. Consequently, Dr. McDougall's patients will lose 6 to 15 pounds a month eating as often as they want to but eating only the low-density starches and none of the high-density fats. They are encouraged to enjoy eating and not be afraid of it, as are so many overweight and obese people. The patients' top priority is to choose the *proper* types of foods.

Another reason Dr. McDougall's patients are taken off fats is that fats are one of the chief causes of coronary artery problems. In order to understand this it is necessary to review the nature of fats and see what they are and what they do. Fats are a fuel; they are stored energy. The body can synthesize fats; they are part of the cellular structure and are found in people's hormones, enzymes, and brains.

Essential fats are those which must be obtained through diet because the body does not produce them. The primary source of these essential fats is plants. They also come from meat, but meat is only a secondary source. The animal from which the meat (or meat and dairy products) is obtained has the essential fats because it ate plants containing them. People could choose to bypass the animal altogether and go directly to fat sources in the form of vegetables, grains, and legumes to fulfill the essential fat requirements. If you choose to eat the meat, however, you are getting a highly saturated fat that is far rougher on the cardiovascular system than are the polyunsaturated plant fats.

One of the first effects of fat in the system is to make people obese. This is why half the people in the United States are overweight and the other half are on diets and exercise programs to avoid becoming overweight. This obsession with obesity would be entirely unnecessary if people restructured their eating habits and lifestyles. People living in central New Guinea, Japan, and other places where the inhabitants primarily eat plant foods and wholesome, unprocessed carbohydrates are not concerned about their weight even though eating plays a key role in their cultures. They don't need to be, because the cause of obesity does not exist for them.

Fat makes people obese because it is easily transported to body fat tissue once it has been consumed. Carbohydrates, on the other hand, become a stored energy in the form of glycogen in the muscles and liver. Only with great difficulty does the body convert carbohydrates into fat. In victims of heart and artery disease, fat, especially animal fat, plays a sinister role by causing a sharp rise in *cholesterol*. The presence of excess amounts of cholesterol in the blood damages the inner walls of the arteries. The high incidence of cholesterol in the American diet is directly proportional to the epidemic of heart disease that people in this country now face.

Specifically, cholesterol is linked to arteriosclerosis and is probably its chief cause. *Arteriosclerosis*—hardening of the arteries—occurs
when the epithelial layer of cells lining the inner arterial walls is
scratched, injured, or damaged. This damage is usually caused by
cholesterol, which collects on the arterial walls, creating lesions in
them. Cholesterol deposits then embed themselves into these wounds,
causing the arterial walls to become inflamed. The resulting plaque
buildup clogs the channels through which the blood flows, causing
atherosclerosis. When the main arteries become blocked in this way
in advanced stages of atherosclerosis leading to severe occlusion or
closure of the blood flow channel, the patient may suffer heart attacks,
angina, strokes, and intermittent claudication (severe leg pain).

A sufficient supply of blood and oxygen is critical to the body. In
the case of heart attacks and angina, blood flow is severely reduced
through atherosclerotic and occluded arteries leading to the heart.
Strokes, which cause severe brain damage and senility, may be
brought on by the inability of the oxygenated blood supply to pass
freely through the arteries leading to the brain. Peripheral diseases—
those affecting less vital parts of the body farther away from the heart
and brain—are caused by the same mechanics. Poor blood flow
through the legs can cause intermittent claudication. Patients with
this problem are frequently unable to walk more than a few feet
before stopping because of the pain.

Arteriosclerosis provides a sad but clear example of how cardiovascular disease is closely interwoven into the fabric of lifestyle and
diet. It is estimated that by age three practically all American children
have arteries that are lined with fatty deposits—the initial stage of
arteriosclerosis. As this condition becomes advanced in the adult years,
it can lead to associated degeneration. This may take the form of
atherosclerosis and arterial occlusion, angina and heart attacks, peripheral disease of the legs, strokes, and senility. All these conditions
can be avoided by steering clear of meat and dairy products.

A less severe and more generalized indication of insufficient blood flow through the circulatory system is lethargy. This is fatigue that may be created by various degrees of oxygen reduction in the bloodstream. When fat-laden blood cells cannot pass through many of the tiny capillaries in remote parts of the body, the body is deprived of a portion of its required oxygen supply and feels tired and sluggish. Even a single meal of greasy meat and heavy dairy products may make the body respond with this tired, drained feeling. After one has rested sufficiently and the fat starts getting digested through the system, the blood begins to thin out and flow better. When more acceptable oxygen levels are restored, a person's energy level rises. Eating this way habitually, though, may result in a constant feeling of sluggishness—a condition of chronic fatigue.

While all these and other related conditions may be brought on by high-fat, high-cholesterol, low-fiber diets, they can be stopped and even reversed by changing one's diet. This is the basis of Dr. McDougall's therapeutic approach to coronary vascular disease. The diet that Dr. McDougall blames for a large proportion of heart disease in this country consists of approximately 45 percent fat, mostly animal fat; 15 to 20 percent protein; and 40 percent carbohydrates, mostly processed carbohydrates and simple sugars. The American Heart Association (AMA) and other national councils have finally begun to concede that this sort of diet contributes to coronary artery disease. They now suggest that a moderate diet be adopted. By moderate, they mean a 30 percent fat intake instead of 45 percent. As noted earlier, Dr. McDougall contends that these moderate changes result in only moderate improvement in one's condition. And when one's life is at stake, one must adopt drastic alterations. He suggests a diet consisting of only 5 percent or 10 percent fat.

Many cardiologists tell their patients to eat white meat instead of red meat, but Dr. McDougall points out that this will not reduce fat and cholesterol levels significantly. Beef may be 70 percent fat, but chicken is still 40 to 50 percent fat. While eating chicken is an improvement, it will not reverse arterial blockage and heart conditions. If a patient is suffering from too much fat intake, why should that patient be told that it is all right to eat food that consists of one-third fat? Why not instead consume foods that range from 1 to 10 percent fat at the most? To get an idea of the relative fat contents of various foods, consider chocolate, a food with a 55 percent fat content, whole milk at 50 percent, eggs at 65 percent, cheese between 70 and 90 percent, a "good steak" at 81 percent, and luncheon meats—cold cuts—up to 90 percent. Compare these high-density saturated fats with low-density, polyunsaturated vegetable fats like that of the potato, with a meager 1 percent fat, rice at 5 percent, and fruits ranging from 2 to 10 percent fat content. Realizing that these fruits and vegetables also contain high-quality fiber, which is essential to free-flowing blood and arterial health—something that is altogether lacking in meat and dairy items—it becomes clear that choosing complex carbohydrates over animal fats lays a solid foundation for recovery from heart disease. After all, the very causes of the heart disease are being eliminated almost entirely from the diet.

While the fat content of white meat may be less than that of red meat, the cholesterol levels may actually be higher. While 3½-ounce servings of beef and pork have 85 mg and 90 mg of cholesterol, respectively, turkey has 83 mg and skinned white chicken has 85 mg. Patients told by their cardiologists to switch to fish may also be victims of misinformation, since some types of fish have as much cholesterol as meat or poultry. Many people with coronary and/or vascular problems are deceived by inaccurate information into thinking they are choosing the best possible therapeutic diet when in fact they are not.

There has been quite a bit of discussion about the merits of fish oil in relation to heart disease in recent years. Dr. McDougall believes that the highly touted benefits of these fish oils are taken out of perspective, misleading cardiologists and patients alike. The only people benefiting are the drug companies that manufacture and market expensive fish oil capsules.

The fish oil scenario seems to have its origin in the finding by researchers that Eskimos have a very low incidence of heart disease. Since they live primarily on fish, whale, walrus, and seal, it was surmised that fish oil reduces the risk of heart disease. This fish oil is a plankton fat called EPA (eicosapentaenoic acid), which stimulates hormones called prostaglandins. The prostaglandins in turn reduce the incidence of blood clotting by thinning the blood and thus preventing it from sticking, clumping, and sludging. In this way, the fish oils are indeed responsible for lowering blood pressure and serum cholesterol and for lessening the risk of heart disease.

But thin blood can cause serious bleeding maladies, and deaths from nosebleeds are not uncommon among Eskimos who have high quantities of EPA in the blood. Moreover getting EPA from fish oil rather than directly from the plant source—the plankton—means you are getting it high on the food chain thus you will also get a high concentration of pollutants and possibly toxic levels of vitamins A and D. Also, taking an excess of animal fat may increase the risk of gall bladder disease and colon cancer.

Rather than look to a panacea—bypass surgery, diuretics and digitalis, or fish oil—Dr. McDougall believes people need to change their diets and lifestyles radically. This is not a simple solution and you cannot passively sit by and expect a single substance, an operation, or a good cardiologist to cure you when everything you take into your body is harmful. You must understand the causes of coronary and vascular disturbances and actively work to avoid them.

Dr. McDougall found the earliest recorded reference to this sort of healing approach in the Bible in the book of Daniel. Daniel's men had become sick from eating rich foods, and rather than offer them some magical cure or secret medicinal concoction, he had them ingest only vegetables and water. This high-starch, high-fiber diet helped them regain their normal health in only 10 days. At Dr. McDougall's hospital, practically everyone in the program is able to get off drugs and experience drastically reduced cholesterol, triglyceride, and blood sugar levels in a mere 12 days—the duration of the program. Their diet is similar to the one Daniel's men were given over 2,500 years ago.

There is no quick cure, however. The disorders plaguing these patients have been arrested, but the reversal and restoration of coronary and arterial health takes months to accomplish. The special diet used in the program is not a temporary one but must be continued after the patient leaves St. Helena and for as long as the patient wishes to avoid reestablishing heart disease and vascular dysfunction. In other words, the new eating habits are not really a diet but—along with a structured and progressive exercise program—constitute a whole new lifestyle.

During the 12-day live-in program at St. Helena people with heart disease are taught how to let go of their high-fat diets and how to choose and prepare high-quality complex carbohydrate meals that are high in starch and fiber. At breakfast, coffee, ham and eggs, and white buttered toast with sugar jam might be replaced by oatmeal with strawberries. A whole-grain bread without the fat-laden butter—maybe topped with a real fruit jam instead of sugar jam or jelly—might be paired with herbal tea or a hot beverage derived from grains rather than coffee beans.

Patients are taught to distinguish simple from complex carbohydrates. The simple sugars may be called glucose, fructose, maltose, or lactose: they are found in honey, corn syrup, milk, molasses, maple syrup, and fruit juices. They provide the body with quick-burning fuel which does little to sustain energy levels evenly or over an extended period of time. In a processed state, they do not even retain their fiber and nutrient values and become little more than highly concentrated sugars full of calories with little nutritional value. These types of carbohydrates should be avoided, but not as much as the fats and animal products.

Complex carbohydrates, on the other hand, provide a very slow burning fuel that is stored in the muscles and provides a steady energy supply throughout the day. Potatoes, rice, and vegetables such as peas, corn, and asparagus contain ideal forms of carbohydrates.

Dr. McDougall offers a variety of suggestions regarding starch-based meal planning, preparation, and variation using a carbohydrate-centered diet: "The foods we suggest are corn, pasta, rice, most vegetables, grains and all fiber-rich foods. For breakfast, you can have oatmeal or other hot whole-cereal meals, grains, waffles, and pan-cakes. For lunch you can have all kinds of soups, such as lentil soup, bean soup, tomato soup, onion soup, or pea soup, as long as you make the soup yourself. Main entrees for dinner can be spaghetti with marinara sauce, curry vegetable stew, brown rice casseroles, baked potatoes, bean burritos without lard or oil, Indian curry dishes, and all kinds of Chinese and Japanese dishes. You can have all these foods as long as they are not processed in any way and are made fresh."

All the foods Dr. McDougall recommends are high in starch and fiber and have naturally balanced amounts of minerals, vitamins, and other nutrients. When these foods are eaten in the whole, natural state, they provide a highly nutritious source of calories and essential nutrients. They contribute to overall good health and a trim, easily maintained body weight. People who adhere to these dietary changes have experienced great and rapid success. According to Dr. McDou-gall, during his patients' brief stay at the clinic, their "blood choles-terol drops down an average of 18 points. Their triglycerides drop and blood sugars drop in a matter of 4 or 5 days. These people change from cardiac cripples who can't walk 15 or 30 feet to people who are walking 3 or 4 miles and exercising."

Dr. McDougall cites a patient who was suffering from severe restriction in the legs caused by arteriosclerosis. "He could not walk 15 feet without leg pain. He left the clinic 2 weeks later, and he was doing 4 miles on a bicycle and a mile and a half of fast walking without pain in his legs. It wasn't because he reversed his arterioscle-rosis—that would take months or even years to do—but he increased the ability of the blood flow.... So he dramatically increased the amount of effective circulation to his tissue. This is an example of what you can do."

Besides the symptoms of their diseases, many people suffer greatly from the medications they are taking to treat these diseases. "With high blood pressure," Dr. McDougall relates, "we take people who come in on high-blood-pressure medications, and they just want to get off these medications because the side effects are so horrendous. They may even be on 10, 12, or 15 medications. It's rare that we can't get them off."

Here is an example of such a patient: "I had an accountant come into my office and state that he was on 20 drugs and wanted off them. Actually, he was on 12 high-blood-pressure pills, one diabetic pill, and several heart pills. After 4 days on a healthy diet consisting of no salt, low fat, and no cholesterol, he was off all his medication; his blood sugar, which was 235, fell to 168, and his blood pressure, which started at 190/110, became 150/70."

High blood pressure is not in itself a disease. It is a condition or symptom which may accompany a more generalized disease state, specifically, heart and arterial disease. Blood pressure rises when arteries damaged by excessive dietary fat, oil and cholesterol begin to close up and occlude. The presence of salt attracts even more fluid into the bloodstream, and the pressure gets even greater. Decreasing the area the blood can flow through is like putting your thumb over part of the opening of a garden hose: The pressure increases, and the water squirts farther. If you increase the amount of water flow at the same time—say, by turning the faucet on higher—the pressure becomes even greater and the water squirts still farther.

To treat high blood pressure, the most obvious step is to clean out the arteries by eliminating fat, oil and cholesterol ingestion. In other words, you take your thumb away from the hose nozzle and the pressure is reduced. Can you imagine leaving your thumb there while trying to reduce the pressure? You would be overlooking the obvious cause of the pressure buildup. Dr. McDougall says that this is exactly what happens in the traditional treatments of high blood pressure: "We treat blood pressure," he says, "by lowering it, which makes as much sense as giving aspirin to someone with an infected toe. We've lowered the fever but did not cure the infection. When there is a sign that the blood vessel system is diseased, we use blood pressure pills to eliminate the sign, but the disease stays. What we should do is deal with the cause. So far only a half-dozen people in our program have not been able to eliminate blood pressure medications. Over the last 10 years, I have treated over 7,000 people.

"Let me tell you about a minister at the church I've gone to for several years. This young man, who is only 32 years old, had blood pressure problems for 10 years and had been taking blood pressure pills for 2 years before I saw him. He was recently married and was having problems with sexual function. He was being treated by a doctor who gave him the standard line: 'You're on high-blood-pressure pills, we don't know what causes the problem, and you'll be on them for the rest of your life with no chance of getting off them.' He finally decided to see me, and when he asked what could be done for him, I told him to stop taking the blood pressure pills and told him how to do this (he was taking the kind that can't be stopped immediately). He changed his diet. This was over a year ago, and his blood pressure went down from high levels of 160/95 to 110/70 in 2 to 3 weeks. He lost 30 extra pounds he'd been carrying around since his teenage years, and he's absolutely drug-free and feels wonderful. He still sees the doctor who told him he'd never get off blood pressure pills and gloats a bit as the doctor takes his blood pressure and finds it perfectly normal. The doctor's response to all of this is 'It was a coincidence.'"

Dr. McDougall says that this sort of "coincidence" occurs in more than 90 percent of the cases where patients have changed their diet dramatically. This is because his patients all make the required dietary changes. Frequently, people are not willing to undergo these changes. Probably the biggest obstacle to improving people's heart conditions once they have been taught how critical diet and exercise are is their reluctance to make such vast changes in their lifestyles.

Dr. McDougall recalls one of his most stubborn cases, a man who only after a severe debilitation finally decided to make the changes he had been told to make years earlier: "The person involved is my father and therefore is probably my most important case. I had been working on him for at least 10 to 11 years, trying to get him to change his diet. I even went to the University of Michigan to lecture to the physicians at the medical school there for 4 days. Since my dad respected the University of Michigan Medical School, if he saw me present this information to the doctors there, I hoped that it would make a big impression and that he would finally change his diet. Well, it did make an impression, and he did believe what I said, but he couldn't turn down Joe's kielbasa (Polish sausage). Joe would bring down kielbasa once or twice a week, and my dad had to have a pizza on Friday nights, but otherwise he followed the diet strictly. His blood pressure continued to rise and in fact went to 190/130. He gained an extra 50 to 60 pounds over what he should have weighed, he became very swollen, his cholesterol and triglyceride levels were both over 330, and he had such bad arthritis in his joints that it was difficult for him to get around. That still didn't get him to change his diet. He didn't decide it would make a difference in his life until one day when he got out of his car and tried to hobble to his office. He suddenly developed a pain in his chest which he described as feeling like there was an elephant sitting in the center of his chest. This scared him.

"I got a call from him about 2 hours later asking me what he should do because his physicians wanted to take an angiogram and were talking to him about bypass surgery. In this very emotional setting I told him, 'You know Dad, I've been telling you for the past 8 years that you had to do something about your diet. I really think this is the way for you to go. It's your decision; it's your life, and you'll have to decide what you want to do, but you can't play around anymore.' So he decided that he didn't want a foot-and-a-half long hole in his chest and didn't want to risk the brain damage associated all too frequently with bypass surgery; he didn't want to be sick anymore. Therefore, he went home and with the help of my sister, who happened to be living with him at that time, changed his diet drastically: no kielbasa, no meats of any kind, no dairy products, and so on. He had chest pain for the first 4 or 5 days that was so bad he couldn't walk more than 10 or 15 feet. We're talking about a man who had been fully functional all 60 years of his life and who now was essentially crippled with arthritis and heart disease. Within 15 days after he changed his diet he was walking around without chest pain, and in 4 months he lost over 40 pounds. His cholesterol and triglycerides were below 180, a drop from 330, and his blood pressure fell from 190/130 to 110/70. This all took place over 3½ years ago. Since that time, when I go home to his farm in the fall and we load hay into the barn or do whatever else is necessary to get the farm ready for the winter, I find that this 65-year-old man can outwork me. This man who was almost dead 3 years ago now lifts heavy bales of hay and works longer than I can."

## The Results

Dr. McDougall's treatment of his father is not unusual. Most of his patients have had similarly resounding success. The attention he pays to the broader perspective of heart disease has culminated in a therapeutic approach that goes beyond the cover-up of symptoms and gets to the basic, underlying issues. When diet, exercise, and overall lifestyle are dealt with in an informed, constructive manner, coronary artery problems can be arrested and reversed rapidly. General health, outlook, and vitality improve. Not only can your life be prolonged, your enjoyment and appreciation of it and your ability to partake of it more actively will certainly be enhanced.

As cardiovascular research continues, as we learn more about the causes and progression of heart disease, potential new approaches to treatment are indicated. We have always known that sugar can be damaging to the body. In "Glucose linked to hypertension" by Dr. Norman Kaplan, published in the March 11, 1991, issue of *Medical Tribune*, glucose intolerance was linked to elevation of blood pressure. Those individuals that have elevations of blood sugar, especially after a "glucose load," can have a significant increase in blood pressure as they age. It is also possible sugar consumption can damage the heart and the blood vessels through the release of insulin. In "Hyperinsulinemia may set stage for cardiovascular disease;" by Dr. Lewis Lundsberg, published in the March 15–31, 1991, issue of *Family Practice News*, oversecretion of insulin was found to be a contributor to vascular cell damage. This can lead to atherosclerosis and high blood pressure.

Low levels of nutrients such as vitamin E, C, and Beta Carotene have been associated with an increase in angina and coronary heart disease. Moreover, patients with heart disease on Beta Carotene had as much as a 44% reduction of all major coronary events including heart attack and sudden death ("Low vitamin levels linked to higher risk of angina in men" [study from *Lancet* 337:1–5, 1991], *Family Practice News* 21:15, 1991). In an article by Dr. L. Cohen published in the *American Journal of Clinical Nutrition* (30th Annual Meeting, 512:18, 1990), antioxidants such as vitamin C are inversely correlated with diastolic blood pressure: increases in vitamin C are associated with decreased diastolic pressure.

### Choosing a Therapy

Having reviewed the material in this chapter, you should know enough about the available alternatives to radical surgery and drug treatment to decide whether you prefer to seek traditional or alternative care for cardiovascular distress. Whatever sort of care you seek, you should monitor the progress you are or are not making to determine whether it may be feasible to abandon one course and embark on another. If you seek alternative treatments, you can find references in this book. In either case, select a competent physician and weigh his or her advice carefully remembering to give serious consideration to your own observations of your response to the treatment. Don't be afraid to demand the best and most appropriate care available. When you are dealing with heart disease, your decision could be a matter of your own life or death.

# CHAPTER THREE

# Chelation Therapy

For the past 30 years, one of the most promising, exciting, and healing therapies available has been viciously attacked by the medical establishment. This treatment, called chelation therapy, could be saving hundreds of thousands of lives a year and improving the quality of life for millions more by treating strokes, cardiovascular disease, diabetes, and peripheral vascular disease, memory loss and senility, and damage due to smoking, drinking, and environmental toxic exposure to heavy metals.

Hundreds of thousands of people have undergone the therapy, more than 400 doctors now use it, and more than 4,000 scientific articles have been written on various aspects of the process. Chelation is nontoxic when properly administered, and yet it has been kept from an objective review until now because it threatens the economic stability of the multibillion a year cardiovascular and coronary bypass industry, which profits from the very illnesses that chelation treats.

The Food and Drug Administration has approved two careful clinical studies of chelation which are now being conducted at the Walter Reed Hospital and Letterman Army Hospital, with the results to be published upon their completion. Yet mainstream doctors, for the most part, still ignore the possibilities of chelation treatments. It is the height of arrogance for physicians to decry a therapy as quackery and demean its advocates as misguided and uninformed charlatans when they have never tried the treatment on their own patients, have never attended the comprehensive seminars its practitioners offer, and have never reviewed the medical records of patients who benefited from it.

But there are no better experts on the therapy's safety and effectiveness than the pioneering doctors who administer it and the patients who receive it. This chapter tells the story of such doctors, and of their patients, all of whom have well-documented records to prove the extent of their improvement from chelation therapy.

### What Is Chelation Therapy?

Chelation therapy is a safe, easily administered alternative to drugs and surgery in the treatment of heart disease and other illnesses. The term is derived from the Greek root "chele" meaning claw, and refers to a molecule which is able to grab onto, deactivate, and remove a mineral from the body. The process involves the infusion into the bloodstream of the amino acid EDTA, which moves through the blood vessels and removes excesses of iron, copper, and various other metals that are implicated in the formation of plaque. As the plaque is reduced, and through a variety of other biochemical mechanisms, blood flow all over the body improves.

When combined with a change in lifestyle, this treatment may benefit a person in other ways as well. For example, it may slow down or reverse the aging process by keeping free radicals in check. It can also strengthen oxygenation to the heart and blood vessels thereby helping major organ systems to revitalize. In addition, it can help to reverse many disease processes, like strokes, Alzheimer's, diabetes, etc., and to eliminate heavy metals which poison the body, like lead and cadmium.

In contrast to most conventional methods which address symptoms only, chelation therapy treats the basic causes of underlying illness, thereby reversing the disease process and restoring health. Dr. Michael B. Schachter, of Suffern, New York, President of the American College in Advancement of Medicine (ACAM) explains how this may occur:

> We know that EDTA removes metals and that it is not metabolized in the body at all. It just comes in, grabs a mineral, and goes out through the urine. In so doing, it brings about a number of profound reactions in the body that result in the therapeutic effects. For example, as people age and disease occurs, we get an accumulation of calcium in and around the cells of the soft tissues, and the EDTA helps to remove this excess calcium from the wrong places. In other words, we like calcium in our bones but we don't like it in our arteries and our joints, and EDTA helps to get rid of that. It also helps stop excessive free radical formation, which results in destruction of cell membranes and serves as a common pathway for diseases such as multiple sclerosis, arthritis, cancer, arteriosclerosis, and so on. So, EDTA does a number of very remarkable things in the body.

### The History of Chelation

Chelating agents were first used by the German textile industry in 1935 to remove calcium from hard water, which was staining and ruining fabric. After considerable research, a synthetic amino acid known as Ethylene Diamine Tetra-acetic Acid (or EDTA) was found to be excellent for that purpose. So, its first use was a commercial one.

Soon afterwards it was discovered that chelation therapy could promote healing by removing heavy metals from the body. During World War II, when an antidote for poison gas was being sought, it was found that chelating agents could be helpful by chelating arsenic, an essential component of some poison gases. One chelating agent that was particularly helpful was BAL or British antilewisite. After the war, chelation therapy was used in the treatment of radiation poisoning, for heavy metals like strontium and uranium. And soon afterwards it was found that in cases of lead poisoning EDTA could effectively and quickly reverse the condition.

At the same time, an unexpected benefit of chelation was discovered. In the early '50s, Dr. Norman Clark, Sr., was treating some auto workers for lead poisoning, when he found, to his surprise and amazement, that many of those suffering from heart disease, including angina pectoris, a pain from coronary insufficiency, reported that while they were being treated for lead poisoning, their heart condition seemed to improve as well. As a good scientist, he then began to explore this phenomenon, and he published a number of studies showing that patients with various forms of cardiovascular disease improved. Dr. Clark is now considered the father of EDTA chelation therapy for cardiovascular disease.

## The Physiology of the Heart and Heart Disease

Basically, the heart is a pump composed of four chambers and works through the contraction of muscle. Blood enters the right major chamber of the heart and is then contracted to both lungs where it picks up oxygen. It then returns to the left chamber of the heart and is pumped out by the left ventricle into the arteries in order to deliver oxygenated blood to all the tissues of the body. After passing through the tissues, blood returns to the heart through the veins and the process repeats itself.

When coronary arteries become clogged because of atherosclerosis, the circulation of blood going to the heart is impaired. This is detrimental because the heart muscles need oxygen from the body in order to contract properly. Therefore, when the circulation of blood is impaired the function of the heart is damaged as well. The heart may then have problems with electrical conductivity, which could result in abnormal heart rhythms.

Another factor important for the normal beating of the heart is magnesium. A lack of this mineral may cause the aorta or the coronary blood vessels to go into spasm. This in turn causes poor functioning because it reduces the amount of blood to the heart muscles. When the body is unable to pump as well as it might because of poor or uncoordinated muscle contraction, the body receives signals from the heart in the form of pain, called angina.

It is also important to realize that the arteries are more than pipes delivering fuel to the body. Dr. Savely Yurkovsky of Westbury, New York, who specializes in cardiology, emphasizes that they are living structures with other vital functions:

> The arteries are not just some type of dead pipe whose only purpose is for something to flow through them; they are very much living structures. Their linings have about 98 different enzymatic systems, whose purpose is not only to prevent blockage buildup damage, but to allow oxygen and nutrients to permeate freely through them into the heart muscle or other tissue.
>
> Quite often the degree of the arterial disease present is oversimplified with an overly mechanical approach to the problem. It is simply judged by the size of the blockage in the arteries. If the blockage is big then it is said you have severe problems with the circulation and if it is moderate or if no blockage is seen, you are usually given the impression that no circulatory disease exists whatsoever. But this is not necessarily true.
>
> Ninety-eight enzymatic systems are responsible for maintaining health in the lining of the arterial wall, and it has been found that in circulatory diseases, usually 46 out of 98 enzymatic systems are destroyed or limited. This leads to the deposition of heavy metals, calcium, and free radical pathology which further leads to the formation of insoluble complexes being deposited and injuring the intima (inner lining) of the arteries.

Dr. Yurkovsky goes on to explain that these insoluble complexes bind to lipids of the outer membrane of the arterial walls leading to an overall increase in collagen, a scar tissue, which prevents oxygen or nutrients from permeating the lining freely. This destroys the integrity of normal circulatory physiology since the final objective of this arterial supply system is to deliver the right amount of oxygen to the cells.

If nutrients and oxygen are not delivered to the heart muscle, it will begin to degenerate. First, the metabolism of the heart muscle cells will switch from aerobic to anaerobic. The body uses this as an alarm system to try to preserve the function of the cells, like a backup mechanism. This eventually leads to a buildup of acid between the cells, in the interstitial spaces. In the long run, cells devoid of oxygen become exposed to free radical activity, which causes them to weaken and die. Very often, accompanying this process is an increase in nerve sensitivity, and the person experiences the pain of angina.

In the early stages of this pathology, where the permeability and transport of oxygen is impaired, a patient may have classical angina symptoms suggesting blockages in the arteries but have normal angiographic studies. In other words, no coronary artery blockages are seen on the angiogram. At that point, he or she is usually told that no circulatory disease exists and that perhaps the problem is one of depression, life stress, etc.

For this reason, Dr. Yurkovsky believes that chelation therapy should be used as a preventive measure before heart disease becomes evident: "I think anyone after the age of 30 should be getting chelation therapy, as I do myself. That certainly is the most effective, rejuvenating, circulation restoring therapy I know of."

### Chelation Therapy in the Treatment of Heart Disease

Chelation therapy helps the heart in a number of ways. First, it cleanses the body of toxic material and moves the calcium out so that normal contractions can resume. Dr. Murray Susser, of Santa Monica, California, says that according to researcher Hans Selye calcium goes to the site of an injury and acts like an internal scab. When you heal the calcium goes away, but if you keep on injuring yourself, like smokers do with cigarette smoke every day, it builds up and arterial sclerosis forms around it. EDTA can go in and take out that calcium, and when accompanied by a change in lifestyle, it can reverse some of the effects of continued injury.

Another way chelation can help the heart is through the injection of magnesium along with the EDTA. More magnesium helps the coronary arteries to relax and open up so that a greater amount of blood can flow through them.

EDTA also acts as a calcium binder. As serum calcium decreases, the body responds by secreting parathyroid hormone, which helps mobilize calcium from abnormal soft tissue sites and move it into bones where it is needed. In this way, chelation is an indirect treatment for osteoporosis.

In addition, by acting as a calcium channel blocker EDTA may cause the blood pressure to go down 10 to 20 points and high blood pressure medications may become unnecessary over time.

Dr. Kirk Morgan, Director of the Morgan Medical Clinic and Assistant Clinical Professor at the University of Louisville in Kentucky, has been using chelation successfully on heart patients since 1982 with 90% or better improvement in people with hardening of the arteries. His recently published article, "Myocardial Ischemia Treated with Nutrients in Intravenous EDTA Chelation: Report of Two Patients," documented the results of two patients with exercise-induced angina pectoris treated with chelation. After the administration of less than 40 treatments, electrocardiographic heart tracings (EKGs) were taken. They showed abnormalities to become normal on repeat stress testing 15 months after beginning the treatment. Both patients demonstrated total resolution of symptoms and renal function did not deteriorate in either subject. The article concludes, "Though only two such cases are described, there is increasing evidence that chelation using EDTA is a relatively inexpensive, effective, safe, and even preferential, but often neglected technique for medical management of cardiovascular and related diseases."

Most other studies in this area show equally dramatic results. Dr. Albert Scarchilli, of Farmington Hills, Illinois, former co-chairman of the education program at the ACAM, was involved in a study of 19,187 retrospective cases of patients with peripheral vascular disease. It was revealed by thermoscan that 87.5 percent of all patients who received chelation therapy showed significant improvement.

Dr. Michael Janson of Cambridge, Massachusetts, a member of the Board of the ACAM, says that, almost invariably, pain from angina pectoris is relieved in 90 percent of the heart patients who are given chelation therapy. He gives an account of one patient's condition before and after treatment:

> Before treatment, this man could not walk from his golf cart to the tee to do his golfing and he told his buddies he was not going to be with them next year. He noticed some friends of his getting better and went to their doctor. He said, "Doc, I don't know what you are doing for these people but I have got to have some of it." After chelation, he is free from angina. He is golfing a full golf course and walking the course now instead of taking the cart.

The amount of infusions necessary to correct a cardiovascular problem varies. According to Dr. Stephen Elsasser, of Metamora, Illinois, circulatory problems due to blockages in small arteries show more rapid improvement than blockages in larger arteries, such as the aorta or the iliacs, which are the large arteries that go to the legs. Therefore, it is not uncommon to see someone with significant blockages of the big arteries to require 50 to 100 infusions before really getting better. Dr. Dan C. Roehm, of Pompano Beach, Florida, adds that a rough rule that he has found to apply is that the further from the heart the blockage is, the slower the response rate will be. In other words, coronaries respond the earliest, carotids second, and arteries in the legs third.

### Chelation Therapy and the Removal of Toxic Heavy Metals

Heavy metal toxicity is a growing problem as it is everywhere present. It gets into your food and drinking water. Additionally, if the air you breathe contains metal, you will pick that up as well. Dr.

Murray Susser sums up the situation: "The average civilized human being now has a body burden of lead which is 1,000 times greater than primitive people had 500 years ago. We are all, to some extent, lead poisoned, some much worse than others."

As mentioned previously, chelation therapy is approved for the removal of these heavy metals. However, mainstream medicine would like not to see it used except when levels in the body are very, very high. The problem with this thinking is that since toxic substances, like lead, are very dangerous and have no biological function, they do not belong in the body at all and should be removed at any level.

Unfortunately, heavy metals do not show their tremendous burden to the body until a great deal of harm has already been done. Only when damage is in its acute phase will symptoms like headaches and dizziness appear. When chelation therapy is used, it usually lowers the level of toxic metals in the body significantly after only 5 to 10 treatments. In one man's experience:

> I went to Dr. Yurkovsky with many complaints. I had some days where my thinking was foggy and I felt like a car with a clogged fuel filter. It was as if my brain wasn't getting enough oxygen or enough blood. And I kept losing weight.
>
> Dr. Yurkovsky discussed the weight loss as a possible mal-absorption and as a possible result of heavy metal toxicity, maybe from mercury which was suppressing pancreatic function. He asked me about my amalgam fillings and when I told him that I had a lot of them, he suggested I take them out.
>
> I had a chelation test where you get one treatment followed by a 24-hour urine test for heavy metals, and I was found to be high in cadmium, mercury, and lead. Then we started a program of chelation, and after 25 treatments all the metals were down within what is called a reference range. In addition, I had my amalgam fillings out. As a result I have started to gain weight and I feel much better.
>
> It was a good experience all around and I am continuing with the treatments because my doctor has encouraged me to get all the metals out even though I am below what is considered a dangerous level.

## Other Conditions Successfully Treated with Chelation

Chelation practitioner Dr. Serafina Corsello, of Huntington, New York and New York City, notes that unlike coronary bypass operations, which work only on the heart, chelation therapy can benefit the entire circulatory system:

> You often have atherosclerotic plaque of the little vessels of the kidneys even before the heart is affected and this weakens the body's cleansing process. By regulating the amount of EDTA accordingly and adding vitamin C to repair the tissues, the little vessels of the kidneys will get cleaned out. Then we can increase the amount of EDTA, and ultimately clean the whole vascular system, the heart, kidneys, liver, pancreas, and brain.

Chelation is especially helpful to diabetics since diabetes generally involves the arteries. The blood sugar simply happens to be an indicator of how rapidly the disease is progressing. Chelation will open up insulin receptors and may decrease the body's need for extra insulin. Dr. Dan Roehm relates his experience with one patient: "To take him off of 60 units of insulin after 7 treatments I thought was unusually good, and I am sure a good half of that insulin was not ever necessary. It is an interesting thing to turn a diabetic around that way."

Additionally, chelation improves circulation to the brain and may prevent the onset of a stroke or aid in alleviating the effects of one. A large study has indicated that an imbalance of facial circulation is indicative of those people who are prone to have strokes. Chelation softens the arteries in the neck and brain and improves the blood flow causing abnormal thermography scans (infrared scans of the face, hands, and feet) to return to normal.

Some people with Alzheimer's disease also do well with this therapy. They function much better, are more alert, and are able to fit into their family setting more appropriately than in the past. Dr. Dan Roehm explains that in people who succumb to this disease, delicate nerve tendrils, which are responsible for allowing one part of the brain to talk to another, short out and are responsible for a loss of short-term memory. He has given chelation therapy to his brother diagnosed with Alzheimer's:

> My brother, Paul, was losing his way home from a golf course that he had gone to for many years. He was having little fender bender accidents. He used to be polite and well mannered and he was turning into this rather difficult, irascible person.
>
> His life has largely turned around in a 6- to 8-month period using chelation. . . . Even though he had no obstructive arterial disease that we could grossly recognize at the capillary, arterial, and prearterial levels, he may have had significant reduction in blood flow [before chelation], and there are studies showing that cerebral blood flow goes up in people with Alzheimer's disease following chelation therapy.

One study on the effects of chelation on the brain was performed by Dr. Edward McDonagh in which an independent psychologist tested 35 senile people with a battery of psychological tests prior to 30 treatments of EDTA chelation and 20 treatments of hyperbaric oxygen, which were given concurrently. When retested, every person showed improvement in mentation and their IQs went up about one point per bottle.

Tens of thousands of people have also been successfully treated with chelation for intermittent claudication, the name given to a type of peripheral vascular disease involving poor circulation in the legs, which may produce pain in the calf muscles upon walking. Dr. Michael Janson reports his experience with peripheral vascular disease. "We have seen dramatic results with people who have vascular disease to the legs where they had sores from diabetes or other causes. Some of them had ulcers that had not healed for up to a year. But these ulcers healed during chelation therapy."

Gangrene often responds as well. Over the years, Dr. Sessions has seen people with gangrene, people who were supposed to have had their legs amputated days later. Some of these people are now still walking on their own legs.

Another disease which responds well to chelation therapy is macular degeneration, a disease of the eye which causes blindness. Dr. Martin Dayton, a board certified practitioner of family medicine from North Miami Beach, Florida, reports that: "Although many ophthalmologists do not believe there is a treatment for this condition, chelation practitioners have found that many of these patients improve significantly and can read where they couldn't read for several years before treatments."

The detoxification aspect of chelation therapy is quite remarkable and is responsible for the alleviation of a myriad of other conditions, such as migraine headaches, scleroderma, hypertension, arthritis, impotence, kidney calcification, high cholesterol, and multiple sclerosis. Dr. McDonagh's Kansas City, Missouri, clinic even had success with people who had been poisoned by Agent Orange in Vietnam:

> These men were severe, tough cases. They were unable to get their wives pregnant after 10 or 15 years of marriage and they were depressed, suicidal, and alcoholic, with all kinds of organ damage, sores on their skin, and so on. Over the years they had been treated with every kind of treatment with no improvement. In every case we were able to bring them back to a normal situation with a 19-month program of chelation.

### An Ounce of Prevention is Worth a Pound of Cure

Studies reveal chelation therapy to be effective preventive medicine. It is believed that it helps prevent disease by removing toxic substances that inferfere with natural physiological processes and by stimulating the immune system. In one Swiss study, for example, Dr. Walter Blumer compared the cancer incidence of his patients, who had undergone 10 to 15 chelation treatments 18 years prior to the study, to the cancer death rate of people living in the same area who had not had chelation therapy, and found a decreased incidence of cancer among his patients.

Dr. Edward McDonagh has noted a decreased cancer incidence in his chelation patients as well:

> We have treated approximately 20,000 patients. We should have seen thousands of cases of cancer develop by this time compared to the national statistics. However, we have not. We have seen 3, 4, or 5 cases total in 28 or 29 years. I think it boils down to the fact that once you stimulate the immune system back to a normal position the body can heal itself. The body has tremendous powers of rehabilitation even in far advanced cases where people are told their conditions are hopeless.

Dr. Trowbridge, of Humble, Texas, says that chelation helps to correct the problem at the cellular level:

> Calcium builds up around the little energy batteries, called mitochondria, within every cell of our body. What happens is a little change here and a little change there add up to an injury pattern. The work of Peng in 1976 showed that if you flush an injured heart with EDTA, calcium will get out of those energy batteries and they will work better making your heart stronger. This is molecular medicine, which will actually change the way people get old and die.

The treatment may also benefit those who are younger and in relatively good health as the blood vessels have to be 50 percent occluded or more before any noticeable loss of function is seen. In an interview, Dr. McDonagh commented:

> Young people are like a time bomb; these processes are sneaking up on them. During the Korean war, 40 percent of the autopsies done on the GIs that were killed showed significant narrowing of the arteries. We're talking 65 percent occlusion or more. After the Vietnam War it was something like 70 percent had 65

percent occlusion. So we know that this is a disease that is striking our younger people and these people would definitely benefit from having a treatment to clean out and reverse the disease process.

As a vote of confidence, most chelating physicians utilize this treatment on themselves. For example, Dr. Serafino Corsello, who has been using chelation therapy in her practice for 10 years, says:

> Chelating physicians practice what they preach; I also utilize this
> on myself preventively. My patients see me walk around with a
> bag and pole [attached to my arm], and when they wonder
> where I get all my energy and stamina in spite of the multiple
> things that I have to do, the answer is chelation therapy.

### How Chelation Therapy Slows Down Free Radical Activity

Toxic materials in our body cause an acceleration of free radical activity, which quickens the aging process by causing cells to die. By pulling out excess copper, iron, lead, cadmium, and other poisons, free radical activity is reduced and the aging process slows down and often reverses. Dr. Sessions reports that his own father who was white-headed before therapy had his hair turn black and white after 30 chelation treatments.

### Improvement from Chelation Treatments

After chelation therapy most people are given functional tests to see how much their arteries have deoccluded rather than arteriograms and other tests which can be dangerous. One of Dr. Session's patients had an arteriogram after bypass surgery that showed that he was still occluded in all the arteries. After chelation therapy he was able to pass a treadmill test with flying colors, which means he was getting enough circulation back to the heart muscle to carry on the strenuous activity.

Other patients elect to go back for an arteriogram to see if all the plaque is gone, with differing responses. Some will develop marked collateral circulation around the blockage, which gets the needed blood supply to the heart or other area even though all the blockage itself has not disappeared. This is because chelation therapy does not always work like a Rotor Rooter treatment. What it is doing, however, is helping the body to reestablish the proper amount of blood flow to any given area of the body.

There are other objective data on the effectiveness of chelation therapy as well. A new noninvasive MRI angiogram, done with magnetic imaging and of superb quality, can now document the before and after results of chelation quite accurately. Other tests which can be performed involved ultrasonography, the use of ultrasound to determine the degree of opening of arteries, and through thermography, the measurement of temperature on the surface of the skin. Temperature rises when circulation improves. In addition, changes in the color of the extremities can be seen; and one can objectively see changes in a person's ability to walk distances as well. Also, an echocardiogram may show the heart's improved ability to pump blood following chelation, and a thallium stress test can also substantiate that chelation works.

### Controversy

Chelation therapy for heart and blood vessel disease has been considered controversial since the early 1960s, shortly after the articles about the treatment first appeared. As mentioned earlier, one of the early pioneers in the field was the late Dr. Norman Clark, Sr., Director of Research at Providence Hospital in Detroit, who researched the utilization of EDTA for heart and circulatory diseases. His landmark article, which had great potential for shaping the course of medical treatment, was published in the *American Journal of Cardiology* in August 1960:

> For several years we have been administering intravenously to patients with advanced occlusive vascular disease 3-5 grams of

EDTA. An accumulative experience with several hundred patients has demonstrated that overall relief has been superior to that obtained with other methods. In occlusive vascular disease of the brain there has been uniform relief of vertigo and the signs of senility, even when advanced, have been significantly relieved. In summary, the treatment of atherosclerotic vascular complications with the chelating agent, EDTA, is supported by a large volume of information.

Unfortunately, Dr. Clark's research and future chelation work were dealt a heavy blow shortly after his article appeared, and the treatment became the object of a carefully waged and highly damaging attack from nearly all components of the medical industrial complex: physicians, their professional organizations and journals, government regulatory boards, and insurance companies.

On what is this controversy based? Is it based upon something that has been proven, or upon American Medical Association and American Heart Association propaganda whose aim is to put chelation therapy out of business so that costly medicines, products of biotechnology, and medical procedures like coronary bypass operations can be marketed? In other words, who is being harmed by chelation therapy? Dr. Serafina Corsello believes part of the problem stems from the use of cardiovascular medication being diminished and ultimately often eliminated after chelation. "Herein lies the danger. We are creating less money for the pharmaceutical industry, so why should they love us?" The precedent for this viewpoint can be traced back to 1969 when Abbott Laboratories' patent on EDTA ran out and they decided not to invest in further research on EDTA because without exclusive rights to produce the drugs there was no way that Abbott could get back the amount of money necessary to prove to the FDA's satisfaction the effectiveness of EDTA chelation therapy for cardiovascular disease.

Opponents of the procedure call chelation therapy a dangerous process when, in fact, there is no evidence to support this claim. All

94

clinical research on EDTA is positive, and the only negative articles are opinions and editorials. The most popular published myth concerning chelation is that it is going to ruin the kidneys. In truth, however, published articles substantiate the fact that chelation actually improves deficient kidney function when administered properly; there are over 200 drugs listed in the PDR far more dangerous to the kidneys. Dr. Sessions confirms this in his experience with dialysis patients where at first ". . . the kidneys were functioning at 5 percent" and after treatments, "they were able to cut down on their dialysis from three and four times a week to one and two times a week." In addition, their lifestyle improved; they could go back to exercising, mowing the lawn, and having a more acceptable lifestyle.

Another myth is that chelation therapy makes bones weak by taking out calcium. According to Dr. Sessions, this is a half truth since chelation does pull out many minerals including calcium that are found in the bones. However as mentioned previously, the lowering of serum calcium stimulates parathormone production by the parathyroid gland, which wakes up the bones and causes them to put calcium and other minerals back into the bones. The net result is that bones are far stronger and far harder than before chelation. Dr. Kirk Morgan feels that as we get older we tend to accumulate calcium in the soft tissues of the body, such as blood vessels, joints, muscles, and skin. This calcification contributes to the aging of the cells and tissues and interferes with their proper functioning. Chelation therapy, by helping to remove this excessive calcium in the wrong places, can help to reverse this aging, degenerative trend.

In actuality, conventionally approved therapies like bypass surgeries are the extremely hazardous ones, especially with people 65 and older. The mortality rate from the procedure is about 5 percent a year, and a large percentage of those who do get the surgery need another bypass procedure approximately 6 to 8 years later. Many of these people do not live longer than 6 or 7 years from the time of their first operation. Dr. Chris Calapei, a fellowship member of the

American College of Nutrition and a professor of Family Practice at New York College of Osteopathy, comments:

> Mainstream doctors often have blinders on. They think the only thing to do for blockage of the arteries is to scoop it out and go for this high-tech procedure, but they do not realize that there are phenomenal risks to even the smallest surgical procedures when you are talking about the blood vessels and trying to remove or strip off this cemented type of plaque. When you compare the risks from surgery to the absolutely nil possibilities of having adverse affects from chelation, it almost boggles the mind as to why doctors are constantly pushing for all these surgical modalities before trying something like chelation.

Dr. Sessions, who has given the treatment to over 3,000 patients in 13 years, agrees that no one has ever been harmed by the treatment when given in the proper way by a physician trained in its administration. As mentioned previously, he has used the therapy on his own father:

> I have seen some of the most astounding and gratifying results. Specifically, my father had about 10 treatments and was then able to get rid of his walker and walking cane. In 30 treatments he went back into his business of raising cattle and farming and bought new equipment.

Bypass surgery is also more expensive than chelation therapy, which costs approximately $90 to $110 a session, or approximately $3,000 to $4,000 for a course of 30 infusions. In contrast, a coronary artery bypass surgery procedure costs $35,000 to $50,000. In addition, coronary bypass surgery has never had a good study done on it to prove long-term benefit to its recipients. In fact, studies published in the *Journal of the American Medical Association* (JAMA) and other journals have shown that most patients getting bypass surgery should not have received it. In a 1987 study done at Brigham Hospital in Boston and published in JAMA, cardiologists were asked to give a second opinion on people recommended for bypass surgery. Thirty-five to sixty percent of the time they said that patients should not have it.

Chelation therapy has been approved for some period of time for the use of heavy metal detoxification. And once a drug is approved for one purpose by the FDA, physicians are permitted to use it for other indications provided that there is some medical justification for its unapproved use. Following this logic, there is nothing illegal about using chelation therapy in the treatment of cardiovascular disease and other degenerative diseases. There are only some special interest groups in medicine which would like to see this fact kept secret from the general public.

Dr. Sessions believes that some of the controversy also dates back to early research done in the field when chelation was given to people without nutritional supplementation. Since chelation therapy removes many important nutrients from the body, some of the early patients became deficient in zinc and other minerals during the course of treatment.

### Nutritional Supplementation

A patient undergoing chelation therapy but on a poor diet will probably not experience significant improvement from the therapy alone. Chelation practitioner Dr. Stephen Elasser notes: "If a person comes in and just wants to be hooked up to an IV for chelation therapy but wants to continue to smoke and eat filet mignon and whatever else, that is the person I would refuse to take care of because there is not any one modality that is so good that it can overcome the toxic onslaught people put their bodies through."

While the purpose of chelation is to remove toxic material from the blood, the addition of various nutritional supplements can help to correct deficiencies and keep the body as healthy as possible. Therefore, chelation practitioners usually give nutritional supplements along with the therapy.

Dr. Morgan advises his patients to drink a lot of good quality water unless they happen to have inadequate kidney function. He also suggests a diet high in fiber.

> I simply tell [my patients] to think of cereal for breakfast, vegetables for lunch, and beans and lentils at supper. I ask them to keep the fat down in the diet similar to what Pritikin has said and I ask them not to skip meals, particularly the overweight patients. In addition I suggest exercising. I try to teach them to count grams of fiber and grams of fat, not so that they will have to do this but so that they will get some idea of how much fiber and how much fat their various choices have.

Dr. Dan Roehm also recommends a diet high in complex carbohydrate fiber and the avoidance of animal fats. He has found that his patients on a macrobiotic diet respond particularly well to the therapy.

In Dr. Session's practice all patients are given an organic multivitamin that is well absorbed and well tolerated. Then a hair analysis is done, and a history and physical findings are taken into account. In this way patients can be treated on an individual basis. Some patients need more zinc, others more selenium. Only in very rare instances is a patient given copper or iron. In contrast, most conventional physicians often give an iron tablet even though it is now known that iron can accelerate the aging process. Dr. Sessions also uses fish oil supplements, omega oil supplements for improving circulation, and antioxidants to reduce free radical activity.

It is important for the specialist in chelation therapy to be well versed in his understanding of how supplements can benefit the patient if he is not to make the patient worse than when he started.

### Educating the Patient

One of the prime cornerstones of a chelation therapy practice is education. In Dr. Sessions' office, every member of the staff works with patients. "You can't just tell someone who has been eating sausage for breakfast for 50 years not to eat sausage, but if you sit down and explain to him or her what the fats are doing, how they are causing free radical activity, what a free radical is, and how he is going to benefit by following our instructions, then you will get a fairly good [rate of] compliance."

## Why More Doctors Are Not Using Chelation Therapy

Dr. Sessions categorizes doctors who do not use chelation therapy into three types:

First there are the pompous ones. These are the people who claim to have discovered one thing or another and they don't want to come down from their lofty post. They are the ones responsible for some of our artery surgery.

Then there are those who are just simply ignorant. This is not faulting them in any way; they are just busy and they don't have time to learn what is new. Also, since most of the articles received on chelation and other alternative therapies are rejected by the major medical journals, these findings cannot reach the mass of doctors. All they hear is that it is dangerous and ineffective. At the same time, these people are pressured from the standard-setting bodies. If they say something good about chelation they may lose their hospital privileges and their referrals from other physicians.

Lastly, there is the group motivated by greed. If a physician is doing bypass surgery and making a million dollars a year, he probably would not want to reduce the number of coronary bypasses he does when he learns that chelation therapy is a viable alternative for many of these patients.

## Why We Need Chelation Therapy Today

Most people today are suffering from a deficiency of oxygen and a toxic overload from some 60,000 man-made chemicals in the environment, which we can eat, breathe, and drink in substantial quantities. Over 130 of these chemicals can be found in our food supply each day and end up in our bodies. Many of these include heavy metals such as lead, cadmium, mercury, arsenic, zinc, and chromium. They can lodge in various tissues of the body and disrupt the enzyme activity of the tissue and hence disturb metabolic functioning. As a result, the amount of chronic degenerative disease in the world is higher than ever. For example, millions of people are suffering from cancer and Alzheimer's disease, which at one time were relatively unheard of.

Dr. Dan Roehm comments on the situation:

> When we look at the misery of millions of people having Alzheimer's disease and we realize the utter insanity of the medical profession's approach of saying, well there is now a gene for Alzheimer's disease and we are going to work on that gene, well obviously our genetic makeup has not changed in the last 500 years. It is our environment. So, there could be a predisposition genetically to the disease but the medical profession's approach goes more and more in the direction of nonapplicability and lack of ability to confront the fact that we have millions of people who are losing their memory and are experiencing a living death.

Dr. Roehm concludes that he is very confident that people who go through an initial program of chelation therapy and change their lifestyle will probably not die of the disease they came in to be treated for in the first place.

### The Future of Chelation Therapy

Despite all the controversy surrounding chelation, there are inroads being made suggesting that this may be a more standard and accepted therapy in the near future.

One indication of this was a unanimous Florida Supreme Court decision to make chelation therapy legal without question. In fact, the judge in this case was very complimentary to the doctors who were persecuted by their peers, saying that their pioneering spirit was refreshing and that without people willing to take on the establishment medicine would not progress. This decision has set a precedent in the United States and, based upon this ruling, many of the state boards in different areas of the country will now think twice before persecuting doctors using chelation therapy.

In addition, as previously mentioned, the ACAM has been able to get the FDA to cooperate with a double-blind placebo controlled study on the use of EDTA in peripheral vascular disease now being conducted at Walter Reed Army Hospital in Washington, D.C., and Letterman Army Hospital in San Francisco. The organization's president, Dr. Schachter, explains why he believes the FDA is now open to positive results and what that will mean to the American public:

> Magnesium EDTA was accepted by the FDA as a new drug, so there are some commercial interests, and that probably is part of the reason why we have been able to get the studies going. . . . If the results are positive, we have real hopes that the package inserts will be changed so that EDTA will be approved for use in cardiovascular disease and maybe for general use. Insurance companies would then need to pick up the tab when people are getting helped for their conditions. Right now, most insurance companies will not pay for it because the FDA has not approved it for these purposes.

If findings are positive in this new study, millions upon millions of Americans may be able to receive chelation therapy as it becomes an accepted mainstream practice.

## Patient Experiences

*Lee Sherman:* I have had two bypass operations, one during Christmas 1975 and a second in July 1981. In September of that year Social Security forced me to go back to work at the Post Office once a week. Even though I was working with great constant chest pain, they removed me from social security because I looked so healthy. They had a local clerk say that as far as they were concerned there was nothing wrong with me even though I had blocked arteries and constant pain shooting throughout my chest.

A year and a half later I ended up in the local VA hospital. While there, they told me I had four arteries blocked 100 percent. I was only able to get from my bed to my bathroom. That was it. I was given a handful of pills and told to go home.

Three weeks later I had a real bad spell where I had to sit up in the chair the whole night because I couldn't catch my breath. My arms, legs, my whole body, swelled up like a basketball and I turned just as blue as the car that I drive. I had to concentrate to get every breath. I felt like I had one foot in the pine box and the other one on a banana peel. I promised myself that if I woke up in the morning I would go to see Dr. Sessions, whom I had known for about 10 years.

I did start to see Dr. Sessions, who gave me chelation treatments. I can't tell if it was psychological or physical, but the very first bottle I was given removed the shooting-star chest pain that I had for over 5 months.

I have learned from Dr. Sessions that previous to treatment I had an unbelievable amount of iron, zinc, cadmium, and lead in my system. Now I have changed my diet. Previously I was a heavy beef eater but I no longer eat red meat.

*Claude Miley:* I had a blockage in the bend of my leg. My leg circulation was so bad that I could hardly walk. After running an arteriogram on me the doctor said I should take an aspirin a day. Then I went to Dr. Sessions and I have had no trouble since. I have had 95 chelation sessions and I can now walk. My legs don't hurt me like they did and I can do almost anything I want to. I believe that Dr. Sessions' chelation therapy kept me from having my leg amputated. I was also right on the verge of a stroke when I went to him and he straightened that out. I am over 81 years old.

102

*     *     *

*Randolph McCormick:* I am 66 years old. Back in 1989 I had artery blockage for which I had an operation. After the operation I still had blockage in my main artery because it was that bad. A friend of mine told me about chelation. I have had 40 treatments; a treadmill test given by my cardiologist shows no sign of blockage anymore.

Chelation therapy has made a substantial difference in the quality of my life. Before I took chelation I couldn't walk a block. Now I have no problem walking. I can walk two miles three times a week. Also, my eyesight has gotten better. In fact, I hardly have to wear glasses at all, even to read, whereas before I had to have them with me all the time. I would start chelation all over again if I needed to.

*Mr. Hill:* Approximately 12 years ago I suffered from diabetes, hypertension, high blood pressure (250/110), glaucoma, and kidney stones. There were weeks of time where I did not get out of bed. Evidently my condition was terrible. My kidney stones were so large that I was told they could not be removed except surgically. Dr. Sessions suggested that he might have a treatment for me and I started taking it right away. After the twentieth treatment I began to feel better and I have continued to take chelation ever since once a month. In all, I have had 300 treatments.

I am 83 years old and currently I have no kidney stones. This morning my blood pressure was 130/60 and I feel great. This afternoon I am going to go back on my ranch, take the horse, and try to find and kill a wild pack of dogs that are attacking my calves and cows.

In addition to chelation treatments I have changed my diet. I take vitamins and do not eat fats. I exercise as well.

If it had not been for chelation treatments I do not believe I would be alive today. I intend to take one treatment each month for as long as I live.

I have seen many, many people come through Dr. Sessions' office, and almost everyone, including those who were facing amputation, have suffered no ill effects.

I think this is a treatment most of us need since all of us have been contaminated in some manner with lead and other chemicals that chelation removes.

*Dr. Bush:* I was going through a period in life where a lot of my friends, who are in the over 50 age group, were experiencing heart attacks, angina, and associated symptoms. That prompted me to think about my own condition, so as a precautionary move I took a thallium stress test.

To my surprise, they found a blocked major coronary artery. The hospital recommended at that time that I do an angioplasty where they open up the artery. I felt that that was an invasive procedure which should be used as a last resort.

I discussed this with Dr. Corsello, who suggested I try chelation for a year or so. She said I could always have the angioplasty done later because it was not yet at a serious stage. I agreed. In fact, I had wanted to take chelation therapy for another reason. As a dentist I had been exposed to a lot of heavy metals over the years.

I went through a year's chelation therapy. During that year I had a tremendous increase in my energy level. I had younger looking skin and I felt younger and everyone said I looked great. A year later I went back for another thallium stress test and to the doctor's surprise the blockage was no longer there. I have had two successive thallium stress tests since then with the same results. I have maintained a schedule of having chelation therapy once or twice a month since that time and my heavy metal level has decreased almost 80 percent. I feel great.

Some of my patients have used chelation and the results are equally positive. It alleviates tiredness and it restores the immune system. I have even seen people suffering from Lyme's disease have equally good results. Other people who were intoxicated with heavy metals have all had very favorable experiences. We had one person with Epstein Barr who was walking around with a cane for years because nobody was able to ascertain what he had or give him a definitive treatment. He calls me up every month to thank me.

*Don:* When I first came to Dr. Corsello I had lead toxicity that measured in the upper 300 category. She brought it down during a period of less than a year to about 77 or so, at which point I decided to stop chelation for awhile. One of the curious by-products of the treatment was that it has a remarkable effect on alleviating the bilateral carpal tunnel syndrome that I was suffering from for almost 10 years. After chelation, it disappeared.

*Chris:* I am 75 years old. In 1975, I had a massive heart attack that left me practically a cripple and forced me into early retirement. I could hardly walk even one city block; the pain would get so bad that I would have to stop and wait approximately 15 minutes before going another block. I went to see one of the famous cardiologists in New York and the diagnosis was that if I lasted five years I would lose both legs. I didn't like those odds at all.

In the meantime I heard of something called the Dr. Rinse formula and I started with that. It seemed to help a bit but I still had no pulse in either ankle.

Then I finally heard about a Dr. Levin at the World Health Center and I went to him. I went through his course of chelation and I suddenly realized that I was able to walk as many blocks as I wanted. My angina disappeared. My bursitis, which had made it very painful for me to get into or out of a shirt, just vanished. At the end of the treatments with Dr. Levin I was able to walk several miles with no leg pain and I have a pulse in both ankles. It has worked wonders for me. I am positive I would not be alive today if it were not for chelation.

*George Forton:* Before therapy I had a heart attack. They found that two of my blood vessels leaving the heart were restricted, one 95 percent and one 45 percent. After leaving critical care, I was not able

105

to walk without experiencing pain. They had me on a couple of drug programs to control my blood pressure and heart action and they told me I should take nitroglycerin for the pain. I couldn't walk more than a half mile without pain after my heart attack.

After I had between 9 and 10 treatments of chelation therapy I was able to walk without pain. I could walk 3 miles in 45 minutes. My cardiologist is monitoring me and my injection fraction (which is the cardiac output) has gone from 49 to 54 percent. This astonished the cardiologist, who still to this day will not acknowledge the fact that my progress is due to the chelation therapy.

Originally, I was a firefighter and I built houses in my spare time. Since the chelation therapy I have been able to maintain activities similar to that. In fact I recently helped a friend put up a building. I have done carpentry work in my own home and I have completely finished my basement.

*Lester:* I had open heart surgery twice in less than 9 years. I went to Dr. Scarchilli for chelation therapy and now I have a lot of energy. I sleep very little, about three or four hours a night, and I have a lot of pep. I am going to be 69 in October.

*Paul Hoisington:* My blood pressure was elevated all the time so my doctor suggested I take a stress test; it showed that I indeed had some problems. I ended up having a catheterization and they found some blockages in my heart.

Having had 28 years of experience in the pharmaceutical field, and having heard of chelating agents, I started inquiring about them. Dr. Scarchilli was recommended to me by my family physician. He took tests prior to my treatment and there were several things that were wrong other than blockages in the heart. He put me on a program of chelation therapy and diet and exercise. I rode an exercise bike all winter long, 45 minutes each night, while doing some weight lifting exercise and maintaining a very rigid diet.

I have made progress. I notice my memory has improved. I do power walking now at the doctor's suggestion and I can walk one and four tenths of a mile in 18 minutes. I take my pulse immediately afterwards and it is 88. That is excellent and indicates that my blood flow and overal physical condition is good. I have stopped using my heart medications almost altogether. I carry them with me just in case I need them, but I'm going to stop carrying them pretty soon because I feel a whole lot better.

*Ziegfried Roy:* I had a massive heart attack on February 15 that left me in the hospital for months. One artery was 100 percent blocked and the other two were 60 percent and 40 percent blocked. Of course, the doctors recommended a bypass operation, which I was not very keen on doing. I thought I would try other possibilities with chelation being at the top of the list.

Since that time I started taking chelation therapy and am now on my 23rd treatment. As a result I feel a lot better and I have increased my walking ability. When I first started I couldn't even walk 100 yards without getting chest pains. Now I can walk three to four miles every morning.

I changed to a completely vegetarian diet and cut out all my fat intake. It took a little getting used to but after three to four weeks I was able to adjust. I have lost 42 pounds in the last three months just from changing my diet.

*Male Caller:* My experience with chelation is that the doctors who offer it tend to be just as greedy as the drug companies and I'll tell you why. I am 30 years old with no history of heart problems, carotid artery problems, etc., but I would like to take it as a preventative. I have spoken to a number of doctors who insisted that I should come in first for a $300 visit. They then want to send me out to a lab for an additional $600 worth of blood work before getting treatments. They also want me to come back every three to four months for another $200 worth of tests. I am finding it very difficult to find a doctor who will offer the treatments alone without all these additional tests, and I believe it is because they cannot make money from my coming in just once a month for a $90 chelation treatment.

*Response from Gary Null:* You have raised a legitimate issue. I too am disappointed because there are only a few sensible doctors who have the good judgment not to become enticed by the large sums of money they could make, and they are in large demand.

Realistically, most doctors today need to charge about $100 a visit. Their rents are high, their malpractice insurance is high, and they have to pay a nurse and other personnel, so it is not profitable for them to see a patient for a half hour at $50.

Many of them are good doctors and you can be helped by them. It's just that they can get excessive. Without testing they are making approximately $60–70,000 a year before taxes, which is not a lot considering their overhead and the standard of living today. But if you start to add all the tests, you can triple or quadruple that income and that, in my opinion, can be exploitative because most of the tests these doctors run are overpriced and not actually necessary to help the patient.

I do believe there are certain tests healthy people should get as a preventive measure. These tests can be gotten at a reasonable cost. You can get a full spectrum blood chemistry, a complete mineral analysis and a glucose tolerance test, all for under $200. Then you don't have to get them for awhile. And most of your allergy testing can be done at home. Once you have these tests done you can present them to your physician; you don't need to have them done over each time. Of course, if a person is very sick with cancer or some other problem, other tests are then necessary.

It is helpful to know how to interview a physician before going to see him or her. You can ask questions such as, how much is my initial visit? How much time do I actually spend with the physician? Can I have these tests done anywhere else where they will cost less?

So just keep calling until you find yourself a doctor who is willing to give you what you want and to work with you. If there is a test that he feels is necessary, challenge him. Have him explain to you a legitimate rationale for your having the test taken.

*Woman Caller:* My husband has Parkinson's disease and he has had 13 chelation treatments in a year so far with much improvement. The main thing I have noticed is that his arthritis is not bothering him and that he can move around much better. In fact, he's mowing the lawn right now. Also, his Parkinson's hasn't advanced or worsened at all since the treatments and that is great because as you know it usually gets progressively worse.

*Leo Levy:* Approximately 2 years ago, I was suffering from dizzy spells, which at times were just unbearable. I went to see a few physicians who couldn't find out the cause of my trouble. Finally, one suggested that I go to a vascular surgeon and I did. He gave me a thorough examination with all his technology and equipment and then told me that my condition was very discouraging as one carotid artery was 100 percent blocked and the other was blocked 75 percent. He said my condition was inoperable and that I would have to wait for the inevitable to happen. That was in February 1990.

I then heard of chelation therapy through a friend of the family who gave me the name of Dr. Dan Roehm in Florida. I have since received between 75 and 80 treatments, and as of March 1991 the results have been remarkable. My right carotid artery has gone from 100 percent to 83 percent blocked and the left one has gone from 75 percent to between 44 and 48 percent blocked.

All in all, I have found that this has done me a world of good as I am able to get around and do my work. I can highly recommend the treatment to anyone in the same position as myself. I am 85 years old and feel that chelation therapy has added quality to my life. In fact, I feel I would be dead today without it because they couldn't operate on me and I was going downhill at the time.

*Steve:* I had a couple of heart attacks about 6 or 7 years ago and I pulled through those in fair condition. Then I had a bad one where I had an infarct and I checked into a hospital with that. After that I couldn't walk too far or do too much work because I would get angina and a heavy chest.

I accidentally heard about Dr. Schachter on the radio. I went to see him and after several chelation treatments, I began to feel a lot better. It took a little time, but after a couple of years, I could reduce the treatments from two a week to one a week, to once a month.

Now I am feeling fine and can do a lot of work around the yard. I do gardening, I walk better, and I don't have the angina the way I used to have it. I used to walk half a block and take nitroglycerin. Now, I'm doing pretty well on the supplements that they instructed me to take plus the treatment. I recommend chelation highly to anyone with a problem of the vascular system.

*Joseph:* I went to various cardiologists and other doctors for my angina and they would give Corgard and stuff like that. But even with all the medication, I couldn't walk more than 20 or 25 feet without angina pain. I would have to stop and take nitroglycerin. My color was a yellowish green and I was bent over. The last cardiologist I saw wanted me to have an operation because I had 74 percent and 45 percent blockages and I was pretty down about that.

I heard about chelation, read a pamphlet about it, and decided to try it. After all, I could always go for bypass surgery. I started going twice a week to Dr. Schachter's office in 1983 and noticed that after 25 or 30 treatments my color came back. I was getting a pinkish reddish color on my face and body and I was able to walk a mile or so. I continued with two treatments a week until I had 40 treatments and then the treatment was stopped for three months to see how I would react to no treatment. After that I had another examination and was asked to come in once a month.

Since starting chelation I have been feeling progressively better. I am 72 and can still play tennis, whereas before treatments I couldn't even walk. I'm not on Corgard or nitroglycerin. I keep it in my pocket but I never take it. I can walk straight and I look like a human being again.

*Charles Fromm:* In 1984, I was diagnosed as requiring a quadruple bypass. My left ventricle was 85 percent blocked and the rest of my body wasn't too good either.

I was barely able to walk when I started out. Now I am 71 and can walk 2 miles without any great sweat. Also, I can exercise for 45 minutes or more every day, and I do. I also found that what little arthritis I had left me and I am free from pain. I hardly ever have any angina now.

I have had over 80 treatments by now and I still continue maintenance treatments once a month. I would say that chelation, coupled with exercise and supplements and keeping control of your diet, is pretty much the path to success.

*Irving Berman:* In 1987, I was taken to the intensive care unit of a hospital for a heart attack. While there, I had another heart attack and I barely made it. In fact, my cardiologist told my wife that I was not expected to live.

When I left the hospital, I could barely walk across the room; with every step, I found it difficult to breathe. The cardiologist never spoke to me about exercise or diet. All she did was give me a lot of medications. She gave me Procardia and Isordil, which brought my pressure down to 90/60 and kept me chilled all the time, even in the warm weather. Also, she suggested bypass surgery.

Being a long-time listener to your show, I knew that was wrong so I was able to ask her an intelligent question. I asked if there was any difference in longevity between bypass and nonbypass patients and she said no, so I decided not to take it. I remained under her regimen for about a year with very unsatisfactory results.

One day on your show I heard you mention Dr. Yurkovsky and went to see him with some miraculous results. After 30 some odd treatments, I am able to play singles tennis and I can walk an hour every day. Although the doctors told me I was going to have a stroke at any time, since seeing Dr. Yurkovsky everything has been great for four years. At 77, going on 78, I feel like a new person. With Dr. Yurkovsky's help, I think I will make it to 100.

*Mrs. Knowles:* My husband is a patient who, 2 years ago at the age of 70, had many strokes which affected his mental capacity. He couldn't remember things and was having difficulty in general.

We took him to our local doctor who gave him an MRI test and sent him to a neurologist. The outcome was that they decided he had atherosclerosis. When I asked what could be done for that, he said there was really nothing except medication for high blood pressure. We had him on five pills a day until one day I decided that perhaps, since both my husband's parents had lived well into their nineties and had been well and sharp, I should try to do some research to see what I could do with diet and other means.

A year ago last May I found a book on chelation in the library and read about what it could do for the brain. I called medical establishments in Nassau County but they gave me no information on it at all. They thought I was talking a foreign language. Then I found out about Dr. Yurkovsky through a friend and we went to see him.

My husband has had about 40 half treatments and I have seen major improvements in his condition. On a scale of one to ten we have gone from about three to eight and that makes life much more comfortable.

\*     \*     \*

*Florence:* My problem was a clogged carotid and I think that chelation therapy saved me from having a stroke. I went for chelation after the Mayo Clinic wanted to put me on Valium for a change of life. I asked the doctor there what tests they took to show I had a Valium deficiency and we were downhill all the way from that point.

My husband had severe rheumatoid arthritis and after five treatments he improved tremendously. We had no idea this would do anything for arthritis. He also started to go for treatments after the Mayo Clinic told him to take 15 aspirins a day and that he would be in a wheelchair in six months to a year. Since the treatments, he has worked 11 years without missing a day.

We met a young man with a calcified pancreas. The Mayo Clinic just sent him home to live with it until death. We told him about the chelation. The last time I spoke to him he said he was 85 percent improved and that his wife was 125 percent improved because she wasn't worried about him like she was before.

I can't praise this enough and I just can't believe that the doctors and insurance companies are not allowing this to be spread and accepted.

*Mitch:* I started chelation therapy in March 1987 after having had three open heart surgeries from 1975 to 1987. In all, I have had a total of 11 bypass operations. In March 1987, I went to my cardiologist and he told me to have a heart transplant. I would not hear of it and he just said that I should go home and get my affairs in order.

I heard about chelation therapy from Dr. McDonagh's book *Chelation Can Cure* and got an appointment the day after talking to my cardiologist. By the way, I am 54 years old and was 50 at the time. I had my first heart attack at 36. By the time I got to Dr. McDonagh's office I was taking 29 heart pills a day and my total bill for medication was $394 a month.

In January 1988, Dr. McDonagh began taking me gradually off all my heart pills. Since that time, I have had 100 chelation sessions; I no longer take even one heart pill, and I have never been in the hospital. I work between 12 and 15 hours a day and I travel over 80,000 miles a year making my own deliveries. I do carry nitros but I do not use them. I go back to Dr. McDonagh three times a year for maintenance and I take three bottles every time I go back. I never get a cold or flu or anything like that.

*Ed:* I started with Dr. McDonagh in 1978. Previously, I had a history of severe leg itching where I would scratch my leg so much that it would sometimes bleed. And I would get out of breath from walking 15 minutes or longer.

I finally decided to do something to help my body so I made an appointment with a well-known physician in Kansas City and had a physical. He diagnosed me as having hardening of the arteries and said that I was 50 to 60 percent blocked. After some tests, he recommended that I have bypass surgery.

I gave it some thought and decided it would be better to get a second opinion so I went to another well-known cardiologist who likewise diagnosed my condition as being 50 to 60 percent blocked in the left femoral artery. He suggested immediate bypass surgery as well. A third opinion was the same.

I decided instead to try chelation therapy. That was in December of 1978 and since that time I have had about 60 chelation treatments. As a result I have never in my life felt better.

*Saul Ziff:* In 1977, I was 57 years old and I didn't realize anything was happening to me although I felt tired, had weak legs, and I would fatigue very easily. Then one day while I was on the job carrying a 50-pound sack, I just had to drop it at one point because I couldn't breathe.

I went to see a cardiologist who put me on a treadmill and I couldn't last for 15 seconds. He did a catheterization on me and found that I was totally occluded. They scheduled me for surgery in the next several days where they did five bypasses on me.

They never told me that my arteries would block up again and it took several years, but I did have another heart attack. My wife found me on the kitchen floor and they rushed me to the hospital again. They did a catheterization and found that I was once again occluded. They built me up for about a week and then did five more bypass operations. This lasted for five years.

Then last June I didn't feel right and went to see the cardiologist. He did a catheterization on me again and said, "Saul, there is nothing more we can do for you." I just point blank asked him how much time I had left and he said, "I don't have a crystal ball, thank God." He turned and walked out of the room. In other words, I was sent home to die.

I had heard of chelation and made an appointment with Dr. McDonagh the very next day. I have since had 49 sessions and my state of health today is very good. Now when I go to my cardiologist I don't tell him I'm taking chelation but he scratches his head and says, "Saul, whatever it is you are doing, just keep on doing it."

*Barnie:* My trouble started in August 17 when I had the hiccoughs for 10 days and felt like I was choking. I was put in the hospital but they couldn't stop them. My bill was well over $100,000 and in 2 months time, I lost 65 pounds from not being able to swallow.

I have had 40 treatments as of today and am once again eating, gaining weight, and working everyday. Chelation therapy helped my condition, which otherwise cost me $100,000 and a lot of weight.

## Phone Numbers of Chelation Physicians

| | |
|---|---|
| American College of Advancement in Medicine | 1-800-532-3688 |
| Dr. Chris Calapei, East Meadow, NY | (516) 794-0404 |
| Dr. Serafina Corsello, Huntington, NY | (516) 271-0222 |
| New York, NY | (212) 399-0222 |
| Dr. Martin Dayton, Miami Beach, FL | (305) 931-8484 |

Dr. Stephen Elasser, Metamora, IL　(309) 367-2321
Dr. Michael Janson, Cape Cod, MA　(508) 362-4343
　Cambridge, MA　(617) 661-6225
Dr. Edward McDonagh, Kansas City, MO　(816) 453-5940
Dr. Dan Roehm, Pompano Beach, FL　(305) 977-3700
Dr. Albert Scarchilli, Farmington Hills, MI　(313) 626-7544
Dr. Michael B. Schachter, Suffern, NY　(914) 368-4700
Dr. John Sessions, Kirbyville, TX　(409) 423-2166
Dr. John Trowbridge, Humble, TX　(713) 540-2329
Dr. Savely Yurkovsky, Westbury, NY　(516) 333-2929

# CHAPTER FOUR

# Cancer

In today's society, cancer is epidemic and the single most important medical issue—an issue inseparable from politics and economics. Tens of billions of dollars and an entire industry in which over 800,000 people work full time are involved. The "war on cancer" has led to the formation of an enormous army consisting of the National Cancer Institute (NCI), the American Cancer Society (ACS), and other major research centers throughout the United States.

Each year, just before the ACS's annual fund-raising drive, we are bombarded with news stories of an imminent breakthrough that could change the lives of millions of sufferers. Months after the collection pots have been passed, there is still no breakthrough and the human toll in suffering continues to rise: 150,000 deaths one year, 480,000 the next, and estimates of over 550,000 in 1991. While we are told that improvement in the treatment of various cancers is just around the corner, in reality we see only an increase in the incidence of cancer deaths. While there have been gains in treating a few forms of cancer, overall we are losing the war.

Part of the reason lies in the strategy of the people who are leading the fight. Their view of the disease is determinedly myopic. To them, cancer is a localized disease represented by the tumor. By excising, poisoning, or irradiating the tumor, the traditional oncologist attempts to kill it in order to save the patient. The allocation of research funds depends on who controls this battle. When the head of the NCI is a chemotherapist, money goes into chemotherapy; if he or she is a radiologist, the money goes to radiology. Unfortunately, the same small group of people have continued for nearly 30 years to dictate where the money goes. At no time has this cartel been receptive to physicians who experiment with more progressive, nontoxic, noninvasive, and most important, unpatentable and hence nonproprietary treatments.

This is not to suggest that established cancer researchers are not interested in finding a cure for cancer. They are dedicated and sincere but are equally eager, I believe, to have *their* cancer cure be the one that is ultimately accepted. And every company is pushing for its drugs to be the ones of choice.

Forgotten, overlooked, even maligned and denigrated in this pell-mell rush for dollars, power, and control of the golden goose is the fact that a small number of highly qualified physicians and scientists have been able, through a lifetime of work, to succeed in curing and otherwise improving the prognosis of cancer in a certain percentage of their patients. They do not use the word "cure," and I use it only on the basis of the establishment's definition of a cancer cure: alive and well 5 years after being diagnosed with the original tumor. In fact, I have tracked down and interviewed hundreds of alternative practitioners' patients and have found them alive and well 5 years, 10 years, and even 20 years after diagnosis and treatment, even for terminal cancer.

It is true that money and self-interest stand in the way of research on innovative cancer therapies. It is also true that a basic misunderstanding of the nature of cancer prevents the acceptance of innovative therapies. The cancer community has barely recognized that a person's attitudes, beliefs, and diet can affect the outcome or causation of cancer. Only recently have some scientists acknowledged that environment can be a determining factor or that cancer represents a breakdown in the body's overall immune system. Traditional physicians are more reluctant still to acknowledge that treatment that consists solely in removing the tumor with surgery or killing the cells in the tumor with radiation or chemotherapy may end up killing the patient by releasing extra toxins while doing little or nothing to stop the progress of the disease.

This chapter will focus on the alternative view that the tumor is merely a symptom and that the therapy should focus not on the symptom but on the underlying causes. This would lead to treatment aimed at rebuilding the body's natural immunity and strengthening its ability to destroy or control cancer cells. This is no longer a theory, as you will see from the following case histories.

The cancer puzzle has not been completely solved. There are still failures in the treatment results of each of the therapists described in this chapter. However, in total, these therapies represent the most logical and advanced perspectives and the best chances for success in the treatment of cancer.

### Dr. Livingston: The Cancer Microbe

The lump in Dr. Owen Wheeler's neck was not large, but it was a lot more than a swollen gland. Closer examination confirmed the physician's worst fears. He had a cancer of the lymph glands that had wrapped itself around the major arteries nearby. An attempt at surgery would be the equivalent of slitting the doctor's throat.

As a physician, Dr. Wheeler had seen a great deal of cancer in books, in laboratories, and in his own and other doctors' patients. Now he had to choose a treatment for himself. For him, since surgery was out, it had to be either radiation or chemotherapy. As a medical doctor, he would be in danger of losing his license if he ordered any treatment other than surgery, radiation, or chemotherapy for a similarly afflicted patient. However, from his own experience he knew that the improvement rate for these treatments is 15 percent at best.

Radiation, the doctor soon discovered, would be almost as damaging as surgery to the major blood vessels near his cancer. However, he did not feel ready to subject himself to chemotherapy. Just a few years previously he had watched his father die of the same type of cancer, suffering horribly from the side effects of the drugs used to combat the disease.

Like many other physicians, Dr. Wheeler refused chemotherapy when his own health was involved and began looking into alternative therapies. Ultimately, he decided to go to Dr. Virginia Livingston's clinic in San Diego, California, which featured an innovative treatment based on an unorthodox theory of the nature and cause of cancer, a theory with far-reaching implications for public health. At Dr. Livingston's clinic, Dr. Wheeler's cancerous tumor gradually disappeared and has stayed away for the past 12 years.

## The Discovery

Dr. Wheeler did not make the decision to go to San Diego lightly. He knew his life was at stake, but he also knew he was not going to undergo a Johnny-come-lately treatment of uncertain background and unpredictable outcome. He knew that Virginia Livingston was a remarkable physician whose interest in and work on cancer went back two generations. One of only four women to graduate from New York University-Bellevue Medical College in 1936, she was one of the first women residents appointed to a New York City hospital. Her interests then were tuberculosis and leprosy.

Her path to cancer research began indirectly in 1947, when she was asked for a second opinion on a case diagnosed as Raynaud's phenomenon, a circulatory condition that causes ulcerations on different parts of the body. While many of the patient's symptoms resembled those of leprosy, Dr. Livingston thought a more likely diagnosis was *scleroderma*, a skin disease characterized by hard, knotty patches, which can be fatal if it spreads to the internal organs.

Curious about the apparent similarity of scleroderma to leprosy, Dr. Livingston tested some smears with a special dye designed to detect the presence of tuberculosis and leprosy microbes. The tests were positive, suggesting that these scleroderma microbes were closely related to the tuberculosis and leprosy bacteria.

Livingston went on to test these organisms on chickens and guinea pigs. To her amazement, almost all the chickens died while the guinea pigs developed hardened patches of skin, some of which looked cancerous. Since cancer in guinea pigs is nearly unheard of, these results raised unsettling questions: Could this microbe from a human being cause disease in chickens and guinea pigs? Could this same microbe transmit disease from animals to humans? Was cancer perhaps infectious? Was it caused by bacteria?

From various hospitals, Dr. Livingston gathered samples of human cancers removed during surgery and put the pathological tissues under the microscope. The microbe was indeed present in every one of the samples. When she isolated and cultured the microbe from the cancer tissues and injected it into mice, the mice developed cancer in about 20 percent of cases. Dr. Livingston decided to call this microbe progenitor cryptocides

After several years of careful research at Newark Presbyterian Hospital, Dr. Livingston published her findings in the *American Journal of Medical Sciences* in 1950, much to the verbally expressed dismay of many members of the cancer establishment. After all, they had long accepted as an article of faith that cancer is caused by a virus. Medical technology has long been able to develop antibiotics to deal with bacteria but has yet to find any consistently effective protection against viruses. The fact that cancer might actually be caused by a bacteria thus should have come as good news, but the medical establishment refused to give credibility to Livingston's findings by setting up testing procedures to verify or disprove her findings. Instead, the traditional researchers simply continued to voice denial of the credibility of the microbe theory.

Both Dr. Livingston and her opponents—including the ACS—

cited as evidence in their favor experiments performed by Dr. Peyton Rous in 1910 which demonstrated that roughly 90 percent of the chickens sold in New York City contained cancers caused by a microbial agent small enough to pass through a filter designed to catch bacteria while allowing viruses, which are much smaller, to pass through. Although Dr. Rous did not conclude this "filterable microbial agent" was a virus, scientists who came after him assumed this to be the case. Dr. Livingston, however, believed her progenitor cryptocides (PC) was in fact the cancer-causing agent discovered by Dr. Rous.

Since PC bacteria are highly pleomorphic (i.e., often assume forms that do not resemble bacteria at all) and have different growth requirements depending on the stage they are in, Dr. Livingston proceeded with extra tests to make certain that she was not dealing with a virus. She discovered that PC would indeed pass through Dr. Rous' filter just as viruses were supposed to do. But then she took samples of the filtered microbes and regrew them in cultures, something impossible to do with viruses, since they are unable to survive outside of living organisms. Dr. Livingston also discovered that unlike viruses, both PC and Dr. Rous' cancer agent could be dried, stored indefinitely, and then reactivated to produce new tumors. For Dr. Livingston, the PC cancer-causing agent was not a virus but was only viruslike. The PC bacteria had to be reincubated and made larger in order to be kept from passing through very fine filters that usually hold back bacteria.

In the course of her research, Dr. Livingston reached another conclusion that put her at odds with the cancer establishment, especially the part of it which believes implicitly in surgery as a first recourse. PC, as Dr. Livingston found out, was present not merely in the cancer but throughout the patient's entire body. In her view, cancer is not a localized disease. Rather, it is a generalized or systemic illness affecting the entire body, not just the particular area manifesting symptoms. Thus, while surgery can be helpful in that by removing cancerous tissue it helps the immune system fight the disease, it is a serious error to think of the tumor or lesions as constituting the disease and of surgery as being the cure. Indeed, from Dr. Livingston's viewpoint, it was no surprise that a patient could develop cancer in a totally different site after a "successful" operation, despite the surgeon's having "gotten it all." Since surgery does nothing by itself to enhance the body's immune system, it may even make another onset of cancer more likely—and more serious.

Dr. Livingston might have concluded that once a drug to combat or at least control PC bacteria was developed, a cure for cancer would be on its way. Careful research on the microbe in laboratory animals, however, convinced her that the solution was far more complex than finding a "magic bullet" to strike down PC. The PC bacteria, she discovered, are a normal constituent of every cell in the human body.

"The microbe is present in people from the time of conception," she stated in a WBAI radio interview in 1987. "It is not always harmful. It is useful, for example, in the knitting of wounds. But when it begins rampant proliferation, it produces a hormone called chorigonadotropin, which promotes tumor growth and is present in abnormally large amounts in cancer tissues."

Dr. Livingston went on to explain that PC normally remains dormant in the cell and emerges only to help in healing after injury to the body. Ordinarily the immune system monitors the production of PC, keeping it at the amount needed to cope with the damage. But when immunity is weakened by stress, poor diet, old age, surgery, and/or other debilitating factors, the body may no longer be able to regulate PC production and PC bacteria may begin to proliferate, releasing chorigonadotropin as it multiplies.

Dr. Livingston pondered this evidence for many years beginning in the 1940s and 1950s and continued gathering data and doing research until she evolved a program of cancer treatment that she could put into practice at the San Diego clinic, which opened in 1969. According to Dr. Livingston, since that time more than 10,000 people have been treated with a combination of her Anti-Cancer Diet, antibiotics, and a therapy she calls autogenous vaccines. Eighty percent of them have improved. Recently, while on vacation in Europe, Dr. Livingston died. We all mourn her loss. But the challenge her work presents to the medical establishment lives on.

## The Anti-Cancer Diet

The Anti-Cancer Diet is not in itself a cure for cancer, nor is it intended as such; however, it works with the other aspects of Dr. Livingston's therapy to strengthen the immune system. A healthy immune system not only keeps normally present PC under control but combats any disease-causing PC taken in with food. Meats, especially chicken, beef, and pork, are the most likely sources of dietary PC.

Since the immune system of a cancer patient is already seriously depleted, it is necessary to avoid these kinds of foods in order to minimize the influx of pathogenic cancer-causing PC. For this reason, Dr. Livingston's diet goes beyond the usual tenets of sound nutrition. It emphasizes raw or very lightly cooked fresh foods full of vitamins, minerals, and enzymes for rebuilding the body. Refined or processed foods are dispensed with as far as possible. Most animal products are excluded, both because of their suspected ability to transmit pathogenic PC and because they are often full of toxins, hormones, antibiotics, chemicals, and pesticides that deplete the immune system and may interfere with treatment. In fact, the diet Dr. Livingston developed is basically the one which the ACS is now only beginning to promote: primarily vegetarian, low in fats and cholesterol, low in animal products and protein, and high in fresh fruits, vegetables, whole grains, and legumes.

Dr. Livingston stipulated that her patients do the following:

- Avoid the obvious carcinogens and immune system depleters, such as cigarettes, alcohol, caffeine, and drugs, both recreational and prescription.

- Avoid the empty calories of foods that are high in white flour and sugar or that have been deep fried.
- Cut down on salt and on foods high in sodium while increasing consumption of potassium-rich fresh fruits and vegetables.

As patients began to recover, Dr. Livingston allowed them to eat some fish, but chicken, eggs, beef, and milk products remain prohibited, since her research has led her to believe that these foods have a high potential for transmitting cancer to humans. The PC microbes in their pathogenic state are in the animals, and when the animals are eaten, the microbes are transmitted and proliferate in humans.

The most unusual aspect of Dr. Livingston's diet, however, is its focus on abscisic acid, an essential immune nutrient forming part of the vitamin A molecule. As Dr. Livingston stated in her 1984 book, *The Conquest of Cancer: Vaccines and Diet* (Franklin Watts, New York, 1984), "Abscisic acid is the keystone upon which all cancer immunity is built in your body. If you already have cancer, *abscisic acid* is absolutely critical to your defense, because it actually *stops cancer cells from multiplying.* If you don't have cancer (or if it is latent in your system), it is imperative that your diet contain high amounts of vitamin A and abscisic acid if you are to immunize yourself against it."

Of course, raw juices, especially carrot juice, and fruits and vegetables high in vitamin A have a prominent role in the Anti–Cancer Diet. However, because many cancer patients have extensive liver damage and therefore are unable to break down vitamin A to obtain abscisic acid, Dr. Livingston's diet also includes a number of foods such as mangos, avocados, tomatoes, and green leafy vegetables that are naturally rich in abscisins. To break down the vitamin A in carrot juice, Dr. Livingston recommended adding a tablespoon of dried liver powder (from organically fed cattle, of course), which contains enzymes that predigest the carrot juice and thus make the abscisic acid available.

Besides the diet, Dr. Livingston developed an autogenous vaccine made from the PC in the individual patient. "We make the vaccine," she reported in the 1987 interview, "and as the body builds immune bodies to the organism, the deleterious effects of the progenitor cryptocides are nullified. But each time we make it, we make it for the individual. It cannot be made for your neighbor, and it cannot be sold."

Since PC microbes are bacteria, they are vulnerable to antibiotics, and Dr. Livingston found that the administration of safe, nontoxic antibiotics such as ampicillin and penicillin G can reduce the *excessive* amount of PC in the bloodstream and thereby cause cancerous tumors to shrink. The term "excessive" is used here because, as has been noted, normal amounts of PC do not cause a problem in the healthy body and in fact contribute to one's well-being. It is only when they become excessive that they contribute to cancerous growth in the body.

Other elements of this completely safe, nontoxic program include the following:

- Transfusions of fresh whole blood, preferably from a healthy family member, to reduce the risk of contamination, increase oxygenation, and replenish the body's enzymes
- Injections of gamma globulin to provide fresh antibodies
- Injections of spleen extract derived from immunized animals to increase the patient's white blood cell count. White blood cells play a critical role in arresting foreign substances and toxic intruders into the blood.
- Injections of nonspecific vaccines, such as one containing numerous mixed bacteria, for use in respiratory infections and to increase general resistance.
- Supplements and/or injections of vitamins C and $B_{12}$ plus tablets of vitamins such as A, C, E, $B_6$, and $B_{12}$ and minerals to stimulate the immune system.
- Oral supplementation of hydrochloric acid where needed to correct overly alkaline blood caused by digestive difficulties.

Dr. Wheeler's visit to the clinic had a special fringe benefit in that he found a new wife as well as renewed health. But while only one patient could marry the director of the clinic, thousands of others have regained their health and have come home with a regimen that has kept them cancer-free over the ensuing years.

## Transmissibility

Theories about the transmissibility of cancer have alarming implications for public health. The doctor's experiments convinced her that cancer can be transmitted from human beings to chickens and guinea pigs. This conclusion raises the disquieting implication that the transfer mechanism may work in the other direction as well, allowing cancer to pass from animals to humans.

For obvious reasons, the poultry industry finds such an idea unthinkable. However, Dr. Livingston's chicken vaccine was licensed in California in 1985.

"Cancer is a very serious disease in chickens," Dr. Livingston noted in her radio interview. "Each year many thousands of chickens are lost to cancer. The organism is carried from chicken to chicken, even in the unhatched egg."

If all of these birds were simply "lost," the problem would be confined to the poultry industry, but there is considerable evidence, Dr. Livingston stated, that many infected fowls are finding their way into supermarkets. She believes that the chickens we consume today are just as cancer-ridden as the ones Dr. Rous examined in 1910 when he determined that 90 percent were so afflicted. A March 1987 report on *60 Minutes*, while not concerned specifically with cancer, certainly supported her contention that FAA enforcement is both lax and ineffective in keeping questionable poultry off the market.

The question of whether cancer can pass from animals to humans takes on even wider dimensions when one considers that livestock, often living in cramped and unhealthy conditions, are frequently fed chicken manure because of its high protein content, and are thus exposed to the infectious cancers so prevalent on the poultry farm. But avoiding eating beef and pork, while desirable, is not sufficient, according to Dr. Livingston. Even drinking milk is risky, she asserted, since "about 80 to 90 percent of cattle are carrying leukemia," according to the cattle industry's own literature.

The doctor's views on milk are met with as much skepticism in the dairy industry as her views on meat and poultry are in the meat and poultry industries. But Dr. Livingston's legacy is not without support. Her views are accepted in Europe. In Switzerland and Sweden, where dairy is the number one industry, milk from leukemic cows is not permitted to reach the market because the authorities consider it a serious risk to the public health. Such strictures have not been imposed in the United States in part because the U.S. dairy industry simply doesn't believe, and no government authorities will test, Dr. Livingston's theories. The doctor never denied that the expense of enforcing strict quality control and rejecting milk or meat from diseased animals would be tremendous. However, it would also alleviate a great amount of human suffering.

### The Results

Dr. Livingston's ideas about the treatment and prevention of cancer are not purely academic. They have been put to the test in her clinical practice as well as in her laboratory. In *The Conquest of Cancer*, she lists over 60 cases of patients she treated; these were pulled at random from her files. Of course, not every story is a success story, but the sample does show an improvement rate of 82 percent, a statistic that conventional therapists can only dream of.

*Example 1:* A 66-year-old man came to the clinic in 1978, diagnosed with inoperable cancer of the liver. By 1980 the patient reported feeling much better, and tests showed that his tumor had shrunk 50 percent. When Dr. Livingston contacted him in 1983 while writing her book, he said that he was still following the program and was in general good health.

*Example 2:* In April 1981, a 12-year-old boy was diagnosed with

Hodgkin's disease. His mother, however, refused to subject him to chemotherapy and brought him to Dr. Livingston's clinic instead. By January 1982 his lymphoma was in remission. Follow-up testing revealed that he was totally clear and that a lesion on his liver had disappeared. He went back to school, gained weight, and was soon participating in sports.

*Example 3:* A 51-year-old woman could no longer endure the side effects of radiation and chemotherapy for cancer of the ovaries which had spread to her colon, causing a tumor about the size of a baseball. Her prognosis was terminal when she started treatment at the clinic in February 1981. A computed axial tomography (CAT) scan and an ultrasound test taken the following year showed no abnormalities. She went back to work, and in 1983 she was still free of cancer.

*Example 4:* Cancer of the pancreas that had metastasized to the liver brought a 67-year-old man to the clinic in May 1979. His physician had given him 6 weeks to live. By May 1981, however, CAT, bone, and liver scans showed that the tumor was in remission, as was the liver lesion. In February 1982 a biopsy showed that his liver was normal.

None of these case histories, of course, constitutes experimental proof that Dr. Livingston's therapy is effective. Such proof is not likely to be forthcoming, since it is not morally feasible to establish a control group of cancer patients, give them a placebo, and see how many of them die. However, Dr. Livingston always stood ready to put researchers who wished to verify these stories in touch with these patients or any others in her files.

The doctor's work continues in San Diego. Whether her theories will ever find acceptance and be applied in the wider arena of public health in the United States remains to be seen.

### Dr. Burzynski

Twenty-five years ago a medical student in Poland took a different approach to cancer research: he decided to find out why all people don't have cancer. Everyone is exposed to the same known and unknown causative agents of this disease. What is different about the people who never contract it? Is this difference the key to developing a cure?

Dr. Stanislaw Burzynski, M.D., Ph.D., believes so. Now working out of a research facility he founded in 1970 in Houston, Texas, Dr. Burzynski has treated about 2,000 patients with advanced cancer with impressive success since 1977. Most of these people turned to him as a last resort when conventional treatment with radiation, chemotherapy, and surgery had failed. What they found was a therapy based not on the abuse of the body's built-in defense systems but rather on the transformation of cancerous cells into healthy, normal tissue.

### Peptides and Antineoplastons

Dr. Burzynski's solution lies in a group of chemical substances, part of a larger group of chemical compounds called *peptides,* that exist in every human body. His research points to a severe shortage of these substances—called Antineoplastons—in cancer patients. Simply stated, Antineoplastons are a special class of peptides, found in the body, that combat neoplastons—abnormal cells or cancer cells. Antineoplastons could be the vehicle needed by the body to ward off and even reverse the development of these cancerous cells.

Dr. Burzynski has put this theory into action, treating patients by reintroducing Antineoplastons into the bloodstream either intravenously or orally with capsules. In many cases, tumors shrank in size or actually disappeared. Some patients even experienced complete remission of the cancers, and years of follow-up study have revealed no sign of any return.

Such results are almost unbelievable. Dr. Burzynski appears to have tapped the power of Antineoplastons to naturally "reprogram" cancer cells. His approach could virtually eliminate the need to destroy these cells or remove the tumors they create.

This therapy was not developed overnight. It has taken Dr. Burzynski over two decades of research, first in Poland, then at the

Baylor College of Medicine in Houston, Texas, and ultimately at the Burzynski Research Institute in Houston. During this time, Dr. Burzynski has zeroed in on the substance he named Antineoplaston. But to get back to Dr. Burzynski's original concern, why do tumors develop in the first place?

According to his theory, cancer is due primarily to an information-processing error. Good information produces healthy cells; bad information results in cancerous cells. Antineoplastons are important because they carry "good" information to the cells. They can "tell" the cells to develop normally.

All cells start out with specific goals: Some to turn into skin, some into blood vessels, some into bone or other body tissues. However, they will never go on to perform these highly specialized functions in the body unless they go through a process called differentiation. Cancer cells, or neoplastons, which everybody produces regularly, never differentiate. They are abnormal cells that the healthy body rejects and destroys because they have not received good information and so have no constructive role to play. When the body is in a weakened state, these neoplastons are not destroyed but rather are left at the mercy of cancer-causing agents that invade the system and "turn them on." They begin to multiply, forming large, constantly growing lumps. They are victims of bad information and assume a destructive role in the body.

This is where Antineoplastons come in—as a means of relaying positive messages. Forming various combinations of the substance, Dr. Burzynski sends instructions to the cells that can allow them to differentiate or specialize. He seeks to correct the information-processing error and restore the body's normal defense mechanisms. The beauty of the treatment is that harmful drugs, radiation, and surgery are not required. The body virtually heals itself.

According to the research done by Dr. Burzynski and others in this country as well as abroad, Antineoplastons are components of a biochemical defense system which parallels our immune system. Unlike the immune system, which protects us by destroying invading agents or defective cells, the biochemical defense system protects us by reprogramming, or normalizing, defective cells. Errors in cell programming may lead to such diverse disorders as cancer, benign tumors, certain skin diseases, AIDS, and Parkinson's disease.

How did Stanislaw Burzynski evolve this amazing therapy? The doctor's progress in medical research is characterized by a rare ability to look further, to take that extra step onto an untried path and go beyond the status quo. Considering that the doctor was born into a family with a passion for learning, these traits aren't altogether surprising. His parents had university degrees, his father a total of five before retiring as a university professor. Stanislaw followed suit, becoming at age 25 one of Poland's youngest men ever to earn both an M.D. and a Ph.D. He began his research at one of Poland's finest medical schools, the Lublin Medical Academy. Its prestigious faculty provided the mentors he needed to shape his embryonic theories on anticancer defense mechanisms.

The Polish government eventually granted him leave to emigrate to the United States, and by 1970 Dr. Burzynski had become a staff member at Baylor College of Medicine. Since his research had been interrupted by obligatory military service, nearly a decade had passed since he had fixed on the notion that the human body must possess a built-in system to resist cancer and similar diseases. He believed that without this system, no one could hope to ward off the cancer-creating "sea of carcinogens" that surround us. Of course, believing that a natural defense system exists does not explain what it is made up of and how it works, but mentors from his university days offered some clues.

From a former chemistry professor Burzynski had learned about the information-carrying peptides, which are related to the Antineoplastons he had yet to uncover. Other clues had come from Dr. Marian Mazur, professor at the Polish Academy of Science and a widely acclaimed authority in the cybernetic field of science. Cybernetics looks at how systems work; one of its key elements is feedback, which provides a way to control and communicate within a system. If cancer cells become destructive because they have received only bad information, the task is not to kill them but to get the right information to them to make them normal and healthy. Cybernetics provides insight into the nature of improving communication within a system so that the desired information or feedback is properly transmitted. A household thermostat is an example of a feedback device: a tool used to close the gap between an *actual* result—say, room temperature of 90 degrees—and a *desired* result—a more comfortable 70 degrees.

Dr. Burzynski concluded that an active ingredient of the body's cancer defense system might be found in the family of peptides—small blood proteins—which were known to communicate with and affect the growth of cells. Within that system, these substances could operate as a feedback device to correct the difference between actual cancer cells and the desired healthy cells or to reprogram cancer cells with good information so that they could become constructive and vital instead of pathogenic.

Peptides are a popular subject of modern medical research. Nearly 50 different types have been found that can stimulate cell growth. One known as peptide T, is attracting attention for its potential in treating AIDS. Dr. Burzynski is thus by no means the only scientist exploring the potency of peptides, but he has been at it longer than most and has achieved findings unique to cancer therapy.

An early discovery involved the level of peptides in advanced cancer patients. Their blood samples reveled only 2 to 3 percent of the amount typically found in healthy bodies—a drastic difference. If peptides, as Dr. Burzynski assumed, played a role in the body's natural defense system, these cancer patients had at some point been disarmed. They were victims of misinformation, since there were not enough peptides to carry good information to the cancer cells.

The next task was to determine exactly what *kind* of peptide cancerous bodies lack. Burzynski put his doctorate in biochemistry to good use, studying the makeup and structure of the deficient substances and uncovering an interesting effect. When applied to tissue cultures, the peptide missing from cancer patients actually suppressed the growth of human cancer cells.

## The Treatment

But while progress was evident, the puzzle was far from solved. It was not enough to know that Antineoplastons *could* carry appropriate information to cancerous cells; it had to be determined how to get them to do it in order to ameliorate tumor growths. Dr. Burzynski turned to his knowledge of systems, cybernetic science, and information theory. The idea of using feedback to adjust and correct an obvious imbalance seemed appropriate to the possible role of Antineoplastons in treating cancer.

The concept constitutes a scientific leap, yet it appears amazingly simple in light of the most basic function peptides perform: They transmit information to the cells. Some aim to spur on, others to inhibit, cellular growth—but they all do it by sending messages the body can obey.

Dr. Burzyhski likens the process to the use of the alphabet: "It's like having 26 alphabet letters—you can create an infinite variety of words." Using the right "code" becomes the key to reprogramming cancerous cells. Theoretically, it is possible to stop a peptide messenger carrying dangerous, damaging goods and hand over a more beneficent, favorable package for it to deliver instead.

The best time to change the peptide code is when cells are new and immature. Guided by good information, the cells can successfully pass through all the normal stages of development. They can gradually take on the special traits they need to serve different parts of the body, in other words, differentiate. When cells differentiate, they have reached maturity.

Imagine being stuck in childhood or puberty, never given the means to change and grow into a fully functioning adult. This is the state of a cancer cell. It doesn't know how to differentiate and mature, because its genetic code is garbled. In a healthy body with a sufficient level of peptides and Antineoplastons, good information is quickly communicated to the cancer cell, and the cell is rendered harmless. But when these levels are low, the cancer cell continues to be victimized by the wrong information. Dr. Burzynski's treatment is aimed at ending the cancer cell's confusion. He puts Antineoplastons into the bloodstream to carry the proper genetic code, halt the growth of useless tumors, and encourage cancer cells to differentiate.

Antineoplastons are not foreign substances. Because they appear naturally in the body—and evidently are found at a much higher level in healthy bodies—they don't pose a toxic threat. This fact alone sets Dr. Burzynski's approach miles apart from traditional cancer therapies. Radiation treatments and chemotherapy destroy cancer cells but also destroy any other cells in their path.

Other scientists are testing newer methods which have the same objective as Antineoplaston therapy, that is, to encourage cancer cells to differentiate. Researchers at Johns Hopkins University, for example, are examining the substance HBMA (hexamethylene bisacetamide). But HBMA is an artificial chemical. The body can be expected to react with greater resistance to a substance it does not produce naturally.

Two significant observations have been made about the side effects of Antineoplaston treatment. First, most patients experience virtually no side effects. The few that have appeared have been minor, short-lived, and easily controlled, such as skin rashes, chills, and fever. The second and more remarkable observation is that the treatment can actually create positive side effects in decided contrast to traditional medical treatments. Patients have shown increases in white and red blood cell counts, decreases in blood cholesterol, and stimulate skin growth; these and other effects are known to aid the body's natural healing powers. Antineoplaston therapy has tremendous promise not just in theory but in practice.

However, a new medicine or medical treatment is not accepted overnight. The medical and scientific communities as well as certain governmental bodies set rigid testing standards to ensure the safety and effectiveness of every supposed curative. Antineoplastons are no exception.

For over 14 years Dr. Burzynski has been subjecting his theory to the testing procedure required to "prove" its worth, and it is holding up well under pressure. More than 60 percent of the patients treated during the Burzynski Research Institute's phase 1 testing showed considerable improvement, whereas the norm is only 3 percent at best.

Each phase of testing has different goals. Phase I of Dr. Burzynski's therapy is designed to examine any side effects that may occur and to determine proper dosages of Antineoplaston "medicine." Phase II entails a more specific study of whether and how the medicine acts to reduce or eliminate cancerous growth, and phase III would take an even closer look at these issues, among larger groups of people with the same types of cancer.

When phase I clinical trials began, Dr. Burzynski didn't expect much in the way of an anticancer effect. His aim was to find out how much medicine patients should be given, starting with very small doses that could be increased over time. He had no way of knowing but could only suspect which kinds of cancer would respond best to his treatment. What he expected and what he got were two different things.

The results in the best cases of 20 different phase I trials showed significant anticancer activity. In the most successful trial, not only did more than 60 percent of the patients respond to treatment, more than 20 percent remained cancer-free for over 5 years. These patients suffered from some of the most serious and difficult to treat forms of cancer, including advanced lung and bladder cancer, and malignant mesothelioma, a type of cancer that results from asbestos exposure and is especially resistant to traditional medicines.

To conduct these phase I trials, Dr. Burzynski had to have some of his medicine on hand. Since Antineoplastons are a specific kind of peptide, he and a research team first concentrated on isolating peptides. The substances then were separated into testable fractions to find the traits unique to Antineoplastons, specifically, the ability to inhibit the growth of cancer cells.

Once the Antineoplastons were located, knowing the coded information in these substances became important. One group seemed effective against specific types of tumors. A second group had a broader effect. One group was labeled Antineoplaston A, and was strained and purified until five new coded combinations were found: A1, A2, A3, etc.

These numbered A's proved to have the greatest effect on tumors and the least toxic or potentially harmful properties, but one seemed especially powerful. Patients given the Antineoplaston A2 in phase 1 tests had the highest number of complete remissions from cancer. Based on these results, the team decided to purify this A2 substance even further, and A10 was born.

These efforts to isolate the right Antineoplaston for certain types of cancer took place while phase 1 tests were under way. The generalized goals at this stage—to study side effects and proper doses—had yielded some very specific findings. Antineoplaston A3, for example, produced complete remissions of advanced prostate cancer and encouraging results in cancer of the pancreas. Some A combinations were more effective with lung, bladder, and breast cancers; others with malignant brain tumors, for which surgery is usually the only and often futile alternative.

Dr. Burzynski and his team were clearly on firm ground as they entered the next phase of testing. Phase II trials began in 1985, as many as 51 are planned. Here patients are grouped according to their basic type of cancer. However, depending on how and where those basic types develop in the body, different phase II treatments are tried. For example, in current trials with breast cancer, treatment varies depending on whether the disease has spread to the lungs or to the liver or bones.

Twenty-four patients with malignant lymphoma (cancer of the lymphatic system) have already been treated in phase II trials. Chemotherapy had failed to help nearly 70 percent of these patients. Only certain forms of this cancer, such as Hodgkin's disease, have ever shown real success from conventional treatment. But with Antineoplaston care, 85 percent showed vast improvement.

The most impressive results have been in brain cancers (astrocytoma stages III and IV and glioblastoma) and metastatic cancer of the prostate.

In a small phase II trial of atrocytoma conducted by Dr. Burzynski, 20 patients were enrolled—13 with astrocytoma stage IV, five with stage III, and two with stage IIB. All diagnoses were biopsy confirmed. All but one patient had received (and failed) one or more prior standard therapies.

Four patients achieved complete remission and two others partial remission. The responses of 10 patients were classified as objective stabilization (less than 50 percent decrease of tumor size). Since the end of this study in May 1990, some of these patients have achieved partial and even complete remission. These are preliminary results, since the first patient was enrolled only three years ago, in 1988. Nonetheless, the results are impressive in this type and stage of cancer.

In another phase II study of stage IV prostate cancer refractory to hormonal treatment, two complete and three partial remissions were reported in a group of 14 patients. Seven patients obtained objective stabilization. These, too, are preliminary results, as the study began in 1988.

Dr. Burzynski is currently in the process of locating the funding to do a trial in the U.S. independent of his clinic. This phase I study titled "Treatment of Advanced Breast Cancer with Antineoplaston A10" will be conducted under Dr. Burzynski's IND #22,029 issued by the Food and Drug Administration March 16, 1989.

Most of Dr. Burzynski's patients, during all phases of testing, are treated without being hospitalized. Checkups are conducted every day or every other day for the first 2 weeks and then less frequently depending on the improvement of the individual patient. The Burzynski clinic in southwest Houston operates on an outpatient basis, with the average period of care ranging from 6 months to 3 years.

The Antineoplastons which have been responsible for the dramatic results mentioned above are manufactured in Burzynski's plant in Stafford, Texas. According to Dr. Burzynski they are considered a form of chemotherapy since a chemotherapeutic agent is technically any "organized mixture of chemicals that fight a malignancy." However, they do not have the devastating side effects of the traditional class of chemotherapeutic drugs because they are formulations that are identical to proteins that are present in the body. Natural Antineoplastons are small proteins isolated from human urine or blood. Synthetic Antineoplastons are chemically identical to natural proteins but are synthetically derived. Synthetics are easier and cheaper to manufacture and are even more efficacious in treating specific cancers, such as brain and prostate cancer. Other cancers, though, respond better to the natural substances.

Dr. Burzynski uses a deliberately coordinated assortment of Antineoplastons, both synthetic and natural, as the case requires. When he thinks it is appropriate, he refers patients for other types of treatment (chemotherapy, radiation, or surgery) to augment the Antineoplaston injection or capsule therapy. While he has had little success with cancer of the testicles and childhood leukemia, he has had astounding results with brain tumors, malignant lymphomas, and cancer of the bladder and prostate.

Other groups have reproduced and are expanding Dr. Burzynski's preclinical work, including researchers at the Medical College of Georgia, the Imperial College of Science and Technology of London, the University of Kurume Medical School in Japan, the University of Turin Medical School in Italy, the Shandong Medical Academy in the People's Republic of China, and the Uniformed Services University of the Health Sciences in the U.S.

The front page of the July–August 1990 issue of *Oncology News* featured an article on Antineoplastons, "a completely new type of antitumor agent that is nontoxic and seems to make malignant cancer cells revert to normal." The report was from Geneva, Switzerland, where the prestigious 9th International Symposium on Future Trends in Chemotherapy was held in March 1990. A special session was devoted to Antineoplastons where seven papers were presented, including preclinical and clinical results by researchers from Japan, Poland, China, and the U.S.

Some of the most exciting preclinical research was reported by Dvorit Samid, Ph.D., from the Uniformed Services University of Health Sciences in Bethesda. She reported that "Antineoplaston AS2-1 profoundly inhibits oncogene expression and the proliferation of malignant cells without exhibiting any toxicity toward normal cells." Dr. Samid explained that AS2-1 does not kill cancer cells, rather it reprograms them to behave like normal cells.

Clinical results of Antineoplastons in patients with cancer refractory to other forms of therapy included reports of complete remissions from Japan and the U.S. in inoperable metastatic ovarian carcinoma and advanced stage prostate cancer, respectively.

### The Patients

*Example 1:* Mavis once earned her living installing asbestos tiles. In 1970 she learned she had developed malignant mesothelioma—cancer resulting from exposure to asbestos. She was 27 years old.

Surgery was first performed at New York's Memorial Sloan-Kettering Hospital. Some of the tumors pervading her abdomen were removed, along with part of her colon. The operation brought relief but no guarantees and the cancer returned. In May 1979 Mavis underwent less than successful surgery at Methodist Hospital in Lubbock, Texas. More tumors were found, and the disease continued to spread. No conventional cancer treatments could help.

Six months later Mavis came to the Burzynski Institute. She was

36, weak and in intolerable pain. Treatment began with Antineoplaston A. Within weeks she had no need for her steady diet of morphine and other drugs. The pain was gone.

Something was obviously going well, though her abdominal tumors were surprisingly unchanged. New treatment was tried with Antineoplaston A2. This time more than the pain went away. By April 1980 Mavis was in partial remission from the cancer, with only a few tumors left, and those less than half their former size. By year's end no signs or symptoms of the cancer remained.

Mavis continued to take low-dose Antineoplastons for a while, mostly as a precautionary tactic. Treatment stopped in March 1981. Close to a decade of "fatal" disease and pain had ended. As of March 1991, Mavis remains in complete remission.

*Example 2:* Rebecca was a heavy smoker; in fact she still is. She is not therefore an ideal patient. Her case is not uncommon, though, and is instructive in that whatever success she has had could be amplified if she would stop smoking. Nonetheless, the lung, liver, and breast cancer she once suffered from is gone.

Rebecca became a patient at the Burzynski Institute in June 1980. She was then 56 years old. Radiation and chemotherapy had failed to arrest the malignant tumor in her lungs, and the cancer spread into her lymph nodes and liver. Her Antineoplaston treatment began with intravenous injections of a synthetic preparation called AS2-5.

The results were quick and nearly miraculous. No signs of lung or liver cancer remained after only 2 months of treatment. Most doctors would expect a rapid return of Rebecca's type of lung cancer, especially because of its spread to the liver, but Rebecca was not a typical case. Her Antineoplaston preparation was not typical either, just effective. She's been completely free from this cancer since the end of 1981.

A completely separate breast cancer was first detected in August 1981. A week later she underwent excision of a nodule in the left breast, and on September 11, 1981, she had a modified radical mastectomy for her breast cancer, which was still in its early stages. She was treated with Antineoplaston A10 capsules from September 1982 until June 1983 to prevent recurrence of the breast cancer. As of March 1991, her breast, lung, and liver cancers still appear to be clear.

*Example 3:* Reuben was told by his doctor in March 1978 that his severe bladder tumor could probably be helped only with radiation treatments followed by surgery. He got an affirmative second opinion and underwent treatment.

Surgeons removed as much of the tumor as they could, but Reuben's symptoms became worse. By April he had arrived at the Burzynski Institute—age 47, weak, losing weight, and experiencing painful urination along with blood in the urine. He was given Antineoplaston A by intramuscular injection.

Harmful symptoms went away in two weeks; the tumor was reduced to half its size within a month. Over the next year seven cystoscopies—screening procedures for the bladder or tumorous growths—revealed no return of the cancer. Examinations by two consulting specialists in urology supported this evidence, and the Antineoplaston treatment was ended in September 1979.

Unfortunately, Reuben's nightmare was not over. Other less severe tumors appeared. Treatment began again in February of 1980, this time with Antineoplaston A3. He was given injections daily; over a year's time they were gradually reduced to one a week.

In the end Reuben did triumph over his disease. His last treatment was in 1982. A decade has come and gone since then. Dr. Burzynski doesn't expect to see him back for more.

*Example 4:* Nick could have predicted he would develop cancer if family history was the predicting factor. He had lost two grandparents to the disease, his mother to stomach cancer, and his father to prostate cancer. His son, only 8 years old, had died of malignant cancer that started in the skeletal muscles.

In this case the tragic loss of a child may have helped save the life of the father. At age 39 Nick developed lymphoma, cancer that affects the body's tissue-cleansing fluids, white blood cells, and general circulatory system. His symptoms were widespread: extreme swelling in the legs and stomach; enlarged lymph nodes, liver, and spleen; and a damaging buildup of body fluids. Remembering the agony of his son's chemotherapy and radiation treatments, Nick turned instead to Dr. Burzynski.

Improvement was rapid after treatment began in March 1980 with A2 injections. The swelling was reduced, and fluids decreased in his abdomen. However, the most amazing result showed up in June: Nick's liver and spleen were almost back to normal just weeks after his liver had been so enlarged that two x-ray films had been necessary for a complete "photograph."

Nick felt good and returned to work part-time. Only one concern remained: His lymph nodes still had signs of disease. When he examined the pathological reports on his body tissue, Dr. Burzynski found poor cell differentiation that had not been corrected by treatment. A combination of Antineoplastons AS2-1 and A2 was tried on Nick with success. Lack of cancer and any related symptoms pointed to a full remission by June 1981.

However, the struggle resumed the following year when cancer reappeared in the lymph nodes. Nick came to the Burzynski Institute in May and was responding well to Antineoplastons when he fell into a behavior pattern that blocked his progress. He kept making decisions to start and then stop treatments; in addition, an addiction to the drug Dilaudid (hydromorphone) got in the way.

Nick had been on Dilaudid, a painkiller, before coming to the Burzynski Institute, and Dr. Burzynski kept him on it for a while afterward. Later, Nick obtained it illegally and abused it. This addiction led to his failure to maintain the recommended maintenance treatments and resulted in the development of pneumonia after Nick slept in the rain under the influence of drugs.

Despite these complications, treatment continued and a complete remission was finally achieved in late 1984. Nick died in September of 1990 of pneumonia. According to his wife, medical reports showed no signs of recurrent malignant lymphoma.

## Future Possibilities

Prevention is the focus of several studies Dr. Burzynski has undertaken. In one study, two groups of mice were exposed to the main cancer-causing agent from cigarette smoke. One group was given food containing an Antineoplaston preparation; 80 percent of these mice avoided lung cancer. Among the group that was not given Antineoplastons, 100 percent got the disease.

The next step in this research is to use Antineoplastons as part of a preventive treatment among humans. Dr. Burzynski believes that this would best be done with apparently healthy individuals who have low levels of Antineoplastons. Smokers may well benefit in this respect since they fit this requirement and are therefore prime candidates for cancer and so are in dire need of a preventive program.

The possibilities of Dr. Burzynski's "new medicine" appear endless. Antineoplastons correct (i.e., stop) cancer development in a way the body understands and easily tolerates. Even with phase I treatments, which aren't intended to produce maximum benefits, some patients have emerged cancer-free.

Of course, successful outcomes result from traditional approaches as well. Careful surgery can aid recovery, and chemotherapy has had particular success with rarer types of cancer such as Hodgkins disease and childhood leukemia. The regrettable part is that these "answers" to cancer can also cause more harm. Typical and devastating side effects accompany methods to which many patients never respond. Surgery and radiation can lead to serious damage to organs and tissues, and radiation and chemotherapy may drastically undermine the ability of the immune system to fight off even the simplest bacteria and toxins.

What Dr. Burzynski offers is an opportunity to use and strengthen the body's natural defense system. The need to explore and develop

Antineoplastons and other safe remedies will continue as long as people are exposed to air pollution, radiation, chemicals, ultraviolet rays, and the like.

### The Immuno-Augmentative Therapy of Dr. Burton

The majority of patients arriving at Dr. Lawrence Burton's Immunology Research Center (IRC) on Grand Bahama Island have been pronounced terminal by orthodox medicine. Many are crippled and unable to walk, others bloated beyond recognition with ascites, an abdominal fluid buildup that is a common symptom of malignant carcinomas. Some have been bedridden for long periods, others are mentally disoriented, and many are in such constant pain that the simplest outing is unthinkable. They come to receive the Immuno-Augmentative Therapy (IAT) developed by Dr. Burton, a Ph.D. in zoology who also has a strong background in cancer research.

In 1983, Curry Hutchinson was one of Dr. Burton's patients. He recalls that after he had suffered 4 years from a malignant melanoma that had been partially "removed" from the middle of his back, his doctors and practically everyone else had given up on him. Mr. Hutchinson did not want to continue with traditional medical treatment after the surgery because he knew of too many people who had suffered miserably from chemotherapy and radiation. He investigated the possibility of several unorthodox therapies before deciding to try the Immuno-Augmentative Therapy of Dr. Burton.

His mother took him to the Bahamas as he stood at death's door. She "took me down there in a wheelchair," Hutchinson recalls. "I had about 90 pounds of body weight. I looked like the most pitiful survivor of Buchenwald you can imagine."

At first Dr. Burton was hesitant to treat someone so deteriorated, but finally he relented.

Hutchinson remained bedridden for the first 2 months there, but then he became strong enough to get up and around and even went to the grocery store. "It is hard to imagine," he remarked, "what a thrill it is to walk into a grocery store when you have not been out of bed for a year. It's like going to Disney World. My mother went home. I started taking care of myself, preparing my meals, and went on with it, slowly but surely." He is still up and around and reports feeling well to this day.

What is going on at the IRC that makes it a fortress of hope for so many cancer "immigrants," most of them outcasts deemed hopeless by established medicine? On Grand Bahama Island, the IRC has taken in people considered doomed. Many are still alive, long after the terminal prognoses given by their traditional physicians and oncologists have come and gone. Others have died but were enabled to survive longer than anyone had imagined possible. Many now lead happy, fruitful lives with much less pain than they had come to accept as an inevitable accompaniment of illness.

"Desperate people came through our doors," says Lynn Austin, head nurse at the IRC for 7½ years, during which time she has seen about 2,500 patients come to the clinic. "Many," she continues, "have been handed a death certificate with the date written in." But they came to Dr. Burton because they had heard about some of the miracles his IAT has worked. Not everyone can be accepted for treatment, unfortunately. Dr. Burton and his staff must first be reasonably sure the treatment they offer is the right thing for the prospective patient's condition. But "for those who were accepted," Austin recalls, "something new appeared: a restoration of hope. Many were told that they were dead, and all had life-threatening cancer. Now someone was holding out some small promise."

That someone is Dr. Burton, who is quick to note that IAT "is not by any means a cure for cancer." However, he also relates how "cancer patients who have been treated with IAT . . . often respond with cessation of tumor growth and, in some cases, with no tumor growth. In many there is actual reversal as well as necrosis [complete stoppage] of the cancer growth."

The man who has made such startling progress in the treatment of cancer has had a long career in research. Burton decided to go into cancer research after seeing "firsthand the many horrors of cancer" while assigned as a pharmacist's mate to the U.S. Navy's Cancer Center at Brooklyn Naval Hospital in 1944. In those days, he recalls, "the accepted procedure for cancer treatment was radical surgery. If you had a cancer of the foot, the leg was removed at the hip."

After World War II, Burton studied genetics, cancer etiology (the cause of cancer), oncolysis (destruction of cancer cells), and immunology. This culminated in his receiving a Ph.D. in experimental zoology from New York University in 1955. "My training and experience are classically those of a medical researcher," he says.

After graduation in 1955, Dr. Burton became a research associate at the California Institute of Technology and began to publish the results of his work in leading scientific journals such as *Cancer Research*. Back in New York, he became a research associate at New York University in 1957, moving up to become an associate in oncology in 1964 at St. Vincent's Hospital, a noted teaching hospital. In 1966 he became a senior investigator and oncologist at the cancer research unit while still at St. Vincent's.

### The Discovery

Burton's Immuno-Augmentative Therapy has its roots in this period of his career. In 1959, Burton and a team of cancer researchers accidentally discovered a tumor-inhibiting factor that reduced or eliminated cancer in a special breed of leukemic mice. Their research progressed well enough so that in the November 1962 issue of *Transactions of the New York Academy of Sciences* they reported on certain substances that were capable of causing remission in over 50 percent of the leukemic mice treated.

In the fall of 1965, Patrick McGrady, Sr., science editor for the American Cancer Society (ACS), observed Dr. Burton's experiments and was amazed. In a radio interview, McGrady told my audience,

147

"They injected the mice and the lumps went down before your eyes—something I never believed possible."

McGrady had Dr. Burton and his associate, Dr. Friedman, also with a Ph.D. in zoology, repeat the experiment at the ACS's 1966 Science Writers Seminar. The two doctors, in the presence of 70 scientists and 200 science writers, injected mice having mammary cancer with the serum they had isolated during their research. An hour and a half later, the tumors had disappeared almost completely.

The next day, the result of these experiments received front-page coverage throughout the world. The *Los Angeles Herald Examiner's* headline read "Fifteen Minute Cancer Cure for Mice: Humans Next?"

Unfortunately, this enthusiastic publicity backfired. As Dr. Burton recalls, "This caused a misleading specter of 'cure' to which no researcher would ever dare lay claim . . ." Furthermore, when word about the experiments spread throughout the medical community, many traditionally trained physicians questioned their validity, suggesting that the results had been accomplished by trickery.

In September of the same year, Drs. Burton and Friedman were invited to repeat the experiment before the New York Academy of Medicine. This time, in order to avoid accusations of fraud, they had the mice selected by independent oncologists and pathologists. Again, an hour or so after the injections with the newly isolated tumor-inhibiting factors, the tumors started to disintegrate. However, there was still little interest in the efficacy of the tumor-inhibiting factors.

During 1970 and 1971 Burton and Friedman were assisting Dr. Antonio Rottino, a medical doctor on the cancer research team, in treating his cancer patients at St. Vincent's with their antitumor serum. In 1972, however, Dr. Rottino announced that the treatment had to cease. The IAT treatments were considered experimental and therefore unproven and so were not appropriate to use in providing regular medical care.

Also in the early 1970s, Long Island psychologist Martin Goldstone's wife was being treated with the Burton-Friedman technique.

She had enjoyed such promising results that when they learned that the treatments had been stopped at St. Vincent's she and her husband and other prominent people in the Great Neck, Long Island, community raised enough funds to establish the immunology Research Foundation to continue the work of the two doctors.

In 1975, *New York* magazine published an article on the work of Burton and Friedman entitled "The Politics of Cancer—Why Won't the Medical Establishment pay Attention to These Two Men?" The article drew considerable public attention and inquiry. Senator Howard Metzenbaum of Ohio, whose wife had just died of cancer, wrote a letter to the NCI demanding to know why the public was being kept in the dark about this treatment. He was informed that the NCI was of the opinion that the Burton-Friedman work was nothing new, couldn't possibly be effective, and was therefore not worthy of further investigation or testing.

Perhaps the most important result of the article was that after extensively investigating Drs. Burton and Friedman, Champion International, a philanthropic organization interested in alternative medical therapies, decided to fund the two men's work. Champion International's patronage became all-important 3 years later, when Dr. Burton decided to relocate his clinic.

### The Therapy

The Immunology Research Center moved from Great Neck, New York to Freeport on Grand Bahama Island in 1977. Since then, over 2,500 terminal cancer patients have undergone treatment there. According to Dr. Burton, 50 to 60 percent of these patients experience tumor reduction. Many are able to resume normal lives; frequently they survive 5 years and more beyond the initial diagnosis (usually made by a traditional attending physician prior to Burton's involvement in the case) of cancer. The 5-year survival period is sufficient for the American Cancer Society and the National Cancer Institute to consider a patient cured.

I had visited Dr. Burton's clinic on a number of occasions and have analyzed the records of many of his patients. This investigation has confirmed the remarkable success that IAT continues to have on a regular basis. In sharp contrast to the depressing environment of most cancer hospitals in this country, the attitude of patients at the IRC is one of optimism and hope. Most patients are off drugs and free of pain and report that they feel well. Perhaps the most telling endorsement comes from the family members of non-surviving patients who have continued to support the clinic with financial contributions and moral backing.

Dr. Burton does not believe that we should use the word "cure" in relation to cancer. "Immuno-Augmentative Therapy," he explains, "augments the immune system and enables it to control and combat cancer." But it does not totally eradicate cancer. No therapy does that. Cancer patients, no matter how long the cancer is under control, must always be watchful of their condition to be sure that the cancer does not begin growing again or growing somewhere else. Cancer is not a localized condition, but a systemic disease. While it may clear up in one organ, it may flare up in another.

Immuno-Augmentative Therapy consists of injections of four blood proteins that Dr. Burton discovered and is able to isolate. These proteins are essentially responsible for the control and even shrinkage of tumors. When injected in the proper amounts and at proper intervals, they can help the weakened body do what it would do normally: control the growth and proliferation of cancerous cells. Dr. Burton believes that cancer is primarily a matter of immune impairments. When the immune system is working properly, the cancer cells that occur are quickly arrested and disposed of.

Two questions arise from this explanation. What exactly are cancer cells, and what causes an immune system to be impaired to the extent that the body can no longer defend itself against them?

The body's cells are constantly dividing as a normal part of the living and growing process. Each cell has two sets of chromosomes and a single nucleus. For a healthy cell to reproduce, the sets of chromosomes hearing the unique genetic information that makes the cell what it is split and form four sets of chromosomes, while the nucleus splits into two. The single cell then divides into two—a process called mitosis—so that there are two cells instead of one, each with a single nucleus bearing two sets of chromosomes with the same genetic code. This is an endless life process that occurs thousands of times every moment. Dr. Burton's theory posits that approximately 1 out of every 10,000 such cell divisions is endomitotic, or abnormal. In these instances, the cell begins as usual by separating into four sets of chromosomes and forming two nuclei. The problem begins when these nuclei become encased in a single cytoplasmic mold, thereby forming a single cell with a double nucleus and four sets of chromosomes each. This single cell is called a supercell, or neoplaston. It is a cancer cell, usually recognized as being abnormal by the healthy body, which proceeds to destroy it.

This leads to the second question. In cases of cancer, what causes the lapse in the body's immune system that allows the proliferation of these supercells? What allows or causes a person to become vulnerable to the ravages of cancer? Dr. Burton believes that the immune system is overtaxed by the presence of intruders such as viruses, bacteria, and toxins, but he also believes that the greatest damage is done by a person's inability to cope adequately with stress. Although he has not done scientific studies to verify this belief, he is convinced from observation of cancer patients in his care that the damaging effects of stress and negativity are the chief cause of dysfunction within the immune mechanism. According to Dr. Burton, the overly stressed body "stops making antibodies, stops making alpha-macroglobulin, the deblocking protein. Without enough antibodies to attack cancer cells and without enough deblocking protein to restart the process once the waste products of tumor cell destruction are cleared, the cancer grows unchecked. That, I think, is the 'cause' of cancer."

If cancer is indeed caused by stress and other suppressants to the immune system in general and if its occurrence is in the form of abnormal cells that may grow rapidly throughout the body or within specific locales, one is brought back to the matter of how to control this abnormal growth and proliferation. Endomitotic cell division can occur at any time, producing a primary tumor or metastasis. A *primary tumor* is one where the cancer develops at a particular site; *metastases* are abnormal cells that have migrated away from the primary tumor and resettled elsewhere in the body. "But," Dr. Burton explains, "it does not matter what the primary [tumor] is; cancer is an affliction of the immune mechanism. When the four proteins of the immune mechanism are operating properly, they can shrink the tumor whether it is primary or metastatic." It is thus necessary to examine the four proteins discovered and isolated by Dr. Burton.

One is a tumor antibody that can destroy tumors; another is an antibody complement that stimulates the tumor antibody. Without the stimulation from the complement, the antibody will remain inactive. The other two proteins have a direct effect on the destruction of tumors: The "blocking" protein inhibits the antibody to give the body a chance to clear away the toxic waste of tumor destruction; otherwise the body would go into toxic shock. The blocking protein is itself then inhibited by an antiblocking protein. When the blocking protein is prevalent, the antibody and tumor complement are prevented from attacking tumors, which therefore may grow; when the antiblocking protein is prevalent, the blocking protein is held in check, enabling the tumor antibody and complement to actively seek and destroy cancerous cells.

In his IAT therapy, Dr. Burton has applied his discovery of these blood fractions to create a harmonious balance in the patient's internal chemistry. The immune system is directed by different proteins (peptides) in the blood. The four discovered by Dr. Burton are blood fractions or components—necessary for the immune mechanism to function properly. There may be others that have not been discovered, but at this point Dr. Burton has found that at least these four must work together to maintain a normal balance in immune function capabilities.

Once this balance has been established, the patient's body is able to defend itself naturally against the continued proliferation of cancer cells and frequently is able to attack and begin to reduce existing tumors. Dr. Burton's therapy does not attempt to shrink a tumor directly or intervene in the growth of a cancer. It is designed only to "augment an immune mechanism in the patient." The stimulated immune mechanism itself is then responsible for attacking the tumor.

IAT therapy involves two separate stages. The antibody, antibody complement, and antiblocking proteins help the body fight cancer. Every time a tumor cell is destroyed by these three proteins, the fourth one—the blocking protein—is released to inhibit further destruction of the tumor. The role of the protein, as noted above, is not to protect the tumor but to give "the liver a chance to eliminate the waste by-products of cell destruction." The blocking protein actually helps the body recover from the toxic shock caused by killed cancer cells. It plays a vital role not in the actual destruction of cancer but in the body's ability to recover afterward.

IAT involves a careful consideration of the alternating roles of tumor destruction, on the one hand, and the body's recovery from toxic breakdown, on the other hand. The timing of these two processes is all-important. While the blocking protein is eventually deblocked by the antiblocking protein, this process may take too long. During therapy a decision must be made as to when and how aggressively to intervene in this process. The body—especially the liver—must be protected from the toxic waste of the destroyed cancer cells, but it must at the same time be protected from the ravages of the tumor. The attending physician has to decide when the blocking process has given the body enough recovery time. The system is then deblocked by the intravenous introduction of specific amounts of the antiblocking protein, and the cancer destruction continues. The immune mechanism may be bolstered further by the injection of the tumor antibody and tumor complement.

The timing and the quantities of protein introduced are the critical issues. As Dr. Burton explains, "In time, the patient's own body . . . deblocks the system [enabling cancer destruction to be resumed]. But if there is a large amount of tumor, we cannot wait indefinitely while the process is repeated. The patient has a limit. He or she can produce only so much antibody and so much deblocking protein. Thus we have to *augment* these proteins—once a day, twice a day . . . as many as six to eight times a day. If the augmentation is done properly, we can produce, to quote the National Cancer Institute, many, many 'spontaneous remissions.' "

### The Clinic

Ms. Elaine Boise, whose husband, Jack, died in 1985 after more than half a year of treatment at the IRC, talks about pictures she has that remind her of Jack's final months in the Bahamas: "pictures that have surprised doctors . . . pictures that showed him outdoors, singing, playing the guitar, sailing on a yacht, playing a slot machine at a casino." She recalls "Jack driving a car, going Christmas shopping with me, having dinner out several times in Freeport restaurants."

This is not what most people think of when they are told someone is dying of cancer. They expect instead the kind of person Jack was when he first arrived in Freeport, when none of those activities was possible for him, since he was heavily drugged, sedated, and in a wheelchair. Ms. Boise and her children were amazed by Jack's rapid physical improvement. "It was enough," she recounts, "for us to know that Burton's approach to killing tumors by augmenting the immune system is a valid one clinically, and it is one that should be pursued further."

Perhaps the most remarkable thing about the treatment program of the IRC is that it is essentially nontoxic and noninvasive, unlike chemotherapy, radiation, and surgery, which are either toxic or invasive or both. Chemotherapy, for instance, essentially poisons the body in order to kill the tumor. It is toxic because it introduces a poison into the body, and it is invasive because the poison aggressively invades the cells and tissues of the body. The problem is that the poison is indiscriminate: It kills not only cancerous cells but healthy ones as well. In fact, its invasion of the body is systemic (total), not local, and therefore seriously damages the immune system. It is because of such invasive and/or toxic therapies that cancer is associated with horrible pain and sickness, hair and memory loss, and a general miserable life.

Dr. Burton's patients frequently avoid these side effects because IAT uses substances (blood fractions) that occur naturally in the body to bolster the immune system. One patient, Dr. Phil Kunderman, discussing his experience with cancer, explains: "I was so impressed [with IAT], since it seemed such a logical approach. I also was particularly impressed because it had no deleterious side effects, in contrast to radiation therapy and chemotherapy, both of which modalities I had turned down because my own experience as a surgeon proved that these measures were, in an advanced disease at least, [not] all that great."

Dr. Kunderman's story is particularly interesting because he was a leading cancer specialist at the time his cancer was diagnosed. In 1979 he discovered that he had prostate cancer and that it had spread to his bones, particularly the sternum and shoulder, rendering the cancer essentially inoperable. Surgery could do no more than relieve his obstructive symptoms. He had the surgery but he was told that his prognosis was only 1 to 3 years survival.

Dr. Kunderman began therapy at the IRC in 1980. Six years later he reported that he was doing very well and admitted being "just amazed" by the success Dr. Burton is achieving with cancers usually considered hopeless. "For instance," he says, "I know of carcinoma of the pancreas, which in my experience was such a lethal, terrible carcinoma, with remission for as long as 8 or 9 years [as a result of IAT therapy]. In carcinoma of the larynx, the young woman [treated by Dr. Burton] is at least 10 years postlaryngeal. These were such horrible cancers that we never seemed to be able to control; the prognosis was so very bad, and the life span was so short thereafter."

Dr. Kunderman recalls Dr. Burton's associate showing "an x-ray one day of a chest and asking, 'What do you think of that film?' "

"I said, 'Well, it's certainly a big cancer of the left lower lobe, and there is nothing you can offer this patient surgically or by any means.' "

"Then he showed me another film. It was completely clear. He had been on therapy for 7 or 8 months. . . ."

"I said, 'Well, is this before or after therapy?' "

"He said, 'This is after therapy.' "

"It was an amazing thing. I had never encountered anything like it."

Many people would like to be treated by Dr. Burton, but unfortunately, not everyone falls within the entry guidelines set up for prospective patients. Dr. Robert John Clement, a British physician licensed to practice in both England and the Bahamas, joined the IRC in 1977 and has attended over 1,500 patients since that time. During a congressional hearing in 1986, he outlined the criteria for accepting patients at the IRC:

One: Does the patient have a confirmed diagnosis of cancer? This is required by the statutes of our license.

Two: Is the type of cancer one we have treated successfully in the past?

Three: Is it one that cannot successfully be treated by other methods?

Four: Is the condition one which has failed [to be helped] with other treatments?

If a patient's condition can be successfully treated by surgery alone, we strongly advise them to have the surgery performed.

If it is something which can be treated successfully by orthodox therapy, we would not accept the patient. However, if the patient has personally refused orthodox therapy but has a confirmed diagnosis of cancer, he or she may be accepted.

Nurse Austin recollects how "each morning, in addition to those who arrive wishing to become patients, there were the previous day's group awaiting the physician's decision. The reaction of those who were reluctantly informed that the physician did not feel that IAT could help them remain vividly in my mind despite all my training and experience in maintaining professional distance."

Patients who are accepted are attended by a staff of 4 medical doctors, 2 registered nurses, and about 10 laboratory assistants. The nurses collect the medical records the patients have brought with them, try to appraise their general attitudes toward their situation, and then draw blood for the initial immunocompetency test. The clinic's procedures are then explained carefully and in detail to the patients before they are released to meet the attending physician.

Dr. Burton explains the initial stages of treatment from this point on: "When patients get here, we take their blood to test for AIDS and hepatitis, and we use our own tests to see whether their immune systems are functioning. Then they have an interview with one of the four M.D.'s. Part of the reason for this is to make sure they are not phony. So far, the ACS has sent three fakes, which the doctors picked up. The ACS and NCI always say that we just want to take the money and run.

"After that, I talk with one of the M.D.'s to decide whether to take each patient. Does the patient have a chance [to get better with IAT] or not? If there is no chance, they go home. We don't win any prizes for just taking patients.

"The first 3 days, they are treated with subefficacious doses [amounts designed only to test a reaction to the substance]. The first day, we give one-fifth of the effective dose. On the next day, if the immune system is working and the patient is killing tumor, that means the immune mechanism has recognized the proteins in the serum and used them as a signal to begin functioning.

"On day 2 one of the proteins is elevated to the effective dose. We do this in stages to determine whether the patient is allergic to any of the individual proteins. Although we have never had a case of this, if there were an allergy, we would want to know which protein was the allergen."

If the patient responds well to the increased dosage of one protein, his or her immune system should be elevating one of the two proteins to the effective dose by itself. The next day, two of the proteins are increased to the effective dose, and "If that patient then supplies the amount of the third protein, this is a patient who will probably be able to stop the shots fairly soon, because his or her immune mechanism is good enough that he or she shouldn't have gotten cancer to begin with," says Dr. Burton.

"After the third day," he continues, "the patient gets into another program using the computer, which determines the appropriate doses the patient should receive of each of the three proteins. If the patient has a very high tumor kill, he or she will get only one *augmentation*. Then, as the tumor goes down, the patient will get two, three, or four . . . augmentations depending on which protein is elevated in the blood and how much of the tumor is being killed. If the patient's immune mechanism is not responding to the augmentations within a couple of days, we will take more A.M. and P.M. blood samples to see if we can spot something wrong.

"The doctors meanwhile test the tumors by x-ray and by palpation. If the tumor begins to soften and shrink, the case is put back in my lap. When the immune mechanism is stable enough that I think the patient can make it, the patient goes home."

Treatment with IAT at the clinic costs about $5,000 for the initial month of treatment and observation and then $500 for each subsequent week. Once a patient's immune mechanism is sufficiently strong and the cancer is under control, the patient goes home and is self-treated at a cost of $50 a week. This does not present a problem since these patients are taught early on to inject themselves, using disposable diabetes syringes. Every 6 months or so, such patients return to the clinic for a week's follow-up to determine whether alterations in the serum are required. Does the patient need more tumor complement and less blocking protein, for instance? If the tumor is breaking down too fast and creating high levels of toxicity, the blocking protein may be increased instead.

Dr. Burton has had particular success with mesothelioma and metastatic colon cancer, two supposedly "incurable" cancers. *Mesothelioma*, or "asbestos cancer," typically attacks the lungs (the pleural cavity), sometimes the stomach (peritoneal cavity), and occasionally the heart (pericardial cavity). It is characterized by a number of tiny tumors initially resembling shotgun pellets that spread and grow rapidly. There is no treatment for mesothelioma according to an NCI treatise on the subject, only pain management. The survival rate is zero. The prognosis is only 4 to 11 months' survival.

The use of asbestos in building has decreased sharply because of the associated health risks. Nonetheless, the treatment of mesothelioma will continue to be a major health priority for many years because of the unusually long latency period of asbestos cancer.

There are no known survivors of mesothelioma in the traditional medical health care system. Dr. Kunderman, a board-certified surgeon who is chief of surgery at three New Jersey hospitals and chief of thoracic surgery at two others, has had considerable experience with the disease since his office was located near Johns Mansville, the asbestos producer. He was eventually afflicted with the cancer himself and chose to place himself under Dr. Burton's care. As mentioned earlier, Dr. Kunderman recovered after being diagnosed as terminal.

It is no wonder that Dr. Kunderman left the United States to seek a nontraditional therapy in the Caribbean. Even though he is a traditional physician, he admits that "our experience with mesothelioma was so horrendously poor. . . . We just threw up our hands toward the end of my years of practice with mesothelioma; we had tried everything, including such radical surgery as removing a whole lung and removing all of the pleura, but still these tumors recurred."

Dr. Burton reports that the average survival rate of his mesothelioma patients is already 47 to 48 months, and a number of survivors are currently residing at the clinic. Some have been released and now live normal lives since, "in contrast to other types of cancer, once you get rid of all tumor cells containing asbestos, the patient is safe," says Dr. Burton. This is due partly to the fact the mesothelioma is strictly an environmental disease and is in no way genetic.

Eleven IRC peritoneal mesothelioma patients were the subjects of a recently published report by Drs. Burton and Clement. They had suffered such physical defects as abdominal distension, obstruction, and ascites. The four women and seven men had an immune profile typical of advanced cancer populations: elevated levels of blocking proteins and suppressed levels of deblocking protein and tumor complement. All were "augmented" with injections of immunoglobulin serum antibodies and deblocking protein. The results of the study were as follows:

"Four males and one female are alive, with survival among the five ranging from 22 to 80 months. The mean survival for those living is 43 months, and the median is 52 months. Of the other six cases, mean survival was 23 months and the median was 16 months, with a range of 7 to 50 months. The total subject population represented mean (or average) survival of 35 months and a median survival of 30 months, with a range for all cases from 7 to 80 months."

Dr. Burton's mean survival and survival range results can be compared with those obtained by other researchers working with peritoneal mesothelioma patients who had undergone traditional medical therapies. In 1957 four patients studied had an average survival of 12 months, with a range from 1 to 26 months. A 1960 study showed 12 patients with an average survival of 18 months; survival among these patients ranged from 1 to 60 months. Twenty-one patients surveyed in 1965 had an average survival of 15 months; 45 patients studied in 1972 had an average survival of 6 months, and 68 patients studied in 1974 had an average survival of 9.5 months. Finally, a 1979 study conducted by the University of Missouri dealt with eight patients who had an average survival of 7 months and a survival range from 9 days to 16 months. Clearly, IAT achieves survival rates two to three times those of traditional therapies.

Dr. Kunderman has become convinced "that this approach to the control of cancer in far advanced disease is the right approach . . . in terms of what we know about cancer right now." He spoke of IAT "to a number of my colleagues back home, and they know nothing about it." His surprise is clearly justified: "It just shows how little we out in the field know about this particular type of therapy." He himself was a leading practitioner in the cancer field and had never heard of Dr. Burton until he became a patient himself.

Dr. Burton has had equal success in treating metastatic cancer. He notes that "Dr. DeVita, director of the NCI, announced on television around December 1984 that the 5-year survival rate for metastatic cancer of the colon is zero. This means that nobody under traditional treatment survived 5 years. But we have over 10 patients [who have metastatic cancer of the liver] who have lived past the 5-year mark and are still alive today."

One of those surviving patients is Robert Beasley, who in 1975 was diagnosed with colon-to-liver cancer (meaning that the cancer metastasized—traveled—from the site of the primary tumor, the colon, to a remote site, the liver). Beasley says that his doctor "not only could tell I had liver trouble, he could hold the tumors in his hand. That's how bad it was. So he sewed me up and he said, "Take him home . . . I will not offer him chemo. He has three months to live." Eleven years later, after being treated for this condition by Dr. Burton, Beasley reported that he was in perfect health.

Dorothy Strait is another survivor of colon-to-liver cancer. She was diagnosed in 1976, and her surgeon told her that her case was hopeless. Having seen and biopsied her liver metastases and having viewed her live scans, he gave her a prognosis of 3 months of survival or less. After being treated by Dr. Burton for a few months, she returned to her surgeon, who was surprised to find no trace of the tumor in her body. Today, 12 years after the original diagnosis, she is alive and healthy.

There are many other cases of metastatic carcinoma survivors among Dr. Burton's patients, with some patients living 7 to 10 years after having received prognoses of less than 12 months' survival. But the traditional physicians who are informed of these dramatic turn-arounds in their former patients frequently write them off as "spontaneous remissions" rather than giving credit to the "unproven" therapy of immune augmentation. Still, neither the NCI nor the ACS has been able to explain why their "spontaneous remission" rate is zero while Dr. Burton's is about 1 out of every 10 patients. Dr. Kunderman observes: "That is always the point that is brought up. But in all my years of practice and hundreds of cases of cancer, those remissions in advanced cases have been [so rare that] it's with difficulty that I can recall any.

"So when somebody speaks about spontaneous remission, it's almost like saying, 'Well, it's a miracle' . . . I am sure that it happens . . . but I think the cases are few and far between."

Despite its successful pioneering work in cancer treatment, the Immunology Research Center came under attack from the traditional medical establishment in 1985. The ACS and NCI regard cancer "cure" as their exclusive province, heavily supported by public funding. Many outside efforts were regarded as intrusions and trespasses, and when they departed significantly from traditional treatment approaches, they were suspected of being quackery.

### Congressional Testimony

The American cancer establishment finally convinced the Bahamian government that Dr. Burton's therapy might have involved the use of contaminated blood. The clinic was forced to close on July 17,

1985, but was reopened the following spring after investigation proved that these allegations could not be substantiated. While the clinic was closed, a group of Dr. Burton's patients formed an association dedicated to reopening the IRC. Since most of these patients were Americans, they sought the assistance of the U.S. Congress. A congressional hearing on the matter was conducted in January 1986 by Representative Guy Molinari for the purpose of fact-finding and to make these complaints public. During the hearing, many members of the patient association had a chance to tell the public about their personal experiences at the IRC.

One of the witnesses was Sherry Costaldo, who was diagnosed as having breast cancer in 1978 at the age of 28 after many doctors had dismissed her, insisting that she wasn't sick. She underwent a radical mastectomy at Sloan-Kettering and then 5 weeks of daily radiation and 19 months of chemotherapy, which she was told at the time was only experimental. She recalls that "I was not told that beforehand." Subsequent radiation treatments continued on a regular basis before she suffered a massive seizure on May 31, 1983, resulting from the spreading of her cancer into the brain.

Displeased with what she had come to learn was experimental treatment at Sloan-Kettering, she went to Nassau Medical Center. There she underwent surgery to remove a brain tumor and then endured 5 more weeks of radiation treatment while she was on Dilantin (phenytoin) and prednisone. She remembers being "extremely ill from the treatment and medication, and seizures occurred periodically." She was "almost always dizzy, disoriented and nauseous, and very ill." She was told she might go on to chemotherapy administered through a shunt in her skull or through the spine, but she would have to suffer even greater pain, and the results were not guaranteed. She returned to Sloan-Kettering, where her ovaries were surgically removed (oophorectomy) in the hope that once estrogen production was stopped, tumor growth might be halted. But on February 10, 1984, a brain scan confirmed that four tumors were lodged in her brain. Her oncologist told her that nothing more could be done. On

April 28, 1984, she headed for Freeport and Dr. Burton's IRC, which she had heard was helping many cancer patients.

Although her husband was vehemently opposed to her being treated by Dr. Burton, she underwent IAT therapy for 14 weeks. During that time she was able to get off prednisone completely and eventually found herself "swimming, walking with confidence, and able to take care of my family and myself." She noted her progress from that point on during the congressional hearings: "The improvement has been almost unbelievable, and I am now living a fairly normal life.

"I have taken aerobic dancing, organized and directed a children's choir, and seldom need to rest. I run circles around my husband.

"On May 17, 1985, I repeated the neuromagnetic resonance [brain] scan. . . . My neurologist and I compared the 1984 scan and the 1985 scan; there was no trace of the four lesions, and much of the scar tissue from the massive tumor had depleted."

Ms. Costaldo's neurologist was skeptical about IAT but was both "thrilled and amazed" to see how her health had turned completely around. And Sherry is equally thrilled that IAT not only "saved or extended my life" but accomplished this "without destroying the quality of my life." When the oncologist from Sloan-Kettering contacted her to ask if he could use her recovery as one of his success stories, he was surprised to learn that she had been on IAT. "Oh, my, you mean I am going to have to give Dr. Burton credit for this?" he quipped.

Mary Yevchak began treatment at the IRC in the spring of 1984, only months after being diagnosed as having a large-cell lymphoma of the right lung. Ms. Yevchak had found her traditional medical treatment psychologically distressing as well as ineffective and painful.

"When they started intravenous chemotherapy, my family was told to leave the room," she states. "This was against my wishes because it was such a difficult time for me. The nurses who administered the chemotherapy proceeded to tell me about all the side effects. It would cause hair loss, and I would become sterile. This was especially traumatic to me, since I had just been married 2 years and was looking forward to starting a family. This procedure continued for 8 full days around the clock."

She was released in February, but further complications set in the next day. She was put on a combined chemotherapy-radiation program to reduce severe swelling in her head and neck. She soon found it painful to swallow, developed bacterial pneumonia, and was bloated beyond recognition by the large doses of steroids that were introduced to offset the radiation damage. During her treatment, Ms. Yevchak was told by her doctor that the "chemotherapy had very little effect, if any, on the cancer," and the radiation, while it did reduce the tumor somewhat, was extremely damaging. During her hospital treatment she was taking 14 oral medications a day, was bloated to nearly 200 pounds, and was completely bedridden. She had already given up when she learned of Dr. Burton's treatment center in the Bahamas. She says, "I was apprehensive at first, but my fears left as I could see a gradual improvement in my appearance and general condition.

"I was immediately taken off steroids, and the bloating started to subside. I became stronger and enjoyed walking short distances for the first time in months, since I was bed- and wheelchair-bound at the time.

"As time went on, I enjoyed more activities, and my outlook on life improved. I was there a total of 2 months and returned home to continue my daily injections at home. Two weeks later I returned to my job as a schoolteacher and secretary on a full-time basis.

"I visited my oncologist . . . who gave me a thorough examination, and he could find no trace of the disease, even though he had told me previously that without chemotherapy the disease would spread and tumors would grow throughout my body. It would then be too late for any treatment at all. He also advised me at the time that I had less than a 2 percent chance of living 6 months. . . .

"At the last visit he could find no evidence of the cancerous condition and stated that it may have been a misdiagnosis; that it could have been a thymoma instead of lymphoma, which is a much less serious condition."

According to Ms. Yevchak, when she told her oncologist that she was going to see Dr. Burton, he stated, "The guy is a quack. He is not going to hurt you, it's only blood fractions, but the rest will do you good. Go down there and have a good time." Says Ms. Yevchak, "He thought I was going to have a nice vacation and come back and die." When she returned and walked into the oncologist's office, Ms. Yevchak quotes him as saying, "Oh, I am in trouble."

Kate Banner was diagnosed with malignant cancer in 1977, with a third of the lymph glands in the lower portion of her colon affected. "So they [the doctors] just did not think that I had too much time," she recalls. Unwilling to suffer through chemotherapy, she insisted, "Keep me comfortable and I will take it from there." She opted for IAT treatment and reported feeling fine at the congressional hearing in 1986. In fact, when she returned home for adhesion surgery, her doctors could not find any sign of the cancer that had threatened her life in 1977. The way Kate Banner sees it, "They have been in my belly, and they can't find any cancer. I think I will stick with Burton."

Besides IAT's effectiveness against cancer, "Dr. Burton's clinic also provided an ambiance" to Elaine Boise and her family, including her husband, Jack, who did not survive his bout with cancer. She recalls that the clinic "encouraged the most intimate, emotional, psychological, philosophical, and spiritual exchanges between us and among us and our four children, with the result that we are newly bonded now.

"Does it matter, then, that the 7 months we spent fighting for our lives in the Bahamas are now counted among the best experiences of my life? It matters. It matters very much. . . .

"The strength and the wisdom—that we could never have obtained through conventional medical treatment. Essentially, at the

166

Immunology Research Center we were not dying of cancer, as we had been at home. We were living it, with many other people. And we savored life with an intensity and a passion that we have not known before, which would have been impossible in an orthodox hospital setting.

"This was the gift, the gift of life that Dr. Burton gave us. Our children and I will be forever grateful."

### Ganzheit Therapy: The Whole-Body Approach of Dr. Issels

The operation to be done that morning at the Maria Hilf Hospital in Monchengladbach, Germany, in 1931, was routine. The head surgeon, Dr. Sickmann, would perform a mastectomy in the hope of saving a young woman from breast cancer. The operation was nothing out of the ordinary in those days, yet two lives would be changed forever.

Dr. Josef Issels, who had just begun an internship in surgery at the hospital, assisted, first with professional interest and then with growing horror. "The breast was truly a thing of beauty," he was to write in a letter cited in Gordon Thomas' book, *Dr. Issels and His Revolutionary Cancer Treatment* (Peter H. Wyden, Inc., New York, 1973), "perfectly formed with the nipple glistening from swabbing with antiseptic.

"Satisfied that everything was positioned properly, Sickmann started to cut. A line of spurting blood marked the progress of his knife. He kept on staring intently at the incision area. I wiped the area clean with surgical sponges and pinched shut the main bleeding points with blood-vessel clamps. Then Sickmann went on cutting.

"Nobody spoke. The only sounds were the rustling of a nurse's gown as she passed over instruments and the click of one instrument following another into the discard tray.

"In 10 minutes, it was all over. Ten minutes to destroy what had taken 20 years or so to form. With a last snip, the breast was cut away like a piece of meat and thrown in the waste bucket."

Dr. Issels was appalled. A few minutes before the patient had been a complete woman. Now she was disfigured forever, not by some ghastly accident but by a skilled surgeon working in a modern hospital. Was the operation necessary? the doctor asked himself. Had anyone thought of its aftereffects on the woman, hideously marred for the rest of her days?

The psychological results of the operation were every bit as severe as Dr. Issels had feared. The woman suffered a nervous breakdown, and her husband, not understanding her suffering, divorced her within a year.

Dr. Issels did not waver in his commitment to become a surgeon, but he resolved that he would never assist at or perform another radical mastectomy. Along with his resolve came an implacable hatred for the disease that caused such suffering, a hatred that would lead the doctor over the next 20 years to develop his *Ganzheit* therapy and to open the Ringberg Clinic in Germany, where that therapy is practiced today.

For more than a century the orthodox medical establishment has adopted the position that cancer is a localized disease, indistinguishable from its symptoms—the cancer tumor. A brief overview of medical history reveals that this has not always been the case. In fact, until the mid-1800s the prevailing view of cancer was that it was a chronic systemic disease affecting the entire body of the cancer patient.

The tremendous advances in the development of symptom-oriented treatments, which include surgery, radiation, and chemotherapy, have benefitted some cancer patients. However, these benefits appear to have plateaued in the mid-1950s, and notwithstanding the stunning array of new high-tech surgical procedures and chemotherapeutic drugs, traditional medicine has been unable to attain more than a paltry increase in the real survival rates of its patients.

For over 40 years Dr. Josef Issles, founder of the Ringberg Clinic in the Bavarian Alps of southern Germany, has been aware of the need for traditional medicine to broaden its horizons with respect to the treatment of cancer. Trained as a traditional surgeon, Dr. Issels became aware of the limitations of orthodox therapy when he began treating cancer patients. After much research, Issels is convinced that the successful treatment of cancer lies in the return to the whole-body approach to the disease. According to Dr. Issels, "Cancer is not just a local disease confined to the particular place in the body where the tumor manifests itself but is a general disease of the whole body." Consequently, the treatment that offers the best chance of success in combating cancer is one which treats "not merely the tumor but also the whole body, which has produced the tumor." Based on this whole body approach to cancer, Dr. Issels has developed a broad-spectrum therapy to restore and regenerate the body's natural defense mechanisms that complements the specific measures of traditional medicine directed at the elimination of the localized tumor. With this dual approach to cancer, Dr. Issels has achieved a degree of success in treating his cancer patients which is unparalleled in traditional medicine.

After 10 years of practice, by 1947 Dr. Issels felt sufficiently confident in whole-body anticancer therapy to begin putting some of his theories into practice in what he would later call a "*Ganzheit*," or "whole-body," approach to healing. He required that all his patients have infected teeth or tonsils removed, since he strongly believed that they release poisons into the body which lower natural resistance and trigger disease. Proper diet was also considered critical. The usual foodstuffs had to be replaced by biologically adequate ones adjusted to fit the actual organic conditions of individual patients. Chronically ill patients usually had to receive *lactobacillus acidophilus,* a cultured milk product which served as a ferment substitute to compensate for a loss of efficiency in their digestive systems. Tobacco, alcohol, coffee, tea, and other substances the doctor considered harmful were banned. Whenever possible, longstanding emotional stress was relieved or eliminated. In the meantime, the doctor went ahead with treatment of the particular disease organ, confident that he was also addressing the root cause of the patient's sickness.

Dr. Issels was soon getting remarkable results with this combination of *Ganzheit* Therapy, homeopathy, dietary control, and other therapeutic techniques. His practice became the largest in the town, although it did not make him a rich man, since his fees were low and he treated for free those who were unable to pay.

Yet these successes contrasted grimly with his inability to help cancer patients. He knew that his colleagues were equally baffled by the disease, but that knowledge did not ease his frustration. Surgery and radiation seemed to bring temporary improvement, but it was clear that they did not get at the cause of the cancer and could not protect the patient from further occurrences. Surely, Issels thought, there had to be a way of applying the principles of *Ganzheit* Therapy to the treatment of cancer to produce not just remissions but genuine cures. There had to be an alternative to disfiguring surgery, toxic chemicals, and poisonous radiation.

### Historical Theories of Cancer

The antipathy Dr. Issels had felt toward cancer in his early years became almost an obsession with the disease. He read everything he could find on cancer and in the process became an expert in medical history. He discovered that cancer, contrary to popular opinion, was not a modern affliction but had been observed by Chinese and Sumerian physicians and described in manuscripts dating back 3,000 years before Christ as resulting from a malfunction in the body's regulatory mechanisms that was to be treated with acupuncture and drugs.

Hippocrates (460–377 B.C.), the founder of western medicine, was the first to use the word "carcinoma" in referring to malignant tumors, which he believed arose from a "separation of the humors" (blood, bile, and phlegm) and was to be treated with surgery and drugs. But what Dr. Issels found especially noteworthy was Hippoc-

170

rates' recommendation that the entire body be detoxified and that cancer patients be put on a special diet. Further research showed that for the ancient Greeks, *diata* or "diet," referred to far more than what a patient was to eat or drink. The term was closer in meaning to "way of life" or "lifestyle" and strongly suggested abstinence from anything that might be spiritually as well as physically harmful.

The Roman physician Claudius Galen (A.D. 131–200), the founder of scientific physiology, whose authority had gone unchallenged in western medicine for over 1,000 years, had also turned his attention to cancer, as Dr. Issels soon discovered. The doctor's interest became more than academic when he read Galen's opinion that cancer is a disease of the entire body, not confined to the site of the tumor.

Moving forward in time, Dr. Issels encountered the world-famous doctor of the Renaissance, Philippus Aureoulus Theophrastus Bombast von Hohenheim, better known as Paracelsus, who also felt that the physician's role in treating cancer and other diseases was not to interfere with the body but rather to stimulate the healing processes nature had provided to correct the imbalances in the body that result in illness. Dr. Issels also encountered the pioneer surgeon Ambroise Pare (1510–1590), who shared Paracelsus' view of cancer as a disease of the entire body, and the French thinker Rene Descartes (1596–1650), who thought cancer was caused by abnormalities in the lymph glands. He pored over the work of Percival Potts, the eighteenth-century British physician who was among the first to describe cancer as an "occupational" malignancy when he noticed an abnormally high rate of cancer of the scrotum in young chimney sweeps. In short, no one who might have something useful to say about cancer escaped Issel's scrutiny.

The work of Dr. Edward Jenner, the English physician who had developed a vaccination and checked the scourge of smallpox, seemed to offer special promise in regard to body theory and practice. Although Dr. Jenner had not been successful in treating cancer, he had produced vaccines which had shown promising results against other disorders. Equally important for Dr. Issels, his British predecessor believed that cancer stemmed from inadequacies in the immune mechanisms and that it could have a fatal effect only when the body's natural immunity had broken down completely.

Following this line of thought, Dr. Issels searched for a vaccine that would bolster the body's immune system to the point where it could fight back successfully against cancer. Neoblastine, a vaccine he developed by culturing cancer tissues in a controlled medium many times over a long period to insure safety, seemed to offer some promise. After testing the vaccine on laboratory animals, he tried it on a terminally ill lung cancer patient, together with his *Ganzheit* Therapy involving extraction of infected teeth and tonsils and strict dietary control. Although the patient lived 3 months longer than expected, the results were ambiguous, since there had been no cure and it was impossible to attribute the patient's improvement to any single factor in the treatment.

Another case, on the surface equally disappointing, occurred when Dr. Issels agreed to treat a woman with an enormous uterine tumor who had already been given up on by her doctors. Heeding her husband's pleas, Dr. Issels agreed to see her, but he could do nothing beyond prescribing painkillers and ordering a change in her diet. Nonetheless, the fact that Dr. Issels had undertaken to treat her gave the woman a much better outlook. Until her death 2 months later, she maintained steadfastly that Dr. Issels' treatments had freed her of pain that drugs had been unable to eliminate.

These patients and others all succumbed to disease and left Dr. Issels little cause for optimism. Yet these cases did serve to convince him that *Ganzheit* Therapy had been helpful and to confirm his longstanding belief that cancer is not a mysterious ailment but a chronic systemic illness, to be treated like other diseases of this kind. The tumor, he became convinced, was merely a late-stage symptom, accidentally triggered off but able to grow only in what he described as a "tumor milieu," the result of prior damage to organs and organ systems, especially those involved in maintaining the body's resistance to disease. The disease would never gain a foothold unless the body's defenses were depleted.

Once it had gained a foothold, conventional treatments, Dr. Issels decided, could usually provide only temporary relief. While surgery, by removing large masses of tumor, might stimulate the immune system to regenerate, it was not likely to provide a cure by itself, since the operation could not get at the underlying cause of the cancer. Radiation and chemotherapy, while often initially successful, frequently provided only temporary relief. Nonetheless, Dr. Issels did not offer *Ganzheit* Therapy as a substitute for the usual treatments but as a supplement which he believed would make the conventional therapies more effective by rehabilitating the entire patient, not just attacking the tumor.

### The Treatment

As the number of his cancer patients continued to grow, Dr. Issels began specializing in that disease. In 1950, he took charge of a 30-bed cancer unit at a small suburban clinic, where he put in 17-hour days, treating patients with a combination of traditional and unconventional methods. Surgery was used to remove large tumors. Drugs were administered to improve the functioning of various organs, especially the liver and kidneys, which usually are severely damaged in advanced cancer patients. The body was detoxified through the use of purifying drugs; mild purgatives; a diet high in fruit, vegetables, and grains; and the consumption of large amounts of water, juices, and herbal teas. Homeopathic remedies were used along with vaccines to stimulate antibody production.

Dr. Issels' cure statistics were not numerically impressive, but there was no lack of patients for treatment. Those who came to him were not in the early stages of the disease but were for the most part patients whom the medical establishment had been unable to help.

For them, Dr. Issels offered the proverbial "last, best hope" of staying alive, a hope he was sometimes able to fulfill in ways that bordered on the miraculous.

When he was asked to treat Kathe Gerlach in October 1950, Dr. Issels hesitated, since she lived an hour's drive from the hospital and he was reluctant to take the time from his other patients. When he finally acceded to requests from the 41-year-old patient, her husband, and her physician, Issels was dismayed at her condition. She had an enormous tumor in her uterus which a biopsy had shown to be malignant and inoperable. Edema in her legs had left her unable to walk and she was expected to live only a few days.

Even though the case seemed hopeless, Dr. Issels agreed to treat her at home, since she was far too weak to be moved to the hospital. By mid-October she began to show definite signs of improvement, and by November her pain had subsided. The edema in her legs diminished, although the tumor remained very large.

Dr. Issels drove Mrs. Gerlach to the hospital as soon as she was well enough to be moved. There she began to improve rapidly. Pieces of the tumor were being eliminated, the edema decreased continually, and her circulation improved markedly. By November 25 it was clear that the tumor was regressing. In February of the following year she left the hospital with no detectable signs of cancer.

Mrs. Gerlach, however, was not the only one impressed by this remarkable turn of events. Her surgeon, Dr. Lothar Ley, examined her in March 1951, confirmed Dr. Issels' findings, and offered to refer more cancer patients to him for this unorthodox but clearly successful treatment.

Nearly a quarter of a century later, when Dr. Issels contacted Mrs. Gerlach in connection with his own book, *Cancer: A Second Opinion* (Hodder and Stoughton, London, 1975), he found her leading a normal life with no indications that her cancer might return.

In the spring of 1951, Dr. Issels went to Holland to consult with the Dutch shipping magnate Karl Gishler, who was suffering from prostate cancer that had metastasized to his spine and left him bedridden. His prognosis was terminal.

After much deliberation, Mr. Gisher decided to undergo *Ganzheit* Therapy under Dr. Issels' supervision, and the treatment began in mid-May. Over the weeks that followed, Mr. Gishler, despite the progress of the disease that ultimately took his life, remained attentive and alert, interested in every aspect of the treatment. His friendship with and respect for Dr. Issels also grew steadily as he came to know his physician better and understand his deep-seated desire to alleviate human suffering.

These feelings, however, were not shared by the conservative hospital administration, which expressly forbade Dr. Issels to treat any other patients according to his methods. This rebuff led indirectly to another incident that changed the direction of Issels' career.

On a visit to Mr. Gishler's bedside, Dr. Issels found the patient in tears not just from the pain of his tumor but from the humiliation of being slapped by a nurse who felt he was troublesome. Dr. Issels was aghast, but all Mr. Gishler said, as reported in Gordon Thomas' book about Dr. Issels, was that Dr. Issels had to find his own place where he could hand-pick his staff:

In answer to Mr. Gishler's questions about the cost of such an institution, Dr. Issels answered without thinking that 150,000 marks would be about right.

In postwar Germany, 150,000 marks was a considerable sum, close to $500,000 in today's purchasing power, but the tycoon was undaunted.

"Then you will have the money," Gishler assured him.

### The Ringberg Clinic

On September 21, 1951, the Ringberg Clinic opened in a former hotel in the Bavarian town of Rottach-Egern. Here Dr. Issels finally had a free hand in treating cancer, and here he was able to spend nearly four decades treating patients whom other doctors had not been able to help.

The first patient, Mrs. Lydia Bacher, arrived in an ambulance, bald from radiation therapy and so debilitated by the effects of an inoperable brain tumor that she could no longer speak, hear, or see. She was paralyzed in both legs and in the right arm, and her bladder and rectum no longer functioned. Her physicians had discharged her with painkillers, saying that no further treatment was possible. *Ganzheit* Therapy, supplemented with daily injections of Toxinal (oxytetracycline), an immunotherapy agent, was started at once.

Within a month Mrs. Bacher's speech had returned, she was able to read a newspaper, her hearing was improving, and her bodily functions were almost normal. By mid-December she was walking, and on March 17, 1952, she left the clinic, completely recovered. Her amazed doctors explained this recovery as a "spontaneous remission," but Mrs. Bacher was only the first of many terminally ill patients to have such a remission at the Ringberg Cinic. She was also the first clinic patient to survive symptom-free past the critical 5-year mark which conventional medicine accepts as proof of a cure.

The treatment which practically brought Mrs. Bacher back from the grave and has saved many others from death is not a magic pill or simple potion that produced overnight wonders. Rather, it is a complex and carefully thought out regimen that takes into account every aspect of the patient and the patient's illness and seeks relentlessly to find and correct the imbalance in the patient's being that made it possible for the cancer to arise in the first place.

Patients arriving at the Ringberg Clinic find that the old hotel was abandoned in 1981 in favor of a sophisticated medical facility, staffed by 4 doctors and 25 nurses and outfitted with the latest equipment for diagnosis and treatment. The documents the patients bring with them pertaining to their illness are checked, and the patients are carefully examined to verify the diagnosis. An exact case history is taken, stretching back not only over the course of the disease but over each patient's whole life and, if possible, the lives of the patient's ancestors as well, since Dr. Issels believes that it is necessary to construct a complete nutritional health profile before an effective treatment can begin. The weak points that made the patient vulnerable to cancer must be found and strengthened if a relapse is to be avoided.

Although about 90 percent of the patients have already been designated as incurable and beyond the help of orthodox medicine, Dr. Issels will continue conventional treatment if it is possible and appropriate, since he views *Ganzheit* Therapy as a supplement to make these treatments more effective rather than a substitute for them.

Once the examination is complete, the doctor tailors the treatment to the patient's individual needs and a regular appointment schedule is set up. The patient gets a chart that is filled in every morning and evening, listing the patient's symptoms, whether there is pain, changes in the tumor, the amount excreted, and whether there is vomiting, sweating, etc. When the patient comes in for an appointment, he or she shows the chart to the nurse, who then enters the data on a 4-week chart so that the doctor can judge whether the treatment should be stronger or weaker.

All the patients must part with infected teeth and tonsils, since Dr. Issels views these as sites of infection that place an unnecessary burden on the immune system and act to lower the body's general defenses against disease. Scars and the sites of old injuries are treated with Dr. Huneke's Neural Therapy to eliminate them as sources of infection. Both patients and doctors find tonsillectomy and tooth extraction a strange treatment for cancer and the injection of Novocain (procain hydrochloride) into parts of the body far distant from the tumor even stranger. But Dr. Issels, although not a devotee of Dr. Huneke's abstruse theories, has seen many cases in which these procedures, often undertaken just to relieve pain, have cleared the way for other treatments to attack the tumor.

A healthy diet is also a critical element in *Ganzheit* Therapy at the clinic, as it was from the very beginning of Dr. Issels' practice. Most meats are avoided, since meat is difficult for advanced cancer patients to digest and is usually filled with hormones, antibiotics, and pesticides that place further strain on the body. The recommended diet is primarily vegetarian, focusing on organically grown whole grains, fruits, and vegetables, supplemented by enzymes, minerals, and vitamins, with emphasis on A, B-complex, C, and E. Yogurt and acidophilous supplements are used to eliminate abnormal intestinal flora.

Serum activator is administered to bring the metabolism of red blood cells up to normal levels, allowing the release of additional hemoglobin and thus increasing the supply of oxygen to the body's cells.

Organ extracts are supplied to help repair secondary damage to organs and improve their functioning, while a high fluid intake backed up with herbal extracts, DNA, and RNA is used to detoxify the body, improve kidney, lymph, and liver functions, and bolster the excretory systems.

Since *Ganzheit* Therapy entails the treatment of the entire patient, individual group psychotherapy is an important element. Through this treatment, Dr. Issels hopes not only to help the patient come to terms with the disease, but also to remove, or at least alleviate, the psychic stress which he feels can help bring on cancer and hinder its cure.

The second part of this two-pronged attack is aimed at the tumor itself and is essentially a highly sophisticated form of immunotherapy, geared specifically to fighting cancer and supported, where necessary, by surgery, radiation, and chemotherapy. This immunotherapy also involves a twofold approach: specific immunization against the particular type of cancer to be fought around a general effort to augment the body's natural immune responses.

"Specific immunization works on a well-tried principle," Dr. Issels wrote in his 1975 book, *Cancer, A Second Opinion*. "Once a particular cancer antigen has been identified, it is administered under conditions most favorable for the induction of an immune response that will destroy cancer cells bearing that antigen. This is really no more than an extension of the standard vaccination technique against any infectious disease."

For specific immunizations against the tumor, Dr. Issels often administers a vaccine shown to cause regression of malignant tumors which was developed by Dr. Franz Gerlach, a Viennese scientist who has been working at the clinic since 1958. Other tumor-specific immunization is effected with standard nontoxic vaccines such as Centanit for carcinoma, Sarkogen for sarcoma, and Lymphogran for Hodgkin's disease.

General immunotherapy is used to bolster the patient's overall immunity and to destroy the "tumor milieu" that makes it possible for the cancer to sustain itself and grow. Here the primary means of attack consists of autovaccines prepared from extracts from the patient's own teeth and tonsils as well as other nontoxic vaccines designed to boost general resistance to disease.

Ozone therapy, although not a direct aid to the immune system, also is used as a means of increasing the oxygen supply to the cells and destroying viruses and bacteria in the bloodstream. This method of systematically exposing portions of the patient's blood supply to medically pure ozone is almost unknown in the United States but has been used against blood-borne infectious diseases in Germany for more than 25 years. Dr. Issels has also found the therapy to be effective in purging the blood of oxidation-resistant pesticides and other toxins.

Hyperpyrexia, homeopathy's long-sanctioned induction of fever, is also used in much the same way as ozone therapy to make life uncomfortable for the tumor. Once a month patients get a "fever shot," which can raise the body temperature as high as 105 degrees Fahrenheit, where it stays for 2 hours or so while the patient is under constant medical supervision. In the evening the body's temperature is lowered again.

While Dr. Issels may not share the enthusiasm of the ancient Greek physician who remarked, "Give me a chance to produce fever, and I can cure all illness," he knows that fever is a natural reaction of the body to foreign invaders and that it makes these invaders more vulnerable to attack. He has also discovered that the number of disease-destroying leukocytes in the patient's bloodstream rises enormously after each fever shot and that the patients uniformly report feeling much better afterward, as their bodies are detoxified. Even localized heating of the tumor area, Dr. Issels has discovered, can have effects which, while not as spectacular, are clearly beneficial.

### The Patients

To medical practitioners who firmly believe that cancer is largely an incurable disease, Dr. Issels' theories and methods are simply bizarre. To them, the notion that cancer is not a localized illness but a chronic disease that manifests itself as a tumor only in its advanced stages is simply unthinkable, as is the idea that the body, once restored to its normal physiology, is capable of destroying the malignancy. This low opinion of *Ganzheit* Therapy, however, is not shared by the patients who have seen it work.

*Example 1:* Nineteen-year-old Thea Dohm arrived at the Ringberg Clinic on October 29, 1952. Surgery and radiation had been ineffective against a malignant fibroblastic sarcoma (skin and muscle cancer) that encircled her spine like a snake. Her physicians had sent her home to die and advised her parents to call a priest to administer the last rites. She was not even expected to survive the 600-mile trip to the Ringberg Clinic. But 16 days after beginning therapy, she began to show strong signs of recovery. By January 1953 her x-rays showed considerable reduction in the tumor, and 1 month later she was released from the clinic to return home, where her family doctor had agreed to administer maintenance therapy.

Thea's story seemed well on its way to a happy ending, when she was returned to the hospital in Monchengladbach, suffering from a secondary fibrosarcoma. Since Dr. Issels happened to be in his home-town visiting his brother, he went to see Thea in the hospital and found her completely resigned to dying. After some questioning, he learned that Thea had been engaged to be married, when her fiancé canceled the engagement, leaving her desolate. The cancer recurred almost immediately afterward, convincing Dr. Issels that it had been psychologically triggered.

Since radiation had been ineffective in treating the tumor, Dr. Issels suggested that Thea return to the Ringberg Clinic, and her parents agreed. Dr. Issels began treating her in November with No-vacarcin, a newly developed immunotherapeutic agent, and by January there was considerable reduction in the size of the tumor. But Thea still lacked the will to live, and Dr. Issels now knew that without a change in her attitude, long-term remission would be impossible.

After carefully considering the options, Dr. Issels decided to visit Thea's former fiancé and tell him about her condition. The man went at once to the clinic to see her, and there was a reconciliation. Thea began to improve rapidly, her tumor shrank, and she was able to return home. Five years after the original diagnosis of cancer Thea got married, and as Dr. Issels notes in his case files, "There has been a complete disappearance of the secondary tumor. The original one remains dormant. Patient is entirely free of any active cancer."

More than a decade later her family doctor found Thea's lung free of malignancy and the original spinal tumor still dormant. His opin-ion, as given in Thomas' book, was simple and straightforward: "She leads the usual busy life of a mother of three children, and has every reason to expect a full life span."

*Example 2:* Mrs. K. G. was 40 years old when she was first diagnosed as having inoperable stage III uterocervical cancer. At first she responded to radiation treatment, but in July 1950 an egg-sized recurrence appeared and was unresponsive to radiation. The tumor grew, filling her pelvic area with a solid cancerous mass and blocking her rectal passage so that a palliative colostomy was required. She was admitted to the Ringberg Clinic in October 1950, barely alive.

*Ganzheit* Therapy and immunotherapy were started at once, and within 5 months all tumor symptoms had disappeared. When Dr. Issels contacted Mrs. K. G. again in 1973 while researching his book, he learned that she was still symptom-free and without any signs of cancer.

*Example 3:* In July 1952, a right-sided mastectomy was done on S. G. to remove a breast tumor. Since biopsies of the cancer tissue revealed that she had a penetrating adenocarcinoma, she was given follow-up radiation treatments that failed to halt the spread of the disease. By January 1953 the cancer had metastasized to both lungs, and the prognosis was hopeless. In April of that year she was admitted to the Ringberg Clinic and was started on *Ganzheit* Therapy and immunotherapy. Within 2 years all the lung metastases had disappeared. When she died at 69 of a heart attack, 15 years after completing the treatment, she was still cancer-free.

*Example 4:* Twenty-nine-year-old K. K. was diagnosed in December 1954 with seminoma, a cancer arising from the uncontrolled proliferation of sex cells. His right testicle was removed, and postoperative radiation was recommended because of several palpable lymph nodes in his right groin. He refused the radiation and went to the Ringberg Clinic early in 1955 for *Ganzheit* Therapy and immunotherapy. Although his symptoms did not respond immediately to treatment, he ultimately had a complete remission. Subsequently, he married and fathered two children. In 1974, when Dr. Issels last spoke with him, he was symptom-free with no signs of cancer.

While skeptics may mutter about "spontaneous remissions," it remains true that three independent studies of Dr. Issels' medical records conducted by highly reputed experts have confirmed a 16.6 percent cure rate among all the terminal patients treated with *Ganzheit* Therapy, a figure that no doctor or hospital anywhere in the world comes close to matching. The other alternative therapies mentioned in this chapter have success rates (5-year complete remissions) ranging from 5 to 15 percent.

To understand the significance of this figure, it is necessary to recall that all these patients were terminal, already given up on by conventional medicine. In the United States, for example, such a patient has virtually no chance of survival, let alone of cure.

The distinction between survival and cure is also crucial. For conventional medicine, "cure" simply means that the cancer patient has survived 5 years after the initial diagnosis. It says nothing about the state of the patient during the time or at its end. Dr. Issels uses a different standard. For him and for the doctors who have studied his work, a cure indicates that the patient in question is free of any detectable sign of cancer. A man or woman who fully expected to die of cancer is now alive, healthy, and free of the disease 5 years or more after beginning treatment.

While even Dr. Issels does not think of *Ganzheit* Therapy as the be-all and end-all, his indisputable successes bring one face-to-face with some uncomfortable facts. The tremendous advances in the development of symptom-oriented treatments, which include surgery, radiation, and chemotherapy, have been of benefit to some cancer patients, but these benefits appear to have peaked in the mid-1950s. Notwithstanding the stunning array of new high-tech surgical procedures and chemotherapeutic drugs, traditional medicine has not been able to attain more than a slight increase in the survival rates of patients. Despite the expenditure of billions of dollars in the war on cancer, there is growing evidence of the limitations of conventional therapies and evidence that statistical manipulations have inflated the amount of actual progress.

Of course, the shortcomings of conventional therapies do not by themselves constitute proof of the accuracy and efficacy of Dr. Issels' theories and methods which he continues to refine today. But at the very least these limitations should indicate that it is time to take a long, hard look at conventional therapies and the theories behind them. Before the medical establishment is allowed to brand *Ganzheit* Therapy as "weird," it should explain why it works in so many cases in which orthodox treatments have failed. Until then, Dr. Issels' explanations are the best one is likely to find.

### Gerson Therapy: Rebuilding the Body's Natural Healing System

With the advance of technology, an ever-increasing number of new substances are introduced into the environment each year. These substances range from chemicals, pesticides, and drugs to the by-products of nuclear weapons and energy. There are also new agricultural and manufacturing techniques such as genetically engineered microorganisms and food irradiation. Until relatively recently the human body, which has evolved over thousands of years, seemed to do a fairly good job of adapting to the changes within the environment. Within the past century, however, the rate at which people have been exposed to new and toxic substances has accelerated so rapidly that the result has been a breakdown in the body's natural adaptation and defensive processes. Certain physicians view this breakdown as one of the major contributing factors to many of today's most dreaded diseases, especially cancer.

The theory that cancer is triggered by environmental factors which deplete the body's natural adaptive and defensive capabilities is not a new one. In fact, Max Gerson, M.D., took an "environmental" approach to cancer therapy over 60 years ago. The cornerstone of Dr. Gerson's therapy is the detoxification of the body through diet designed to rehabilitate the body's natural immunity and healing process.

Although Dr. Gerson died in 1959, his work is being carried on by his daughter, Charlotte Gerson, in the new Gerson clinic located on the western coast of Mexico about 30 miles south of San Diego. Dr. Gerson was eulogized by Dr. Albert Schweitzer, whose wife Gerson cured of lung tuberculosis in the 1930s. Schweitzer wrote in a letter to Ms. Gerson, "I see in him one of the most eminent geniuses in the history of medicine. Many of his basic ideas have been adopted without having his name connected with them. Yet he has achieved more than seemed possible under adverse conditions. He leaves a legacy which commands attention and which will assure him his due place. Those whom he cured will now attest to the truth of his ideas."

## The Use of Diet

Dr. Gerson was born in Wongrowitz, Germany, in 1881. The roots of his work date to his early days as a young intern and resident before World War I. At that time he was suffering from severe migraine headaches, which were considered incurable. But Dr. Gerson, after a fruitless search through the medical literature, turned to nutrition to change his body chemistry and gain relief. Gerson was already convinced that contamination of foods by artificial fertilizers and processing has a deleterious effect on body chemistry. He felt that by restoring normal metabolism through a healthy diet, he might be able to improve his migraine condition, and so he started to experiment on himself with certain foods. His first experiment was with milk. He thought that milk, being the first food, was something that even a baby could handle, so that his body should have been able to utilize it properly. But when he drank nothing but milk, his headaches became worse. Then it occurred to him that milk is not normally consumed by adult animals other than humans anywhere in nature and that maybe milk is a foreign substance rather than a natural nutrient in the adult human diet.

He decided to conduct his next experiments using foods that were more suited for the human type of build and body chemistry, namely, fruits and vegetables. (Contrary to popular belief, human physiology is basically vegetarian and not carnivorous. The human intestinal tract measures 30 feet in length and as such is unsuited to the proper digestion and elimination of meat.) When Dr. Gerson found that he did not experience migraines when he ate nothing but grains, fresh fruits, and vegetables, he began experimenting with single foods to discern their particular effect on his physiology. He found, for instance, that when he ate cooked foods, they often did not agree with him. But it turned out that it wasn't the cooking but the added salt that made the difference. When he ate the same cooked foods without salt, he was able to handle them very well.

Little by little Dr. Gerson began to piece together a menu of foods that he could safely consume, together with a list of foods that would almost invariably give him migraines within a few minutes of his eating them. In the end he arrived at a diet very high in fresh fruits and vegetables and freshly prepared vegetable and fruit juices and very low in fats. Later, in his treatment of tuberculosis patients, Gerson would use a small amount of raw, fresh unsalted butter because it is a good source of the phospholipids which form an important part of the body's defense mechanism, but otherwise the diet was largely free of animal fats, especially cooked fats, and totally free of meats and cooked animal proteins of any sort.

By the early 1920s, Dr. Gerson had succeeded in completely curing himself of migraines with his special diet. He then started extending his findings to patients who came to see him suffering from migraines. They too benefitted. Eventually, although by accident, Dr. Gerson began to use his "Migraine Diet" in the treatment of tuberculosis as well. His daughter, Charlotte Gerson, relates how this occurred:

"One time, a patient came to him suffering from migraines and was given what he called his 'Migraine Diet.' When the patient came back after 3 or 4 weeks, he told Dr. Gerson that along with his migraines, he also had been suffering from lupus vulgaris, a form of skin tuberculosis, and that with the diet, not only had his migraines disappeared but the lupus had also begun to heal. Dr. Gerson found this almost impossible to believe, because he had learned that lupus was *really* an incurable condition. But there was the proof before his eyes. He saw that the lesion was healing, and he verified that it had been properly diagnosed and that there had been bacteriological studies showing that, in fact, the man had skin tuberculosis.

"After that, he was able to cure many other patients with skin tuberculosis. This therapy was later verified in large experiments in Munich, involving 450 terminal or incurable cases of skin tuberculosis treated with this Gerson dietary therapy. The treatment was shown to cure 447. From there, Dr. Gerson felt that if tuberculosis could be influenced by nutrition, then why only skin tuberculosis— why shouldn't other forms of tuberculosis respond? He applied this same dietary treatment to people with lung tuberculosis, bone tuberculosis, kidney tuberculosis, etc. One of the most famous patients he had at that time was the wife of Albert Schweitzer, who had contracted TB in the tropics. She had been given up because her TB had spread to both lung fields and was quite extensive. Well, among others, she too recovered and lived many, many years, until age 80 or so."

As a result of this healing, Drs. Gerson and Schweiter became friends and remained so throughout their lives. Dr. Schweitzer followed the progress of the Gerson Therapy as it was later applied to a wide variety of diseases, and when he developed adult diabetes, he found relief through Dr. Gerson's treatment. Unfortunately, the American medical establishment has never shared Dr. Schweitzer's high opinion of Dr. Gerson. Instead of being praised, he was persecuted and harassed by his colleagues. Today, more than 30 years after Dr. Gerson's death in 1959, his therapy still remains on the American Cancer Society's "Unproven Methods" list.

### The Treatment

Before discussing Dr. Gerson's therapy, it is important to look at its theoretical basis. Like the other alternative cancer approaches discussed in this chapter, it differs fundamentally from the traditional medical treatment in that it deals with cancer as a generalized rather than a localized disease. More specifically, it is related to the balance or imbalance in the body's internal chemistry and physiology. According to Dr. Gerson (author of *A Cancer Therapy: Results of Fifty Cases,* 4th ed., Gerson Institute, Bonita, California, 1986):

"A normal body has the capacity to keep all cells functioning properly. It prevents any abnormal transformation and growth. Therefore, the natural task of a cancer therapy is to bring the body back to that normal physiology, or as near to it as possible. The next task is to keep the physiology of the metabolism in that normal equilibrium.

"A normal body also has reserves to suppress and destroy malignancies. It does not act in that manner in cancer patients, where the cancer grew from the smallest cellular unit freely, without encountering any resistance. . . .

"In short," says Dr. Gerson, "what is essential is not the growth itself or the visible symptoms; it is the damage of the whole metabolism, including the loss of defense, immunity, and healing power. It cannot be explained or recognized by one or another cause alone."

Dr. Gerson's therapy aims at rebalancing and revitalizing the cancer patient's entire physiology in order to rectify this systemic disorder. It looks for the cause of the illness, works to correct it, and thus not only causes the cancer to regress but prevents it from recurring. Traditional cancer therapy, as has been seen, is not very successful at eradicating symptoms and fails abysmally in preventing recurrences. Furthermore, while the traditional therapies of chemotherapy and radiation may be effective in treating the symptoms of certain relatively rare forms of cancer, they not only do nothing to revitalize the body's immune system, they actually work to suppress it. Gerson Therapy attempts to detoxify and rebuild the body's natural immunity and healing power, while traditional medicine administers highly toxic substances which destroy the immune system and often cause secondary cancers. In fact, Dr. Gerson was often forced to turn away cancer patients who had received traditional medical treatments and whose bodies had been damaged beyond hope by these very treatments, not by the cancer.

According to Curtis Hesse, M.D., former director of the Gerson Therapy Center (personal correspondence to Charlotte Gerson), "Ironically, the main problem we actually have in this treatment is not always cancer or disease but the other medications and treatments that the patients have already undergone. . . . In cancer therapy, we do not as a general rule accept any patient who has undergone chemotherapy. From past experience, we know that liver damage and damage to other organs, as well as the immune system, have been such that they do well for a 2- to 3-week period but then go downhill."

The core of Gerson Therapy is a regimen consisting primarily of a saltless and fatless diet of organically grown fresh fruits and vegetables which are usually served raw or as juices. The primary objective of the diet is to detoxify the entire body and rebalance the whole metabolism, not simply to eliminate the symptoms of the disease. "The treatment . . . has to penetrate deeply to correct all vital processes," says Dr. Gerson. "When general metabolism is restored, we can again influence the functioning of all organs, tissues, and cells through it."

Since detoxification and normalizing the metabolism are major factors in Gerson Therapy, Dr. Gerson placed particular importance on the condition of the liver, which is a primary regulator of metabolism. According to Dr. Gerson: "The problem of the liver was and still is partly misunderstood and partly neglected. The metabolism and its concentration in the liver should be put in the foreground, not the cancer as a symptom. There, the outcome of cancer is determined as the clinically favorable results, failures, and autopsies clearly demonstrate. There the sentence will be passed—whether the tumors can be killed, dissolved, absorbed, or eliminated, and finally, whether the body can be restored.

"The progress of the disease depends on whether and to what extent the liver can be restored."

The liver's many functions, coupled with its constant interaction with all the other organs of the body, give it a crucial role to play in the maintenance of health. Dr. Gerson and many other scientists have noted that in all degenerative diseases, including cancer, there are varying degrees of liver dysfunction and deterioration. Fortunately, however, while the liver is not easily destroyed and liver damage may not even be detected until liver function his been greatly impaired, the liver is also one of the organs that has the greatest capacity for regeneration. Consequently, the restoration of the liver is a significant objective of Dr. Gerson's diet.

Dr. Gerson's liver therapy is multifaceted. First, animal proteins are eliminated or greatly reduced in the diet because they have been found to interfere with liver medications and impede the body's detoxification.

The ideal diet of patients on liver therapy is the same as that described above for the cancer therapy: low in salt and fat and high in potassium and fresh fruits and vegetables, mostly in juice form.

The juice is also rich in iron and potassium as well as hormones and vitamins which aid in regenerating the liver. The juice is always prepared *freshly* and is not mixed with other medications which could alter the pH and thereby decrease its efficacy. The restoration of the liver, which may take from 6 to 18 months, depending on the severity of the illness, allows it to detoxify the body and produce its own oxidative enzymes.

Other aspects of liver therapy include liver injections and lubile and pancreatin tablets. The liver injections are composed of liver extract and are given daily for 4 to 6 months. They too provide important vitamins, minerals, and enzymes which aid in restoring the liver to its proper functioning. These liver injections are usually combined with vitamin $B_{12}$ injections, which Dr. Gerson believed are important for proper protein synthesis. Cancer patients are often unable to combine amino acids properly in order to form proteins within their bodies.

Lubile (defatted bile powder from young calves) was used more frequently in the earlier stages of the therapy; it is not used for most patients today. However, it is beneficial in cases where the liver is extremely damaged and the whole bile duct system is impaired.

Pancreatin tablets are given during and after the detoxification program is completed as a backup source of digestive enzymes, since these are also deficient in most cancer patients.

According to Dr. Gerson, patients on the therapy actually begin to break down, assimilate, and eliminate cancer tumors. This is accomplished when the repaired liver is adequately producing oxidative enzymes, the general detoxification process (of which the liver is a critical part) is active, and potassium levels throughout the body are adequate.

During the period when the body is killing, absorbing, and eliminating the tumor, detoxification is of the utmost importance. Dr. Gerson admits that in the early stages of development, the therapy did not contain adequate detoxification techniques. "After a tumor was killed," he says, "the patient did not die of cancer but of a serious intoxification with 'coma hepaticum' (liver shock) caused by absorption of necrotic cancer tissue." Thus, in addition to the other cleansing aspects of the therapy, Dr. Gerson began to prescribe frequent coffee enemas, which at the outset of treatment can be given as often as every 4 hours. This prescription derives from the work of two German researchers who found that caffeine administered rectally causes an opening of the bile ducts, releasing accumulated toxins and causing an increased production of bile, which flushes out these toxins. After these enemas, Dr. Gerson noticed that patients were often relieved of pain such as headaches, fevers, and nausea and could easily discontinue sedation. On the other hand, Dr. Gerson noted that coffee taken orally seemed to have exactly the opposite effect: It caused the stomach to go into spasm and produce a "soaping" over or contraction of the bile ducts. Hence, while regular coffee enemas are an indispensable part of Gerson Therapy, drinking coffee is discouraged.

Muscles, the brain, and the liver normally have much higher levels of potassium than of sodium. Early in his research, however, Dr. Gerson noted that in cancer patients this ratio is reversed; that is, he found that sodium is elevated in cancer cells and that in the ailing body, potassium is often inactive and/or improperly utilized. He felt that at the beginning chronic disease is caused by the loss of potassium from the cell system; accordingly, another primary objective of Gerson Therapy is to reestablish proper levels of potassium in the body.

Because of the specific relationship between sodium and potassium, in which an increase in one mineral causes a decrease in the other and vice versa, one of the first things Gerson advocated is the elimination of salt and sodium-rich foods from the diet.

Additionally, all patients on Gerson Therapy immediately begin receiving large amount of a potassium solution which Dr. Gerson developed after 300 experiments. The potassium compound he used, which is still used at the clinic, is a combination of potassium gluconate, potassium acetate, and potassium phosphate monobasic. This is administered in the form of a 10 percent potassium solution, which is added to juices 10 times daily in 4-teaspoon doses. The potassium solution is *never* added to the liver juice because Dr. Gerson believed that it can alter the juice's pH, thereby decreasing its efficacy. After a month, the amount is decreased by about half. The fluid retention or edema (caused by a sodium overabundance) is usually the first thing to disappear when patients are given high amounts of potassium in juices.

Dr. Gerson noted that even in a healthy person, it is very difficult to restore potassium deficiencies. In seriously ill people, it may take as long as a year or two before normal levels in major organs are reestablished.

In patients suffering from dehydration, potassium is added to the fluids therapeutically administered in the form of GKI (glucose, potassium, insulin) solution. According to Ms. Gerson, this solution is not specific to Gerson Therapy but is recognized and utilized by the

American medical establishment in general. "Dr. Demetrio Sodi-Pallares, a world-renowned cardiologist from Mexico City," says Ms. Gerson, "very much recommends this solution." He agreed with Dr. Gerson that disease is systemic or metabolic. His own research in heart disease has shown that it is not a disease of the heart but a metabolic disease that must be treated with a high-potassium, low-sodium diet. (For further discussion on heart disease, see Chapter 2.)

Dr. Sodi-Pallares found that giving GKI to heart patients with fluid retention is also very helpful. Ms. Gerson noted that "This solution helps restore potassium to the cell system. . . . Energy is required in order for potassium to go back into the cell system, and this energy is supplied by the glucose and insulin. We use this solution quite successfully in two ways: first to replenish the patient with fluids but also to restore potassium to the cells and reduce edema."

All aspects of Gerson Therapy revolve around the diet, which is designed to support all the other efforts to rebalance the internal body chemistry. At the clinic, all meals are prepared with fresh, organically grown produce. Nothing is canned, jarred, pickled, frozen, or preserved in any way. Between the juices and the three meals, the total average intake of food for each patient is approximately 20 pounds of fresh raw food a day, mostly via juices.

All refined, processed, and empty-calorie foods are avoided. This includes obviously treated foods such as white sugars and flours and smoked, sulfured, packaged, or mass-prepared products. Other obvious taboos include cigarettes, alcohol, drugs, and caffeine, which are known to deplete the immune system and act as carcinogens. All animal proteins such as meat, poultry, and dairy products are avoided, since they are difficult to digest and hinder rather than promote the restoration of the liver.

Both animal and vegetable fats are also avoided as they too can be difficult to digest and can impede detoxification. Additionally, Dr. Gerson found that dietary fats actually have the effect of promoting tumor growth. This accords with cancer research indicating that the higher the level of cholesterol and fats in the blood of cancer patients, the less chance of their surviving. Dr. Gerson slowly eliminated all fats from the diets of his cancer patients and found that the results improved substantially. On the other hand, whenever he added fats (even oils which are low in cholesterol) to the patients' diet, he observed regrowth of tumor tissue. Essentially through trial and error, Dr. Gerson found that he was able to control the growth of cancer tissue. With an external tumor, say, a lesion of the breast or skin, when the tumor was practically healed, if the patient was suddenly given a little butter, the lesion would often break open again or a new cancer would begin to grow. When the butter was eliminated, the tumor would begin to regress and heal again. Consequently, for cancer patients receiving Gerson Therapy, fats of animal or vegetable origin are eliminated as much as possible. The only exception is linseed oil, which Dr. Gerson found is particularly well tolerated. For patients suffering from other illnesses, while the diet is essentially low in fat, some raw fresh butter, egg yolks, and low-cholesterol vegetable oils such as safflower oil and sunflower oil may be eaten in small quantities.

Dr. Gerson was a strong believer in the importance of organically grown produce, and as mentioned above, all food used at his clinic must be grown in this manner. Chemical pesticides and fertilizers, he said, essentially poison and denature fruits and vegetables by altering their chemical composition. For instance, he found that many chemical fertilizers cause the sodium content in the affected foods to rise while decreasing potassium levels, which is precisely contrary to what the body requires to restore its healthy metabolic function. Consequently, the benefits of eliminating salt and sodium from the diet while supplementing potassium could be counteracted by consuming foods which had an altered chemical composition because of the manner in which they were produced. Furthermore, chemical pesticides and fertilizers are not washed off most foods by water but actually penetrate the food and thereby poison it. Eating these treated foods brings toxins into the body, where they accumulate, weaken the immune system, and interfere with detoxification.

Part of Gerson Therapy for many people is learning how empty refined calories can be replaced with nutritious foods and condiments. For instance, different types of whole-grain breads are used instead of refined white breads; maple syrup, molasses, date sugar, or honey may be substituted for white processed sugars; and certain spices, such as garlic, and foods can be combined so as to enhance their flavors without salt.

### The Clinic

Gerson's clinic occupies facilities on the western coast of Mexico. The clinic is about a block from the beach and has several rooms with an unobstructed ocean view. The other rooms face into a courtyard garden filled with tropical flowers and trees, benches, and walkways.

Most patients come from the United States by air. They are picked up at the airport by a member of the staff, driven back to the clinic, and assigned a room (all rooms are private). Starting immediately and continuing throughout their stay, all patients receive a glass of freshly prepared juice every hour on the hour, except for one glass which is given on the half hour in order for 13 glasses to be served in a 12-hour period. Within the next hour or so, a staff doctor arrives, examines the patient, looks at his or her records, makes an appraisal, and orders the appropriate course of therapy. Patients who are not in condition to go into the dining room have meals delivered to their rooms. During the day patients are given cod liver oil and vitamin $B_{12}$ shots and any other prescribed treatment, such as ozone therapy.

The base cost is $295 per day plus a 15 percent Mexican tax, for a total of $340. This covers everything that is part of the basic Gerson Therapy. A few items which are not considered part of the therapy include certain intravenous potassium drips, items such as blood transfusions that may be necessary in extreme cases, and ozone treatments.

Ozone therapy, used in Europe for over 20 years but still considered an unproven method in the United States, is one of the most effective new techniques added to Gerson Therapy. In a telephone interview Ms. Gerson stated that "Ozone actually, in chemical formula, is $O_3$. Plain oxygen that we breathe all day in our air is $O_2$. Now, that little, extra oxygen atom that's loosely attached . . . comes off easily and is highly active. . . . It circulates very quickly through the bloodstream and attaches very quickly to the red blood corpuscles and is released, among other places, at the tumor site. The ozone molecule [is] extremely active and can directly attack and destroy malignant tissue. . . .

"The ozone can be used in many ways. We have used it, for instance, as an insufflation into the rectum. . . . The patients can easily hold it, and it is then absorbed . . . directly into the bloodstream. It is also extremely effective in colon cancers. . . . It can be put into the vagina for tumors in the cervix or uterus. It can also be given intravenously; ozone gas can be injected into the veins without any adverse effect. This is something that makes people worry a bit, because they still remember the horrible exterminations done on prisoners in concentration camps. By simply injecting air into the vein, you can cause spasms of the heart and death. But this isn't air; it's oxygen and ozone. This has to be done properly, with very, very thin needles so that the bubbles that go into the vein are very, very tiny. And they disperse very quickly in the blood and are picked up very rapidly by the red blood cells. If it's done slowly, there is absolutely no adverse effect. To be quite sure of that, I'm usually the first one to get any of these new techniques done on me. I've had it done a couple of times; I've had as much as 20 cc of ozone gas put into my veins, and I'm here to talk to you about it. We also use room ozone generators, so you can breathe air augmented with ozone; it goes through the lungs very quickly and into the bloodstream.

"Ozone has proved to be very effective at killing viral and bacterial infections. The ozone can be used, and has been used, by pediatricians, for instance, in cerebral infections. They have removed a little bit of cerebral fluid and put it into the spine, and it works very well. So ozone happens to be one of the best and totally nontoxic antibiotics. In some patients infections and even certain anaerobic parasites can be quite easily eliminated with these ozone injections. Besides that, there is a feeling of well-being in the patients who are given ozone because it increases oxygenation and energy. Ozone is also, with its extra single oxygen atom, an excellent scavenger of free radicals, in other words, a very good detoxifying agent. It's altogether a wonderful material, and we feel that since we started using it quite extensively within the last 3 or 4 years, we have vastly improved our results."

Besides the therapeutic techniques, the clinic has excellent facilities and staff to go along with a carefully designed individually tailored dietary regimen. While the new clinic has space for 30 patients, generally the population stays below 25 because of the tremendous amount of work involved in the care of each patient. There is a staff of about 40 people, which includes the kitchen personnel, groundskeepers, doctors, nurses, and cleaning persons. Each patient has a personal doctor assigned upon arrival. There is also a staff doctor on 24-hour call for emergencies.

In addition to medical records and basic personal items, patients are asked to bring a tape recorder for the lectures that are given to help them learn and understand the therapy and to continue it when they return home. The lectures are on food preparation, juicing, the specific medications, the typical healing crises that occur on the program, and restoration of the body's normal healing functions.

### The Diet

Three full vegetarian meals are served each day. Usually, breakfast is served at 8 A.M. and consists of freshly squeezed orange juice, oatmeal with fresh stewed fruit, and a special whole-grain rye bread. This bread is made mostly of rye flour with a small amount of wheat or another whole grain. It is unsalted, made with very little yeast, and served toasted without butter.

At breakfast patients also receive the first of their special juices. Along with the potassium supplement, in 6 of the 13 daily juices there are three drops of half-strength Lugol solution (an iodine/potassium compound). A small amount of thyroid extract is also added. Dr. Gerson felt that the iodine and thyroid supplementation is extremely important in helping to reactivate the immune system. He found that this iodine-thyroid combination is especially important in the first couple of weeks. The patients receive 5 grains of thyroid, the full regular extract with Lugol's solution, not thyroxin or eytomel or any of the fractionated materials.

Four times a day starting at breakfast, patients also receive three tablets of pancreatic enzyme (pancreatin), which helps restore the stomach acid, as most patients with chronic degenerative disease have low stomach acid and need to have supplementation of these materials in order to be able to digest properly. In addition, they receive a 50-mg tablet of niacin six times a day.

After breakfast and from then on during the course of the day, a glass of juice is served every hour on the hour (except for the one served on the half hour). There are five glasses of apple and carrot juices in a 2:5 and 3:5 proportion, and four glasses of various green leaves juiced with a little apple to make them more palatable. All the juices are supplemented with the potassium solution.

Lunch, served at one o'clock, begins with a large plate of fresh mixed raw salad which contains a wide variety of greens and other vegetables. It is spiced with a little bit of apple cider vinegar and mixed with a few herbs and a little water so that it is not too strong.

In the very last year of his practice Dr. Gerson found that cold-pressed, good-grade linseed oil was very helpful to his patients and that it was the only oil or fat they were able to handle and digest. This was important because during all the years he had been treating cancer he had looked for an oil that would help the body transport vitamin A, which is an oil-soluble vitamin. Since the carrot juice and the liver and green juices all contain very high levels of vitamin A, which cancer patients need to reactivate the immune system, Dr. Gerson felt that he also needed some form of fatty substance to transport the vitamin. He finally found that linseed oil filled the bill since his patients could handle it without any new tumor growth. Gerson Therapy thus includes a few tablespoons of linseed oil in the diet. Usually patients are started on 2 tablespoons daily (it can be used as an oil dressing for salads at lunch and dinner). After about a month the oil is cut down from 2 tablespoons to 2 teaspoons daily.

The second item at lunch is a soup that Dr. Gerson called Hippocrates Soup. Dr. Gerson found that certain combinations of foods and herbs have a very beneficial and detoxifying effect on the body. This soup is a combination of celery, onion, leek, potato, and tomato; it is cooked and mashed and is quite tasty. Garlic can be used for extra flavor.

The soup is followed by a cooked vegetable plate, usually two vegetables and either a baked potato or potato salad that is made without eggs or mayonnaise but may consist of diced potatoes in a vinegar and flax oil sauce. Neither salt nor butter, cheese, nor any fatty substance are added to the foods, but most patients report that after a while they lose the need for these condiments and enjoy the natural flavors.

In the course of the day, patients also receive a shot of crude liver extract with $B_{12}$, which is important for helping to restore the damaged liver.

Recovery under Gerson Therapy can be very dramatic. Usually the first thing to occur is the reduction of fluid retention as a result of the large amounts of potassium supplementation. Additionally, says Ms. Gerson, who now oversees the clinic, "we see in cancer patients, usually within the first 24 to 48 hours, a reduction if not a disappearance of pain. Occasionally there will be a patient whose pain is more resistant, but in most cases, even when patients come in on high doses of pain relievers (including morphine), we see the pain disappear within a very short period."

The next phase in the therapeutic process is what Dr. Gerson described as a healing crisis. This is an activation of the body's defenses, and it often takes the form of fever as the immune system begins to be functional again. Ms. Gerson says that "almost invariably, once the patient begins to produce a fever, this is followed by a tumor reduction. It seems as though the fever helps the body break down and dissolve the tumor tissue. Along with the fever comes flulike symptoms such as aches and pains all over the body. If, for instance, the patient has had symptoms of arthritis, the arthritis often flares up during this period. Usually within 24 hours or so, the healing crisis abates, the arthritis, for instance, is gone, and the tumor tissue is reduced.

"This healing crisis can be quite severe in cases where the body is getting rid of accumulated heavy toxic materials. These toxins are removed through the coffee enemas, but sometimes the patient will have a very irritated colon because these materials literally burn as they are being released. In those cases, we alter from the coffee to chamomile tea enemas, which are soothing and help the body release any toxic materials which have built up. We see that type of problem with patients who have been medicated a lot with tranquilizers and antidepressants. The latter are especially toxic. When they have been used a fair amount, the patients suffer a lot as they are released from the body. We have to give these patients chamomile tea enemas, peppermint tea and chamomile tea by mouth, and oatmeal gruel—all are soothing."

Usually these reactions last no longer than 3 to 4 days, and when they are over, the patients claim to be much relieved and improved, with a better appetite. Sometimes, if patients have experienced a good deal of weight loss, they become ravenously hungry. This is part of the body's normal healing process. Ms. Gerson tells of a 38-year-old patient with liver and pancreatic cancer who had been told in October 1986 that she would not survive past Christmas. She was on 12 morphine tablets a day and had lost 25 pounds. In 2½ days she was free of pain and off the morphine, went through a healing crisis with fever, came out of it after about 6 or 7 days, and started to be very hungry. Every time she went to dinner, she took food back to her room so that she could have an extra meal or two in the middle of the night. This patient not only survived past Christmas but told Ms. Gerson in mid-1987 that she was feeling wonderful and had resumed most of her normal activities.

## Case Histories

Cancer patients have been treated with Gerson Therapy for over 30 years, and the results have been amazing, especially in contrast to those reported by conventional cancer specialists and agencies. The therapy was administered at treatment centers in New York and then California before the establishment of the new Gerson Therapy Center in Mexico in 1977. It was at this time that statistical analyses began to be recorded. A 40 to 50 percent improvement rate was recorded in terminal patients, and an 80 percent improvement in early to moderate cancer cases. The following are examples of the types of improvements patients have experienced using Dr. Gerson's therapy. In 1946, Dr. Gerson appeared before a Senate subcommittee considering appropriations on cancer research. The four cases described here are those presented by Dr. Gerson at the hearings; he was then treating cancer patients at Gotham Hospital in New York City.

*Example 1:* A 15-year-old girl had been treated for a tumor in the spinal cord. She had been paralyzed, and her father had been told that she would die. When she came to Dr. Gerson, she couldn't walk or feed herself. In front of the Senate, approximately 8 months after beginning Dr. Gerson's treatment, she could move her arms and hands, and her tumor had vanished. Now, over 40 years after her appearance before the Senate, this woman, who in 1945 was given approximately 6 months to live, is still alive. "I have been tested throughout the years," she writes, "and there is no sign of any tumors." She concludes by saying, "I truly hope that our government will soon open its eyes to the truth even if it does hurt the canned food business.''

*Example 2:* A young soldier had basal-cell carcinoma of the neck that had grown into his skull. He had been operated on but could not receive radiation therapy because of the risk of brain damage. After about 6 weeks of Gerson Therapy he showed improvement, and at the time of his appearance in front of the Senate subcommittee a year later there was no sign of cancer at all. He remains well to date.

*Example 3:* In this dramatic case, the patient had a malignant lymphatic sarcoma that had resulted in very large tumors of the abdomen, neck, groin, and other areas. After going to two hospitals, she was informed that nothing more could be done. A year on Dr. Gerson's diet changed her life completely. When she was presented to the Senate, there was no sign that she had ever had cancer.

*Example 4:* A woman had had recurrent breast cancer. She had undergone mastectomy and radiation treatments but then had been told that nothing more could be done. Three weeks after she was started on Dr. Gerson's diet, her cancer began to disappear. Nine months later it was completely gone.

Additional cases, 50 of which are discussed in detail in Dr. Gerson's book, are no less dramatic.

In one, a 17-year-old girl was admitted to the hospital with a tumor on her upper lip, which had grown progressively larger since age 2 years. She had undergone two operations to remove the tumor, but it continued to undergo ''rapid growth and possible development sarcoma.'' She also had a lung tumor and she said that ''12 tumor specialists told Mother that I would never get well and that there was nothing they could do!'' A few years later 12 smaller tumors were discovered all over her body (on her jaw, eyelid, arms, etc.). Within 1 month on Gerson Therapy the tumors were no longer palpable, and a month later they disappeared.

She went off the diet for 2 years when she got married, and 3 years later she developed a brain tumor which caused dizziness and impaired vision. She decided against the operations recommended by her doctors and began intensive treatment with Dr. Gerson. One month after she had begun the therapy her eye specialist noted "a phenomenal improvement." The last report received by the patient's mother noted further improvement of the overall well-being of the patient.

A 47-year-old man was diagnosed as having a brain tumor which caused severe headaches and loss of vision. The patient refused to be operated on after discussion with his brother, a medical doctor. When Dr. Gerson first saw the patient, he was almost blind and had headaches and trouble walking. Within 2 months he was free of pain and was walking normally. Within 5 months his vision had improved markedly. He went off the diet for a while, and his vision deteriorated, but he recovered when he began therapy again.

Two years later he reported feeling well, no complaints. A year later he was studying and working.

A 30-year-old man was diagnosed with melanosarcoma (a skin cancer) which was spreading over his body. He had undergone surgery once for removal of tumors. New nodules appeared 2 months later, and doctors recommended radical surgery of both axillae and removal of the left half of the neck and neck muscles as well as removal of glands in the groin. Refusing surgery, the patient started Gerson Therapy, and within a few weeks all glandular nodes had disappeared. Three years later the patient wrote the following to Dr. Gerson:

"I am now more vigorous and stronger than ever. The long 18 months to 2 years which we spent in following your orders have paid off with the very best of health. At present I weight 187 pounds and am full of pep and health. I have worked harder this year than in any year of my life and eat a well-balanced diet of all normal, healthy food." He remains well today.

Ms. Gerson relates some of the cases which have been treated with success at the new clinic. She notes that all these patients arrived at the clinic with independently confirmed cases of cancer and with complete medical records from their physicians (x-rays, tests, and surgical and full diagnoses). She stresses that the primary reason that the clinic does not do its own medical reports is that the results are often so striking that when the clinic did records in the past, doctors did not believe them and tended to accuse the clinic of falsifying the records.

*Example 1:* An 8-year-old boy, Teddy, arrived at the clinic blind and completely paralyzed. He had undergone surgery in March 1985 and had been diagnosed as having a malignant brain tumor, the same type of tumor which recently took the lives of baseball's Dick Howser and ex-CIA director William Casey. By the middle of summer of that year his condition had deteriorated substantially. When he arrived at the clinic, although he had had surgery, an external tumor had started to grow from the back of his head and he had lost speech, sight, control of his bladder and bowel, and the use of his limbs. He had been given up as hopeless by his attending physicians and was not expected to live more than a month or so.

He was put on Gerson Therapy at the clinic and remained on it upon his return home. A year and a half later his mother wrote to Ms. Gerson that Teddy had regained all functions with the exception of his eyesight. Two years later she reported that there was a slight improvement in the acuity of his vision; he still could not see, but otherwise he was doing very well. Notwithstanding his handicap, Teddy was not enrolled in a school for the blind but was put in a regular school, in which he was doing exceptionally well. At the end of the school year in 1987, Teddy received a letter from the principal of the school congratulating him on his academic performance and announcing that he had made the honor roll. Teddy remains alive.

*Example 2:* A man with the same type of brain tumor arrived at the clinic in mid-1986. He also had had surgery. His doctors had told him that they had been unable to remove all of the tumor because it had "runners" which had spread throughout his brain. They said that he had about 2 months to live.

He went to Dr. Gerson's clinic, was started on the therapy, and at the end of 4 months had a new brain scan which revealed that 65 percent of his remaining tumor had disappeared. After 18 months he had another brain scan, which was completely clear. He is alive and well six years later.

*Example 3:* A woman arrived at the clinic with a confirmed diagnosis of breast cancer with bone metastases. She had had a mastectomy, but subsequently the cancer had spread. When she arrived at the clinic she had six "hot spots" in the spine and one in the shoulder. Her outlook was extremely poor, and she was in considerable pain. She started on Gerson Therapy around October 1985. In September 1987 she reported to Ms. Gerson that not only did she have a clear scan, she was horseback riding three times a week, was in excellent shape, and had plenty of energy. These results should be compared with those of orthodox treatment, in which a breast cancer with bone metastases does not have any chance of recovery no matter what type of therapy is used (surgery, chemotherapy, or radiation).

Recent medical literature is providing overwhelming support for the use of vitamins to both prevent and treat various cancers. Dr. Hannes Stahelln at the University of Basel in Switzerland reports that in a 12-year study involving 3,000 men, low blood levels of vitamin A and Beta Carotene increases the risk of lung cancer and other cancers as well. Low blood levels of vitamin C is associated with an increased risk of stomach and intestinal cancer.

Studies done at the Sloan-Kettering Institute in Manhattan have utilized a vitamin A derivative in the treatment of leukemia. This derivative has induced remission in 80 percent of subjects with acute promyelocytic leukemia. Patients were able to leave the hospital in a few days with minimal discomfort. Those individuals utilizing chemotherapy stay much longer and are often very sick from the treatment.

In an article published in the *American Journal of Clinical Nutrition* (52:909-15, 1990), low Beta Carotene levels were associated with an increased risk of breast cancer. And in an article published in the *American Journal of Epidemiology* in 1991, researchers at Loma Linda University reported that fruit consumption appears to protect against lung cancer.

# CHAPTER FIVE

# Arthritis

The orthodox treatment for arthritis includes rest and exercise, heat, surgery, including the replacement of entire joints, rehabilitation, and the use of various drugs. Arthritis medications are primarily painkillers and anti-inflammatories. They do little to stop the progress of the disease and many of them have severe side effects. The arthritis establishment that promotes these treatments has branded as quackery all other approaches, particularly chiropractic and those involving diet and nutrition.

While there certainly are worthless treatments for arthritis, the alternative approaches highlighted in this chapter have been shown to be beneficial and can be substantiated scientifically.

Nearly 40 million Americans have arthritis; over 16 million have osteoarthritis with painful symptoms. More than 250,000 children suffer from arthritis, and the prevalence of this disease is rapidly increasing. Women between the ages of 20 and 40 are the primary sufferers of rheumatoid arthritis, while x-rays reveal osteoarthritis in most people over the age of 65. Over 1 million American men are afflicted with gout. Arthritis costs Americans in excess of $13 billion a year. It is high time to take seriously affirmative treatments that are safe and effective.

This chapter reviews Dr. Robert Liefman's balanced hormonal treatment for arthritis, Dr. Marshall Mandell's allergy-related approach, and the nutritional approach of Betty Lee Morales, who has helped many people overcome arthritis and other degenerative diseases through the use of whole foods.

There is evidence from various disciplines that the westernization of culture worldwide is responsible for the rapid global increase of arthritis and other degenerative diseases. The underlying causes of arthritis include the nutritional deficiencies of commercially grown, processed foods; the presence of pesticides and other toxins in the environment, and the quality of the soil in which food is grown. Thus, detoxifying and cleansing both the body and its external environment are issues relevant to the long-term prospects for overcoming arthritis.

## The Arthritis Industry

A few years ago the *New York Times* ran an article on arthritis in its Sunday business section. The title, "Arthritis: Building an Industry on Pain" (August 18, 1985), together with its placement in the business section (as opposed to the health, lifestyle, or human interest sections), gave the article a uniquely realistic point of view. For many people arthritis is seen not as a health issue per se but rather as a very lucrative growth industry. Using the example of Ann, a fairly typical arthritis sufferer, the article reveals how the symptomatic approach to arthritis of traditional medicine offers little in the way of health benefits while providing tremendous profit-making opportunities for those involved in the arthritis industry.

Ann began to suffer from arthritis at age 28. She was walking downstairs when her knees suddenly gave out, followed by a sharp burning pain. Ann's doctors diagnosed her as having rheumatoid arthritis and started her on an arduous and expensive journey through the maze of treatments used to battle arthritis in the United States. According to the *Times*, Ann spends more than $200 a year on medication (this is probably a very conservative estimate compared with the amount most arthritis sufferers spend for antiarthritics). This includes a daily dosage of 8 to 10 Ecotrin (aspirin) tablets, a prescription pain reliever, and 5 mg of the steroid prednisone. She visits the doctor at least once a month, at $20 to $50 a visit. Even with all this medication and regular medical attention, Ann is physically incapacitated. She has found it necessary to acquire a number of new arthritic devices designed to replace her ever-decreasing mobility: $35 for a walker, $25 for a set of canes, $15 for a reacher to get objects from shelves or retrieve them from the floor, and $130 for a padded bathtub seat. Ann has also had four of her joints replaced at a cost of $15,000 per joint. "And so," the article concludes, "Ann . . . is one of the nearly 40 million consumers of the arthritis industry. It may sound odd to label arthritis as an industry, but in fact any disease—cancer, diabetes, AIDS—is not only an affliction, it is an employer. For thousands of people and scores of companies, battling arthritis is a livelihood."

The *Times* estimates that arthritis costs this nation $8 to $10 billion annually in medical bills and adds to those figures another $7 billion in lost wages and taxes resulting from absenteeism.

Arthritis medications are one of the pharmaceutical industry's biggest and most lucrative products. In 1982, the *Times* estimated in another article (also in the business section) that the projected $717 million in industry sales that year for prescription arthritis drugs would continue to increase at a phenomenal 20 percent annually. Additionally, according to the *Times*:

"Drug company estimates suggest that arthritis relief accounts for anywhere from one-third to one-half of the $900 million in annual aspirin sales.

"Some arthritis sufferers gulp down as many as 10,000 aspirin tablets a year, 30 a day. The extra-big bottles, with as many as 1,000 tablets, are earmarked for arthritis sufferers.

"It is hard to pinpoint how much drug-makers earn from arthritis because anti-arthritis products also are taken for headaches, trick knees, and the many other guises of pain. But when one considers all the drugs that find use in fighting arthritis, the market bulges to something close to $3 billion in retail sales, according to analysts. Over-the-counter sales make up more than half of that total, but the swiftest growth comes from prescription drugs."

According to the *New York Times* (August 18, 1985) article, a spokesman for Upjohn, the manufacturer of Motrin (ibuprofen), one of the best-selling prescription antiarthritics, says about the market for arthritis products: "Every new drug that comes out seems to expand it. Since no one has a cure for arthritis and it's such a debilitating disease, people seek everything that comes along, hoping and praying that this may be the ticket."

One reason the arthritis industry is so lucrative is precisely the attitude expressed above. The arthritis establishment, which includes the pharmaceutical companies, special interest organizations such as the Arthritis Foundation, and specialized medical personnel such as rheumatologists, physical therapists, and surgeons, has consistently maintained that arthritis is an incurable disease. Therapeutically, this translates into physical therapy, ad hoc surgical intervention to replace joints, and a lifetime of medication which, even if it is effective at relieving pain, does nothing to address the cause or arrest the progression of the disease. Economically, addressing arthritis as an incurable disease is a prescription for steady, long-term profits.

### The Nature and Treatment of Arthritis

While a whole variety of aches and pains are commonly attributed to arthritis, the term technically refers only to an inflamed condition affecting the joints of which there are 68 throughout the body.

Bones cannot move upon themselves without creating a great amount of friction which would not only make movement awkward but would also cause the bones to wear down very rapidly. The joints, which are the connections between two bones, make smooth and efficient movement possible. Within the joint are the two bone ends covered with a spongy substance called *cartilage*, which becomes slick when lubricated. Between the two bones is a cavity containing *synovial fluid*, which is manufactured and contained within the joint to lubricate the cartilage and thereby ensure proper movement. The cartilage-covered bone ends, the synovial cavity, and the fluid are encased in a fibrous layer called the capsule. The capsule in turn is covered by ligaments which stretch across the joint and connect to the two bones on either end.

When the joints function normally, movement is smooth and effortless. However, if any part of the joint becomes injured or damaged, ease of movement may be replaced by pain, swelling, stiffness, and often disability and deformity. In osteoarthritis, the most prevalent form of arthritis, the cartilage may be worn and brittle so that it ceases to act as a shock absorber and fails to provide the cushion of support between the two bones. In rheumatoid arthritis, another very common form, the membrane that produces the synovial fluid becomes inflamed and extra fluid is leaked into the joint; the result is swelling and pain in the entire joint.

Before turning to alternative methods of treating arthritis, it is important to look at the manner in which this disease is treated by the orthodox medical establishment.

Typically, arthritis is diagnosed on the basis of a patient's symptoms, which most commonly include pain or swelling in the joint areas or some limitation of movement. There are some diagnostic tests, and x-rays may show abnormalities in the joints, but often these tests are not accurate. Thus the patient's symptoms are the central factor in determining the diagnosis.

Because medical students have been taught that there is no cure for arthritis, as doctors they do not look for the cause of the disease but rather focus on alleviating the symptoms. This approach can be very dangerous because many of the drugs used to counteract pain and swelling can have serious side effects. Even aspirin, which is ordinarily considered one of the least toxic medications and normally constitutes the first line of attack in the traditional treatment of arthritis, is not without side effects. In the treatment of arthritis, aspirin is given in large doses on a constant basis. Consequently, arthritis patients have consistently high levels of aspirin in their systems; this can result in dizziness, ringing in the ears, intestinal tract bleeding, and kidney damage.

When aspirin does not work or an arthritis sufferer develops adverse reactions to it, newer medications called nonsteroidal anti-inflammatory drugs (NSAIDs), such as the widely advertised Motrin, are used to control inflammation. Since these drugs are nonsteroidal (i.e., do not contain cortisone), they are less toxic than some medications commonly used to combat inflammation, but they nevertheless have side effects.

The NSAIDs came onto the market as effective alternatives to aspirin, which had caused intestinal bleeding in many long-term users. Ironically, while the NSAIDs are less effective than aspirin as anti-inflammatories, they also have side effects which include gastrointestinal bleeding and peptic ulcers. Other side effects include dizziness, nervousness, nausea, vomiting, and ringing in the ears. If these drugs are unsuccessful, doctors will often prescribe cortisone-derived drugs such as prednisone. These drugs are notorious for their severe toxicity. They interfere with the immune system, leaving the patient defenseless against infection and other diseases. Cortisone-type drugs also interfere with the body's healing ability, and it is not uncommon for a person taking these drugs to have bone fractures or wounds that do not heal for long periods of time.

Some rheumatologists, or doctors who treat arthritis patients, also use gold injections. This method of treatment was abandoned years ago because it was considered too dangerous, but today gold treatments are finding their way back into vogue with the medical establishment. Another technique gaining acceptance among arthritis doctors despite its tragic consequences is the use of chemotherapy drugs. The theory behind this drastic measure is that when a patient's immune system is knocked out, the patient's body is no longer able to form the antibodies which may be causing the inflammation in his or her joints. Other expensive and highly dangerous techniques include radiation therapy in the area of inflammation, again with the intent of destroying the patient's immune response, and plasmapheresis, a procedure by which a patient's blood is drained out, filtered to remove antibodies, and then reinjected into the patient.

While the traditional medical approach to arthritis is undeniably becoming more sophisticated, it also appears to be totally missing the mark. Not only do these treatments fail to get at the cause of the disease, they are becoming more expensive, invasive, and toxic and lead to the inevitable question, Do the ends justify the means? When traditional medicine begins to turn to anticancer therapies to treat arthritis—therapies which often are cancer-causing themselves and result in such radical side effects as nausea, hair and weight loss, and total devastation of the immune system—this question becomes even more pressing.

The remainder of this chapter will discuss alternatives to the traditional approach to treating arthritis. These are not the only alternatives. There is also cod liver therapy, exercise and swimming therapy, and anti-nightshade-diet therapy. These therapies will not be discussed here because they have not shown consistently favorable results. In this chapter the focus is on therapies that have had a consistently high success rate, are not toxic or expensive, and in some cases may actually get to the cause of the disease rather than merely masking its symptoms.

### Dr. Robert Liefman: Holistic Balanced Treatment

Holistic balanced treatment (HBT) is derived from the work of the physician Dr. Robert Liefman (1920-1973). Dr. Liefman first used this treatment in 1961, after 20 years of research. Since that time over 30,000 arthritis sufferers have received the treatment, and many of them are living pain-free, normal lives.

HBT is based on the results of Dr. Liefman's research, which showed that many arthritis sufferers, especially those with rheumatoid arthritis, have specific hormonal imbalances. Within the body there are naturally occurring hormones called glucocorticoids whose role is to reduce inflammation and raise the level of simple sugars in the blood. One of the ways these hormones raise blood sugar levels is by converting nonglucose molecules such as protein into glucose. If unchecked, these glucocorticoids can be responsible for the collagen breakdown or cartilage in joints, which, as we discussed above, may be a contributing factor in the development of arthritis. The gluco-corticoids are balanced within the body by other hormones such as testosterone and the feminizing hormones, which include estradiol; these hormones induce tissue building and hence balance the tissue-wasting effects of the glucocorticoids. If the body is not regulating these hormones, there are therapies to correct these imbalances. Dr. Liefman developed formulas consisting of various amounts of three basic ingredients: (1) prednisone, an anti-inflammatory steroid, (2) estradiol, an estrogenic hormone, and (3) testosterone.

According to the proponents of HBT, the anti-inflammatory property of the steroid prednisone and the healing properties of sex hormones can be used to treat arthritic conditions with minimal side effects because of the balancing action between the different compo-nents. The anabolic, or building, quality of the sex hormones acts to control the catabolic, or devastating, effects of the steroidal drug therapy (these include infection, decreased immunity, improper heal-ing, suppression of pituitary and adrenal gland function, and fluid retention). On the other hand, the feminizing and androgenic activ-ities of sex hormones are kept in check both by the catabolic nature of the glucocorticoids and by careful adjustment of the concentration of the sex hormones in accordance with specific requirements of the individual patient during treatment.

### Early Research

Dr. Liefman, an American married to a Canadian, was graduated from McGill Medical School in Montreal, Canada. During World War II he was drafted into the U.S. Army. A doctor in the medical corps, he was left relatively free to do research on endocrinology. After the war, Dr. Liefman continued his research in endocrinology, focusing in particular on the hormones estrogen and progesterone. Around that time cortisone was being researched and developed at the Mayo Clinic by Dr. Philip Hench, who won the Nobel Prize in physiology and medicine in 1950 for his work on this wonder drug. In the early stages of research, cortisone was hailed as the miracle cure for arthritis for which scientists had been searching for many years. This fanfare caused many sources of research funding to begin funneling grant money into research on cortisone; accordingly, Dr. Liefman also began to explore its potential uses and effects.

Early on, it became apparent that cortisone produces dangerous side effects when used alone. Dr. Hench and his associates continued their work to see how they could counteract the effects of cortisone. Even as early as the 1950s, Dr. Hench and his associates observed that there were fewer side effects when the drug was used concurrently with estrone (the estrogens include estradiol, estrone, and estriol) and that side effects were almost nonexistent when testosterone was used with cortisone. It is unclear why Dr. Hench apparently discontinued his research into the benefits of combining hormones with cortisone to minimize potential side effects. However, around this time both Dr. Liefman and another American physician, Dr. W. K. Ishmael, and his colleagues were conducting similar work which essentially confirmed the finding of Dr. Hench, namely, that the side effects of cortisone could be reduced greatly when it was administered in conjunction with the proper balance of sex hormones.

Parenthetically, 30 years later, in November 1975, another group of researchers would confirm these results in a paper presented at the Southern Medical Association's 69th Annual Scientific Meeting in

Miami Beach, which followed the direction of the work done earlier by Drs. Hench, Liefman, and Ishmael. In their study the researchers measured the responses of 14 women with severe rheumatoid arthritis who were given estrogen and progesterone in amounts similar to those present in pregnant women. (In 1948, Dr. Hench had observed the effect of pregnancies on 34 women. In 30 of the 34 pregnancies, the women experienced substantial or total relief from arthritis symptoms during pregnancy. He also noted that the disease rarely began during pregnancy.) In the 1975 study researchers found that the response to the hormones was often very rapid and dramatic. Not only were decreases in pain and swelling, together with increases in mobility and strength, noted, but objective test results also improved. The degree of inflammation decreased, and 6 of the 14 patients had normal sedimentation rates (which indicate the extent of inflammation) at the time the paper was presented. Before treatment, 12 patients had been moderately anemic; after the hormonal treatment, their blood tested normal. Also, x-rays indicated a lessening of soft tissue and bone softening (osteoporosis) and increased calcification of bones.

### The Treatment

When, in the 1950s, he received an offer from the Arthritis Hospital in Sweden to apply the results of his work, Dr. Liefman decided to leave Montreal. For a year he was given carte blanche to put to clinical use the research he had done on balancing the body's hormonal system. Much to his surprise, almost all the rheumatoid arthritis patients he treated showed great, if not total, improvement. A paper he wrote on his work was published in one of the leading medical journals in Sweden. Quite naively, Dr. Liefman expected that when he returned to North America he would be acclaimed for the fine work he had done. He was sorely disappointed when his medical professors and colleagues were not interested in his findings. He attempted to sell his treatment to one pharmaceutical giant after another, but no one was interested because his hormone compounds could not be patented and hence could not generate the type of profits to which the drug companies were accustomed. These companies told Dr. Liefman that instead of bothering them, he should give away his medication to the government. He went to the Veteran's Administration (VA) and offered to treat the veterans with his hormonally balanced formulas, but the VA rejected his offer because this medication had not been approved by the Food and Drug Administration.

Knowing the value of his treatment, Dr. Liefman began quietly treating patients in his home in Montreal. His first patient was a doctor who suffered from rheumatoid arthritis. After several days on the hormonally balanced treatment, all the doctor's crippling symptoms disappeared. The doctor in turn sent a child who was suffering from juvenile rheumatoid arthritis, and the same thing occurred. Word began to spread, and before long Montreal newspapers were running stories on this "miraculous" new treatment for arthritis discovered by a local resident.

The news of a miracle cure for an "incurable" disease was met with considerable skepticism in the United States. *Look* magazine even sent two investigative journalists to Montreal to "expose" this "quack" doctor who had bamboozled the Canadian press into believing that he could treat arthritis successfully. The journalists spent a week or so outside Dr. Liefman's home, where they observed people entering in wheelchairs and on crutches. After spending a few days there, many of these people left without their wheelchairs or crutches. Based on the personal observations of these journalists, *Look* did a very favorable report on Dr. Liefman's work which explained his method of treatment and told of the high degree of success he was having. Following that article, people from all over the United States and Canada flocked to Dr. Liefman for treatment. With this mass migration came the wrath of the medical establishment, which was outraged that an individual doctor could succeed where they had failed.

Over his lifetime, and notwithstanding persistent harassment by the medical establishment, Dr. Liefman treated over 20,000 arthritis patients with a very high level of success. These were for the most part people who had tried orthodox medical treatment to no avail and had been essentially abandoned by the medical establishment as hopeless. Professor Henry Rothblatt, an attorney and a close friend of Dr. Liefman who was to defend Liefman throughout the many legal battles waged against him, recounts how they met:

"I came to know about Dr. Liefman from a woman physician who learned about his treatment through *Look* magazine and went up to see him. She was literally left to die by her colleagues. She had been rheumatoid for 25 years. She had been in one of the leading hospitals in New York, and her colleagues said, 'Doctor, we have done everything that medical science can do for you. You are just going to have to suffer your last few years and make the best of it.' Well, she decided not to suffer. She went up to see Dr. Liefman, and within one week her crippling symptoms came to an end. She became one of his biggest fans and one of his most zealous disciples. It was through her that I met Dr. Liefman at a time when the Canadian bureaucracy finally decided to go to work on him. . . ."

The persecution of Dr. Liefman was unfortunate since his treatment has been so effective for an illness that affects so many people. The fact that it is innovative and unconventional is probably the main reason for its unpopularity within the medical establishment.

### The Success of HBT

In contrast to the symptom-suppressing approach taken by the traditional medical establishment, HBT is designed to address the causes of arthritis. It does this first by restoring a positive protein-building balance within the body through the administration of the trihormonal formulas described above, which at the same time works to stop pain and inflammation. Secondly, according to Dr. Rothblatt, "HBT is never administered without considering the particular need of the individual patient. The medication is adjusted for every patient . . . so that the proper tissue-building and healing response can be obtained. Respect for the uniqueness and unique need of the individual patient is one of the essential principles of the holistic approach to health." Dr. Liefman developed four basic formulas to account for the different requirements of each individual using HBT: (1) White Cap, which contains prednisone, testosterone, and estradiol, (2) Black Cap, which has only prednisone and estradiol, (3) Red Cap, which contains prednisone and testosterone, and (4) Green Cap, which contains only prednisone and is used only to allow women to shed the endometrium proliferation caused by the intake of the estrogen-containing preparations. In turn, the proportions of these different compounds may vary from individual to individual and may also be altered for the same person during the course of treatment. If, for example, a female patient begins to exhibit an adverse reaction to the treatment, such as the growth of excess body hair, the testosterone level in the medication will be reduced to eliminate these reactions. The same holds true for men who experience breast development or other sex-related changes as a result of the medication's estrogen content. Patients who exhibit some of the typical side effects of cortisone-type drugs will have the amounts of prednisone in their medication decreased, or appropriate increases in one of the sex hormones will be made to counterbalance the wasting effects of the steroids. Generally, the adverse reactions to any of the elements in the compounds disappear within a short time once the proper balance among the hormones has been attained.

In addition to the importance of balancing the anti-inflammatory hormones with the sex hormones to establish a healthy protein-rebuilding environment, Dr. Liefman explored other biochemical interactions within the body which play important healing roles in arthritis. For example, he discovered that growth hormone, which is produced in the pituitary gland, acts synergistically with estradiol and testosterone to stimulate bone growth. He looked at the health of the pancreas to determine whether adequate insulin was being produced to ensure the efficient breakdown of sugar within the body, because without proper sugar metabolism, the body lacks sufficient energy to build and repair bones.

HBT also incorporates principles of nutrition and stresses the importance of regular exercise. The diet recommended in HBT eliminates "junk foods" such as sugar and sugar products and salty and processed foods such as luncheon meats, canned goods, and fried and refined foods. The diet is essentially low in protein, especially animal proteins, and emphasizes high-fiber complex carbohydrates in the form of fresh fruits and vegetables, whole grains, and legumes. Vitamin and mineral supplements are used to bolster the patient's immune system and enhance the body's natural healing abilities. For instance, vitamin D is important for strong and healthy bones because it regulates the absorption of calcium from the stomach into the bloodstream, which carries it to bone tissue. Vitamins C and A are important for the maintenance and repair of *collagen*, the gluelike substance that holds the tissues together and is essential for joint and muscle stability. Vitamin E and B-complex vitamins are important for bone growth. Among the minerals, adequate supply and absorption of calcium, phosphorous, and magnesium are essential for the formation of healthy bones, while zinc and selenium are important immune nutrients.

Exercise is also an important adjunct to HBT and is recommended to restore joint and muscle mobility and function as well as muscle mass lost during periods of inactivity. However, patients are generally told not to exercise until they are free of pain, swelling, and stiffness and feel confident enough to engage in it. Walking may be the first exercise; then, as patients improve, they are given specialized exercises for the hands, knees, fingers, shoulders, and other areas which may have been affected by arthritis.

The medical establishment has basically ignored, attacked, or criticized HBT therapy, even though its basis is drugs already widely used by the medical establishment. All Dr. Liefman did was combine certain commonly prescribed drugs so as to maximize the benefits and minimize the side effects of each component drug. The balanced hormonal approach to arthritis did, however, do one unorthodox thing: It challenged the rigidly held position of the medical establishment that arthritis is an incurable disease. Was it for this reason alone that before his death in October 1973 Dr. Liefman faced considerable opposition from the American arthritis community and was actively prosecuted by the FDA?

### The Patients

The following are some examples of the results arthritis patients have had from using HBT:

*Example 1:* Malcolm had his first attack of arthritis when he was 21 years old. By the time he was 44, the pain had become constant. Deformities started to appear in the joints of his shoulders, hips, knees, upper and lower spine, and breast bone. He was diagnosed with Strumpell-Marie disease (spondylitis), a form of arthritis which causes such deformities in the spine that the patient is literally bent over double.

Malcolm also had severe iritis, an inflammation of the eyes which is not uncommon in rheumatoid arthritis patients, and later extensive retinal hemorrhages were found in both eyes. During the year before his treatment with HBT, he was taking 12 to 14 aspirin tablets daily, received cortisone injections in his knee once a week, and had tried another medication which had no effect.

Malcolm began treatment with HBT in August 1962 after reading the aforementioned *Look* magazine article in May. He experienced almost immediate relief. According to his physician, his arthritis had almost disappeared and his eyes were normal. When he was unable to get his medication in 1968, his symptoms began to return, but they subsided upon resumption of the HBT. About his treatment, Malcolm writes:

"In August 1962, when I started the medication, I weighed 149 pounds and was using a cane. I could not turn my head and could do no physical work. Today I weigh 190 pounds (I am 5 feet 11 inches tall), show absolutely no sign of arthritis, and maintain an active schedule 7 days a week. I have had my blood checked three times, and each time I have been pronounced to be in top physical condition.

"I would like to add that in 1961 I was in the hospital for tests and observation. X-rays showed that my hips were so clouded with calcium that the joints could not be seen and five vertebrae in my back were fused. I was told that in about 5 years I would be so bent that I would not be able to sit in a wheelchair. About 5 years ago, for my own information, I had a set of x-rays taken and was told that my back and hips were in better condition than the average person's."

*Example 2:* In 1972, at age 19, Cynthia began to experience the symptoms of rheumatoid arthritis. Initially the arthritis was confined to her jaw and elbows, but over a period of 2½ years, while she was undergoing treatment by a traditional physician, the arthritis spread to nearly every part of her body. Five years later Cynthia was so crippled with pain and stiffness that it took her a half hour to get out of bed in the morning. The morning after she started HBT, her pain had almost disappeared except for some stiffness and soreness, which also went away during the following 3 days. About her condition and her subsequent treatment at the Arthritis Medical Center in Fort Lauderdale, which administers HBT, Cynthia says:

"I was getting worse and worse. When I first went to my doctor, I had it just in my jaw and elbows. After 2½ years, I had it in just about every place except my hips and knees. I couldn't turn my head at all.

"The doctor actually told me once that he felt really bad, that he had tried everything and didn't know what else to do, and that I had better go to the crippled children's center in Palm Beach. To tell a young woman that . . . I just wanted to drive off a bridge. But I thank him for saying it because if he hadn't, I don't think I ever would have tried this place. I did it in desperation."

At the time Cynthia started HBT, she was taking 30 aspirin tablets a day, which were causing headaches, ringing in her ears, and ulcers. She was spending approximately $1,000 a month on painkillers alone. While Cynthia found that she bruised and bled more easily after starting HBT, she notes that she had the same symptoms while taking large doses of aspirin. On the other hand, while the aspirin and other treatments did nothing to arrest the progression of Cynthia's arthritis, a day after she started treatment with HBT, her pain virtually disappeared and returned only when she forgot to take her medication. At present Cynthia is pain-free and works out three times a week at a health spa. She continues on her medication, but in much smaller dosages than when she started treatment with HBT.

*Example 3:* June also suffered from severe crippling arthritis for 2 years before starting treatment with HBT. Over that 2-year period, June received almost every form of traditional arthritis treatment available: gold injections, penicillamine, Butazolidin (phenylbutazone), small doses of prednisone, and 16 aspirins daily. June says that she was spending over $100 a week for medication alone. In the meantime she kept getting worse, and when she started HBT, she says, "I was immobile in my hands and shoulders. It was at the point that I thought, 'What's the use of living?' I couldn't even turn my head." Additionally, her liver, stomach, and kidneys were damaged by the large doses of medication. She was forced to give up her business because she was too weak and in too much pain to work. Her medical bills were ruining her financially. The second day after June received HBT in July 1979, her pain disappeared. June says about her progress with HBT:

"I woke up and I could move my ankles, I could move my hands and my feet. When I stood up, the pain wasn't there. I said to [my husband], 'My God, there's been a miracle.' It got better and better, and I guess within 2 months I didn't even know I had rheumatoid arthritis. I got a bicycle, and I started dancing again and going to the beach again. It used to be if I lay on the sand, I couldn't get up again."

June continues to be pain-free, leading a normal life, and her medication has been reduced by more than half the initial amount.

*Example 4:* Carolyn had complained of arthritis since she was in high school. In 1964, at age 27, she was diagnosed with rheumatoid arthritis. It had begun in her knees and had spread to every joint in her body except her spine, although she also experienced neck stiffness at times. In 1970 some deformities were noted, and in 1971 she had synovectomies (an operation which removes portions of the synovial membrane in the affected joint) on both knees.

From July 1973 until August 1976 she was receiving biweekly gold injections and taking Indocin (indomethacin), aspirin, and cortisone, but her condition continued to deteriorate. She was in constant pain, movement was greatly impaired, deformities were developing, and she was suffering from weakness, indigestion, nausea, and lack of appetite as a result of the medication. She was semibedridden and required splints.

Four hours after starting HBT on October 13, 1976, she experienced almost total relief from pain. Swelling and stiffness decreased, and within a few months she was able to perform all her regular activities.

### Dr. Theron Randolph and Dr. Marshall Mandell: Environmental Allergies

A second alternative approach to arthritis is clinical ecology, or as it is called, environmental medicine. This branch of medicine was developed by Theron Randolph in the 1940s and 1950s when he observed early in his medical career that food allergies and sensitivities to environmental chemicals were a major contributing factor in a wide range of diseases, including arthritis. Dr. Randolph also noted that the causal relationship of allergy to disease was a very individualized phenomenon: One person could eat beef every day and never have an adverse reaction, while another patient could develop a food allergy to beef even when consuming it only on rare occasions. Similarly, people with an allergy to the same product did not necessarily manifest the same symptoms. One might break out with hives while another developed depression and still another became arthritic. Dr. Randolph also found that seemingly innocuous chemicals found in the home, workplace, or school could in certain individuals trigger symptoms ranging from mental problems to aching joints to chronic fatigue.

The work of Dr. Randolph was applied to arthritis by Marshall Mandell, M.D., a board-certified physician from Norwalk, Connecticut, and one of the country's leading clinical ecologists. He has found that a considerable number of patients who come to him with arthritis or arthritislike symptoms are in fact suffering from a form of environmental allergy such as the ones outlined by Dr. Randolph. According to Dr. Mandell, "The basic process that underlies many causes of arthritis is a completely unrecognized or unsuspected allergy or allergylike sensitivity to substances that are part of daily life, including the food we eat, the liquids we drink, including the water supply, the chemicals that are deliberately or accidentally introduced into a diet, and the various forms of chemical pollutants in the indoor and outdoor air that get into our bodies." From his clinical experience, Dr. Mandell has found that more than half the patients he treats who would by standard medical diagnostic techniques be confirmed arthritics can be helped by means of simple dietary or environmental changes.

"My approach and that of my colleagues in the field of environmental medicine and clinical ecology, supplemented by the benefits of nutritional therapy, begins by looking at the person who is predisposed to having arthritis to see if there are identifiable substances in the diet and environment which can trigger or cause the episode of illness," says Dr. Mandell. "We deal with demonstrable cause and effect relationships. . . . What we do is study the patient.

"First, we take a carefully formulated history which is designed to help identify people who have problems with foods, with various chemicals, with pollutants, and perhaps with seasonal airborne substances. From this, we are able to get a fairly good idea of what we're dealing with."

Before patients are actually tested for food or environmental allergies, Dr. Mandell often will have them fast or go on a restricted diet for 4 days to 1 week to rid the body of any residue of substances suspected to be responsible for the symptoms.

"Next," says Dr. Mandell, "we test these people using a technique known as 'provocative testing,' to determine their response to extracts prepared from all the foods in the diet. . . . The most commonly ingested foods are often the culprits, so it shouldn't come as any surprise that wheat, corn products, milk, beef, tomatoes, potatoes, and soy are leading offenders.

"The most common technique used for provocative testing is to place a few drops of the test substance under the tongue of the patient, where it is almost immediately absorbed. This is called 'sublingual' provocative testing. When we test in this manner, only small doses are used, so the effect is brief, but since the solution enters the bloodstream, the entire body is exposed. Symptoms can show up in the joints, muscles, brain, skin, or any other part of the body.

"If we are able to produce joint pain, stiffness, or swelling or redness within a few minutes after placing the solution under the tongue for absorption into the bloodstream, we know that we've found something that must be important, because we have flared up the patient's familiar symptoms—we have actually precipitated an attack of the patient's own illness.

"Many people will have what we call 'postsymptomatic illness,' meaning that many bodily structures, organs, or systems can be involved at the same time. The arthritic person's whole body may be sensitive, and this is why such patients may have a headache or fatigue or asthma or colitis, although they may not actually have any of the well-known allergies such as hay fever, eczema, or hives.

"We also find that many people react to chemicals. We have some people whose arthritis may be due in part or exclusively to the chlorine that is in the water supply, or perhaps to an artificial flavoring or coloring which is used very frequently, or perhaps to a preservative. We have people who have trouble because they are inhaling fumes, such as tobacco smoke. We have people who, in heavy traffic, have trouble because the exhaust fumes will travel, along with the oxygen, through the walls of the lung, into the circulation; once again, the whole body is exposed."

After Dr. Mandell determines the substances in the patient's overall environment which he suspects are responsible for arthritic symptoms, he double-checks with test meals of the specific substances.

"I confirm the results of our testing in the office with feeding tests," he says. "Three foods can be tested during the course of a day; however, for the test to be accurate, the food to be tested must be out of the person's system for at least 5 days. Sometimes we can get away with it for 4 days, but it is even better if that food has been completely omitted from the diet, in all forms, for 5, 6, or 7 days. We give patients a single food as the test meal; since we want to test the food all by itself, we don't put any ketchup, pepper, mustard, sauce, or anything else on the food. Instead of a usual portion, we allow patients to consume as much of the single food as they can comfortably eat as an entire meal. . . .

"Then we observe them for at least 4 hours. If we're able to reproduce that patient's specific symptoms, if we can actually turn the symptoms on and off like a switch, we know that we have nailed it down, because we have demonstrated a cause and effect relationship that can't be questioned. Should food be the primary causative factor, we will design a diet that eliminates all of those foods. Then, depending on how well they follow the diet, the patients will be either well or sick."

## The Patients

Dr. Mandell provides some examples of how allergic reactions can result in arthritis or arthritislike symptoms:

*Example 1:* Sarah was a rabbi's wife who began to have arthritis in her hands, but the flare-ups would take place only on Saturday mornings and then disappear during the course of the day. Using Saturday as a starting point, Dr. Mandell began to explore the possible sources of Sarah's "Saturday arthritis."

"Since she woke up with the arthritis in the morning," Dr. Mandell explains, "we knew it was not caused by something she was doing in the morning, so we went back 24 hours to explore Friday. What did she do on Friday? What did she eat? Drink? Breathe? What came into her system? Could it be, perhaps, the paraffin fumes from the candles on the table which were lit ceremonially every Friday night? Or could it be something they ate? Was it caused by something she was exposed to when she went to temple on Friday night, perhaps from clothing just taken out of the dry cleaner's? Or was it hair spray, perfume, cologne, or men with after-shave lotion? Was it that the temple perhaps had had the rug shampooed the day before the services or that the furniture was polished? I had no way of knowing, but I retraced all her activities, and then I tested her systematically.

"This actually turned out to be an easy one, and it was humorous, because the great 'Jewish penicillin,' chicken soup, was the thing that was undoing her. When I placed a few drops of chicken extract under her tongue, within minutes the knuckles that were affected by arthritis swelled up and became painful and red. I did this on a few occasions, and so we were able to demonstrate this. It is rare to find a patient in whom a single substance is the factor, but it does happen now and then. So here is a rabbi's wife with chicken and chicken soup arthritis—Friday night ingestion, Saturday morning appearance of arthritis."

*Example 2:* Dr. Randolph treated a surgeon who became so

incapacitated by arthritis that he had to stop performing surgery and had to restrict his medical practice to office consultations. He had developed severe arthritis primarily in the hips, knees, shoulders, and hands and had had traditional treatment for 10 years. While he derived some relief from the treatment, he still was incapacitated. He had to walk downstairs backwards, he no longer had the strength or dexterity in his hands to perform surgery, and he lacked the physical strength even to stand at the operating table.

The surgeon went to Chicago to see Dr. Randolph, who admitted him to the hospital and immediately put him on a pure spring-water fast, free of chlorine and fluoride and without any of the contamination that affects city water supplies. Additionally, he was placed in a special room where the environment was controlled. There were no air fresheners or disinfectants and no bleaches, the floor was not waxed or polished, and the personnel were not permitted to smoke or wear perfume.

Within 5 days the surgeon was free of pain. He regained some dexterity in his hand and reported that if he was a little stronger, he felt he could return to the operating room and resume his normal work. Then he was given single-food feeding tests, and Dr. Randolph discovered that when he was tested with corn (cornmeal with some corn syrup), within a matter of hours he became miserably uncomfortable with severe pains in the shoulders and hips. He had so much pain it felt as if he had been kicked by a mule. A few days later he was tested with chicken extract, and the effect was different. While he did not experience pain right away, the chicken affected his brain. He became so sleepy that he actually dozed off. When he awoke, he was in such severe pain that he was actually crying.

The surgeon found that as long as he avoided corn and chicken, he was virtually pain-free and could resume his regular daily life.

*Example 3:* This example not only documents the dramatic effects which can often be achieved by eliminating an offending food from an arthritic person's diet, it also shows the degree of resistance orthodox arthritis doctors have to accepting this even when it has been unequivocally demonstrated.

In the mid-1970s Dr. Mandell sent out a mailing to rheumatologists in the northeastern part of the country, indicating that he was studying the relationship between food allergies and arthritis and that he was interested in studying some of the patients free of charge. Out of 90 letters, he received six responses, of which three said yes and three said no. Through one of the doctors who agreed to send patients, Janet eventually saw Dr. Mandell. He discusses her testing and the results:

"I want to emphasize that we never tell the patient what the test material is, so we completely eliminate suggestion. When we tested her with pork, she had pain almost immediately in one finger on her right hand, and this was her arthritis joint. We caused the joint to swell up and become red and painful.

"This test was repeated three times, once a week, and after the last test I told her to stay off pork for at least a week and then have a large portion of it one morning as a feeding test. Once again, the same thing happened. However, when she told her rheumatologist, the man who was willing to have her come to me, he said he didn't believe it because we didn't have any controls. This is . . . more than pathetic, it's almost a medical crime! Here the patient had her symptom reproduced . . . and the doctor says he doesn't believe in what has happened to her."

The ironic thing about this skepticism by the orthodox medical establishment is that many of the treatments that it prescribes for arthritis have never been proved either safe or effective. Gold injections are a good example. This treatment is extremely costly, has very high toxicity, and is only rarely of benefit to arthritis sufferers. Furthermore, in cases where gold does provide some relief, rheumatologists are unable to offer a scientific explanation of how it operates within the body. Nevertheless, gold continues to be endorsed by the arthritis establishment, while something as simple as eliminating a food from a patient's diet, even if that food has been demonstrated to cause the patient's symptoms, is totally ignored or criticized as being unscientific.

*Example 4:* Dr. Mandell has a friend, Dr. Bullock, whose wife suffered from arthritis. Dr. Bullock had noticed something strange about his wife's condition. When she would go to the hospital for testing and treatment, her arthritis would improve, but the moment she returned home, the symptoms would flare up again. Her rheumatologist told Mrs. Bullock that he felt that it was all psychological; the "protective environment" of the hospital made her relax, and this in turn had a beneficial effect on her arthritis. The rheumatologist concluded that something was "emotionally" wrong with Mrs. Bullock's home and that she should seek psychiatric help to discover what it was.

Her husband was skeptical about this, and after talking with Dr. Mandell he began to look at possible environmental and dietary changes which could have been responsible for his wife's improvement in the hospital. Mrs. Bullock's problem, it turned out, was very simple. At home, she ate a very limited southern diet which included certain favorite foods eaten either daily or very frequently. When she was in the hospital, however, and was presented with a long list of foods from which to choose, it was like being in a hotel or a restaurant, and she ate an extremely varied diet. For Mrs. Bullock, varying her menu made all the difference in the world. Her husband created a diet that eliminated the major offending foods and rotated a wide variety of foods so that no one food had a chance to build up in her system. Her condition improved enormously.

### The Nutritional Approach to the Treatment and Prevention of Arthritis

In this section the various roles that diet and nutrition can play in treating and preventing arthritis are discussed. As diet and nutrition are integral parts of both Dr. Liefman's therapy and the approach to the clinical ecologists, this section should be considered complementary to the preceding two.

### Buildup of Toxins

Many practitioners of alternative health care who address degenerative diseases (e.g., cancer, diabetes, heart disease, atherosclerosis, and arthritis) in their practice agree that most of these diseases stem from a buildup of toxins in various parts in the body, which in turn result in metabolic dysfunction and eventually in the manifestation of the symptoms typifying the particular disease. As to how these toxins begin to accumulate in the body, Ms. Betty Lee Morales, a long-time advocate of a natural approach to health and disease prevention, contributing editor of *Let's Live* magazine, and member of the National Health Federation, comments that this follows directly from modern lifestyles and realities. "The pesticide sprays, the poisons that are getting into the air, soil, and water," she says, only worsen the conditions that she calls nutritional deficiencies. All these things have a negative impact on what she describes as the weakest link, genetic inborn metabolic errors. "In short," she continues, "the proliferation of processed and refined foods, drugs and man-made chemicals . . . is really at the root of this rapid increase in all degenerative diseases.

"Although it is frightening, it is well to stop and think that there has been no advancement in the treatment or correction or prevention of degenerative diseases in the last 100 years."

One of the specific sources of this problem is the manner in which food is produced and soil is treated in this country. Dr. Max Gerson, one of the first physicians to take an environmental approach to the treatment of cancer (for more on Gerson's cancer therapy, see Chapter 4) and other degenerative diseases, referred to the soil as our "external metabolism." Even at the outset of his career as a medical doctor more than 60 years ago and long before the soil was depleted and stripped to the degree that it is today, Dr. Gerson was a strong proponent of organically grown, unprocessed foods. According to

Dr. Gerson, chemical pesticides and fertilizers essentially poison and denature fruits and vegetables by altering their chemical composition. For instance, he found that chemical fertilizers often cause the sodium content to rise in certain foods while decreasing their potassium levels. As chronically ill patients are very often chemically imbalanced, with excesses of sodium and deficiencies of potassium, the effects of the fertilizers were exactly opposite to what was required by these patients to begin to recuperate and served to exacerbate their metabolic imbalances. In other words, even patients who had the willpower and determination to follow a strict regimen in which, among other things, salt and sodium were restricted and potassium was supplemented could find their efforts undermined simply by eating foods grown in chemically treated soil.

Additionally, says Ms. Morales: "When foods are grown in deficient soil, deficient plants result, and then the farmer poisons them with pesticides in order to bring them to harvest and to market. We must get back to taking care of the soil and regenerating it. It is not possible to keep taking from something without returning. It's just like a bank account; if you kept writing checks and didn't put more money into the bank, you would be bankrupt—and our soil is bankrupt. Through bankrupt raw materials and food, bankrupt animals and their by-products, we are producing bankrupt people from the standpoint of health and nutrition. The United States probably leads the world in excessive consumption of overly processed, overly refined carbohydrates and sugars."

Because of today's agricultural and manufacturing practices, foods once full of vitamins, minerals, protein, and fiber have indeed become bankrupt. Not only does refining wheat and other grains strip them of their fiber, the wheat grown on today's soils contains only a fraction of the protein content it once had. But this is not the only adverse consequence of modern-day food production. Even with thorough washing, many of these chemicals (pesticides, herbicides, etc.) are not removed. They penetrate the skin of fruits and vegetables and poison the body's systems. If you eat meat, poultry, or dairy products, you are ingesting even higher amounts of toxic chemicals with your food. Meat production in the United States is big business, and the bottom line is maximizing profits, not consumer health. American cattle are fed a myriad of drugs ranging from antibiotics to steroids, are given feed contaminated with feces and sprayed with pesticides, and are themselves sprayed with pesticides. All these chemicals remain as residues in the meat when it is consumed. As meat takes an especially long time to digest and is essentially fiberless, these chemicals are not easily eliminated and can accumulate to cause all sorts of toxic reactions within the body.

Because of the specific physiology of the joints, they are especially susceptible to the buildup of toxic materials, which can over time result in arthritis.

As discussed earlier, joints are surrounded by the synovial membrane, which is responsible for the production of synovial fluid, which allows smooth and efficient movement. Between the blood vessels and the inner portions of the joint, the only thing that keeps the blood from the inner surface of the joint is the synovial tissue; there is no structural barrier in this tissue which prevents toxic material from passing from the blood into the joint space. Usually the blood vessels have a surface called a basement membrane, a structural barrier that keeps the toxins in the blood and out of the tissues. In the synovial tissues that structure is not present, and this allows any toxic material from the blood to pass into the joint space. Once it is in the joint space, this toxic material can scratch and irritate the joint.

There are around 31.6 million known arthritics in the United States. Of that number, some 16 million have osteoarthritis and 6.5 million have rheumatoid arthritis; the balance, or a little over 9 million, have what is classified as gout. According to Ms. Morales, "All these things ending it 'itis,' which simply means 'inflammation of,' such as arthritis, neuritis, and bursitis, are really just new and fancy terms for old-fashioned rheumatism. The new names make them appear to be different diseases when they really are not. Among 16 million osteoarthritics, the most common form of arthritis is called the 'wear and tear' disease of degeneration of the joint cartilage. There is much we can do to prevent that. If it has already taken us over, there is a great deal we can do to reverse it."

Ms. Morales gives an example of how detoxification of the body and rebuilding of health with diet can be used to prevent and treat arthritis.

"I work with people who are ready to do almost anything just to get a little relief," she says. "They don't even expect reversal, but sometimes they do experience it. One of my sisters was married to a professor at a leading university who was very skeptical of anything to do with diet and nutrition. When my sister developed rheumatoid arthritis—she also had five other diagnosed diseases including high blood pressure, elevated cholesterol, and heart trouble—her husband took her all over the world; they went everywhere looking for a magic cure. After they had spent over $40,000 she not only failed to get better, she was actually worse. They returned home and got a practical nurse to come in. She could not even wait on herself.

"Finally when she reached the bottom of the barrel, she called me one day and said, 'Well, I would like to try the natural methods way to see if I can get some relief.' At that time, she was on about five or six prescribed drugs and obviously had many problems from them: digestion, assimilation, constipation, etc. I said that I would be very glad to help her. Then she said, 'I'll take these things, but I don't want my husband to know.' I said, 'Hey, back up a minute.' Although it broke my heart, I told her that I could not help her until she had suffered enough and was willing to do whatever she needed to do, especially since not all of it was going to be pleasant. I explained that she was going to have to examine her life closely and detoxify from years of faulty diet. Detoxification is a very important part of regaining health and maintaining it. I also told her that she could not do this on the sly without her husband knowing about it because it becomes a way of life. It begins with what you eat, the way you live, even the way you think, and you certainly cannot do it living in a house with another person and not have that person know what you are doing. 'In fact,' I said, 'he should be doing it too.' Then she got hysterical and said, 'Well, he's not open to it.' But I had to tell her that I couldn't help her by telling her to take these things, which are not drugs. The first thing you need to do is to start educating yourself. I sent her a few books, and I said, 'When you've read some of this and you are willing to say that you will really try anything, I'll give you three months. Then I will be happy to help.'

"She reached that point when she was in bed and could not go to the bathroom alone, could not hold a glass of water or a cup of tea. She called for me, and I went over. They live in a beautiful home, and there is no problem with money, but when I outlined the things that were needed, both she and her husband said, 'Does it really cost that much?' I requested that they buy a juicer, the kind that grinds and presses, because it gives the maximum nutrition. I also wanted to bring in a practical nurse who was trained in this type of thing. I told them to think it over.

"They talked it over and decided that they would try it, so I sent over a juicer and 25 pounds of organically grown carrots. I gave instructions to the practical nurse to throw out everything in the cupboard that was opened and was refined or processed. Anything that was in cans or closed containers was to be given to Goodwill. I made it very clear that nothing was to go into that home that I didn't send in. I got rid of all the salt and sugar and all the easy-mix stuff— this was all a trauma to them because it costs money and nobody likes to throw away money. But I told her that she had to go the whole way or not at all.

"We put her on a 7-day detoxification to cleanse the small intestines and the bowel. She had coffee enemas every day for about a week. She had nothing but the juices, the potassium broth, and water and herb tea—no solid food for 7 days. We broke the fast carefully.

She had massage every day, and I made sure she was taken outdoors at least once a day. I also had the nurse read different things to her every day so that she would understand what her body was going through.

"Before she started the treatment, I sent her to a laboratory to have complete blood tests, and then after the cleansing, I had her do the same tests again. . . . Not that it was necessary in this case, but I knew that if she didn't see the results confirmed by a medical laboratory, she wouldn't believe them. Her cholesterol count was 535, which is incredibly high. Her doctor had told her that she was a walking time bomb. He was keeping her on drugs, but the cholesterol did not go down, although her liver problems increased.

"Three weeks later on this program—remember, this is a woman who could not get out of bed alone—she got up one day, went out to her own car, and drove down to the city to have her hair done. That's very typical of women and probably of men. As soon as they start to feel better, the first thing they want to do is look better. She wanted to have her hair done, and a facial and a manicure. . . . It was a great morale booster. When her husband came home from the university, he did not know his own wife, because she was up, was beginning to start to fix a juice cocktail, and they were so delighted that I never had more arguments or problems out of them. But she also felt so well that she decided not to wait the full 6 weeks to have the other tests done; it had only been 3 weeks. She went back to the medical lab and asked to have all the tests down over. She wanted to send her doctor a copy because she still was under the care of a medical doctor who had told her 'these health food things won't hurt you, but they won't help you. It will only cost you some money, but you can afford it, so go ahead and do it.' When she had the second batch of lab tests [which showed substantial improvement] done and sent to him, he wrote her a letter in which he said, 'If you are going to pursue these quack remedies, I can no longer be responsible for your health, and I am dismissing you as a patient.' She called me up crying and said, 'I don't even have a doctor in case I need one.' She was still laboring under the terrible fear that this doctor had laid on her by saying that she could have a stroke or heart attack at any minute.

"We continued with the program. Within a total of 3 months, she was able to go on a South Pacific cruise with her husband. Today, you won't meet two people who are better advocates of the nutritional way of living. They have gone 90 to 95 percent holistic and no longer feel that they have to be under the wing of a doctor who does not recognize nutrition.

"One of the positive offshoots of this is that my brother-in-law, who was a professor for 50 years at one of the most prestigious universities and a staunch opponent of the natural approach to healing, also turned 180 degrees around. He too had been taking quite a few medications for high blood pressure. He had what is called a deputrience contracture, where the fingers curl down toward the palm and cannot be straightened—this is a classic vitamin E deficiency. After seeing what it had done for his wife, he said that he was ready to go on an intensive program and see what it could do for his fingers. His brother also had this condition and had had his tendons cut, so it obviously ran in the family. Fortunately, my brother-in-law was willing to try the nutritional program first. Today—he has just turned 80—he's in better health than he has ever been in his life. He is vital and virile and active and full of the joy of life, and the two of them are enjoying their life together so much when they could have been crippled and bedridden."

## The Link to Atherosclerosis

Because of the susceptibility of the joints to the accumulation of toxic material which can scratch and irritate the inner linings, leading to the pain and inflammation characterizing arthritis, an analogy has been made between arthritis and atherosclerosis (degeneration of the arteries). In both diseases corrosive substances scratch the inner linings of the body part involved, causing irritation which can lead to degeneration. These substances can come from toxic material in the bowel which gets into the bloodstream. They can also come from food. In the case of atherosclerosis, these substances include cholesterol, fats, and fried foods, which when they get into the blood scratch and irritate the very sensitive inner linings of the blood vessels. The same substances can also pass from the blood into the joint space and irritate the inner linings of the joints. According to David Steenblock, M.D., a physician specializing in the relationship of diet, nutrition, and arthritis, this correlation between arthritis and atherosclerosis is one of the reasons why a low-fat, low-cholesterol, high-fiber diet has been useful in treating arthritis. "Many patients on this type of diet," says Dr. Steenblock, "show substantial improvement because the fiber cleanses the colon and removes much of the toxic bacterial waste products, which frees up the blood system and makes it more pure. This in turn allows for the toxic materials to be eliminated from the joints, and so the joints themselves can begin to heal."

Dr. Steenblock also explains how a diet which eliminates processed foods and focuses on the consumption of high-fiber natural grains, fruits, and vegetables works specifically in the treatment of arthritis:

"We want to eliminate white sugar and white flour products and processed foods and foods which contain food additives because these processed foods cause abnormalities in the state of health of the intestine. When you eat processed foods with little fiber, the bacterial content of the colon changes from the so-called good bacteria, which are lactobacillus vivitus and acidophilus, to organisms which are anaerobic such as anerococci and streptococci and organisms which generally are not healthy and produce many toxic substances themselves. When these toxic substances are present as a result of eating a diet high in refined food and lacking fiber, these toxins pass through the bowel into the blood. Also, refined foods, because they are so easily digestible and do not require work by the intestine, cause the muscle wall of the intestine to atrophy or become thinner; this thinness of the wall allows more toxic material to pass from the bowel into the blood. Once it is in the blood, it can pass easily into the joints and cause more problems.

"The use of the high-fiber, natural diet goes against this trend because the fiber changes the bacterial content of the colon back to normal, and this eliminates many of the toxic materials, the carcinogens and the mutagens which are formed otherwise, which are well-documented causes not only of osteoarthritis but also of cancer of the colon and atherosclerosis. The fiber also strengthens the bowel wall, making it thicker and healthier, and this creates more of a mucosal barrier between the colon's interior and the blood. Thus the diet should be more of a natural and raw foods diet if you want to get a good result."

Dr. Steenblock does warn, however, that people who have spent an entire lifetime eating refined, fiberless foods must approach a change to a raw, high-fiber diet with caution (excess dietary fiber can, for instance, cause calcium and zinc to be washed through the system so that calcium and zinc deficiencies result) in order to give their intestinal tract time to strengthen. A good physician with a solid background in nutritional therapy should be consulted before any drastic dietary changes are made.

### Chelation, Nutrition, and Proteoglycans

While atherosclerosis and arthritis often serve to exacerbate each other, treatments other than diet which are directed at one condition often are beneficial in treating the other. For example, Dr. Steenblock discusses how chelation therapy, an intravenous chemical treatment (discussed more fully in Chapter 3) commonly used for atherosclerosis and heart disease, can also benefit arthritic patients:

"One of the problems with osteoarthritis is that the capillaries of the synovium have become rigidified, or more rigid than they should be as a consequence of the aging process and of atherosclerosis. This

240

limits the blood flow through these joints, therefore, the heat that is produced when the joint is put in motion cannot be taken away because the circulation is poor. As a result pain occurs when you exercise, and conversely, when you are resting, the blood flow through the tissue is poor and toxic materials accumulate and can cause pain. Anything that increases the diameter and the blood flow through these capillaries will aid in the restoration process. This is where chelation therapy is very valuable because it actually gets into these small blood vessels and capillaries and removes the cross-linkage of the collagen and elastin. This makes these small blood vessels more pliable and elastic, gives them more diameter so that more blood can pass through them, and thus helps in the healing process."

Different vitamins, minerals, and nutritive substances can play important roles in the treatment and prevention of arthritis. There is some evidence that the essential fatty acids furnished by substances such as cod liver oil, linoleic acid, and marine lipids, by replacing missing fatty substances in the synovial fluid, can be important in treating arthritis. The synovial fluid consists primarily of mucin with some albumin, fat, epithelium, and leukocytes. When the joint surfaces become irritated and undergo degeneration, some of the fat from the joint itself is lost. This fat acts as a lubricant and keeps the joint surfaces apart so that the cartilage-covered bone ends are protected and can move smoothly. When a person takes extra cod liver oil or other essential fatty acids, the oil goes to the joints and provides more lubrication. Vitamin A, which is found in large quantities in cod liver oil, is also important for the maintenance of the mucous membranes of the body, which manufacture mucous in order to cleanse the body of infectious bacteria and toxins. Without adequate supplies of vitamin A, infection and accumulation of toxic materials can set in around the joints. Furthermore, a vitamin A deficiency can lead to the insufficient production of synovial fluid; when this occurs, the joints lack proper lubrication, the cartilage becomes subject to drying and cracking, and movement becomes difficult and painful.

Because lubrication is vital to the smooth functioning of the joints, vitamin E, whose primary role is to protect against the destruction of the essential fatty acids by oxidation, also is an important antiarthritis nutrient. Both vitamins E and C, which generally act as free radical scavengers within the body, can be especially important in the treatment as they can "clinch" the free radicals present at the site of inflamed or irritated joints, thereby decreasing pain, swelling, and inflammation. According to Ms. Morales, university studies have also suggested that vitamin E can play an important role in neutralizing toxic substances in the air. Furthermore, Ms. Morales notes:

"Many women are stricken about the time of menopause, which suggests that arthritis has something to do with falling production of hormones within the body. Men go through menopause, but about 10 years later than women. If women would take extra vitamin E and make sure that they eat the hormone-precursor foods so that their bodies are fortified and will make the hormones as the hormonal production from the gonads decreases, then they would also be taking a step forward in preventing the diseases that are related to a hormonal deficiency. Hormone-precursor foods include the unrefined whole grains and pollen, which has all 22 free amino acids and is a great hormone-precursor food for both sexes."

Many symptoms of arthritis are alleviated by establishing a proper balance of calcium and phosphorus in the body, since these are the two minerals most responsible for bone formation and healing. This can be one of the most confusing aspects of arthritis because x-rays of arthritic joints often show excessive calcification. Afraid of further calcification, patients mistakenly believe that they must avoid calcium-rich foods. Actually, the calcification is not due to an excess of calcium but rather to malabsorption of existing supplies caused by an imbalance in the calcium-to-phosphorus ratio. This imbalance is caused by two major factors: (1) excessive consumption of foods containing high levels of phosphorus such as meat, dairy products, and soft drinks and (2) the process of joint degeneration, which releases high levels of phosphates. This excess phosphorus at the joint site binds with calcium and results in calcification. Taking extra calcium orally does not contribute to this localized calcification. Rather, by increasing calcium levels in the blood, it draws the excess phosphorus away from the joints to bind with the blood calcium so that both are eliminated; this in turn inhibits calcification around the joints.

It should be noted here that soft drinks are the number one source of phosphorus in the American diet today. These drinks contain more phosphorus than the average food or beverage, and the typical American consumes 456 gallons of them a year. According to Dr. Steenblock, excess phosphorus is one of the major contributing factors to the development of osteoarthritis. He says, "We see this clinically in many people who come with osteoarthritis in their early forties, who are large consumers of soft drinks, who also consume excess quantities of meats and other high-phosphorus foods, and who do not eat enough of the green leafy vegetables which contain calcium." The other problem associated with soft drinks is that most of them contain citric acids, which bind calcium and cause it to be excreted. "So," says Dr. Steenblock, "not only is there extra phosphorus in the soft drinks, they contain the material that takes calcium out of the body. If you want to develop osteoarthritis, that's a very good way of doing it."

Another therapy for arthritis entails the use of naturally occurring substances called proteoglycans, which are molecules made up of approximately 10 percent proteins and 90 percent carbohydrates. There has been very promising research in other countries on these substances, but to date little has been done in the United States. Dr. Steenblock explains this therapy:

"What we are talking about is a particular substance called condroiten sulfate, which is a type of proteoglycan. In the person with osteoarthritis, these substances gradually diminish in concentration in the joint as the joint becomes worn. If the condroiten sulfate could be put back into the joint, this would allow for an inhibition of the calcification process and also smooth out and seal the irregularities, the cracks, and the irritations which have occurred through time with wear and tear.

"Over the past 10 years or so, condroiten sulfate has been used in both Europe and Japan for the treatment of osteoarthritis, rheumatoid arthritis and also atherosclerosis. Again, there is a great similarity between osteoarthritis and atherosclerosis in the sense that both result from the wear and tear caused by irritative substances in the body. We need to protect these collagen surfaces from the irritative substances which circulate in the blood and ultimately get into the joints. . . .

"Condroiten sulfate appears to be one of the best treatments for both arthritis and vascular disease. When you take it orally, it actually enters into the body through the intestinal tract and will selectively go to the joints and all the areas of damage in the blood vessels. It not only acts preventively but also will help reverse the diseases that are present. Unfortunately, this substance is not readily available in this country because of the FDA's rules about the preliminary research which has to be done before it can be made available.

"There are a few companies which are making it from an extract of the trachea called 'mucopolysaccharides.' That is having very good results. Research in Europe and Japan is showing that this substance is probably the best form of therapy that there has been and probably will be for a long time in treating of arthritis and vascular disease. The treatment is not, however, the sort of miracle drug type of treatment where you give the person one pill and get immediate results. What we are dealing with is a natural substance, and it takes time for these natural substances to create the result we are looking for, namely, healing of the injured areas. When you take these mucopolysaccharides, you have to take them for anywhere from 2 to 4 months in order to achieve results. Patients who are sticking with them are having very positive results and report upwards of 80 percent relief of pain and also a stoppage of the degeneration.

"There is another substance, which is derived from the New Zealand green lip mussel. There are a number of trade names for it. This substance is also a mucopolysaccharide, and it is effective in treating osteoarthritis as well as rheumatoid arthritis. This material is available in most health food stores.

"These mucopolysaccharides can also be used preventively to heal the small nicks and irritations that occur routinely in the blood vessels and joints. These substances immediately seal these little cracks and crevices so that they do not get larger. Our bodies are not really capable of doing that on their own, and we need to help them along with a little bit of these substances all the time so that these joints and arteries that we have are protected."

According to investigators at the Albany Medical Center, as documented in a study that was published in Arthritis Rheumatology (33:810-820, 1990), fish oil supplementation can decrease arthritis symptoms: Swollen joints, pain, and morning stiffness were seen to decrease over a two-month period on EPA oils.

Allergies to inhalants and foods have long been suspected as causes of arthritis. In the May 1990 issue of the *Journal of the Royal Society of Medicine* (83:312-314, 1990), in an article entitled "Is there an allergic synovitis," by Dr. D. H. Golding, immune related pathways causing swelling and pain in the joints was identified. And according to an article entitled "Food induced ("allergic") arthritis: clinical and serological studies," by Dr. Richard S. Panush, published in the *Journal of Rheumatology* (17(3):291-294, 1990), researchers agree that allergic people who avoid food allergens can see a significant decrease in arthritic symptoms.

### Chiropractic

The therapies, substances, and diets mentioned in this chapter have all been found to be beneficial in the treatment of arthritis. Since arthritis involves the inflammation and swelling of the joints and since it can lead to deformities in the spine and fusions in the vertebrae, manipulation of the joints and spine is also an appropriate therapy for arthritis. Even if you suffer from arthritis associated with allergens, you may find relief in chiropractic care. Of course, arthritic pain is not the only thing that chiropractic is capable of relieving. Chapter 6 is devoted to the chiropractic alternative in dealing with many diseases, including arthritis. Now that some very effective nonmanipulative therapies for arthritis have been examined, it is time to look at chiropractic as a general and multifaceted healing modality, keeping in mind that it has very specific applications to the relief of arthritic pain.

# CHAPTER SIX

# Back and Leg Ailments: A Chiropractor Is A Doctor Too

I t is no secret that some members of the medical establishment in this country have been trying to eliminate the chiropractic alternative ever since it emerged as a major healing modality and increasingly since it became the chief rival of traditional medical care. Chiropractic is second only to orthodox medicine as the preferred provider of primary health care. Threatened by what is perceived to be a challenge to its professional exclusivity, established medicine determined to get rid of this menace or at least keep it as far away from mainstream health care institutions as possible.

Despite these concentrated, tightly organized, and well-funded efforts to malign and discredit chiropractic, it continues to thrive. Recently, during an 11-year court battle with the AMA it was argued that chiropractic is not an unscientific cult but rather is a drug-free, surgery-free health care system based on the hypothesis that disease can be caused by displacements (which chiropractors call subluxations) of the spinal vertebrae. These subluxations can impinge on the nerves and disrupt their normal functioning. The court decision affirmed that chiropractors are fully qualified to adjust the skeletal system.

Currently, more than 25,000 chiropractors in the United States are treating an estimated 10 million patients a year. The government's statistics on worker's compensation show that chiropractic offers the best care for back and neck injuries. Chiropractors get their patients back on the job twice as fast as medical doctors on average. Chiropractors can help with most musculoskeletal disorders involving mechanical dysfunction.

Besides describing chiropractic treatment, this chapter includes a look at the politics of the AMA's court-documented war against chiropractic.

## How Chiropractic Works

Chiropractic treatment involves the manual manipulation of vertebrae that have become misaligned, causing nerve pressure and energy blocks to various organs. This manipulation is called an *adjustment*. It involves the chiropractor's gentle painless application of direct pressure to the spine and joints. The chiropractor may squeeze or twist the torso, pull or twist the limbs, or wrench the head or back. What the chiropractor is doing is readjusting the spinal column to restore the normal relationship of one vertebra to another. This eliminates the body's energy blocks and keeps life-sustaining energy flowing freely to the vital organs.

Chiropractic is effective in dealing with pain and as a preventive treatment because it relieves nerve pressure as the spine is properly adjusted. The buildup of this pressure is cumulative in its erosion of the health and integrity of specific body organs or regions. If one vertebra is out of relationship to the one next to it, a state of *disrelationship* is said to exist. This disrelationship throws off that vertebra's environment, that is, the blood supply and detoxifying lymphatic drainage surrounding it. When this occurs, a congestion of blood, toxins, and energy creates pressure that upsets both local and systemic homeostasis, or balance.

Tissues all need normal nerve functioning in order to transport required nutrients to the cells. Insofar as the vertebrae are misaligned, the blood becomes congested and slow in its delivery, creating the absence of this nutrient supply. The cell's normal activity is thereby hindered, and it becomes irritated. Moreover, once the cell's metabolic processing is interfered with, its waste-removing lymphatic servicing to that area is diminished. This leads to toxic buildup that causes further irritation and inflammation. The chiropractor is concerned with alleviating all these problems.

### The Battle against Chiropractic

Despite the success that chiropractic has had in relieving pain and chronic disorders, for a quarter of a century the medical establishment has bullied this licensed profession into having to defend itself as if it were a subversive activity. The main reason for this attack appears to have been the desire to ensure the traditional medical doctor the top spot on the ladder of licensed healing professionals. Chiropractors pose a serious threat to this coveted role since, as a federal court judge pointed out, the leaders of established medicine were well "aware that some medical physicians believed chiropractic to be effective and that chiropractors were better trained to deal with musculoskeletal problems than most medical physicians." This is especially scary to medical doctors since they know very little about the musculoskeletal system even though it constitutes nearly two-thirds of the human body.

Unfortunately, this long-standing attempt to inhibit free competition in health care has left countless numbers of people who could be relieved of pain confused and therefore hesitant about going to doctors of chiropractic. Moreover, because chiropractic care often is not covered by major health insurance companies, it looms as a financial burden to many. Even though it is far cheaper, it is frequently not covered by insurance policies, and so the final out-of-pocket expense to the consumer is higher than the cost of far more expensive traditional medical care which is covered by insurance carriers. The administrative law judge of the Federal Trade Commission (FTC) ruled in 1982 that the American Medical Association (AMA)—the largest medical trade association in the nation, representing the interests of half the 500,000 medical doctors—had created "a formidable impediment to competition in the delivery of health care services by physicians in this country. That barrier has served to deprive consumers of the free flow of information about the availability of health care services, to deter the offering of innovative forms of health care and to stifle the rise of almost every type of health care delivery that could potentially pose a threat to the income of fee-for-service physicians in private practice. The costs to the public in terms of less expensive or even, perhaps, more improved forms of medical service are great."

This chapter will give some of the basic information about chiropractic care that has been withheld from the public, but first it is necessary to review the rocky road that chiropractic has had to travel in order to be recognized as the highly effective health care provider that it is.

The AMA was so bent on destroying the reputation of the doctor of chiropractic that in 1963 it formed its own Committee on Quackery almost exclusively toward that end. Shortly thereafter a flood of press releases hit the media; their goal was the total condemnation of chiropractic. *In the Public Interest,* anonymously published in 1972 contained an alleged AMA document which outlined the Committee on Quackery's chief goal: to contain and eliminate chiropractic. Since this attitude and the actions issuing from it were clearly intent on the blatant restraint of trade, a small group of chiropractors decided to fight back. They formed the National Chiropractic Antitrust Committee to fund litigation to help expose this conspiracy. It will be shown later in this chapter how such a legal action was initiated in the Untied States District Court in Chicago in 1976.

Meanwhile, the AMA maintained its assault on chiropractic by working to deny state-licensed doctors of chiropractic the same hospital privileges that medical doctors enjoyed and by trying everything feasible to keep chiropractic colleges from being accredited by state medical organizations while campaigning actively against the inclusion of chiropractic programs in accredited colleges and universities.

A major complaint against chiropractic is that chiropractors rarely research and publish their findings as medical doctors do. Publishing often entails presenting one's findings at a conference of peers to open dialogue and invite constructive criticism, but chiropractors were denied the right to convene with medical doctors on a professional basis in associations or to present research or clinical findings at cooperative meetings. A case in point is a seminar that was arranged by the workmen's compensation board in Oregon. The purpose was to entertain different ideas from health care providers that might help reduce the pain and discomfort of industrial accident victims while accelerating their return to work. Those in attendance were assured by the sponsoring medical societies that they would receive educational credit toward mandated license renewal.

When it was learned that the board had invited a chiropractor to speak, the Multnomah County Medical Society and the Oregon State Medical Society, the sponsors of the event, reneged on their support. They spread the word that attendees would not get education credit after all. Why? Because a single representative from a licensed profession known for years to offer the most effective treatment for industrial injuries was invited to share his experience on the subject.

In a similar situation, Dr. Philip R. Weinstein, a neurologist practicing in California, was pressured into ceasing his efforts to cooperate with doctors of chiropractic for the benefit of both professions as well as that of patients suffering from spinal disorders. Dr. Weinstein had frequently lectured to chiropractors on the diagnosis of such ailments before he came to realize that the AMA was strongly opposed to such cooperative action. He decided to back off from lecturing to chiropractors, explaining to one such group that "this late cancellation [of a scheduled lecture is] due to circumstances beyond our control. We were unaware that delivering medical lectures to your [organization] was prohibited." (Null, "The War Against Chiropractic," *Penthouse,* October, 1986.)

The AMA's attempt to destroy the educational base of chiropractic went much deeper than this sort of harassment. In 1962 attorney Robert Throckmorton authored a master plan eventually put into action by the AMA and representing its general approach to "the chiropractic menace." The plan proposed attacking chiropractic on many fronts. Referring to the chiropractic schools, it states: "To the extent that [the schools'] financial problems continue to multiply, and to the extent that the schools are unsuccessful in their recruiting programs, the chiropractic menace of the future will be reduced and possibly eliminated."

To ensure that chiropractic's financial and recruiting problems multiplied, the AMA tried to keep the government from granting student loans to prospective chiropractors and research-teaching grants to faculty members. It also fought to keep chiropractic students from receiving accreditation. It bitterly complained that chiropractic schools were being operated without proper accreditation while at the same time vehemently opposing the creation of proper state accrediting bodies. To its dismay, national accreditation finally came in 1974 when the U.S. Health, Education and Welfare Department sanctioned the Council on Chiropractic Education to meet this need.

The AMA also fought to keep chiropractic programs out of universities. The idea here was to keep chiropractic in isolation, away from mainstream educational health care institutions. The AMA could then point a finger at chiropractic as being substandard because of its lack of affiliation with these same institutions.

In the early 1970s, when C. W. Post University entertained notions of teaching pre-chiropractic students, pressure was brought to bear. Dr. Ernest R. Jaffe, acting dean of Albert Einstein College of Medicine of Yeshiva University, wrote of the school: "I urge you to take all appropriate measures to terminate any relationship with the Lincoln College of Chiropractic. It can only bring discredit to your university." C. W. Post backed off and to this day refuses to offer chiropractic instruction.

The University of Illinois was urged to discriminate against students and state-licensed doctors of chiropractic by the chairman of the board of trustees of the Illinois State Medical Society. In January 1974 he wrote to the executive dean of the University of Illinois College of Medicine about the AMA's displeasure at learning that the college had collaborated with the National College of Chiropractic on an educational television program. He warned: "Any time chiropractors can gain a foothold by reporting on collaboration with the Medical Center, it will give them status. It might be wise to prohibit any contact of any kind at any time by persons at the Medical Center with any chiropractor. You might wish to discuss this with . . . others who had been involved in this problem."

To further deny status to chiropractors, the AMA has fought bitterly over the last quarter of a century to keep them out of hospitals. If chiropractors were given hospital privileges and if they could operate programs within universities, how could the AMA continue to argue that their educational and professional status was substandard?

The late Dr. Irvine Hendryson, an orthopedic surgeon and one-time professor of surgery at the University of Colorado, had been a trustee of the AMA. He was concerned with the mechanical problems that give women such pain and discomfort in the final stages of pregnancy and during childbirth. These problems are often caused by the dislocation of vertebrae resulting from the heavy burden of carrying the fetus and the strain involved in delivering it. In a report that was ultimately suppressed by the Committee on Quackery, Dr. Hendryson wrote:

"It is commonly known that in the third trimester of pregnancy, unrelenting, unmitigated back pain is one of the prices that is paid for perpetuation of the race. I have learned from personal experience that general manipulations of backs in this particular condition has given these women a great deal of physical relief and has permitted them to go on to term and deliver without having to be bedfast during the latter term of pregnancy.

"I would not for an instant indicate that it is manipulation alone that permits these women to go on and carry on normally, for at the present time we are giving them manipulation to relieve them of their acute symptoms and also fitting them with support, which is well recognized in medical practice. However, I must say that I am impressed by the many cases who are able to go on to term, to manage their households, to lead a comparatively comfortable third trimester without having to be hospitalized or given traction, heat, support, and all the rest of it."

Because this information would lend status and credibility and possibly even give hospital privileges to chiropractors, it was withheld. The AMA took control of hospital policy toward chiropractic through its power over the Joint Committee on Accreditation of Hospitals (JCAH). Without accreditation, a hospital stands to lose its "internship and residency programs, its nursing affiliations, and its automatic check-off for direct insurance payments. Its malpractice insurance rates would soar, and the interest on its financial bonds for building would probably increase."

The threat of withholding or "reviewing" accreditation became an effective means of limiting chiropractic presence in hospitals. This is clearly illustrated in a letter of August 1974 from the JCAH to a hospital administrator: "Any arrangement you would make with chiropractors and your hospital would be unacceptable to the Joint Commission. This would be in violation of the *Principles of Medical Ethics* published by the American Medical Association that is also a requirement of the Joint Commission on Accreditation of Hospitals." Even more blatantly, in January 1973 the JCAH supplied this information to a hospital in Silver City, New Mexico: "This is an answer to your letter of December 18 referring to a bill which may be passed in New Mexico that hospitals must accept chiropractors as members of the medical staff. You are absolutely correct—the unfortunate results of this most ill-advised legislation would be that the Joint Commission could withdraw and refuse accreditation of the hospital that had chiropractors on its medical staff."

### Chiropractors Fight Back

In an effort to return health care to the public and take it out of the clutches of the AMA and the medical physicians, litigation was finally initiated on October 12, 1976. Five chiropractors filed a 38-page complaint in the United States District Court in Chicago. They charged among other things that the AMA had masterminded a years-long conspiracy aimed at isolating, containing, and eliminating its chief health care rival—chiropractic. This conspiracy included fostering a general boycott of chiropractors, discriminating against them in public institutions such as hospitals and universities, manipulating government studies on the efficacy of their practice, and directly pressuring insurance companies to deny chiropractic patients coverage similar to that offered for health care sanctioned by the AMA.

The case was a costly one for the plaintiffs, involving travel, legal expenses, and many hours away from their practices. It took over 4 years to gather evidence before the trial finally began on December 8, 1980. But as the evidence was presented, it became clear that the AMA had operated for years in restraint of trade. It had even manipulated Congress. For instance, a 1967 "impartial" congressional study to determine whether chiropractic should be covered by Medicare was tainted by the very-present influence of the AMA, a clearly biased party. Doyle Taylor, secretary to the AMA Committee on Quackery, wrote to Dr. Samuel Sherman, the AMA representative on the congressional committee, "I am sure you agree that the AMA hand must not 'show' at this stage of the proposed chiropractic study." Five months before the study even began, Dr. Sherman already was reporting to Taylor on the nature of its results. "Dear Doyle," he wrote in March 1968, "There was complete acceptance of the concept of preparing the decision on the basis of lack of scientific merit."

After reviewing the evidence in detail, the court finally rendered its decision in September 1987. Judge Susan Getzendanner ruled that the AMA and its co-conspirators, the American College of Surgeons and the American College of Radiology, had conspired to isolate and eliminate the profession of chiropractic and that in the process they had violated the Sherman Antitrust Law. The American Academy of Orthopedic Surgeons was found to have been a part of the conspiracy until 1986, when it backed away. The American Hospital Association, the Illinois State Medical Society, the American Osteopathic Association, and the American Academy of Physical Medicine and Rehabilitation all settled with the chiropractors before the case ended by agreeing to cease their harassment of chiropractic. However, it was ruled that there was insufficient evidence to convict the JCAH or the ACP.

Judge Getzendanner, in her decision, offered this opinion:

"I conclude that an injunction is necessary in this case. There are lingering effects of the conspiracy; the AMA has never acknowledged the lawlessness of its past conduct and in fact to this day maintains that it has always been in compliance with the antitrust laws; there has never been an affirmative statement by the AMA that it is ethical to associate with chiropractors; there has never been a public statement to AMA members of the admissions made in this court about the improved nature of chiropractic despite the fact that the AMA today claims that it made changes in its policy in recognition of the change and improvement in chiropractic; there has never been public retraction of articles such as 'The Right and Duty of Hospitals to Deny Chiropractor Access to Hospitals'; a medical physician has to very carefully read the current AMA Judicial Council Opinions to realize that there has been a change in the treatment of chiropractors and the court cannot assume that members of the AMA pore over these opinions; and finally, the systemic, longterm wrongdoing and the long-term intent to destroy a licensed profession suggests that an injunction is appropriate in this case. When all of these factors are considered in the context of this 'private attorney general' antitrust suit, a proper exercise of the court's discretion permits, and in my judgment requires an injunction."

The plaintiffs in the case saw the decision as a victory for the American public as well as for the chiropractic profession. Dr. Patricia Arthur, for instance believes that the extraordinary cost of health care is due largely to a lack of fair competition in the health care industry. "The August 1987 edition of a magazine directed to hospital administrators," she says, "predicts that the nation is headed toward a $1.5 trillion annual health care budget. Each person in the country will be expending more than $5,000 per year on health care costs. Chiropractic is a low-cost substitute for certain segments of medical care. That is the result of a monopoly in the health care field centered around the AMA." Another plaintiff, Dr. Chester A. Wilk, thought the decision long overdue: "Eleven years of litigation have demonstrated the folly of allowing the AMA, whose primary purpose for existence is the economic interest of medical physicians, to sit in judgment or control of any other licensed health care provider. . . . Every sick person and every taxpayer in this country has suffered because of the actions of the AMA."

J.F. McAndrews, D.C., former president of the largest chiropractic college in the United States and currently practicing in Harbor Springs, Michigan, agrees that this decision was long overdue, and that its delay caused unnecessary suffering: "As an educator and administrator I spent almost 25 years combating the despicable actions of the AMA now declared to be illegal by the court. How many students, patients, and professionals have had to suffer from the AMA's folly? Perhaps now the government will listen when we point out the corrupt power exercised by the AMA. Perhaps now the people of the United States can get cooperative care from all segments of the health care spectrum."

Now that chiropractic care finally seems to be on the verge of much broader acceptance than it has ever enjoyed in its 92-year history in the United States, it is appropriate to consider more carefully how it can help in the treatment and prevention of various human ailments.

### Chiropractic Treatment

There are two basic types of chiropractors: the "straight" chiropractors, who employ chiefly manipulation of the spinal vertebrae in treating disorders, and the "mixers," who in addition to this counsel their patients on different aspects of diet, stress control, and exercise as it pertains to particular problems and to the overall health profile. Chiropractic considers the body to be a whole, natural organism that possesses its own healing capabilities. These capabilities may be interfered with when the spine is out of place. The movement or shifting of vertebrae creates local nerve pressure, which in turn may block the energy going throughout the system and the organs that correspond to particular vertebrae. The energy interference resulting from improper spinal alignment throws off the whole body. It upsets the body's balance and harmony, or what is called its homeostasis. When one body part begins to malfunction, it is compensated for automatically by another body part, but this compensating body part may then become overstressed. For instance, a weakness in the heart may cause an overstress of the lungs, which are forced to work overtime to bring in extra oxygen to make up for the oxygen loss from the reduced circulation resulting from the heart's weakness. This can cause a chain reaction effect which can continue indefinitely until the entire body system becomes unbalanced, weak, and prone to further degenerative diseases.

It is good that the body is an interrelated organism, because one part can come to the aid of another, as when the lungs help the liver. However, this compensatory feature of whole-body mechanics also means that meticulous care must be taken to make sure that every part is in prime condition to avoid a damaging drain on other parts. The longer a person learns to tolerate nerve dysfunction instead of relieving it, the more problems will accumulate that will begin to impinge on one region after another. Morton Jacobs, D.C., who has been practicing for over a quarter of a century, notes that "if you can minimize or eliminate any type of nerve pressure in your body, you can eliminate any type of body dysfunctions, and therefore you can maintain a higher function, a higher level of adaptability of health and function in your body. That's why chiropractic adjustments are very good for preventive care."

Besides its use as preventive treatment, chiropractic care can also be very helpful in relieving acute pain as well as chronic disorders. Dr. Jacobs states that this is possible because chiropractic does not overwhelm the body as drugs and other methods may. It simply and naturally restores the body's natural ability to heal itself.

A condition with which chiropractors have had considerable success is bursitis, a chronic pain that is actually an inflammation of the bursal sac which cushions every body joint. it can cause severe, ongoing pain in the neck, shoulders, hip, and lower back. The inflammation can be caused by a physical trauma to the joint, as when a person lifts something too heavy or too quickly. It may also result from a bacterial infection or an allergy. Whatever the cause, the site of the irritation becomes extremely painful since the bursal sac has many tiny nerve endings.

The most common place bursitis appears is in the neck and shoulders. The chiropractor will try to locate a pinched nerve in this area and then apply ice to it to reduce the blood congestion and swelling resulting from poor circulation and lymphatic drainage. According to Dr. Jacobs, the ice is followed by the application of moist heat to relax and expand constricted muscles, allowing better blood supply into the area and helping to "regulate the environment of that tissue so it has the ability to start repairing." It should be mentioned here that dry heat should not be used since it creates a thickening and congestion of the blood; this may cause a condition known as hyperemia, or blood blockage.

Rest and exercise follow the ice and heat treatments. Rest give the joint time and the relaxed environment it needs to repair itself. Exercise, including joint exercise or "cracking" (as in cracking the knuckles), stimulates circulation into the joints while reducing congestion, fixations (misalignments of the vertebrae causing trauma and/or spasm), and energy blockages.

Arthritis is another condition with which chiropractors have had good success. This condition seems to be brought on by some sort of allergy, which in turn stimulates the creation of an inflammatory agent that causes swelling, tightness, and pain in the joints. Chiropractic adjustments help stimulate the body's enzymatic, metabolic, and nervous systems. This gives the body the ability to deal better with the allergen and to begin repairing the damage that has already been done.

The tissue or joint directly affected by arthritis is treated in much the same way as bursitis: ice, moist heat, and exercise. Additionally, soft tissue manipulation, or "milking," may force out toxins and wastes while stimulating better blood supply to the joint. Milking also increases joint movement and rotation. This again represents a non-toxic intervention that can help the body reestablish a homeostatic balance without the side effects of drugs. While they may help reduce blood pressure and swelling and help manage pain, the drugs commonly used for arthritis do not treat the condition at its source. They also adversely affect the body's essential functions and processes in several ways. They may, for instance, interfere with vitamin and mineral absorption, so that a whole new set of physical problems will eventually arise from this situation

Stress is a major contributor to most of the ailments a chiropractor is able to treat. The treatment is done partly by helping the patient release this stress. Pinched nerves or energy blockage from pressure brought to bear on nerve areas may be the direct result of stress. It is important to understand why this is so and what a chiropractor can do about it.

The *autonomic nervous system,* which controls involuntary body functions and mechanics, is divided into the *sympathetic* and *parasympathetic systems.* The autonomic nervous system is important because all the vital functions and overall state of health are under its control. Heartbeat, the rate of blood flow, breathing, hormone and enzyme secretion, and so forth are all managed without conscious input by the autonomic nervous system.

The parasympathetic nervous system represents the normal, well-coordinated, balanced functioning of these vital processes. The sympathetic nervous system, though, is called into play when this harmony has been disrupted and special bodily reactions are required to meet specific situations. The sympathetic nervous system can be described by what is called the fight or flight syndrome; when an organism perceives a direct threat to its existence, it must temporarily and spontaneously interrupt all other body functions so that the crisis may be met by all the body's available resources. It must actively resist this danger (the fight response), or it must do everything possible to avoid it (the flight response). Either way, the integrity and harmony of the organism may be restored and the parasympathetic nervous system may resume its normal ordering of those physiological processes which ordinarily sustain life as the sympathetic system retires from the arena.

However, if the sympathetic nervous system is called into action too frequently, the body may suffer from a chronic depletion of its vital energies, and its effort to maintain a state of homeostasis will be negated. Stress is a primary engager of the sympathetic mechanism. Things such as fear, anger, jealousy, and extreme emotional episodes call the sympathetic system, which normally is not needed, into play. When these stressors become chronic reactions for coping mechanisms, stress syndromes may evolve. In this case, certain target organs are most likely to be fatigued and exhausted as a result of the over-

261

activity of excessively stimulated glands, usually the adrenal, thymus, and digestive glands.

Even when stress is not chronic, the body's internal harmony is disrupted spontaneously by hyperactive emotions and response to circumstances and events. If you are angered by a nuisance phone call, for instance, your heart rate is immediately altered, your blood pressure rises as the vascular system constricts, and your normal digestion may cease, allowing stomach acids to harm the inner stomach wall. If you are always angry, these occurrences will become common or even regular as you begin to suffer from a chronically imbalanced body mechanism.

A chiropractor may release stress centers and sites of energy blockage for temporary relief, but more important is a review and modification of the patient's overall lifestyle. The chiropractor may suggest such things as yoga, Transcendental Meditation, and regular exercise as ways to learn to mellow one's reactions to daily problems and confrontations. Meanwhile, the chiropractor can help the body with regular adjustments to keep it in relative harmony, with a free energy flow. This will in effect defuse the sympathetic nervous response and allow the parasympathetic mechanism to resume its task of maintaining the body's vital functions and harmony.

In general, chiropractic is most helpful in treating musculoskeletal disorders. Back pain may be caused by emotional stress, while curvature of the spine may result from physical stress. In either case, the stressor creates nerve pressure that throws off first the spinal alignment and eventually specific bodily functions. Adjustments are helpful here, especially when combined with stress-management counseling and exercise programs.

Exercise to keep the muscles strong and resilient is critical because muscles move bones and thus protect the skeletal system and afford it mobility and ease of activity. Physical or emotional stress in turn may render the muscular system fatigued, spastic, and tight. When this happens, joints—specifically the spinal vertebrae—are more readily misaligned and a disrelationship results.

Muscles must be kept strong through exercise to support the skeletal system against the negative gravitational pull everyone lives with. This is why weakened muscles will lead to poor body posture. This *structural attitude* will ultimately have an impact on the internal organs. Putting undue weight and physical pressure on them. Exercise, then, counters fatigue. It stimulates such vital functions as elimination and respiration, both of which require ease and fluidity of internal body movement and function. Since stress and exercise are so tightly interwoven, the chiropractor will do a thorough stress evaluation before giving the patient a specific exercise program. If it is not done properly and in conjunction with one's general health and state of mind, exercise can lead to chronic and debilitating injury. Done right, it will promote the establishment of a healthy metabolism, burn intramuscular fat, and slow the body's aging process.

In 1992, the resistance against chiropractic from our medical community is still in force, irresponsibly guiding the general public against this important treatment modality.

### Choosing a Chiropractor

There are things to be mindful of when selecting chiropractic care. Chiropractic manipulation is not indicated as a primary treatment for degenerative diseases, although it can be a valuable adjunct to more direct therapies. Fracture and degenerative lesions such as joint or bone cancer may be exacerbated by chiropractic treatment, and such treatment should be avoided in these instances. Acute trauma, such as whiplash, may also contraindicate chiropractic treatment.

When chiropractic care is to be employed, take notice of the following: What type of chiropractor are you choosing? A straight chiropractor may be fine for a disorder such as an injury requiring only manipulative adjustment. A mixer may be preferred for an internal problem that can also benefit from lifestyle, stress, dietary, and exercise counseling.

Whichever type of chiropractor you choose, be sure you are not put through needless, extensive, and expensive batteries of tests. Blood tests, hair analysis, x-rays, cytotoxic tests, allergy tests, and other diagnostic procedures may be needed, but they should be decided upon only after a full, thorough medical history has been taken. The history should include a survey of subjective attitudes, exercise and dietary habits, and a full symptomatic report. Once this background has been established, the chiropractor may prudently offer the patient selective testing based on what seems to be needed.

Chiropractic care has been available for nearly a century, but its potential as a primary and adjunctive health care modality is only beginning to be understood. The recent court ruling showing that chiropractic has for years been maligned and conspired against by the AMA and others should also help pave the way for placing this type of treatment in a better perspective. Chiropractic care is not right for every condition, but it is very effective for many. As a preventive, it may be among the best types of health care available.

# CHAPTER SEVEN

# Allergies

As the industrial world continues to expand, creating new products for consumption, progress in the area of human health will depend on the ability to control and decrease environmental pollution and the medical problems associated with it. More than ever, individuals are reacting adversely to the world around them; these reactions often include the development of sensitivities to food and other natural substances. This chapter will explore the role of the clinical ecologist, a medical specialist who studies the interdependent relationships between people and their environment—office, street, factory, and home.

Clinical ecology looks at allergies and allergic reactions from a perspective different from that of the traditional allergist. It is estimated that from 10 to 30 percent of the American public may be allergic to something in the immediate environment that causes mild to severe reactions and sometimes requires medical attention.

At one time it was thought that the main causes for behavioral problems in adults and children are psychological, sociological, or familial. However, clinical ecologists and experts in environmental medicine have added allergies and nutrition to the list of factors that can cause behavioral disorders.

When you think of allergies, you may think of a person eating strawberries and breaking out in hives or a person who pets a dog or cat and starts coughing and tearing. You may even know someone who smells diesel fuel and comes down with a headache. These are classic examples of allergies that have an immediate effect on various organs of the body. Allergies can also affect the brain, but such cerebral allergies are not easily diagnosed. Most physicians who see mental reactions such as mood swings, anxiety, depression, confusion, anger, and other behavioral problems tend to diagnose various forms of mental illness. This has led to unnecessary institutionalization, over-medication of children, and social stigma in adults.

This chapter describes both the traditional and bioecological approaches to allergies that affect the body and the mind, with special attention to the behavioral symptoms of allergies. The foods and chemicals most likely to cause reactions as well as guidelines to determine which health problems may be environmental are presented.

Home food allergy tests are discussed, along with the more sophisticated testing methods used in the doctor's office. Alternative treatment strategies are the main focus of the chapter.

## The Problem

Whatever disease state is discussed, it is necessary to deal with a weakened immune response and consider ways to strengthen it. The immune system protects the body from sickness and disease by forming an appropriate response to the invasion of foreign substances that may be harmful and by overcoming the deleterious effects of various internal imbalances. It is therefore important to maintain a strong immune system. Think of all the times your immune system's response is there to help you: when you breathe in toxic fumes, from someone who is smoking in the same room, from a car exhaust, or from a nearby manufacturing site; when you ingest irritating or poisonous chemicals, such as additives in processed foods, hormones and antibiotics in meat, and mercury and other metals in fish; or when you are exposed to bacterial and viral invaders when someone in the same vicinity sneezes or when your body creates an overabundance of usually benign bacteria. The immune system is constantly being called into action on your behalf. But if this immune response is overused and the adrenal glands and thyroid which support it are exhausted, the immune system cannot help the body fight off bacteria, destroy cancer cells, and the like. You are then in a weakened state and are highly susceptible to disease or sickness.

It is critical to keep the immune system strong and healthy. This means that it cannot be overburdened. It has plenty to do keeping the body healthy in the face of pollution, viral infections, bacterial invasions and the like. Whenever possible, its involvement should be averted in order to reserve it for the occasions when it is most needed.

One way to help the immune system is by restricting what is eaten. While people have little direct control over the quality of the air they breathe or the amount of bacteria they are exposed to in a given day, people can control the foods and substances they ingest. A considerable strain can be placed on the immune system by ingesting the wrong foods, in particular, the foods people are allergic or overly sensitive to that overstimulate the immune response, thereby overstressing it and in the process creating symptoms that may be mild and irritating but may also be destructive and debilitating. These symptoms may lead to related complications and a generally devolving health profile. Thus it is important to see just how food allergies work, how to determine which foods or substances evoke an undue sensitivity, what symptoms to look for, what complications may ensue, and how to treat the whole problem of food allergies and sensitivities.

### Early Research and Theories

The word "allergy" usually conjures up images of a tickly running nose, itchy eyes, wheezing, upper respiratory and nasal congestion, hives, rashes, and general discomfort. These are the symptoms of

267

the classical, or what may be referred to as type I, allergy. But there is also a type of allergy, closely related to addiction, that has only recently been recognized. This is the type II allergy, which may not manifest any symptoms for hours, sometimes not until the next day or later. Because of this time delay or because the symptoms are not highly noticeable, these reactions usually go unheeded or are attributed to something entirely different from the food or class of foods that is the actual source of the problem.

Research into the nature of allergies began about a century ago. Scientists were interested in learning how people could "exempt" themselves from bacteria and pathogens by building a defense against them. They did controlled animal studies to see how injections of minute portions of offending substances might cause the body to begin defending itself. The immune system, it was discovered, can be activated by these "immunizations" to moderate its overreaction to foreign microbial "invaders." This overreaction is actually an internal reaction (intrareaction), or as it was called at the turn of the century, an allergic reaction or simply "allergy" to the pathogen.

Immunologists and allergies—the scientists who studied these phenomena—keyed in on the classical reactions, such as hives, skin rashes, and increased pulse rate. In the 1920s they determined that immunoglobulins or antibodies were produced in the blood to defend the body against the intrusion of foreign substances biologically perceived as not belonging. Immunoglobulin E (IgE) was the antibody that seemed most active in combating the *antigen*, or offending material, and in forming the classical reaction, allergy, as the body's response to that antigen. Over the next 30 years scientists looked for ways to counter this reaction, principally by introducing small amounts of antigen into the blood so that the body would learn to recognize it and not react so violently to it.

In the 1970s this understanding of allergies began to change. Clinical ecologists—allergists who look to a person's whole environment as having the potential to create an immune-mediated response or reaction—realized that many allergies were a major factor contributing to illnesses and diseases that traditionally had been left out of discussions of allergic responses. Migraine headaches, depression, and arthritis are just a few of the conditions that were found to be allergy-related. While clinical data have supported this work, traditional allergists and immunologists frequently believe that there is insufficient theoretical explanation of these phenomena to accept them as scientifically valid. They continue to be interested mainly in type I allergies and consider the type II responses to be largely speculative.

### The Immune System, Hormones, and Diet

It was mentioned above that type I allergies are characterized by obvious reactions, as in the case of hay fever, asthma, and various skin conditions. These may be responses to inhalants or direct chemical contact. Type II allergies are also reactions to intolerable substances, but they are subtler and more insidious, as in the case of headaches and chronic gastrointestinal problems such as nausea, constipation, diarrhea, and malabsorption. These may be responses to foods to which a person is hypersensitive and therefore intolerant. The type I allergies call on IgE as their chief antibody, whereas type II allergies incite the production of immunoglobulin G (IgG).

Immunoglobulins are proteins that typically protect the body from bacteria, parasites, and pollutants. If you are subjected to a high concentration of an irritant, say pollen, your body will manufacture IgE efficiently. Then, if you directly encounter pollen, the IgE-manufacturing mechanism will be activated quickly. If you inhale pollen, you may sneeze to force it out. In the case of an actual parasite, if it contacts your skin, the IgE will attach itself to the parasite, thereby causing an itching sensation. You will then scratch your skin, and the scratching will kill the parasite. In the case of the parasite, your body's reaction protects you from potential danger. But in the case of pollen, the response is inappropriate because there are no known health hazards related to breathing in pollen. The problem arises when the body overreacts to pollen so that a whole symptomatology develops.

Inappropriate reactions to antigens are caused by the activity of the inducer or helper cells that constitute part of the T-lymphocyte system, which is responsible for scavenging and destroying unwanted substances. In general, the T-lymphocyte system is composed of both T-helper and T-suppressor cells.

The T-helper cells join the so-called B cells in encouraging antibody development, while the T-suppressor cells curb antibody reactions. If you have too much T-helper involvement, you will be allergic and hypersensitive to many things. If you have too much T-suppressor activity, your lymphocyte activity will not be sufficient to ward off truly dangerous and even life-threatening organisms and substances. Dr. Alan Levin, a board-certified physician in immunology, allergy, and pathology and adjunct professor of immunology at the University of California in San Francisco, uses this analogy:

The series of "inducers or helper cells . . . can be compared to an automobile with the accelerator and brake pedals on the floor; the car isn't moving, but the engine is revving. To go from point A to point B, the brake must be removed. To modulate the car's speed as it goes from A to B, you use the brake, which is applied when point B is reached. Thus, the brake pedal is the suppressor cell and the accelerator is the helper/inducer cell. If you lose your accelerator pedal, you have AIDS, and if you lose your brake pedal, you have rheumatoid arthritis. In people with allergies, the brakes are slipping."

Since allergies are the subject here, the primary concern is with the heightened activity of T-helper cells. It is not known exactly what creates a chronic syndrome of inappropriate immune-related responses as is seen in type II allergies, but it is known that some sort of damage to the immune system is an underlying precondition. Immune system damage can be caused by many things. Concentrated and/or prolonged exposures to pesticides, chemicals, toxic fumes, radiation, and broad-spectrum antibiotics are common causes. Viral damage can occur to the immune system from such things as herpes and the Epstein–Barr virus, which has received considerable attention lately. *Candida*, a yeast which is associated with an intolerance condition, has come into focus in the last decade as being responsible for a wide range of immune system dysfunctions related to allergies, especially of the type II variety. Candidiasis (a condition of *Candida* overgrowth) will be discussed later in this chapter.

Sometimes people develop hormonal imbalances that also impair the immune system. Hormones, which are secreted by the endocrine glands, help regulate vital physiological functions. The thyroid gland, for instance, secretes hormones T3, T4, and TSH (thyroid-stimulating hormone). If a person suffers from hypothyroidism, or low output of these three hormones, the cellular utilization of energy and the normal activity of the immune system will be decreased. Low basal temperatures, dry skin, chronic fatigue, and weight-loss problems may ensue. All these symptoms of hypothyroidism have been cited in cases of food sensitivity.

Pancreatic enzyme production, for instance, may be impaired by specific vitamin and mineral deficiencies. These deficiencies may result from insufficient intake of foods rich in specific vitamins or minerals but can also be caused by malabsorption of the nutrients ingested. Malabsorption is a digestive disorder, and it will be discussed more fully in Chapter 9.

Simply stated, malabsorption involves the body's inability to break down foods sufficiently. If, for instance, there is too little hydrochloric acid (HCl, a primary digestive fluid) production, food particles will not get broken down properly in the stomach or intestinal tract. They will then enter the blood as improperly large molecules and as such will be registered by the body as foreign intruders. This will stimulate antibody production, which in turn will prime the lymphocyte cells for overreaction to many substances. The food particle itself will elicit an allergic reaction since it will stay in the blood too long, having been insufficiently digested. It should be noted here that genetics plays a role in allergies, especially type I allergies. Asthma and skin conditions, for example, are frequently passed on genetically. Type II allergy symptoms such as headaches, depression, and fatigue may also be genetically encoded, but the connection is more tenuous. The role of genetics in type II allergies tends to be to create a predisposition for specific symptoms. But even in these cases the most significant factor will be the interplay between environment and organism. In other words, if you are genetically predisposed to depression, you are more likely to develop this problem than is someone who is not genetically so inclined.

What you eat and how you exercise and what coping mechanisms you employ in your daily life will probably play a far more significant role in your ultimate mental health and outlook. But if you are plagued with this predisposition, you will be especially interested in avoiding brushes with cerebral allergies that may throw you into states of depression far more quickly than they would an individual without such a genetic predisposition.

### Diagnosis and Treatment

The diagnosis for food allergies used by most clinical ecologists is based on detailed history taking, testing for specific sensitivities, and physical examination.

"The clinical ecologist," Dr. Levin explains, "would take the patient's medical history the same way the allergist does but would do so in greater depth. The ecologist would ask about periods of depression, loss of short-term memory (making lists and reminders where none were required before), and unexplained irritability. He or she would ask such questions as whether you've found you have to hold your breath around the detergent section of the supermarket or feel spacy and foggy in department stores, forgetting what you went there for. Where these were once considered simple psychopathological situational problems, they are now considered allergy symptoms; they are biochemical phenomena or adverse reactions to airborne environmental agents. The clinical ecologist would also ask about previous use of steroids, treatment of rashes, arthritis, bursitis, repeated antibiotic treatments, whether you have a vaginal discharge or itching around the rectum, whether certain foods cause your palate to itch, and whether you have chronic nausea or are unusually irritable at menstruation.

The history points the clinical ecologist in the right direction in determining what your symptoms and history of immune responses and allergic reactions are. The clinical ecologist then tries to define your problem more specifically by giving you tests. The prick, or intradermal, test is a standard procedure used to identify obnoxious and irritating inhalants. A concentration of the suspected allergen is pricked into the skin of the arm or back. If swelling and itching follow within a few minutes, the reaction is positive and you are considered allergic to the substance being tested. The RAST (radioallergosorbent test) measures the supply of IgE in the blood and can even specify which immunoglobulin (e.g., wheat grass IgE or ragweed Ige) is prevalent. Whatever is present is what you tend to overreact to. The measurement of specific IgG antigens, especially those related to foods (wheat, corn, milk, orange juice, etc.), can form an important aspect of testing for type II allergies.

Treatment for food allergies involves a two-pronged attack: avoidance of the substances to which the patient tests sensitive and at the same time building up and rebalancing the immune response to better deal with offending pathogens. Both are directly related to the diagnostic results, since a patient must know what substances are the allergens before deciding to avoid them. Dietary modification should be the first line of action because it represents the easiest, cheapest, and most direct and efficacious way of altering the patient's environment from one high in allergens to one that is relatively allergy-free.

Besides substituting for specific offenders, it is wise to avoid all high-allergen foods if you have chronic allergic problems of any sort. Milk is one of the most allergenic foods since most people have lactose deficiencies and cannot digest it properly. Hence, there develops a strong sensitivity to it. Corn and wheat have been in the human diet for half a millennium at the most. The human system is still not able to readily assimilate these foods, and so the allergic response to them is high. Sugar, processed foods, and citrus fruits are other items to be avoided, because they have been shown to be very common allergens.

Many foods produce what are known as cyclic allergies, that is, a sensitivity that becomes manifest only with repeated and/or heavy use of the problem-causing food. These foods are usually more difficult to specify because if you have not had them for a while, your symptoms will erode. They tend to be subclinical, that is, essentially undetected given traditional clinical procedures. Only with the most careful scrutiny to they appear as what they are. A good way to try to find a cyclic allergen is to eliminate a particular food, say, dairy, from your diet for 4 to 7 days. Then you have it as a monomeal, that is, a meal comprised almost entirely of generous portions of the allergen, in this case dairy. Then you monitor your body to determine whether there has been a bona fide reaction to it. If you notice, for instance, that your blood pressure jumps, your heart starts beating faster, your throat gets itchy, or your nose or eyes get runny and irritated or if you begin having trouble breathing, this food should be eliminated for about 3 weeks. During that period your body will usually regain a tolerance to it since the main cause of cyclic allergies is consistent overuse of a particular food. After 3 weeks, you can probably reintegrate modest amounts of that food into your diet, being careful to rotate it so that you do not eat it more than every fourth day, or no more than twice a week.

Dr. Levin describes his experience with the rotation of foods that have been "abused" or overused: "The most important foods to rotate are sources of protein, the most immunogenic molecule. Protein is also the easiest substance to rotate because fish can be eaten one day, fowl the next, beef the third, and pork the fourth day. Cereal grains can be rotated by eating wheat today but trying not to eat it tomorrow; try millet, buckwheat or rice instead, rotating them from day to day. The least important foods are the vegetable sources, but they too must be rotated as much as is practical. Because these simple rotation diets cure many symptoms, I call them simple solutions to complex problems. Whenever I'm consulted by a patient with depression, irritability, or chronic GI symptomatology or one who has been to a number of psychiatrists and has taken tricyclic antidepressants, Valium, or other similar medication, I suggest the patient restrict his or her intake of milk. When the patient does this, the symptoms usually disappear. This has happened so often that I can safely recommend that before you see your doctor, you might try eliminating milk products such as butter, yogurt, sour cream, etc., for 2 days. If your symptoms begin to change, try to avoid these foods for a few more days to see if your headaches, chronic depression, irritability, or constant fighting with your husband or wife stops. Between 60 and 70 percent of the time, these problems disappear with a simple change of diet."

The flip side of avoiding harmful foods is of course making sure to get plenty of the foods that strengthen the body and rebalance the immune system. Determining which foods are good and which are bad in terms of food sensitivity is a highly individualized task. Nowhere is it more true than here that one person's medicine is another person's poison. One cheap, easy, and fairly accurate way of making this distinction is through muscle-response testing. With this method, you can put a substance under your tongue and then immediately test the strength of a specific muscle. Usually you would do this by holding your arm straight and having another person gently try to force it down as you resist. When you've ingested a food to which you are not sensitive, your arm will resist strongly, but when you've ingested one to which you are sensitive, the arm will yield much more readily to your partner's pressure. An alternative version for this test is to press the thumb and little finger of one hand together while your partner tries to pull them apart. Kinesiology offers a convenient way to test any food or substance you may suspect is causing a problem. Some physicians as well as clinical ecologists employ this procedure as a standard method of getting a preliminary readout of offending substances.

Even after having determined which foods are eliciting an inappropriate immune response and replacing them with foods which work better with your body and provide the specific nutrients you need, you may still find it necessary to have some type of therapeutic intervention. In simple type I allergies, the standard intervention is desensitization. This technique has been used since 1911, and the procedure is practically the same today. The traditional allergist studies the patient's work and home environments to try to determine the foods, inhalants, chemicals, fabrics, etc., that are causing classic allergic symptoms. The allergist then administers a prick test, waits 10 minutes, and sees if the suspected allergen tests positive or negative. Once the offender is isolated, a batch of antigen is prepared for injection in the patient in order to stimulate suppression of antibody overreaction and effectively desensitize the patient.

The type II allergies are much more complex in terms of both diagnosis and treatment. An appropriate intervention here might involve finding a specific dilution that is just the right strength to shut off, or "neutralize," the allergic reaction. A dilute antigen is introduced in a low dose to build up a blocking factor, preventing the involvement of the B cells, which direct the production of antibodies and immunoglobulins. As in traditional immunology, the idea is to increase the doses progressively to strengthen the blocking factor in stages without causing a potentially dangerous hyperreaction.

However, optimally raising your threshold of tolerance to a substance is not usually accomplished with a simple upgrade of blocking stimulation: The best neutralizing dose has to be found. If you have prepared dilutions of wheat, for example, they may be increasingly potent as you go from dilution 1 to dilution 2, 3, 4, 5 and so forth.

When intradermal provocative neutralizing testing is done, the wheat dilution is injected just under the skin to see if it provokes a reaction. A reaction may mean apparent symptoms, but it also may mean "skin wheel" measurements: If the red circle, or "wheel," around the injection increases in size after 10 minutes, a reaction is indicated and you may need a higher dilution. When a dilution that does not provoke a reaction is obtained and the skin wheel stabilizes, the best neutralizing dose has been found. This may be dilution 1, 3, or 5. It cannot be assumed that the strongest is the best. Whatever shuts off the symptoms most thoroughly is the best.

Through this sort of intervention, you are exposing yourself to antigens in order to raise your threshold of tolerance and train your immune system to assist you. It does this by increasing the supply of T-lymphatic suppressor cells to prevent B cell and T-helper cell involvement in antibody production. This can be done either intradermally or sublingually, although reactions may be more exaggerated in the latter case.

However, intervention through either desensitization or reaction neutralizing is no substitute for dietary modification, particularly for food sensitivities that do not elicit strong, immediate, and therefore readily identifiable reactions. It is very difficult to build up appropriate immune-mediated responses to substances that may not show symptoms for hours or even days and may never show the sort of direct symptoms sought by traditional allergists and immunologists. This is why the best results for cerebral allergies, arthritis, candidiasis, and the like have been obtained first and foremost through dietary approaches. Dr. Levin talks about how critical an issue this is and how it has been overlooked and/or denied by traditional physicians:

"One of my patients, a 35-year-old woman with life-threatening asthma, had been taking prednisone for 16 years. When I first saw her a few years ago, she had typical cushinoid features, that is, a buffalo hump, an acne face rash, and centripetal obesity wherein her body was fat but her hands and legs were thin. She had purple stria on her abdomen and in general was a very ugly lady who had taken steroids to keep her airway open so that she could breathe. She was carefully placed on a very simple, nontoxic, long-term diet, environment, and yeast control program. Within 8 to 9 months she gradually stopped all steroids, and 8 to 9 months after that she was off all medication, even the routine bronchodilators. Her body reshaped itself, and she progressively became her former beautiful self. . . .

"She started her own business, which subjected her to an enormous amount of stress. She soon forgot about her diet and ate ice cream, wheat, milk, and milk products. She gained weight and developed a viral illness, and then she traveled by plane to visit a sister. Once there, she continued her dietary transgressions and in addition was exposed to a dog. She developed respiratory distress and was taken to a hospital, where she stopped breathing. Fortunately, the physicians were able to start her breathing again, and she did reasonably well until she developed another viral illness. She is now out of the hospital and again doing well. However, I warned her that if she wished to continue as my patient, she had to follow her prescribed diet no matter how stressful her business was. Of course, I could have given her steroids, which would have made her cushinoid again, but she had been completely off all medications for 3 years until she succumbed to business stresses.

"This is a clearcut example of how a patient can be weaned off steroids and then have to be placed back on them by transgressing. Of course, one glass of milk certainly will do little or no harm; it's getting back to the nonrotational diet by gradually increasing the dietary intake of offending foods that can kill. Without reservation, I can state that about 75 percent of steroid-dependent asthmatics in this country can be taken off steroids with adequate dietary and *Candida* control. To date I have been successful in getting all my steroid-dependent patients off steroids; it's a long painful process for these patients because they must avoid foods they really like, such as ice cream.

"A male patient I know—thank heaven he's not one of mine—

has been hospitalized repeatedly for respiratory arrest, yet he stubbornly refuses to give up his daily two bars of chocolate. A large number of adults are on antidepressants and are receiving psychotherapy, and many children are taking Ritalin for short attention span syndrome or hyperactivity. They should not have been given these forms of therapy until attempts had been made to control them by diet. If dietary restrictions do not benefit them, only then should the more artificial forms of therapy be given."

It is time for a more in-depth look at some of the more clearly associated complications and diseases of food allergies. Bear in mind that these are examples of basic hyperreactions or allergies to foods. No matter how complicated the symptoms become—and they become extremely complex—once they are put into the simple immune response perspective described here, these diseases may be more effectively handled on a clinical basis.

### Mental Health and Allergies

A teenager steals a car and takes it for a ride. He is spotted by a patrol car, and a high-speed chase ensues, ending with the youth's fatal crash into a telephone pole, His friends can't understand it because he wasn't drinking and never took drugs. His parents are dismayed because they have three cars sitting in the driveway, and he could have used any of them.

This sort of thing happens all the time. You can call it delinquency or crime or antisocial behavior. You can say that the offender is mentally disturbed, psychologically troubled, schizophrenic, or psychotic. You may be right, but you may be wrong.

The late Dr. Benjamin Feingold, M.D., was perhaps the first to suggest that food allergies and sensitivities often form the basis of what people call criminal and delinquent behavior, although he dealt more with learning disabilities and food additives. The Feingold hypothesis is that antisocial, learning, and behavioral disorders—particularly those related to hyperkinesis, or restless overactivity—are frequently related to specific substance sensitivities. These sensitivities are usually diet-related. He concentrated on the chemical additives in processed foods which induce cerebral allergies. For this reason, Dr. Feingold developed a special diet that deliberately circumvents these items.

Dr. Joseph Edgar, a pediatric neurologist studying the food-mood connection in London between 1982 and 1984, supported the Feingold hypothesis but found that the food allergies were more troublesome than the chemical additives. When the additives were stripped away, the basic foods still caused allergic reactions, including hyperactivity. Milk and chocolate were found to be especially allergenic.

Dr. Alexander Schauss has been studying such phenomena since 1970 and has met with considerable opposition from established medicine and the major food industries. Dairy producers, for instance don't want to hear that the human consumption of cow's milk can be, as Dr. Schauss and others have found, closely correlated to the incidence of delinquency. Opposing studies are often done to discredit the findings of those who support nutrition and supplementation as therapeutic devices. One such study, done at a university medical center in Alberta, Canada, was aimed at denigrating the practice of orthomolecular psychiatry (Chapter 1), an alternative discipline which employs nutritional support to treat mental disorders. In a poorly designed study of hyperkinesis, an attention span malady, it was determined that the administration of vitamins on a supplemental basis causes complications and can actually be dangerous. However, the vitamins administered in the tests were improperly balanced in a way that no competent orthomolecular psychiatrist would do.

A group of establishment physicians and nutritionists at the University of California went so far as to conclude that scientific research correlating diet and crime should not even be done. The American Society of Criminology responded that no one should have the power to censor scientific research, even if it is not in his or her best interest. Public interest groups throughout the country, supported by the medical establishment, warn consumers that nutritional advice is quackery and fraud, but they offer only opinions, not scientific evidence, to support their claims. One such group in New York City quickly aired disclaimers to many studies indicating that foods, chemicals, and food additives may be deleterious to one's health. In investigating this group's six staff members, the Center for Science in the Public Interest in Washington, D.C., found they had received donations over $750,000 from 111 food and chemical manufacturers in just 1 year. These companies all manufactured products which were defended by this so-called public interest group.

## The Food-Mood Connection

Dr. Schauss has continued trying to make the food–mood connection public, especially in relation to criminal and delinquent behavior. He states that the Illinois State Penitentiary System, working in conjunction with an analytical chemist, was the focus of a report indicating that there is a definite "biochemical profile." Based on comparative studies of some of the surliest inmates and their siblings who were perfectly good citizens, the study suggested that criminal and antisocial behavior can be drastically modified through dietary change and proper nutrient supplementation. The study is significant because it undercuts the significance of social conditioning, family background, and psycho-social conditioning in that the studied pairs had identical family, school, neighborhood, and socioeconomic backgrounds. The only real difference was a biochemical one.

Dr. Steven Schoenthaller studied 14,000 subjects in 14 institutions in 4 states in an attempt to refute the food–mood connection. Instead, according to Dr. Schauss, his findings confirmed it. These studies were meticulously controlled and double-blinded. Diets that reduced refined carbohydrate intake and provided for supplementation appropriate to specific conditions, it was found, were responsible for reducing all sorts of behavioral and mental disorders, including aggression and even suicide.

Dr. Schauss relates many cases that also support this thesis. He was asked to study a man in his mid-forties with no prior criminal record who for no apparent reason suddenly shot 24 people at his country club. This former airline president had no recall of the event afterward. Dr. Schauss found through his investigation, based on 2 years of testing at New York University, that the man had drunk red wine that day and that the wine induced a severe paranoid-schizophrenic episode in him. This conclusion was the result of a team investigation that included many experts in psychiatry and clinical psychology. It was validated by sophisticated computer testing and electronic encephalogram readouts. The man was able to return to society, where he has been a model citizen.

In another case, a man who seemed to be retarded and was institutionalized in a residence at Berkeley, Oregon, complained that he did not feel good when he ate. Dr. Schauss, along with a psychiatrist specializing in metabolic consumption, studied the results of hair, urine, and blood samples. It was discovered that the patient had severe hypoglycemia and lead poisoning. He underwent chelation therapy to rectify the lead condition and was put on a special hypoglycemia diet to control rapid fluctuations in blood sugar levels. Not only did his behavior stabilize very quickly, when his IQ was retested, his score improved by 25 points. He too now leads a normal, active, productive life and has long since left the institution to which he had been committed.

These cases and many others like them show the great potential of a system of nutritional therapy that takes food allergies into account. If criminal and delinquent behavior can be modified through dietary regimentation, this might be a cheap, safe way to cut down on the $40 billion that is spent each year on criminal justice services. There are nearly 1.25 million people working in the criminal justice system, and only one-third of crimes are even reported. Imagine how a better understanding of the food-mood connection could affect criminal activity at even deeper levels of society, where petty crime, delinquency, violence, and aggression are "normal" ways of coping and surviving. As it is, half a million people are incarcerated in the United States, a figure rising by 32,000 a year and estimated to increase by as much as 100,000 a year by the turn of the century.

By funding nutritionally oriented behavior modification programs in the prison system, it may be possible to reduce these figures considerably. Alabama was the first state to sanction such programs in its state penal institutions. The results have pleased everyone, and Alabama became the first state in U.S. history to have a reduction in the number and percentage of delinquent recommitments. There has even been a declining rate of arrest since the program went into effect.

Criminal and delinquent behavior are not the only results of cerebral allergies. There is also a whole spectrum of noncriminal mental health problems related to the food-mood connection. Dr. Janice Keller Phelps, a board-certified pediatrician, states that food addictions characterized by strong cravings for a certain substance are followed by an endless cycle of withdrawal symptoms alleviated temporarily by reintroduction of the offender into the system. This vicious cycle can leave a person with symptoms of lethargy and depression as well as full-scale psychosis. Unfortunately, these symptoms are often diagnosed as psychic breaks, or schizophrenia, and the patient may be institutionalized.

Dr. Phelps has used nutritional medicine in overcoming these mind-altering food allergies. She describes a 15-year-old girl who was committed to a hospital just after an episode of manic and irrational behavior. There, she was told she had just experienced her first psychotic break. In other words, she was told that she was mentally ill and that this was only the first of an endless series of similar episodes. When Dr. Phelps began to treat the girl, she was taking medication for a bladder infection. Dr. Phelps determined that she had not had a psychotic break at all but rather an allergic reaction to the medication. She immediately took the patient off the medication and administered 8 g of vitamin C intravenously, along with B vitamins and calcium-magnesium supplements to detoxify her. The girl was also put on an allergy-free diet. Both her manic behavior and her urinary tract symptoms cleared up within a week.

Dr. Phelps also treated a woman in a chronic psychotic haze who had been put on all kinds of drugs to control her "psychosis." Eventually she became manic and uncontrollable and was committed to a hospital. Dr. Phelps used the trial and error method to test the woman for food allergies by putting her through alternating stages of removal and reintroduction of specific foods. If she reacted when a substance was reintroduced, she was considered allergic to it. Dr. Phelps also employed cytotoxic tests to help determine the food allergies that were present. The cytotoxic test can measure many foods at one time but tends to be vague and sometimes ambiguous in its results. Nonetheless, once Dr. Phelps had determined which foods the patient was most allergic to, she constructed an individualized allergy-free dietary regimen for her to follow. The woman was also given "appropriate vitamin and mineral supplementation" and was put on an antidepressant drug to which she was not allergic.

The patient's symptoms substantially subsided within 2 weeks. Dr. Phelps' suspicions were confirmed: This patient was not at all psychotic; her mental haze had been the result of a host of food sensitivities, and she had developed an allergy to the therapeutic antidepressants she was receiving.

Many genetic depressives are likely to develop food allergies that greatly exacerbate their conditions and go on to create many other complications, both physiological and cerebral. This occurs because these people frequently have abnormal adrenal gland function, a major factor in addictions. Sugar addiction and intolerance may cause a reactive hypoglycemia that deprives the cells of their required glucose. When normal physiological functioning is disrupted in this way, a whole symptomatology will ensue.

Dr. Phelps tests for adrenal imbalance by observing dexamethasone suppression activity. Dexamethasone causes the adrenals to suppress their normal activity. When the patient is given a 1-mg tablet of dexamethasone at 11 P.M. on a given day, by 4 P.M. the following day the patient's cortisol level should be depressed. The patient is given a blood test at the 4 P.M. interval to determine whether cortisol levels have indeed dropped off. The genetic depressive's cortisol level will remain high despite the suppressive activity of the dexamethasone. This is an indication that the patient has a poorly functioning adrenal response and will probably have many food allergies and addictions. If you are in this category, a sugar-free diet will help you. Dr. Phelps also supplements the diet with nutritional programs that include pantothenic acid, vitamins B and C, and an adrenal extract to repair the adrenals.

Dr. Levin describes cases that indicate that learning disabilities are another noncriminal behavior disorder that can be associated with allergies:

"To say you can cure this problem with diet and environment control is certainly far-fetched. But many children with learning disabilities or autism—and I'm describing five of my patients who initially had been diagnosed as autistic—have had allergies that compromised their ability to learn. My five children have been helped substantially and are now reasonably normal on dietary control alone.

"One child had been normal up to the age of 3 years, when he developed a series of ear infections for which he received a large amount of antibiotics; he became increasingly autistic. He would neither speak to nor look at anyone and was completely out of touch with his surroundings. I saw him 2 or 3 years later and found that he had allergies. His skin test to dust produced an enormous reaction, during which his personality changed dramatically. He became benign, smiled, and seemed to fall asleep in his mother's lap. A large segment of his emotional or central nervous system problems seemed to be related to his allergies. By working very closely with his mother, we determined that he was allergic to *Candida albicans*, a common fungus infection of the GI tract. Eliminating the *Candida* with antifungal agents restored the child to a point where, although he is not yet completely normal, he attends a normal school, is learning, and is functioning with normal children. He's by no means autistic.

"Roughly 5 of 20 children diagnosed as autistic have benefitted from this type of treatment. It is simple to do and is reasonably nontoxic, and if the child responds, it does a lot of good. If it doesn't help, nothing has been lost."

Many researchers and clinicians have verified the correlation between behavioral disorders and allergies, specifically cerebral allergies. Dr. Doris Rapp is one such authority, specifically on the subject of learning disabilities and allergies. The author of *Allergies and the Hyperactive Child* (Simon & Schuster, New York, 1986), Dr. Rapp is assistant professor of pediatrics at the State University of New York at Buffalo. Her work is discussed more fully in Chapter 1.

It is not asserted here that all behavioral problems are related to cerebral allergies. Many are socioeconomic or psychological in nature. But in cases that are due to allergies, no amount of psychoanalysis, social work, or toxic drug therapy is going to help, and it may make the problem worse. It is imperative that your physician explore all the possible causes and effects of a specific condition before deciding on a treatment. If you suffer from any apparently psychological problems, you should seek the counsel of a doctor competent in diagnosing allergy-related disorders before subjecting yourself to possible misdiagnosis and mistreatment.

## Environmental Allergies

While this chapter has focused so far on allergies from ingested substances, it should also be noted that if you are suffering from allergic symptoms, you should look to your environment as well as to your diet for possible culprits. All the allergens discussed in this category can cause the symptoms mentioned in our discussion of food allergies, both type I and type II, such as sneezing and eye irritation, wheezing, and itching, as well as the more complicated areas of arthritis, bronchial disorders, and depression.

Fungal spores are one of the most common and insidious indoor allergens. They are especially profuse in air-conditioned buildings, where they can grow in cool, wet, temperature-controlled environments without being disturbed. People working or living in such buildings are exposed almost constantly to fungi such as *Aspergillus* and *Chlamydiasporium*. If they are not immediately sensitive to these spores, they almost inevitably become so as the exposure is prolonged.

Wherever there is water, fungi and molds can cause problems. The basement is probably the toughest place to get rid of mold because it tends to be damp, especially in areas with high water tables. Try to redirect water channels away from the house. You can accomplish this by having downspouts extended well away from the baseline foundation, landscaping the surrounding area in such a way that water naturally runs away from the house, waterproofing basement walls with a product such as Thoroseal and calking cracks and openings, and finally, if all else fails, installing a sump pump to force water out of the basement. It is important to keep the basement dry because whatever mold, spores, and mildews grow there will end up in the house—and in your lungs.

Because of water from the shower and tub, the bathroom is another place where mold can grow. It must be well ventilated with either a fan or a window so that it is kept dry. The black film that accumulates on the walls and in the grout between tiles is a mold that emits thousands of spores into the air. It must be cleaned periodically with a diluted bleach solution. Look under the kitchen and bathroom sinks too. If there is a condensation or leaking problem, mold will grow. Also look behind the refrigerator where dampness and dust accumulate and can harbor mold and mildew along with household dust.

You can react to mold when you eat it as well as when you inhale it. Eating mold further complicates the problems of breathing it in, an effect that is called concomitancy. If you are eating mold, your reaction to mold in the environment will be heightened. Foods made by fermentation have mold: wine, vinegar, cheese, and foods with yeast, including most breads, cakes, and baked items. Mushrooms are an offender here too. Avoid these foods as much as possible if you are sensitive to mold.

Many people are very sensitive to household dust, both at work and at home. Household dust is a mixture of many things, including the household dust mite. This tiny particle that easily floats around with air movement is a living organism; under a microscope, it resembles a tiny dinosaur. It creates an allergic reaction not unlike that incited by a dog or cat dander. If you have carpeting, you have created a perfect breeding ground for these little fellows: they are also partial to bed sheets, pillowcases, and blankets. If you sleep in a carpeted room or on bedding that is not changed daily, do not be surprised when you wake up in the morning with thick mucous in the mouth, red itchy eyes, fits of sneezing, and so forth. These tiny mites, mixed with other irritants in household dust, have probably been circulating throughout your respiratory tract all night. Carpeting, especially when it has a rubber or foam backing, compounds this problem by holding in mold and spores.

You need to have bedding cleaned daily, shake and air your blankets outdoors frequently, clean the dust off furniture and lamps regularly, and vacuum very thoroughly every day. The bedroom must be given extra care. Make sure to clean well under the bed; keep that area clear of clutter and debris to keep molds and dust from finding shelter and to keep the air circulating properly. Make sure the air is changed in your house at least once a day, even in the coldest weather. This is done preferably by opening all the windows and leaving the inside doors open to create cross ventilation and circulation of fresh air. Again, be especially particular about the bedrooms. Carpeting cannot be cleaned properly no matter what you do, and dirt collects year after year. Don't be surprised if you and the children develop chronic allergies if the bedrooms are carpeted and if you are not meticulous about keeping a dust-free, mold-free environment. Also, keep pets out of the bedroom; they can add to your dust and mold problems. After all, it has been observed that a person who sleeps 8 hours a night spends 24 years in bed by the age of 72.

Another cause of an environmental allergy is cooking gas, a significant household irritant, together with kerosene and other fuel fumes. When any fuel is burned, some residue is always produced, and this can be the source of allergies. Dr. Alfred Zamm, a board-certified dermatologist and allergist, and the author of *Why Your House May Endanger Your Health* (Simon & Schuster, New York, 1980), tells us the following story:

"About 2 years ago, a child was brought to see me. His mother told me that he was in a special class; that is, he had a learning disability He was hyperkinetic and couldn't concentrate or sit still. The principal told the mother that if she wanted her son in a regular class, he would have to take the drug Ritalin. The mother refused to give the child drugs and insisted on finding a physician who would solve his problem. Despite the principal's insistence that Ritalin had produced excellent results in children with the same problem, she could not be dissuaded from seeking medical care for the boy. Somehow she found her way to my office. . . . I found her son was allergic to three or four foods and took away these foods, and the child's problem cleared except between the hours of 5:30 and 7:00 every night. I asked her whether she had disconnected the gas stove as I had told her to do. Since she hadn't, I told her this is a good test. I instructed her to disconnect the gas stove and then reconnect it and watch the child's reactions. When she disconnected the stove, the child was fine; when she reconnected it between 5:30 and 7:00 P.M., he became very agitated and ran around the house. When she again disconnected the stove, he again became very quiet.

"This chid won the school's PTA award for the child who had improved the most that year. After he received the award, his mother showed the result to the school principal and glowingly stated that her son had not taken any medication. Thus the gas stove to me is a symbol of unsafe living patterns; the fumes are dispersed throughout the house, and the homemaker is exposed to them as an occupational hazard. In fact, in my book, I call this the *moody mother syndrome*."

Chemicals such as cleansing agents and sanitizing and disinfectant products are also major irritants. Paint thinner and remover are known carcinogens, so be sure to have ample ventilation if you must use them. Avoid using them if possible or use them outdoors. Floor waxes used at home or in the office give off noxious fumes as they evaporate. Try to get used to low-sheen or even no-sheen floors so that you don't have to wax them frequently, thereby reducing your exposure to the wax fumes. No disinfectant kills germs, so don't waste your money on them. You may even be irritated by their odors, as you may be by any heavy aromatic odors from cleansers, laundry soap, hand soap, scented toilet paper, and the like. The pine scent usually used in odor disguises is especially troublesome to allergy-prone individuals; it doesn't even deodorize but only compounds the problem. Avoid using scented products and strong chemicals and ventilate areas that contain them well and frequently. This is the only way to clear the air.

Gregg Robertson is a chemist who is an expert on indoor air pollution. Having examined numerous buildings, he has decided that many of them are "sick" buildings. He calls them by this name because they make people sick, or more precisely, because the pollutants in them make people sick. These pollutants include ammonia, formaldehyde, ozone, carbon monoxide, cigarette smoke, and glass fibers. Gaseous formaldehyde can be emitted from carpet backing, wood laminate, and the urea formaldehyde foams used to insulate some buildings. Fiberglass particles come from insulation materials used above ceilings and to line the ducts of ventilation systems. When these materials are disrupted by deteriorating ceilings or by being blown around by heating or air-conditioning systems, glass fibers get into the air and can cause severe dermatitis, throat irritation, and violent reactions in the nasal passages. Ozone is given off by some copying machines and air-cleaning electrostatic precipitators; as is the case with all indoor pollutants, this becomes a problem when there is insufficient ventilation. Ammonia is used in many common floor, window, and toilet cleaners. Carbon monoxide—the poisonous gas emitted by idling vehicles—is particularly troublesome in buildings that have underground garages.

Cigarette smoke is the indoor air pollutant that receives the widest attention, and for good reason. Nonsmokers can absorb a high percentage of the smoke emitted into the air by smokers. The smoke is usually highly visible, and it is irritating to most nonsmokers. The fact that cigarette smoke is the only major indoor air pollutant that is visible and obnoxious indicates something very significant, Robertson notes. If air ventilation is adequate, the cigarette smoker should hardly be noticed. Thus we know that whenever smoke is trapped to the extent that it is noticeable, a host of other pollutants must also be trapped in the same area.

People need to realize that cigarette smoke is only one factor—about 4 percent—in indoor air pollution. Many others are invisible and odorless but can cause far more serious harm if people are exposed to them repeatedly. In 31 percent of the buildings Robertson has inspected, molds, mildew, and fungus contamination are a problem; in 9 percent, bacteria; in 6 percent, fiberglass particles; in 4 percent, carbon monoxide from idling vehicles in underground garages or near air intake ducts; and in 4 percent, cigarette smoke. Smaller percentages of problems were found to be related to formaldehyde, ammonia, ozone, and various chemicals.

Robertson also lists some indoor pollutants commonly found in the household environment. Hair sprays containing methylene chloride are known to cause cancer in rats. Odors given off by new carpets are irritating when ventilation is inadequate. Fireplaces and wood stoves accumulate a variety of particulate matter that can become a problem if there is poor ventilation and/or air filtration. Vacuum cleaners act as portable, miniature air-filtering systems, so be sure to replace the filter bags frequently. Otherwise you are trapping dust, bacteria, and spores that will only be pushed back into the air again. Control the humidity levels of your home with high-quality humidifiers or dehumidifiers if necessary and as the situation demands.

Besides eliminating the source of pollution itself, it is advisable to work toward better ventilation and air filtration. "To give you an idea of the range of the ventilation problem," Robertson explains, "we have now investigated over 37 million square feet of buildings in this country, and in no less than 65 percent of the buildings studied we found inadequate ventilation. Far worse than that, in no less than 34 percent of the buildings—these are government buildings, private insurance companies, banks, etc.—no fresh air whatsoever is brought in. As a deliberate policy, building engineers, building owners, maintenance people, and others are shutting off the fresh air supply solely to save energy, and everyone is living with 100 percent recycled air. When this happens, it's inevitable that every type of indoor pollutant will accumulate with time in that building. Eventually, people will begin to get sick, and the only indictor most people will have apart from sickness is smoke accumulation. That is a distinct sign of ventilation problems."

Speaking about the problem of poor air filtration, he offers this: "We have analyzed 37 million square feet of these buildings, and in approximately two-thirds of the buildings we found very poor and very inefficient filters. In 28 percent of the buildings, the filters were grossly inadequate. In some cases the air filters are actually contributing to the dirt levels in the air, with fungus and mold on those filters being recycled in the building. We find filters that are badly installed so that there are big air gaps at the side of the filter that pigeons could fly through; many filters have never been changed in literally years of operation."

The solution to the problem, Robertson explains, involves bringing in fresh air, "a minimum of 20 cubic feet of fresh air per person per minute coming into the building at all times. Under no circumstances should the building engineers be free to shut off the fresh air supply to save a few dollars." This is important for the home as well as the office. Once you shut all the windows and doors to your house, you are approaching zero ventilation. All the dust and odors and molds are then trapped and concentrated like the smog hovering over a freeway.

The solution to indoor air pollution also involves proper air filtration. Both at home and in the office, you should buy the best filters and filtration systems available regardless of the cost. The few dollars extra can save thousands of dollars in medical costs and lost work time. It is just as important to maintain filtration. Filters must be cleaned on a regular basis and should be replaced periodically according to the manufacturer's suggestions to ensure a clean-flowing air supply. Electrostatic precipitators, used to rid the air of electric static from computer systems, are excellent filtrators, but if you don't wash the electrodes periodically, they will be useless.

Cooking, heating, and ventilation systems and ductwork should also be cleaned regularly. If air-conditioning coils, for instance, are moldy or covered with a fungus, they must be cleaned. The same holds true for ductwork.

Remember that whatever is in your air will end up in your system, just like the food you eat. So, as Dr. Zamm warns, you must in effect eat your environment. If you wax the floor, you will take in, or "eat," that wax as it evaporates. If you don't clean the dust under your bed, you will "eat" it all night as it circulates in the air you breathe.

### Candida and Allergies

*Candida* provides a prime example of how food sensitivities can undermine a person's health and yet go undetected. *Candida albicans* was not widely known until 1978, when a scholarly book on the subject by Dr. Orin Truss was first published. More recently, the condition has received popular attention through the *Yeast Connection* (Professional Books, Jackson, Tennessee, 1983), by Dr. William Crook, M.D.

*Candida* is a microscopic yeast that thrives harmoniously in human mucosa. It is normally held in check by friendly intestinal and vaginal bacteria and causes no problems. However, when the immune system is impaired, *Candida* overgrows its typical bounds and increases its normal activity. It overpowers both the T-helper cells of the immune system and the beneficial intestinal flora. It then becomes pathogenic and can be the source of many diverse conditions and diseases.

The earliest definitive studies on *Candida* were done by Dr. E. Water, who first isolated the *Candida* yeast factor in 1970. He found that in its overactive state, when it combined with ingested sugar in the intestine in Japanese subjects, it was converted to alcohol. The symptomatology that developed was similar to that of typical inebriation.

In American subjects, though, the symptoms are far more serious. Instead of alcohol, a profound tissue toxin results from intestinal fermentation in the presence of ingested sugar. This poison, called acid aldehyde, affects not only the nervous and immune systems but also the skin, digestion, hormonal secretions, and virtually all the body's normal physiological processes. This sugar intolerance is one result of *Candida* overgrowth, which is called candidiasis. Yeast insensitivity is another result.

Candidiasis, which can afflict both men and women, can appear with many symptoms, most of which have been related to this specific condition only recently. The common symptomatology begins with simple headaches, muscle pain, fatigue, and depression but can include more serious maladies such as multiple sclerosis, migraine headaches, urinary disorders, and suicidal depression. It can be seen in infants as a patchy white rash called thrush and in women as vaginitis. Sufferers may have gastrointestinal (GI) symptoms such as constipation, diarrhea, gas, nutrient malabsorption, and digestion. Food allergies, primarily sensitivity to yeast and sugar, are the chief culprits in this disorder. Further sensitivities may develop, though, especially if digestion is bad, creating an overexposure to larger than normal food molecules. There may be brain symptoms; mood swings are typical, as are learning disabilities so severe that a person may appear retarded. Hormonal symptoms may include premenstrual syndrome (PMS) and impotence. Vascular symptoms include varicose veins and hemorrhoids.

### The Cause

The most common cause of candidiasis seems to be prolonged or repeated heavy use of prescription drugs such as cortisone and tetracycline. These broad-spectrum antibiotics appear to be the worst offenders, since they invade the whole body system and attack both friendly and unfriendly bacteria as they attempt to get at the specific virus or bacteria suspected of causing an infectious condition. Children with chronic earache, for instance, may receive these antibiotics for months at a time. While the immediate symptoms may be kept in check with this sort of treatment, the body's immune system becomes weakened in the process, paving the way for candidiasis. The same thing may occur during antibiotic or cortisone treatment for long-term teenage acne or chronic bladder infection. These sorts of treatments decrease the activity of the T-helper cells, which among other things direct the body's controlling mechanism regulating the growth and activity of *Candida* cells.

Hormonal imbalances may also precipitate this condition. These imbalances may occur during pregnancy, when normal hormonal secretions may be altered. Birth control pills can also affect hormone balance. Endocrine activity also can be altered by hormones ingested in commercially prepared meat and poultry products.

The foods you eat can create problems with *Candida* in many ways. Commonly used preservatives and pesticides passed on from sprayed produce can adversely affect the body's immune response. Insecticides, pesticides, and other chemical pollutants in the environment can also set you up as an unwitting victim of *Candida albicans*.

Yeast or *Candida albicans* in the body may act as an immunosuppressant, that is, interfere with a cell's ability to protect itself. This general underlying situation is manifested in various specific conditions brought on by immune breakdowns. Individually predisposed weaknesses usually are the first to be exploited. Therefore, if a person has a predisposition to digestive difficulty genetically related, environmentally induced, or due to lifestyle, this may be actualized when the immune system fails or, more to the point in this context, when the immune system is suppressed by the activity of *Candida albicans*. The symptoms may be triggered when a person attempts to satisfy a craving for sweets and sugary foods. The sugar combines in the intestine with *Candida* to cause the toxic acid aldehyde. Mold, which increases yeast activity, may also bring on these symptoms. A moldy house or even damp weather can do this, as can yeast taken in directly through food.

### The Diagnosis

Since there is such a wide variety of symptoms which overlap with particular disease symptoms, it is important to know when these symptoms are related to *Candida albicans* rather than to another condition. If someone acts mentally ill, for instance, how can one tell if that person is truly disturbed or is simply yeast-sensitive? The diagnosis of candidiasis is obviously a delicate matter.

The first thing the physician should do, as with any allergic or addictive condition, is take a good patient history. The history will determine how long the symptoms have persisted, what treatment has been used to control them, and what procedures or medications have been effective in relieving them. If the symptoms are fairly recent and rather acute, they can be the direct result of a developing illness or a sudden exposure to a newly introduced irritant. If they seem to have been around for a long time, i.e., are chronic, they are more likely to suggest a yeast intolerance that has gone unnoticed.

A medical history will reveal what prior conditions have been treated so that the physician can determine if they could have been part of the broader *Candida* problem. Here again it is important to note how effective prior treatments were. If a patient has had a long history of migraine headaches, for example, and if the treatments given have been only temporarily effective, *Candida* may indeed be indicated. The likelihood of this will be greatly enhanced if the history also shows typical symptoms of *Candida*, such as muscle pain and lethargy.

Some laboratory tests may be helpful in diagnosing the condition, although they tend to lack the specificity required for a definitive diagnosis. For instance, antibody tests can show whether high levels of antibodies are being produced in the body to counter the *Candida* offensive. However, this can be misleading because a low readout may indicate that the body is not producing an abundance of antibodies, in which case there is no real *Candida* offensive. However, it may also indicae just the opposite—that the *Candida* offensive has been so successful that it has seriously weakened the immune-mediated response and so lowered the level of antibody production. The antigen test gives better results because it simply shows how much *Candida* is present in the blood, where it does not belong.

Stool tests and vaginal smears are sometimes used to detect the presence of *Candida*, but these too are unreliable if used exclusively. The simple presence of *Candida* cells is not all that significant since even healthy people have *Candida* in their bodies. Besides, the *Candida* cell has two different forms. One type is round and smooth and is easily moved from one spot to another, but the second type has little feet or claws that dig into the mucous membranes. The second type may be overabundant in the body but will not be manifested in stool samples or vaginal smears because it is too deeply rooted in the body's tissues.

Blood tests may show maladies such as anemia; if such maladies cannot be attributed to a particular condition, they may indicate *Candida*. The same can be said if diabetes or urinary tract infection is indicted by urinalysis.

To further confirm the results of the history and laboratory analyses, a physical examination, including a thorough review of all symptoms, should be done. *Candida* may be indicated if the patient is especially sensitive to odors and fumes; has strong sugar cravings; is aggravated by dampness and mold; displays nervous disorders such as twitching and depression or even fatigue and headaches; has chronic digestive irregularities including diarrhea, constipation, and bloating, or, in women, there is an interruption for the normal menstrual cycle or symptoms of PMS.

## The Treatment

Treatment must be undertaken on many levels since, according to Dr. Crook, "*Candida* affects many body tissues through . . . metabolic changes." Dietary modification is a good place to start, since the condition is directly and adversely affected by ingested yeast and sugar. If you have suffered for many years, as most *Candida* victims have without much help from the doctors you have consulted or the medication you have been given, you will be happily surprised to find most of your symptoms disappearing after just 7 days of proper eating. The correct dietary regimen will actually starve the *Candida* cells into submission, as it revolves around total abstinence from sugar and yeast-containing foods. *Candida* thrives on sugar, and at least half of all *Candida* sufferers are allergic to yeast. The two together are devastating if you have this condition, and you will have to completely abandon your intake of sugar, honey, maple syrup, molasses, and even fruit, which quickly breaks down into its high concentration of fructose—the type of sugar peculiar to fruit. Yeast is found in many forms: raised breads or baked goods, beer and wine, cheese, and even mushrooms.

A general rule of thumb is to avoid refined, processed simple carbohydrates. They should be replaced with complex carbohydrates such as vegetables, whole grains, brown rice, oats, barley, potatoes, and fresh nuts. This basic diet should be supplemented with an acidophilus (live bacteria culture), preferably a liquid bacillicus with live cultures that will enhance the ability of friendly intestinal bacteria to suppress the yeast cells. Oils such as fish oils, linseed oil, and Evening Primrose oil (especially when there are PMS symptoms) may also be beneficial, as may any of the immune boosters such as vitamins C and A. Vitamin B is needed to maintain the nervous system, which is in trouble with this condition. Antioxidants, including vitamin E, are required; and the minerals magnesium, zinc, and selenium are known to be helpful.

It is imperative to realize that these dietary modifications are not so much a diet as a permanent lifestyle change. The word "diet" may make you think that you can eat this way for a few weeks or months or until the symptoms disappear and then go back to eating sugars and raised breads. Unfortunately, as soon as you revert to your old eating habits, the symptoms of candidiasis will reappear. You must get off sugar and yeast products and stay off them for as long as you wish to keep *Candida* under control. There may be some slight flexibility here. Since sugar and yeast are nearly universal in the foods available to us, Dr. Crook suggests that after 3 weeks of strictly avoiding all forms of sugar and yeast, you may be able to eat fruit again in moderate portions and that it may be a good idea to try to integrate brewer's yeast back into the diet to see if yeast tolerance has developed.

Some sort of drug therapy is usually indicated. Nystatin has been the most commonly used antifungal medication. It has frequently been employed as the total treatment approach, but with only limited success. Nystatin antagonizes or competes with the *Candida*, and because it is not absorbed in the digestive tract, it is available to kill yeast cells. It has long been considered a safe and fairly effective drug and has been used in many products, including mouthwashes and diaper powder. Dr. Rosenberg at the University of Tennessee, together with Dr. Sydney Baker of Yale, found that *Candida* symptoms were relieved in remote body regions in patients treated with oral nystatin, even though that drug exerts a direct effect only on gastrointestinal yeast.

Dr. Luc Du Shepper, M.D., who has treated many candidiasis patients, points out that although symptoms are relieved by nystatin, this drug fails to kill all *Candida* cells, and so a patient who is helped initially soon hits a plateau in improvement. Moreover, nystatin, which is quite expensive, is a milk byproduct, and so it aggravates people with food sensitivities. He prefers to use caprylic acid or Fungizone (amphotericin B), both nontoxic, antiyeast acid medications. Fungizone has been used improperly in the United States, according to Dr. Shepper, since it is used only in the intravenous form. This produces many more side effects than can result from the oral form. Shepper also argues that it is applied in doses that are too small and over too short a period to be effective. Three to 4 g should be administered instead of the 1 g typically given, and over a period longer than the normal 2- to 3-month course. Shepper's major complaint is that it is used as an exclusive treatment without corresponding therapies to bolster and enhance the immune system. Physicians approaching the problem in this manner are guilty of treating only the symptoms and not the cause of candidiasis.

Dr. Crook suggests that antifungal medication such as nystatin be administered on a trial basis in order to properly diagnose *Candida*. If the patient responds positively, a yeast condition is indicated. He notes that Nizoral (ketoconazole) may be better than nystatin both diagnostically and therapeutically because it purges deep tissue yeast, whereas nystatin antagonizes only gut-level yeast. In addition, he suggests the use of nonprescription antifungal substances such as garlic, which may be the most potent, and Lactobaccilicus acidophilus, which may be bought in a concentrated powder form or obtained from yogurt. If you use yogurt as a *Candida* treatment, though, remember to have it without sugar or fruit, since these ingredients will enhance the condition you are trying to overcome.

The most basic and essential aspect of *Candida* treatment is repairing and bolstering the immune system. Remember that *Candida* begins as a defect in cellular immunity induced by an alteration in intestinal flora. This alteration in turn may be rooted in antibiotic activity or hormonal imbalance. In either case, an immune system dysfunction follows these alterations. The immune system must begin to function normally again before you can restore and rebalance the regular physiological processes. Dr. Shepper has treated thousands of *Candida* victims over the past 10 years, with an estimated 60 percent rate of marked and sustained improvement. He states that those who do not attain or sustain improvement have usually failed to maintain a lifestyle change that is immune-supportive. These changes involve first and foremost the drastic and permanent dietary modifications mentioned in this section. This may be somewhat difficult when the patient is fighting an addiction that may be deep-seated.

Staying completely off sugar and yeast products can cause severe withdrawal symptoms, but there is good news too. The relief of symptoms is very dramatic and encouraging, and it may begin just a few days into the program. Since the patient is not given many drugs, only an antifungal medication at the most, there will be little likelihood of experiencing side effects beyond those of the withdrawal itself. If you are truly determined to overcome the ravages of candidiasis, you will have to let go of your bad eating habits.

Dr. Crook offers some examples of people who have made the necessary lifestyle changes and have undergone the sort of treatment described here. He was seeing two patients in 1982 and 1983 who had multiple sclerosis. One was in such a bad state that he needed antifungal medication just to button his collar. Both patients had been told by traditional physicians that they would have to quit their jobs because their conditions could only worsen. Both were also put on antifungal medication and worked with the special type of diet outlined above; subsequently, they were relieved of most of their symptoms. Today both live relatively normal, symptom-free lives; one is still taking medication and maintaining his diet, and the other is simply maintaining the diet. When they returned to the medical center where they had been initially diagnosed, both were told that they were lucky to have had "spontaneous recoveries." There were no double-blind studies in the professional literature to support the treatment they received from Dr. Crook, they were told. Therefore, they should not think that it was responsible for their improvement.

In another case, a woman with deep muscle weakness could not function normally. She went for many tests at Vanderbilt University and elsewhere but was offered nothing but cortisone to manage her pain. When she came to Dr. Crook, she could not even walk. He diagnosed her *Candida* problem and put her on nystatin and the special diet; and she is now well and pain-free and is operating a gift shop.

A 2½-year-old child brought to Dr. Crook in 1982 had thrush and manifested aggressive, abusive behavior that had become intolerable. He had been on various antibiotics most of his life to combat a recurrent ear infection. Since he has been on oral nystatin and the *Candida* diet, he has had no physical or behavioral problems except when he breaks the rules and eats sugar.

Dr. Crook also tells about the 10-year-old daughter of a Mrs. Sandy Knabb, who was treated by Dr. Richard Bahr in Ohio. She had been using antibiotics for 150 days over a 1½ year period. She was in the hospital five times during that period and suffered from recurrent bladder infections, severe depression, and vaginitis. Dr. Bahr treated her with nystatin and dietary alterations. Her symptoms disappeared almost immediately.

Dr. Crook has treated hundreds of patients and other doctors have had equivalent results using similar treatment. It is a simple, nontoxic, economical, and amazingly efficacious way of handling a problem that could otherwise persist throughout a lifetime.

As research continues, we are learning more and more about the effects of environmental substances, foods, and synthetic chemicals on our bodies. We now know that from pregnancy and birth through our middle and older years, increasing numbers of individuals exhibit allergic reactions.

It has been reported that actions taken during infancy can reduce the chance of allergies occurring later in life ("Treating allergies early can reduce later toll," *Family Practice News*, November 15-30, 1990). For example, breast feeding seems to reduce the risk of allergies later in life. Moreover, if the mother is able to avoid foods to which she is allergic during pregnancy, this further enhances the chances of the child to be free of the allergies. On the other hand, infant exposure to inhalant allergens, smoke, infections, and baby formula in place of its mother's milk, may increase the risk of allergies.

Recurrent ear infections and constipation have both been related to milk allergy. In older children, symptoms as varied as hyperactivity and depression were associated with milk allergy. Individuals may also be allergic to certain substances contained in various types of health treatments. In the June 1991 issue of *Family Practice News*, evidence was provided that a number of people may be allergic to psyllium, a very common natural fiber used in many constipation treatments.

Exposure to car-exhaust fumes can increase allergic disease. In the June 1991 issue of *New Scientist*, researchers say that nitrogen dioxide from car exhaust damages the fine hairs (cillia) of the respiratory tree. When functioning normally, the cillia trap pollen spores beginning in the nostril. When the cillia are lost or damaged, the inhaled allergens pass deeper into the respiratory passages.

### What You Can Do

Most of the problems discussed in this chapter can have relatively simple and safe remedies once they are understood as essentially allergy-related and treated as such.

In the discussion of food allergies and environmental pollutants in this chapter it has been shown there are many things that irritate people. Everybody is affected differently by these allergens. What causes a runny nose in one person can be manifested as arthritis in another. Also, the allergens all come into play with and against one another. If you are allergic to mold, eating mushrooms may aggravate your condition, mold in the basement may make you react much more strongly to the mushrooms, consuming yeast products may make you more sensitive to the mold in the basement, and so forth. Moreover, all your problems with mold may eventually weaken your coping mechanism to the point where you develop allergic responses to other things—wheat or corn, your brand of toothpaste, or the new paint on the front door, for example.

Most important of all, allergic reactions, while they may cause the typical symptoms—stuffiness,headaches, depression, sneezing, wheezing, runny eyes and nose, postnasal drip, muscle aches, and the like—do not have strictly isolated effects. If they are permitted to continue, their effects will become increasingly systemic as the years go by. Whatever your individual weakness—respiratory or vascular, etc.—this will be the point at which your trouble will begin. From there, other organs and physiological processes can become involved. In short, allergies that go undetected or untreated may eventually lead to degenerative disease. It is far easier and less painful to tune in to the way your body is reacting to various foods and irritants now and correct the situation than to face full-blown debilitating diseases later.

# CHAPTER EIGHT

# Diabetes

**B**efore the development of insulin in the 1920s, diabetes had a bleak prognosis. Sufferers saw the condition rapidly go from bad to worse as complications such as blindness and gout mounted. Gangrene and the amputation of affected limbs were common, and the overall life span was drastically shortened. Insulin, a substance that when injected assists diabetics in the proper metabolization of sugar, appeared to be a miracle drug, and in fact it is. Diabetic children used to survive only 6 to 18 months, but the advent of insulin has added decades to their lives. Many childhood sufferers of diabetes now live long, normal, and productive lives because they can control their sugar metabolism with several daily insulin injections which they can learn to self-administer.

However, diabetes remains a prevalent and grave disease in the United States, responsible for at least a quarter of a million deaths a year. Most diabetics' lifestyles are still hampered by serious associated diseases and side effects, including heart disease, high blood pressure, and most diabetes-related deaths result from heart attacks.

Despite its severity, diabetes need not be as debilitating and severe as it used to be. The American Diabetic Association has been open to reviewing the latest research in the field, most of which indicates a need to move away from oral medications and insulin injections and toward general lifestyle changes mainly involving dietary modification and exercise.

Diabetes is more than just a malfunctioning of the pancreas that results in failure to produce enough insulin. Nutrition and allergies as well as genetics play a role in the disease process. There may be no cure for diabetes, but there are certainly ways of enhancing the body's natural defenses and resources to help diabetic patients lead a healthy life in spit of the condition.

This does not mean that insulin is no longer needed or that oral medications should be stopped. But insulin is not a panacea, and there has been too much reliance on it and too little emphasis on the patient's ability to take control of the diabetic situation with the powerful tools of diet and exercise. These tools are readily available to anyone who learns how to use them and confer the additional benefit of putting patients in charge of their health by natural means through a sound, basic, highly efficacious program of lifestyle modification.

### The Problem

If you were to discover suddenly that you are diabetic, you would probably be in for a lifetime of medications and possibly ever-increasing doses of insulin if you were cared for by a traditional physician. Some of these medications may be necessary for a while, and insulin may be an indispensable life-support measure, but avoiding these toxic and invasive treatments should be a major goal of therapy. You could drastically reduce your dependency on these things if you adopted a diet and lifestyle that would help undercut the causes of your illness. This is the nontoxic alternative approach to diabetic treatment offered by some physicians today. An exploration of this alternative begins with an understanding of what diabetes is.

Diabetes is basically a matter of faulty metabolism that involves the body's inability to assimilate sugar properly. More specifically, it may involve the failure of a portion of the pancreas to secrete enough insulin to metabolize *glucose*, the simple sugar molecule to which carbohydrates are ultimately reduced in the process of digestion. To be metabolized, the glucose must enter the bloodstream, at which point it is called blood sugar. It stays in the blood until reaching various *receptor sites*, or *docking sites*. Here the glucose is "loaded" into the body's cells, where it is necessary to provide vital energy and maintenance of normal physiological functioning. If these docks, or receptor sites, are not open, however, glucose cannot enter the cells. The body is then deprived of its critical energy supply, and the glucose stays in the blood and creates hyperglycemia, or a high blood sugar level. This "sugar" is what is diagnosed as diabetes.

How do these receptor sites get unlocked so that glucose can get into the cells? In the normal individual, the pancreas secretes insulin for just this purpose. Insulin accompanies glucose to the dock site and actually "unlocks" the cell so that it can receive the glucose. Several things may interfere with this process and create a diabetic state. The most obvious and most frequently cited interference is a deficiency syndrome. This happens when the pancreas fails to secrete, or does not secrete enough, insulin.

For many years it was thought that diabetes is purely and simply a deficiency syndrome in which the body does not produce the quantities of insulin required for proper glucose assimilation. More recently, researchers have discovered that many diabetics do produce enough insulin but that the receptor sites have become, according to Dr. Julian Whitaker, "plugged up by fat, cholesterol, inactivity, and obesity so that the [insulin doesn't] work and the blood sugar goes up." In these cases there is not a need to increase insulin production but a need to enhance "insulin sensitivity." The diabetic, in other words, needs to work at making his or her insulin more efficient, and simply increasing the amount of insulin will not do that.

A closely related concept is *insulin resistance*. In this case there is also a sufficient or even overabundant supply of insulin, but it is not doing its job; the lack of insulin sensitivity is due specifically to allergens—usually food allergens—that suppress the activity and efficiency of the insulin. Dr. William Philpott, M.D., developed this concept in the early 1970s after a decade of studies indicated that disordered carbohydrate metabolism can be traced to food allergies. It was also learned that specific foods rather than classes of foods can be linked directly to insulin resistance on an individual basis. Thus it is not a matter of finding which foods are insulin resisters and telling everyone to stay away from them. Doctors cannot, for example, tell you not to eat fats or proteins or not to eat peanut butter. Instead, it has to be determined what specifically creates a resistance in a person on a purely individual basis. Wheat, for instance, may create diabetic symptoms of high blood sugar in one person but not in the next. Dr. Philpott cites the research projects of Dr. John Potts to substantiate the concept of insulin resistance. Potts published his findings, including the discovery that "you can isolate the individual foods that cause the insulin resistance," in the *Journal of Diabetes*, the official journal of the American Diabetic Association.

To understand the significance of insulin resistance and insulin sensitivity versus simple insulin deficiency, it is necessary to understand the two different types of diabetes: juvenile, or childhood, diabetes and maturity-onset diabetes. *Juvenile diabetes* is usually considered a genetic disease, and it most commonly manifests in the childhood or teenage years. Also known as type 1 diabetes, it is characterized by a true insulin deficiency that apparently results when the pancreas is damaged by an exotic viral infection or a highly toxic state. Since juvenile diabetics have an insulin deficiency, they must receive regular insulin injections, usually for life. The type 1 diabetic, then, is what is called *insulin-dependent*.

*Maturity-onset diabetes* is more of an acquired disease. It may be precipitated by obesity, poor diet, lack of exercise, overconsumption of stressor foods or other allergens that are insulin resisters, or a combination of these and perhaps other factors. Known as type 2 diabetes, it is characterized by complications of insulin resistance and insulin sensitivity rather than true deficiency. For this reason, maturity-onset diabetics are called non–insulin–dependent.

### Insulin Therapy

For many years insulin was the universal treatment for all cases and types of diabetes. The higher the blood sugar rose, the more insulin the doctor would recommend. But it soon became clear that there was more to diabetes treatment than insulin injections. While insulin addresses the immediate crisis of lowering blood sugar levels, it does little to ameliorate the long-range problems associated with diabetes. In fact, many of these problems can be heightened by aggressive insulin therapy. Dr. Julian Whitaker, who has treated many diabetes patients over a number of years, explains:

"Insulin stimulates the development in the body of antagonists such as epinephrine, growth hormone, and other substances that counteract its blood-sugar-lowering effects. When you give a diabetic insulin, his or her blood sugar begins to fall. The body immediately responds to the falling levels of blood sugar by stimulating growth hormone and epinephrine to keep these levels elevated because the brain needs sugar."

The result of aggressive insulin therapy is a rebounding effect called the *Somogyi effect*. Blood sugar is high, and so insulin is injected. This makes the level plummet, but that drop cues the insulin antagonists to quickly pick it up again to meet what the body perceives as a life-threatening situation. This constant fluctuation of blood sugar levels leads to a wide range of long-term disorders. Two recent studies have shown that diabetics treated aggressively with insulin have a 40 percent greater incidence of eye problems than those treated moderately with insulin. However, it is still common for diabetics with worsening eye problems to be treated more and more aggressively with insulin.

Insulin may also contribute significantly to inner arterial wall damage, a major problem among diabetics. The incidence of heart attacks and strokes is five to eight times greater among diabetics. About 75 percent of all diabetic mortality is due to heart disease, which is brought on by the hardening of the major arteries that is so common among heavy insulin users.

Other complications which may involve insulin are related to damage done to the microvascular vessels, particularly those leading to the eyes, kidneys, and peripheral nerves, which become thickened and brittle. They become less and less functional as it becomes increasingly difficult for blood to pass through. In the eyes, sudden surges of blood sugar and/or physical exertion put extra stress on retinal blood vessels. If the stress is repeated, as it frequently is in diabetics whose blood sugar and hence insulin levels keep jumping up and down, the vessels may finally hemorrhage. This is the most common cause of blindness in older people after glaucoma, which itself can be diabetes-related. In the kidneys a similar succession of events results frequently in renal insufficiency and an inability to eliminate nitrogenous waste from the body efficiently. Kidney disease is a major and serious complication of diabetes. The interference with proper blood circulation involving both large and small vessels is also responsible for the high incidence of neuritis; gangrene, which frequently leads to amputation; peripheral tingling in the fingers and toes, commonly leading to loss of feeling; and sexual dysfunction.

Most of these complications occur after 10 to 20 years of repeated exposure to the fluctuating pattern of high blood sugar followed by insulin injections to bring it down while insulin antagonists coincidentally try to raise it again. This is not too bad when one considers that in the preinsulin days diabetes was generally a fatal disease.

The problem is that insulin has been grossly and indiscriminately overused, even though there are much more natural, noninvasive, and highly efficacious methods of holding diabetic symptoms in check. Type 2 maturity-onset diabetics are non–insulin-dependent and should not be treated with insulin programs as aggressive as those prescribed for type 1 juvenile diabetics, who are insulin-dependent.

Although about 90 percent of diabetics are type 2, they have been clumped together with type 1 diabetics as needing or at least being able to benefit from insulin treatment in cases where blood sugar remains consistently and/or dangerously high. Vast numbers of diabetics do not need to be on insulin at all but are. It is estimated that 50 percent of the diabetics being treated with insulin do not need it. Among those who may benefit from insulin, including juvenile diabetics, a great many could have their amounts of insulin significantly reduced if their treatment programs took into account a wider spectrum of approaches beyond simple programs of blood-sugar-level maintenance.

It is estimated that only 5 to 10 percent of diagnosed diabetics have the classic symptoms, which include (1) excessive urination, where the patient runs to the bathroom several times during the night or is troubled by bed-wetting on a fairly regular basis, (2) excessive thirst, because the fluid lost in urination has to be replaced, (3) excessive hunger, because the food taken in is not getting properly utilized, and (4) loss of weight despite increased food intake, because the glucose is not getting into the cellular sites of the liver, muscles, etc., and so the person is starving to death even as he or she is overeating.

The other 90 to 95 percent of diagnosed diabetics do not have any of these symptoms. Dr. Whitaker has treated about 2,000 patients with heart conditions. He is the director of a Nathan Pritikin Longevity Center and has a solid background in diabetes research and clinical treatment. He describes these other diabetics, who constitute the vast majority of all diagnosed diabetics:

"Generally, these patients are in their early forties, have been gaining weight and are about 10 to 15 pounds overweight, and go in for a routine physical examination in which the doctor finds that the blood sugar level instead of 110 mg/100 ml is now 190 to 220 mg and diagnoses diabetes. These patients are usually placed on some kind of oral hypoglycemic drug or insulin shots. So, for the majority of diabetics there are no symptoms. It is this type of diabetic who should not be given medications, should not get insulin injections, and should immediately be put on a low-fat diet and exercise regimen to correct the condition."

### The Alternative

Considering the fact that regular insulin use over an extended period of time can eventually lead to further complications, it is important to better understand and employ a wider spectrum of treatments, which includes a thorough understanding and application of food allergy and sensitivity analysis, dietary support, and exercise.

Before exploring these alternative approaches, though, it should be noted that insulin is not the only culprit in the traditional treatments that have been developed over the last half century. There is also a group of oral hypoglycemic agents, medications that stimulate the body to secrete more insulin and thus lower the blood sugar level. Some even act peripherally, that is, awaken and increase the number of sensitive receptor sites so that there are more locations for glucose to enter the cells. This peripheral action in effect makes insulin "go further"—extends its potential efficacy—than it could by merely increasing its presence in the bloodstream.

The oral agents referred to here and those which are of concern because of their potentially disastrous side effects include Orinase (tolbutamide), Diabinese (chlorpropanide), Dymelor (acetohexamide), and Tolinase (tolazamide). Specifically, Dr. Whitaker says, it has been found that "these drugs . . . increase the death rate in diabetics by 250 percent. . . . In pamphlets describing the oral antidiabetics there is a warning stating that 'these drugs have been associated with an increased death rate from heart disease.' " Thus diabetes, which is a risk factor for the incidence of heart disease, is treated with drugs that have been shown to drastically increase the likelihood of premature heart attacks. However, the correlation has been downplayed by the pharmaceutical companies that manufacture and market these drugs, and so physicians—not properly alerted to their dangers and sold on their benefits—continue to prescribe them and make them an integral part of diabetes control treatments. The pharmaceutical companies went so far as to discredit a very long-term study conducted between the mid-1960s and mid-1970s that showed conclusively that these drugs are extremely dangerous and highly lethal. In order to protect their enormous profits, these manufacturers have preferred to promote an excessive and inappropriate employment of the oral hypoglycemic agents.

You must, of course, always consult a physician about what medications or treatments are appropriate for you. It can be dangerous, for example, to stop taking medications that are necessary for your condition at any given moment. On the other hand, you should be concerned that the traditional treatment of diabetes has not gone far beyond the insulin and medication route over the last half century. But don't take matters into your own hands. Voice your concerns to your physician. Remind the doctor that the diabetic has a choice of treatment approaches to the disorder and that you would like to explore them. To help you do this, both the traditional and alternative routes are discussed in detail in this chapter.

### The Therapies

Physicians who practice alternative approaches to treating diabetes for the most part employ a program combining exercise and diet modification aimed at both better nutrition and weight loss (where this is indicated). This sort of program has been shown to have considerable success in lowering and stabilizing blood sugar levels in a very short period of time. It also reduces and frequently eliminates the various symptoms of diabetes. By displacing or cutting down the need for insulin and oral hypoglycemic agents, it can help diabetic

313

patients avoid many long-range side effects and debilitating complications.

## Traditional Therapies

Before describing alternative therapies in detail, this section briefly summarizes the traditional therapeutic approach to diabetes that has evolved over the last few decades. This includes first and foremost an emphasis on reducing high blood sugar levels by stimulating increase production of insulin and/or by supplementing the insulin supply with injections of animal-based insulin. The standard type of insulin employed is the regular, or short-acting, type. This unmodified substance remains effective for 4 to 6 hours. Taken before meals, it maintains the patient's required insulin level throughout the ensuing period of absorption of the glucose produced during digestive breakdown and carbohydrate assimilation. Intermediate-acting and long-acting types of modified insulin have been available since the 1930s but have never been widely used, since their action is mild during the earlier and later parts of the extended period that they cover while peaking somewhere near the middle. Long-acting insulin taken in the morning, for instance, will peak around 4 P.M., so that lunchtime and late night meals will not be affected sufficiently. This creates too much blood sugar fluctuation. The most appropriate use for this type of insulin seems to be when frequent injections of regular insulin are impractical or perhaps during sleep, when regular injections may be delayed for 8, 10, or 12 hours. In the last 10 years the overall emphasis has been on using the steadier, short-term insulin, especially in the early morning and after breakfast, when high blood sugar levels seem to cause the greatest trouble. At least two injections a day is the norm.

Although insulin has been at the center of traditional diabetes treatment, there has always been at least minimal attention paid to dietary modification. Unfortunately, the greater part of the dietary advice given has not been well founded and may have contributed to a worsening of the condition. Basically, the diabetic has been told to eliminate sugars and carbohydrates, and this encourages a diet composed essentially of high quantities of fat and moderate to high quantities of protein. Carbohydrates in particular have been banned because they break down eventually into glucose. No distinction is made between simple and complex carbohydrates, and there has been little discussion of the relative qualities of various carbohydrates, or of fats, proteins, or any other classes of foods for that matter. Fiber also has been denigrated because it has been closely associated with the carbohydrates and has itself been considered a carbohydrate, which it is not. There has certainly been no attempt to relate allergic responses to specific foods in individual cases to the diabetic malaise.

The results of the dietary advice given as well as the information that physicians, who usually know virtually nothing about nutrition, have been able to share have been disastrous.

Besides being put on insulin and oral medications, these patients are also told to stay away from fruit, vegetables, breads, complex carbohydrates, and fibrous foods in general. This advice only worsens their condition and is responsible for many side effects and complications. Although complex carbohydrates, like simple carbohydrates, are broken down into glucose, they do not go immediately and directly into the bloodstream as the monosaccharides, or simple sugars, do. They go through a long process of digestion and only very gradually release sugar into the blood. They do not, then, contribute to the high blood sugar levels as do simple carbohydrates. To warn diabetics to avoid all carbohydrates, regardless of the type and quality, deprives them of the very foods they need to stabilize and improve their situation.

Dr. James W. Anderson, professor of medicine and clinical nutrition at the University of Kentucky in Lexington and author of *Diabetes: A Practical New Guide to Healthy Living* (Warner Books, New York, 1983), believes that poor eating habits exacerbate the diabetic condition. He describes the diabetic response to different diets, using the case of Japanese diabetics who eat primarily high-carbohydrate, high-starch, high-fiber foods and eat very little fat. In contrast, American diabetics, with their prescribed low-carbohydrate, high-fat, high-protein diet, were found to have 100 times more gangrene, 8 times more heart attacks, and 4 times more strokes, all resulting from vascular disorders such as arteriosclerosis.

This is not surprising considering that by a high-fat diet one is talking about up to 200 g or about 1,800 calories on a daily basis. Since most of this comes from animal products—both meat and dairy—the diabetic patient can be getting up to eight times more cholesterol than the body would normally produce. Animal fats are high-density saturated fats inordinately high in cholesterol and are a major contributor to cardiovascular disease. When diabetics are told to stay away from potatoes, grain breads, and wholesome pancakes which have very little fat and cholesterol and to go instead with steak, eggs, and cheese, they are being told to jump out of the frying pan and into the fire.

A diabetic limiting carbohydrates to under 50 g a day, as a doctor employing a traditional line of treatment would recommend, has to get the bulk of nutrition from fats and protein. The fat accumulation in the blood will set this patient up for serious cardiovascular disease while clogging the receptor cells and preventing them from responding to and thus taking in insulin. The inevitable insulin resistance and insulin sensitivity will result in elevated blood sugar levels and probably lead the doctor to prescribe more insulin and oral hypoglycemic medications to normalize the blood sugar level. The diet will not be changed, though, because the traditional physician will overlook the fact that insulin resistance, as well as circulatory and heart problems, is enhanced by dietary fats, especially from meat and dairy products.

The large amounts of protein taken in on the standard diabetic diet also cause problems. Protein must be processed by the body; it cannot be stored. If the protein can be used, that is fine, because the body does need up to 50 g daily. But Americans eat over twice that amount, and for the diabetic this means accelerated kidney damage.

Protein that cannot be used must be passed through the kidney, and this puts great stress on the nephron cells, which filter the body's toxins. Diabetics who eat large amounts of protein along with excess fats may find themselves in a constant state of ketosis, leading to kidney damage and a possible buildup of uric acid leading to gout.

A study at Johns Hopkins tracked 17 patients with progressive kidney failure coupled with a degenerative disease such as diabetes. When these people were taken off meat and dairy products and had their intake of protein reduced, their kidney failures were reversed in eight cases. It is ironic that diabetics are taught so much about keeping sugar out of their diets and that the American·Diabetes Association has begun to change its dietary recommendations to include a lower fat intake among other things, but nobody talks about the problems associated with protein. However, excessive protein in the diet sets the diabetic up for significant kidney deterioration, and many diabetics must receive kidney dialysis or kidney transplants. Dr. Whitaker warns that diabetics should restrict their intake of animal protein and protein in general.

Another shortcoming in the traditional treatment of diabetes is the overlooking of the benefits and importance of exercise. Among other things, exercise heightens the body's sensitivity to insulin by lowering cholesterol and triglyceride levels in the blood, making the cells more available for glucose assimilation. This is why the insulin requirements of diabetic athletes always drop while they are engaged in swimming, soccer, boxing, or any other sport. The same athletes will also notice an increase in their insulin requirements when they cease their physical activities for an extended period. Exercise promotes optimum levels of hormone and enzyme functioning, and during activity, the diabetic can actually utilize his or her blood sugar without insulin. This is because the large muscle groups doing the work during physical exertion use serum glucose to fulfill their immediate needs for oxygen and energy.

Again, it must be emphasized that you should never make a

decision to go on or off of any medication, including insulin, without first consulting a physician. With the doctor's direction you may be able to reduce if not eliminate your insulin dependency, but this is not possible in all cases. Check first to see if and at what point in treatment this can be done in your case.

Athletes are not the only ones who benefit from exercise. Dr. Whitaker uses exercise as an integral part of his therapy with diabetic patients "by trying to get them through a program in which they actually exercise for 7 to 10 minutes after each meal. This generally means a brisk three-quarter-mile walk after each meal, which does wonders to reduce the amount of insulin necessary to keep the blood sugar level under control." Dr. Whitaker notes in addition that a proper exercise program used in conjunction with the right kind of a diet can actually make the body insulin-sensitive enough to hold serum glucose levels in check even in a pancreas-damaged patient who is working with only 20 percent of the amount of the insulin a normal pancreas produces. By ignoring the use of exercise in treating diabetes, the traditional physician would have to increase insulin injections to attain the same effects.

### Alternative Therapies

All the therapeutic mistreatments in traditional medicine are very costly to the diabetic patient in terms of poor control of the diabetes and do nothing to prevent further complications. In fact, such treatments all too frequently contribute materially to these complications. However, there are alternative treatments that address these critical issues and offer the diabetic programs to prevent and control the disease and its ancillary complications in a less invasive, more efficacious manner. These alternatives primarily employ diet and exercise in treating the diabetic, using insulin and medications only as second- and third-line approaches. While maturity-onset diabetics are the ones who will probably have the most dramatic results, even juvenile diabetics may be able to reduce their insulin dependency and, more important, alleviate many of the insidious complications that have come to be thought of as virtually a part of diabetes.

The person who is overweight, consumes large quantities of fat and protein but very few complex carbohydrates and little fiber, and lives a sedentary life is a prime candidate for maturity-onset diabetes. The first signs of this acquired disorder are usually bouts with acute serum glucose elevation, followed closely by hypoglycemia. The body rebounds from the dangerously high levels of blood sugar by throwing itself into a low-sugar, or hypoglycemic, state. The sugar is not properly metabolized in this case, possibly because of the presence of food allergens leading to insulin sensitivity or because of a poor-quality diet.

Such a diet can take many forms. Too much animal fat can render the body unable to utilize its available insulin efficiently. Too many simple carbohydrates can lead to a state of glycogenesis or lactogenesis, that is, overly high levels of sugar in the blood. Modest amounts of fat are needed by the body for proper physiological functioning, and a little sugar can be converted into *glycogen*, a storable form of sugar found in the muscles and liver. But a constant overloading of these things, coupled with lack of exercise, creates too great a demand on the pancreas to produce insulin, and a pattern of disinsulinism begins to take shape.

This is when acute high blood sugar develops because of too little insulin, followed by a counteracting hypoglycemic rebound. While a person may not be diagnosed diabetic in the classic sense at this stage, it is just a matter of time before that person will die. This, according to Dr. Philpott, is "the diabetes disease process not yet called clinically significant diabetes, but it is the same disease process. All you have to do is extend it far enough, chronically enough, until the blood sugar stays up overnight. Then you diagnose it as diabetes. Fortunately, many people never quite get to that final stage, but in the meantime they suffer from the consequences of a carbohydrate disorder and a host of associated symptoms."

For a person to avoid being pushed over the edge and joining the ranks of diagnosed maturity-onset diabetics, that person must begin to take more control over his or her diet and lifestyle. Understanding that hypoglycemia is a forerunner of diabetes in that improper sugar metabolism clearly exists, a person showing these symptoms should immediately adopt a diet with a high percentage (up to 75 percent) of complex carbohydrates and a low intake of simple sugars (no more than 50 g a day). As Dr. Anderson explains, the carbohydrates and fiber "smooth out the blood sugar excursions after meals and so help diabetes by dampening the up side of the blood sugar . . . and it also prevents hypoglycemia by eliminating the down side of the sugar."

Diagnosed diabetics might do well to follow a high-fiber, high-roughage diet like the one Dr. Anderson prescribes since fiber cleans out clogged blood vessels and assists insulin sensitivity. It is based on a high concentration—1,200 to 1,500 calories and 300 to 400 g daily—of complex carbohydrates coupled with reduced—no more than 2,500 g daily—fats. While the average American takes in no more than 20 g of fiber a day, Dr. Anderson recommends over three times that amount. He suggests eating foods such as whole-grain cereals, bran, vegetables, fruit, and a variety of beans. Grains, bran, and fruit are especially good sources of fiber, and oats and beans do an excellent job of reducing serum cholesterol.

Dr. Anderson has used this diet since 1974. He claims that he is able to get two-thirds of his patients off insulin and that they generally maintain this state. He also reports a 30 percent reduction in serum cholesterol levels since his diet replaces low-density lipoproteins with high-density lipoproteins, which can lower triglyceride levels.

In 1976, Dr. Anderson conducted a study of 13 diabetics who were on medication at the beginning of the research; 8 were on insulin, and the others were taking oral hypoglycemic medications. All the subjects were eating the standard American Diabetes Association diet consisting of high fat and protein intakes, with only a 45 percent carbohydrate intake. Dr. Anderson put them on a 75 percent carbohydrate diet with reduced fats for a 2-week period, and all of those using oral agents stopped them completely. In all, 70 percent of the patients were able to get off all medication simply by adopting the new dietary regimen.

While the dietary approach of Dr. Anderson may be news to diabetics who are accustomed to traditional care, it can be traced back to 1922. At that time a study was published in which a man who had refused to eat the recommended fat and protein diet offered as part of a diabetes management program was given an alternative diet by a researcher named Sampson. The diet consisted mainly of complex carbohydrates, mostly breads and cereals. The man showed a startling improvement, and it was determined that the carbohydrate diet was preferable to the fat and protein diet in the treatment of diabetes.

An English researcher named Hensworth came to the same conclusion in the 1930s. He determined that far from being a cause of diabetes, carbohydrates could ameliorate the degenerative disorder. Increased dietary carbohydrates heightened insulin sensitivity, rendering it more available in terms of net utilization to hold levels of blood sugar in check. In a series of studies Hensworth was able to show that the lower carbohydrate level and the higher level of fats, the more sensitive the insulin became and hence the more effective in controlling blood sugar levels. Hensworth did not seem to know why this was so, but through a trial and error approach to testing the effects of many different types of diets on the diabetic, he finally concluded that higher levels of complex carbohydrates increase one's glucose tolerance and thus should form the basis of a diabetic's diet.

Dr. Whitaker describes how his dietary approach, similar to most of the other alternative ones, is translated into a daily menu:

"Generally breakfast is the easiest meal to adapt to, and we try to serve hot oat cereal three to four times a week. Oat bran seems to be one of the more beneficial fibers. We use high-fiber cereals, preferably the hot ones; a little bit of nonfat milk, but not too much because we want to stay away from protein; fresh fruit; and some whole-grain toast with a nonsugar marmalade or fruit spread. Breakfast is relatively easy, and the one I have described is also one you should be eating while taking in substantial amounts of vitamins and minerals at the morning meal.

"For lunch, we try to emphasize some of the popular ethnic dishes so much a part of the American culture, such as Mexican, Chinese, and Italian. For lunch we prepare a tostada with non–lard-laden beans, piled with fruit, lettuce, and tomatoes. We thin the bean mixture with a small amount of olive oil or a small amount of walnut oil just for texture. Again, we have some fresh fruit.

"Between breakfast and lunch, we recommend that diabetics snack on the succulent fruits—peaches, pears, apples, and so forth—because these are high in fiber and extremely low in fat. They give diabetics more evenly absorbed fruit sugar because of the fiber intake. We also recommend this kind of snacking after lunch and dinner and between dinner and bedtime.

"We also have our diabetic patients exercise directly after each meal. If they have heart disease, we do not recommend exercise. Often in a heart patient or diabetic patient with heart disease, exercise after eating may precipitate an angina attack because of the transfer of blood from the intestine to the legs, etc. For a diabetic who does not suffer from heart disease, exercise after meals gets the body's metabolism working a little bit faster right at that time so that the absorption of food is more evenly distributed and the blood sugar tends not to go up as high. Exercise after breakfast is most important; it sets the stage for the rest of the day. The exercise need be only 7 to 10 minutes. Studies have shown that 7 to 10 minutes of exercise after a meal in a diabetic patient is a substantial improvement over being sedentary after eating.

"Dinner would be pasta, Chinese vegetables with brown rice, or something from the Mexicans emphasizing beans and grains. Italian dishes made with tomato sauce, olives, and some other vegetables are very popular here. After dinner and before bedtime we give a snack of some kind of fresh fruit. We also recommend that diabetics supplement their diets with additional fiber, and for breakfast we prepare oat bran muffins that are high in oat fiber, which seems to be one of the more beneficial fibers; again, we recommend succulent fruits.

"That about covers nutrition for the diabetic. We're heavy on beans and grains and low in fats and animal proteins. We get protein primarily from vegetable sources, and carbohydrate intake is about 65 to 70 percent of the calories as opposed to 40 or 45 percent of the calories in the normal American diet. Interspersed with succulent fruits as snacks, this is a pretty good diabetic program."

Another factor to consider in talking about diet and the types of foods that should be eaten is the sheer quantity of foods ingested. Diabetes is much more prevalent in times when and places where there are overabundant food supplies. This is why so many cases are seen in the United States, which is one of the wealthiest countries in history. In third-world countries where food supplies are scarce, diabetes is rare. It was similarly rare in earlier times, when only a small privileged class of nobles and aristocrats could afford to eat large quantities of food while the peasantry barely had enough to survive. In those times it was the nobles and aristocrats, not the peasants, who suffered from the little diabetes there was. While it is best to eat wholesome foods, total caloric intake must be controlled. This can be done in part by eating foods that are bulky and not concentrated. For instance, 4 ounces of high-bulk potatoes may have 65 calories, whereas 4 ounces of highly concentrated raisins have about 400 or 500 calories. Overweight is one of the most prominent risk factors for diabetes.

Dr. William Philpott, M.D., has been a prominent researcher of diabetes for many years. He has also had considerable clinical experience and currently practices in St. Petersburg, Florida. Dr. Philpott gives a great deal of attention to the individuals' food-specific allergic responses that create an insulin resistance factor that hinders the ability of insulin to do its job. He searches for these food distressors by monitoring the patient's blood sugar before and after the patient has consumed specific foods. Foods that cause a classical or even subclinical allergic reaction can be isolated and detected once they are found to cause a rise in blood sugar after consumption.

The RAST detects the presence of allergens. (See Chapter 7 for a full discussion of this subject.) If the RAST is given to detect the IgG antibodies, it will show up in the more common immediate reactors. But upon suspicion beyond this level, Dr. Philpott frequently requests a test for the IgE antibodies, which are the late reactors. In either case, the physician is usually looking for subclinical allergens, those which are not symptomatic in the most obvious ways—itching, swelling, congestion, and so forth. If an allergen showed these classical symptoms readily, it would probably have been noted and treated in isolation before the maturity-onset diabetes took shape. It is the insidious, subclinical types that deceive the patient and cause disinsulinism and other disorders over a period of time.

Dr. Philpott finds that dealing directly with weight and insulin deficiency is not as critical as addressing food sensitivities in most cases of diabetes. In a study conducted with maturity-onset diabetics, dietary modification, including detection and elimination of food allergies, resulted in two-thirds of the subjects being able to get off insulin completely. "The third who did continue on insulin," Dr. Philpott explains, "used only a third as much and were in good control. They all were immediately handled before they even lost weight. Weight was not the critical issue in terms of whether you could control the diabetic or not. We're not saying the weight is good for you. The patients all found it easy to lose weight because they weren't eating the food that they had such an addictive-type urge to eat. Actually, the balance of the diabetic state came under control before they lost the weight. What was most important was that the foods themselves were distressors, not just the weight."

Insulin resistance can be due to food allergy, addiction, or hypersensitivity, all of which are closely related. In any case, Dr. Philpott takes the distressor foods or chemicals away from the patient for about 5 days to see if insulin requirements are affected directly. At the same time, he carefully monitors pH levels. Diabetics tend to be acidic rather than alkaline. Fasting can throw them into a dangerous state of acidosis, which is why Dr. Philpott constantly works at maintaining a normal saliva and urine pH. An alkaline vitamin C is administered intravenously, and sodium bicarbonate is given as indicated while the diabetic is withdrawing from food addictions.

If the blood sugar is maintained at a normal level by the end of 5 days, the diabetic can get off and stay off the insulin that was never needed to begin with. Dr. Philpott finds this to be the case two-thirds of the time. The others must stay on the insulin but may be able—as even juvenile diabetics often are—to reduce this requirement. For those staying off insulin, Dr. Philpott describes his standard program:

"By the fifth day and on the sixth, we start our program and find the particular foods that make the blood sugar go high. Then, before the next meal 3 or 4 hours later, we check the blood sugar and make sure it has come down to normal, which we accept at 110 or 120.

"If it hasn't, we have the patient exercise until it comes down. Or we wait until it comes down, sometimes more than the 3 or 4 hours. But most of the time it comes down, and we then can go ahead to the next meal. There are three or four meals, usually four. They are single-food [meals], and a blood sugar test [follows] 1 hour after each [one]. There are a lot of things on the market, such as the little strips you can use to place a drop of blood from the end of your finger. There are even instruments for $400 or $500 to test your blood. In the office we have the more fancy equipment, but the patient does a lot of his or her own monitoring. The patient eats in the office and at home and monitors himself or herself.

"Just like any diabetic would check blood sugar, the patient gets very familiar with how to spot the foods that make blood sugar higher than it is supposed to be. The most vulnerable foods are wheat and wheat-related foods with the gluten. This includes rye, barley, oats, and buckwheat. Routinely, these diabetics react to those substances. One of my early patients was a mental patient who was delusional and depressed. He was diabetic and was on insulin. I decided I would go through the 5 days of avoidance and monitor his blood sugar and pH carefully, and in 5 days he was all right even without the insulin. When I got to wheat, his blood sugar was about 300 and he was delusional again. The doctor who placed him on his diet had him eat one half slice of whole wheat bread three times a day. That was it: it was centered around wheat. Both his mental illness and his diabetes were caused by wheat.

"We find that the gluten-bearing cereal grains are the worst for our mental patients—we see hallucinations, delusions, depression. Very frequently (and we find the same with diabetes whether it is the brain-reacting or pancreas-reacting) . . . these cereal grains [are the cause], and yet it is a good food. It must be rotated, once in four days, to be consumed with no problem. . . .

"Initially, if you do react, you should wait 12 weeks before introducing it into your diet. There is a 5 percent chance that you never should eat it, but there is a 95 percent chance that you can return it to your diet.

"Once we get our patients under control, strange as it may seem, they can eat sugar as long as they rotate it. The answer is the reaction to the substance, not whether it's a free carbohydrate at all. If you get the patients under control, you can put some sweets right into the rotation without any problem at all. It is not an issue of whether you may or may not eat sweets, it is a matter of eating them in such a way that you do not react to them in an allergic, addictive, or hypersensitive manner.

"Naturally, you cannot eat large amounts!"

## Monitoring and Preventing Diabetes

Diabetics and those who wish to prevent diabetes can do a great deal to monitor themselves. They need to look for the presence of antibodies that attack some part of the body to defend against an ingested allergen. This is easy to see if the symptoms are blatant, but not if they are subtle. The thing to look for is a general lowering of the body's immune response. The best way to see this is to go 5 days without eating the food (or any of its relatives) you wish to test. If you want to test milk, abstain from cheese, ice cream, and all other dairy items or processed foods that may contain milk as an ingredient. After 5 days, eat a meal consisting of just milk and eat generous amounts of it. Then tune in to your body's response. If you experience headaches, stomachaches, pulse rate changes, increased heartbeat or blood sugar, depression, lethargy, dizziness, or even delusions, you can see that your body has reacted negatively to this substance. In other words, you have an allergic response to it. You will have to back off from it. Leave it alone for 12 weeks initially. When it is reintroduced into the diet, it must be rotated with other foods. Eat it in modest amounts no more often than once every 4 days.

"Of course, there are a lot of good things about that 4-day basis," Dr. Philpott notes. "You will eat . . . 30 or 40 kinds of foods instead of the half dozen you've been eating. . . . This is a very wholesome thing. To have the necessary nutrition you will have a wide range of foods." It is a good idea to try introducing new foods into your diet, ones that you have never thought to have. Try to eat no foods more frequently than twice a week.

Dr. Philpott recommends that you invest in some diabetic equipment so that you can quantitatively monitor your blood sugar an hour after each meal. "At least 110 is optimum," he says, "and 160 or beyond is high blood sugar. Before the next meal, test your blood sugar again to make sure it is at least 120 before starting your next meal. If not, wait and exercise. Get it down before your next meal. Monitor your pH from saliva—it should be 6.4. If it is below 6.4, you are having a reaction to the food. Measure your pulse; if it varies drastically, you are reacting to the food. Blood pressure is more significant. Physical symptoms, mental symptoms, and blood sugar are the most important. They are absolutely essential. It will take about 30 days to do this."

Besides the detection of specific foods that must be included or avoided to optimize individual health, some general guidelines apply to everyone. Caffeine, beer, and tobacco should be avoided. Coffee is so stimulating that it is easy to mistake it as being uplifting, but the negative depressive reaction—although delayed—is profound and may last up to 3 or 4 hours.

Specific foods cannot be recommended on a general basis, because even the greatest, most wholesome, and most nutritious foods may elicit an allergic reaction in a given individual. This is why it is preferable to speak about classes of foods—complex carbohydrates, fiber, and so forth. It is possible to give good representative examples of these classes, but you must sort them out and test them on an individual basis and at different times.

There are specific dietary supplements that seem to be generally beneficial in the amelioration of diabetes and its complications. Vitamin $B_6$ is important, and at doses of 100 to 150 mg it can stop gestational diabetes, a temporary form of diabetes that sometimes appears during pregnancy and disappears afterwards. From 75 to 100 mg may be helpful for type 1 and type 2 diabetics. Chromium is an important part of the glucose tolerance factor. When chromium is deficient, insulin sensitivity is negatively affected. Chronically elevated blood sugar levels may then result even in the presence of insulin, and diabetes may begin or be enhanced. Dr. Whitaker puts all his patients on at least 400 mg of chromium a day. Diabetics are also low in magnesium, especially in cases that involve retinal complications. They may be given about 500 mg of this mineral to supplement their daily nutritional programs and initially may need additional magnesium injections two or three times a week. In addition to vitamin $B_6$, chromium, and magnesium, Dr. Whitaker says he generally gives his diabetic patients "2,000 mg of vitamin C, vitamin E, selenium, the rest of the B-complex, and manganese in small amounts, balancing these in a multiple formula. That's generally how we handle vitamin and mineral supplements for the diabetics; we try to maximize the micronutrition and to minimize any tendency to its reduction."

### Clinical Experiences

Dr. Julian Whitaker has worked with many diabetic patients as well as heart disease patients. He has had considerable success with diabetics, using a program that emphasizes diet, vitamin and mineral supplements, exercise, and practical education. He describes a 27-year-old patient who was taught to use these essential tools.

This young man returned to the United States from a winter trip to Rio de Janeiro with a blood sugar level of around 300. The condition had apparently been precipitated by a flu that he had gotten in South America. "He was on insulin," Dr. Whitaker recalls, "for about 6 months and was also having hypoglycemic reactions. When we saw him, he was taking only 10 to 12 units of insulin per day and his blood sugar levels were very low. Whenever you have a situation like this, you can cut down on the insulin and then eventually get off it completely. We measured in his blood a protein called C-peptide which measures the body's production of insulin. If his pancreas was not producing insulin, his C-peptide would be zero. This patient had a close to normal C-peptide, meaning that his pancreas was producing insulin. We put him on a program to sensitize his body to the lower levels of insulin his pancreas was producing. This included exercise, a low-fat diet, and vitamin and mineral supplements. . . . It has now been about 9 months, and he has been without insulin. His blood sugar level would go to about 140 or so after breakfast, but then he was told to exercise, and when he keeps up his program, his blood sugar levels stays under control. I think this indicates that you have a very powerful tool in diet, exercise, and minerals which is patently ignored by most physicians treating diabetes as they systematically utilize insulin and the oral drugs in their diabetic patients."

Another case of Dr. Whitaker's illustrates the shortcomings and even abuses of traditional diabetic treatment and at the same time provides an idea of how an alternative approach may be more appropriate and efficacious. It is also safer as the primary treatment itself and helps prevent later complications that are virtually inevitable if the traditional use of insulin and drugs alone is continued for 5, 10, or 20 years.

Dr. Whitaker describes a Denver businessman who had heard of his clinic and alternative therapeutic approach and decided to look into it: "Five years before I first saw this patient, he had had mild high blood pressure for which he was started on diuretics. He used hydrochlorothiazide, a thiazide diuretic. This drug has a tendency to lower potassium and elevate blood sugar, findings that are well known and listed in *The Physician's Desk Reference*, but it is still the most commonly used prescription medication worldwide. The patient's potassium level dropped, he developed some cardiac arrhythmias, his blood sugar level began to go up, and his problem was diagnosed as high blood pressure plus diabetes. He was placed on oral medications that failed to lower his blood sugar, so he was placed on insulin. When a patient like this gentleman, who did not have any diabetes to speak of but had a drug-induced form of diabetes, is placed on insulin, his blood sugar drops to a very low level. The body responds to this low level by generating glucose from the liver and shooting the blood glucose up very high so that when the highs and lows are checked, the physician feels the patient is out of control and increases his insulin level; this, of course, only increases the rebound, or the up and down characteristics, of the blood sugar. This is what happened. He not only was having much higher and much lower blood sugar levels, he was having one or two hypoglycemic attacks a day. He kept going back to the hospital with this problem, and when he arrived there, his blood sugar would be high so that they increased his insulin. He was taking 130 units of insulin daily and was also taking additional medications for cardiac arrhythmias and high blood pressure, which he didn't have, and 17 pills of prescription drugs daily.

"When we saw him, we realized that he had not had any dietary

advice at all. This, I think, is in some way systematic malpractice. . . .
We very rapidly took him off of all of his medications. . . . When we
instituted a low-fat, high-carbohydrate diet plus an exercise program
under close monitoring, we were able to test his blood sugars two to
three times a day. We cut his insulin in half in 2 days and then
eliminated it after another 2 days. For 9 days he went without insulin,
and his blood sugar never went back up again. We stopped the
diuretics and gave him additional potassium. His blood sugar never
went back up again, and he was able to lose some weight in the short
time he was with us. When we went home and continued the low-
fat, high-carbohydrate diet plus exercise, his weight continued to
drop; he lost, I think, an additional 20 pounds. Over this period of
time, he never required medications again. Here he had been treated
by two board-certified, highly specialized, highly respected physicians
in his community, who had been doing—and I went over his chart
very carefully—everything appropriately, according to standard methods of practice. In other words, it is currently acceptable that some
kind of drug is given for mild elevations of blood sugar. That practice
isn't even frowned upon. It's also currently acceptable to prescribe a
diuretic for mild blood pressure elevations, even though the diuretic
may cause problems down the line.

"Following these currently acceptable methods of therapy, the
patient was rapidly deteriorating not from any diseases he had but
from the treatments he was given. We were able to use diet and
exercise to cut through the requirement for medications, and he is
still, a year and a half later, not taking any medications. Now he's
quite a bit healthier. I think the diabetic patient is prone to excessive
drug use not only in the treatment of his initial condition but also in
the treatment of conditions associated with diabetes. But when you
use a diet-exercise program to cut through that, you can eliminate a
tremendous amount of prescription medication, as was done in this
patient."

Dr. Whitaker sometimes uses an initial fasting for a short time,

331

perhaps 3 or 4 days. He has found that this helps detoxify and "reset" the body before a new diet is begun. The fast, which may be partial or a complete water fast, is broken slowly with fruits and vegetables in small amounts until a regular and sufficient caloric intake is established. Dr. Whitaker says that Dr. John Davidson, chief of the Diabetic Department in Atlanta, has used this technique extensively at Grady Memorial Hospital and at Emery University Hospital, where he has treated about 15,000 diabetic patients. Dr. Whitaker relates the story of one of his patients whom he started off with a fast:

"[The patient] was from the Miami area and had been on 60 units of insulin for 13 years. When she was placed on insulin, she was about 40 pounds overweight, and over the 13 years on insulin she added another 20 pounds and so was 60 pounds overweight. She came in with her husband, and as they were sitting in the office I said, 'Well, I think we might be able to get you off of insulin on a special program.' Both she and her husband were horrified, because if you take shots of insulin for 13 years every day, your psychology is that you need it, and anyone who tells you that you may not need it after 13 years' experience taking the injections is going to be suspect. So I backpedaled diplomatically and told them that we were going to put her on a fast. I told her, 'You're overweight, you need to get rid of the calories, and we're just going to give you a little bit of fruit at meals, and we'll cut your calories down to 200 or 300 a day. I want you to force yourself to drink at least a quart to a quart and a half of water a day. When you're on this fast, we can't give you insulin because you're not eating anything that requires insulin.'

"Therefore, we kind of backed her into stopping the insulin injections. When we started—and she was on insulin initially—her blood sugar was around 225, which is what it had been running throughout the entire 13 years; it really never came down much even though she was taking insulin. Her blood sugar after 2 or 3 days of fasting without insulin was about 180 so that it had actually dropped. After 4 or 5 days, we started her eating again but did not give her insulin; as we gradually increased her calorie intake, her blood sugar didn't go up.

"She is now back in Florida, and it's been a year and a half since I put her on the program. I put her in touch with another physician who knew what we were doing at that time, and she is still not on insulin. She and her husband between them have lost 65 pounds over a 9-month period. He lost about 20 pounds, and she lost about 45 pounds; her blood sugar is now still running in the high 100s and low 200s after eating, which is what it was running with insulin. But as she continues to lose weight, that level will continue to come down. Thus her blood sugars are actually a little bit lower now than they were before we saw her, even though she was then on insulin.

"Secondly, the emotional and psychological benefit both she and her husband received from having this kind of program and the energy level increase they experienced made them extremely happy with the overall approach. They have more energy and are more active, neither of them needs the afternoon nap they used to require, they are much more productive, and she's not taking insulin but is still losing weight and is eating appropriately. This is a good example of how a short-term initiation with a fast can be extremely helpful."

Dr. Philpott has treated 200 to 300 diabetics. His treatment is based on the detection of insulin resistance factors in specific food and chemical allergies as they affect the individual patient's ability to utilize available insulin supplies efficiently. He describes what happened in his treatment of a 60-year-old man who was diagnosed type 2 maturity-onset diabetic:

"He was placed on an oral medication which he took twice a day. However, I saw him 11 years after that diagnosis at his present age. His fasting blood sugar was usually around 300. The doctors said, 'We are going to have to go to insulin.' He was very weak—just terribly fatigued and depressed, too. He had read my book *Victory over Diabetes*

(Keats, New Canaan, Connecticut, 1983), and wanted to give it a try before he went on insulin. When he came to me he was not on insulin yet, he was just ready to be put on insulin. I simply put him on foods that he just never would be addicted or allergic to and put him on intravenous vitamin C, B$_6$, calcium, and magnesium for about 4 days in a row. . . . On the sixth day, we started feeding him foods that he more commonly used. One of those foods was wheat, and within 1 hour his blood sugar was 270. At about 3 or 4 hours it had normalized and we were able to give him another meal. With rye, it was 275. On garbanzo beans it was 206, millet was 189, and even milk was 176. Oatmeal was 206. So we had at least a dozen foods that gave him high blood sugar. Actually the most important was the wheat which he ate religiously every day.

"We find the cereal grains containing gluten wheat and rye, oats, barley, buckwheat to be the most serious reactors. . . . Through the years, corn sugar and glucose have been used as the criteria for response, but we found much higher reaction to wheat. . . .

"As we studied him we grew a fungus from his mouth and from his stool and rectal area called *Candida albicans*. He also had rather high antibodies. . . . A lot of diabetics are made toxic by this organism.

"We spotted that and found that he was deficient in magnesium and folic acid. We found that he was using 400 mg of caffeine, by coffee, a day. This was an important factor that was helping to disorder his functions. Now knowing the foods he reacted to, leaving them out of the diet for at least 12 weeks while treating his infection and making his nutrition optimum, we were able to very quickly leave him with good energy, good control, and no high blood sugars at all anymore.

"Instead of going on insulin . . . here we have him strong with no high blood sugars at all and absent of infections. If we had just given him insulin and paid no attention to this fungus infection, he'd still be toxic. . . . If you monitor him from any standpoint you wish, this man doesn't have diabetes. That's the difference between the types of symptom management: just giving insulin to cover this insulin resistance that he had. We measured his insulin, and actually he had a normal amount of insulin.

"It was the same problem of insulin resistance that we see in these cases. Now . . . he knows that the disease process is not deteriorating him any more. The consequences of this deterioration are rapid spreading, depression, weakness, infection by fungi and viruses, and soon the whole degenerating disease process. Now we have him on a high-fiber diet . . . which will feed the right kind of bacteria. There will be good bowel function, moving the toxins out of the body, which is necessary.

"But this is a very small part of what you need to do. People should lose weight and should use this kind of diet, but there is something much more central to this disease process, which is the insulin resistance to the food and your ability to isolate which foods prevent your body from using insulin properly."

### What You Can Do

Drs. James Anderson, Ira Laufer, William Philpott, and Julian Whitaker are some of the physicians currently offering alternative approaches to diabetic care. There are many others throughout the country. What they all have in common is that they try to address the actual causes of diabetes rather than attempt to invasively overpower the symptoms, primarily fluctuations of the blood sugar level. It is up to the patient, along with the physician, to decide which of these therapies suits the patient's needs best or to determine if a traditional approach is preferred. It is clear that the juvenile or maturity-onset diabetic can do a great deal with exercise and diet modification alone to help the situation and reduce or even displace the insulin requirements. The prediabetic also can use these tools to prevent this degenerative disease before it gets started.

A very important aspect of dealing with your diabetes is to understand it in relation to the specific allergies which may exacerbate it. Chapter 7 can help you learn more about the foods and/or substances that should be avoided, thereby helping to ameliorate the condition or at least some of its symptoms. Eating properly and absorbing nutrients fully are helpful to the diabetic. These topics are covered in Chapter 9.

As the number of people suffering from diabetes increases worldwide, we need to grasp with greater clarity what may be causing this disease and the possible ways it can be treated. Balanced nutrition can be a factor. In "Impact of insulin treatment and hypomagnesemia on glycemic control an blood pressure in hypertensive non Insulin dependent diabetes mellitus patients" (*Journal of the American College of Nutrition* 9(5):538, 1990), J. Sheehan suggests that low magnesium levels in the blood increase insulin resistance and cause elevation of blood pressure. Normalizing serum magnesium can improve both the blood pressure and the ability to control blood sugar. And in an article by Dr. J. W. Anderson that appeared in the August 1990 issue of *Postgraduate Medicine* (188(2): 157-168, 1990), entitled "High fiber diet for diabetes: safe and effective treatment," it is argued that a diet high in complex carbohydrates and fiber can help to decrease fasting blood sugar. Lipid concentrations, along with insulin release, can also show a marked reduction. With 35 grams of dietary fiber per 1,000 kilocalories, type 2 diabetics can show a 75 to 100 percent improvement in glycemic control and reduction in insulin requirements.

In the *British Medical Journal*, authors Tuomilehto and Jaakko correlate coffee and caffeine consumption with early triggering of insulin dependent diabetes in an article entitled, "Coffee consumption as a trigger for insulin dependent diabetes mellitus in childhood" (300:642-643, March 10, 1990). Other important diet considerations include chromium and fish oil supplementation. As reported in the March 1990 issue of *Modern Medicine* (58(3):37 March 1990), chromium enhances insulin's effectiveness. And in the March 1990 issue of *Diabetes*, authors Landgraf-Leurs and Martina describe reduced vascular risk factors in diabetics who add fish oil to their diet. It is known that elevations of sugar levels over a long period will damage nerves, tissues, and blood vessels. Many diabetics have recurrent ulcers and circulatory compromise as the disease progresses. Dietary considerations, such as the inclusion of fish oils, may significantly help these problems.

# CHAPTER NINE

# Eating Right to Prevent Digestive Disorders

In examining alternative approaches to digestive disorders, one must realize that there are no special clinics where research and treatment focus exclusively on these disorders and that there are no particular pioneers in the field of digestion. One reason for this is that digestive disorders are not often clearly diagnosed as such. Usually a determination is made that a patient has cancer, arthritis, or renal failure, but these conditions may be directly related to chronic digestive disorders that have gone undetected for a long time. While you may be undergoing extensive, costly, and toxic treatment for a diagnosed disease, it is possible that only the symptoms of your disease are being treated, not the underlying cause.

It is up to you to be aware of the great effect that digestion has on your total health. If you suffer from a disease you must—with the help of a physician who is knowledgeable in this area—determine how maladies related to digestion can cause a variety of disorders ranging from constipation to colon cancer. In fact, virtually every disease can be ameliorated to some extent by taking appropriate steps to correct digestive problems.

However, since few specialists truly understand the complexities of digestive disorders, you should use the information in this chapter to find the sort of health care you need if you suffer from a disease that may be related to poor digestion and nutrient absorption. Even if you do not suffer from any ailment, read this chapter carefully to make yourself aware of what causes and what alleviates digestive disorders.

Many people go through life with chronic digestive problems—fatigue, nausea, and flatulence, for instance—and assume that this is a normal state of affairs. Any complications that result are rarely understood as being connected to the underlying problem with the digestive mechanism. Disturbances that obviously do have something to do with digestion—diarrhea, constipation, and the like are usually dealt with by taking over-the-counter drugs such as laxatives and antacids. You may think that you have a "weak" stomach or that these problems are just "a part of getting older," and so you may end up taking these drugs habitually, unaware that they can exacerbate the problem.

Having read this chapter, you will be in a position to take positive steps toward rectifying any slight imbalances you may have detected on your own or toward preventing these disorders from occurring in the first place. Proper digestion is primarily a *lifestyle* choice: You can use your understanding of this physiological process to take control of your own health and well-being.

### How to Eat

Nearly half of all illnesses in the United States begin in the intestinal tract. Digestive disorders represent a virtual epidemic in this country today and are at the root of many of the most serious diseases, including heart disease and various types of cancer.

The avoidance of digestive abuse and the repair of damage resulting from digestive maladies can often be undertaken by the individual. In fact, a significant proportion of all digestive disorders are overlooked by traditional physicians either because the patient unwittingly fails to report subtle but insidious and progressive symptoms or because the doctor lacks the skill and knowledge to diagnose or treat such disorders until they have become so blatant that they require very aggressive therapies.

Much pain and traumatic, invasive medical-surgical treatment can be avoided by the individual who understands the digestive system and has some insight into what its proper function is. The malfunction of any digestive part hinders, imbalances, and eventually causes disease in the entire system and may, of course, affect the entire body. Since in this case the whole is only as healthy as its parts, it is important to investigate the various parts.

The digestive system is composed of intricately interconnected parts which set into motion the incredibly complicated process of digestion. Every time you put food into your mouth, you unleash a nearly infinite number of clockworklike reactions and interactions. Although it is possible to track and understand this process to some extent, many aspects remain a mystery. Digestion and absorption of nutrients occur harmoniously and simultaneously. The precise nature of this interaction must be reckoned with to gain proper insight into the nature of digestive disorders.

### The Structure of the Digestive System

The digestive system begins with the mouth and runs some 30 feet to the anus. It is essentially a long, hollow canal that mechanically chops, grinds, and transports food mass while chemically breaking it down into molecules fit for absorption into the blood and cells. The teeth and various internal muscular systems provide the mechanical action; the pancreas and liver are the major contributors of the digestive juices necessary for chemical processing.

All foods are broken down into four elements. Three of them—carbon, hydrogen, and oxygen—are derived from foods containing fats and carbohydrates; the fourth—nitrogen—is obtained from foods containing protein. These four units are metabolized through different body tissues and are made available for the body maintenance and physiological functioning at the cellular level.

Chewing constitutes the first stage of digestion. The way you masticate food is critical to the sort of nutritional benefit you will receive from the food you ingest. If you do not chew slowly to break down food thoroughly, the saliva secreted in your mouth will not mix sufficiently with the food. Improper chewing also leaves food in chunks that are too large to pass easily through the esophagus and into the stomach for the next stage of digestion.

When food reaches the stomach improperly broken down, it will create an excess secretion of digestive enzyme. Extra stomach acids such as hydrochloric acid (HCl) must be produced to break down oversized food particles. This means subjecting the inner wall linings of the stomach and intestinal tract to a higher and more sustained acid level. Over the long term, this can be quite damaging since digestive acids are extremely corrosive, can aggravate ulcers, and may cause heartburn and indigestion. Most important, it upsets the digestive process and internal chemical balance, leaving you susceptible to virtually every disease state.

Another problem is that when food is not broken down into small enough bits, it can enter the bloodstream as oversized particles. These particles cannot be utilized at the cellular level, and so they are carried along until they eventually pass out through the kidneys. But during their prolonged stay in the blood they are likely to elicit an immune response through the activation of antibodies that do not recognize them as being compatible with the body's needs. Improper chewing thus can lead to heightened levels of stomach acid and overstimulation of the allergic response.

Fluids do not require chewing, but they have a significant impact on the digestive process. Drinking large amounts of fluids while you eat can create another problem. Fluids dilute both saliva and digestive acids, interfering with their ability to break down food. To make matters worse, drinking while eating encourages gulping down food chunks that you would otherwise have to chew more thoroughly. You may tend to do this if you are in a hurry or if you are impatient with the chewing required by certain foods. "Washing food down" with liquids not only hampers digestion, it is also dangerous. It makes it too easy to get large chunks of food stuck into the throat, and so "choking down" food may lead to just that—choking.

### The Right Foods

In selecting food, make sure to choose foods which facilitate digestion and thereby work with your body and not against it. These include (1) foods that do not cause allergic reactions or sensitivities, (2) wholesome and natural foods instead of processed, chemically altered, or denatured foods, and (3) foods that contain bulk and have a low density or no fat content. Basically this means that you will be selecting many more complex carbohydrates—potatoes, rice, and vegetables—rather than fats and proteins along with mostly nonanimal products, in order to avoid heavy concentrations of fat and protein.

Among prepared foods, get those which are as close as possible to the natural state. Frozen peas, for instance, are much closer to the natural, raw state than peas that have been boiled and canned. Avoid irradiated produce; while it does not spoil as quickly as raw produce, its essential chemical structure has been so altered that it is hardly the same food anymore.

Produce often is doused with pesticides and chemicals or is dirty. Some has been waxed. Wash these foods thoroughly or even peel them. Better yet, don't buy them unless they have been organically grown, that is, grown without pesticides and potentially poisonous chemical fertilizers. You don't need to load your body with any more chemical pollutants than it gets from everyday living in today's society. No amount of washing and scrubbing will completely rid tainted foods of waxes and chemicals. It will cost more money for food of this quality, but consider the money spent a contribution to your health. Eating right means eating to enhance your vitality. Ingesting pesticide-ridden and waxed produce is not much better than eating processed items filled with chemical preservatives, artificial colorings and flavorings, and other additives.

In preparing selected foods, try to maximize their digestibility without altering their essential integrity and cellular structure, since these things are critical to facilitating digestion and keeping the colon and upper gastrointestinal track clear of food mass and toxic buildup and backup. For instance, plant foods with a lot of cellulose (the cellular structure of plants) need to be softened for easier digestion so that the benefits received from the cellulose can be optimized. Celery can be soaked; cauliflower, carrots, and even sprouts can be steamed; and beans and corn can be mashed.

Take care not to overcook so that a food loses too much of the fibrous structure which aids in digestion nor is deprived of too much of its nutritional benefits in the form of its vitamin and mineral contents. Steaming is generally preferable to boiling, boiling in 1 inch of water may be better than boiling in 6 inches, and boiling for 5 minutes is usually preferable to boiling for 20 minutes.

Stress is another integral part of the digestive process. Don't eat when you are tense, upset, or in a hurry. Wait until you have re-laxed. If you come home from work and are worried about something that happened at the office of if you are upset because a friend is sick, take some time to get your emotions in order before you eat. Otherwise you will not digest your food properly. The digestive mechanism is interrupted by stress, and if you are nervous or anxious or hurried, you may not chew your food well to begin with. Digestive enzymes are not properly secreted because your stressful condition has affected normal enzyme production, and you will get little benefit from the meal. If you make a habit of eating on the run or eating while under stress, you are setting yourself up for chronic digestive problems.

If you select, prepare, and masticate your food properly, you have pretty much done the best possible job. After the food is swallowed, the digestive system for the most part takes over.

343

## The Process of Digestion

Many different chemicals and chemical processes are involved in digestion. The most important substance in saliva is protein, including many free-state proteins and amino acids. Besides digesting starch, saliva keeps the mucous membranes of the mouth moist, and its constant flow helps keep teeth and gums clean and free of food particles. Without adequate salivation, you will have dryness of the mouth, bacterial overgrowth, a buildup of food particles and dead cells, and a loss of the ability to taste, leading to appetite loss.

Enzymes are complex organic compounds, usually proteins, that are task-specific; that is, they work in a specific manner on particular foods. Enzymes that catalyze reactions leading to the breakdown of carbohydrates, for instance, have no effect on fat or protein digestion. Complementary sets of enzymes ensure that the cells get sufficient amounts of the specific foods on which they act.

Carbohydrate digestion is the most important in relation to the energy requirements of the body. Plants, grains, legumes, vegetables, fruits, nuts, and seeds—all carbohydrates—offer the greatest source of energy for proper physiological functioning.

All carbohydrates are broken down into one type of sugar or another. In fact, carbohydrates are composed purely of sugars, and they are classified according to how many glucose or sugar units are present in each molecule. Glucose, which produces most of the complex sugars, is the main form of carbohydrate that goes into the bloodstream and enters the cells in the presence of insulin. It plays a critical role in normal brain function and is the chief source of energy for the nervous system.

Carbohydrates may contain either complex of simple sugars. Glucose and fructose are monosaccharides, or single-unit, simple sugars. Starch is a polysaccharide, or complex sugar. Some carbohydrates are indigestible and merely pass through the digestive system to be excreted with other waste products in their original unaltered state. These are the fibers, and even though they are not digested, their action while passing through the digestive system is extremely important. They stimulate *peristalsis*—the wavelike alternating contractions that move food and waste through the digestion and elimination systems. They further enhance the elimination of toxic wastes by absorbing excess water and joining with other residue to create bulk matter which passes more readily out of the system. Fiber, then, while indigestible and containing no nutrients, plays a major role in digestion through its stimulating, cleansing, and detoxifying action.

The carbohydrates that are digestible go through various processes. The simple sugars can enter the blood system almost immediately upon ingestion, even before they are swallowed. The multiple-unit sugars are partially digested in the mouth by salivary enzymes. They are moved along until they reach the stomach, from where they are passed into the large intestine. This is where the greatest amount of carbohydrate digestion takes place. The sugars are broken down into glucose in the small intestine and are finally ready to pass into the blood in that form. Once in the blood, they are absorbed into the cells and used as a form of energy for the brain and the nervous system.

Different classes of foods are digested differently. For example, proteins are far more complicated than carbohydrates, and they vary greatly in their function. All proteins are made up of chains of *amino acids*, the so-called building blocks of life, which make up part of every living cell in the body; they can be enzymes, hormones, or antibodies.

While there is a great deal that is not known about protein digestion, it is known that proteins are far more difficult to digest than carbohydrates. In order to be reduced, proteins must have their bonding *peptide linkages* broken down by the gastric juices.

Some peptides are more difficult to reduce than others. Those with a lot of fat surrounding them, such as those in meat, are difficult to digest, but not nearly as difficult as deep-fried or charcoal-broiled foods, which form strongly bound molecules that are extremely difficult to separate. When proteins that are hard to digest (e.g., meats) are made even more resistant (e.g., by deep frying), they remain undigested longer. In trying to digest them, the body continues to produce gastric juices so highly acidic that if not properly buffered, they can eat a hole (a penetrating ulcer) through the stomach lining.

Digesting proteins is obviously quite different from digesting carbohydrates. Of course, both proteins and carbohydrates provide the body with essential nutrients, and both are sources of energy. There is a substantial difference in the kinds of energy they produce. It is often thought that proteins are synonymous with high energy, and for that reason hypoglycemics (people with low blood sugar and therefore low energy levels) are frequently fed high-protein diets. But if one looks at the way these two types of foods are digested, one sees that a high-protein diet is not what the hypoglycemic needs.

If a hypoglycemic feels weak because of low blood sugar and eats a piece of fruit, 30 or 40 minutes later the fruit is digested and glucose enters that person's bloodstream to restore energy. If the hypoglycemic person eats a lean steak instead, he or she will have to wait 6 hours for the meat to leave the stomach. It will take even longer for the amino acids derived from the meat to be translated into usable energy. The protein meal will feel satisfying because of its saturated high-density fat, which is very slow to digest and therefore delays the hunger mechanism for a long time. In comparison, a carbohydrate meal—fruits, vegetables, pastas, etc.—will pass through all the stages of digestion quickly, and the person may be hungry again an hour later. But carbohydrates deliver the required energy rapidly and efficiently, while protein not only takes longer in getting energy into the cells but even saps energy in the process in order to keep the gastric juices flowing and the whole digestive system working overtime to break down the complex, high-calorie piece of beef.

### Some Digestive Disorders and Their Treatment

Traditional physicians are more used to treating symptoms than correcting the causes of disease. For this reason, one of the most common problems in digestion—because it is a cause rather than a symptom—is one that is rarely considered in traditional medical practice. This is the malabsorption syndrome, or the failure of the body to absorb the nutrients that have been ingested, a failure often related to a digestive lapse. The problem here is that even though a food is eaten and goes through the whole digestive system, the nutrients, minerals, and vitamins frequently do not get into the blood and hence do not penetrate the body at the cellular level. Instead, the undigestible elements are eliminated as waste by-products.

## Dr. Martin Feldman's Innovative Approach

Martin Feldman, M.D., a traditionally trained physician, combines standard medical practice with effective alternative treatments geared toward nutritional therapy. With emphasis on his own concept of soothing, replacing, and repairing faulty digestive mechanisms, Dr. Feldman is a true innovator among alternative physicians.

A former assistant clinical professor of neurology at Mt. Sinai Medical School, Dr. Feldman now practices general medicine, treating a wide variety of conditions including allergy, low immunity, skin problems, arthritis, diabetes, hormonal imbalances, headaches, and other brain-related symptoms such as poor memory, poor circulation, irritability, and sleep disturbances.

Over many years of practice, Dr. Feldman has found that a surprisingly large number of disorders have their source in digestive problems. Rather than taking the traditional approach of waiting for symptoms to develop into full-blown disease states, Dr. Feldman strongly believes in treating sluggish or suboptimal conditions *before* they develop any further. By identifying and treating digestive system disorders when they first begin, he believes that a large number of degenerative diseases may be avoided.

Many of Dr. Feldman's patients have been dissatisfied with standard methods of treatment. They often report that side effects of standard drugs were bothersome and did not correct their condition.

"Through years of observation, I have learned from my patients," explains Dr. Feldman, "and I have found that when more sophisticated methods of testing are used it turns out that inefficient digestion or malabsorption is frequently present and leads to a variety of other problems." He estimates that at least one-third of the patients seeking his help have digestive difficulties. He has found this to be particularly so in regard do to people with osteoarthritis, gum disease, skin problems, anemia, and hypoglycemia. In response to his patients' needs, Dr. Feldman has worked out various nutritionally oriented therapies which have proven successful in the treatment of many of these disorders.

With his focus on early detection and treatment of disorders, Dr. Feldman looks for subtle warning signs that the digestive system is operating sluggishly or suboptimally, even to a small degree. Many of the signs he considers significant might be of minor interest to the traditional physician who tends to focus upon fully developed disease states.

Dr. Feldman sees himself as a *complementary* physician, whose techniques and philosophical approach to health differ significantly from many traditional physicians. As he describes it, "You use the best of traditional medical science, but you complement it with more natural approaches, many involving nutritional substances." A clear understanding of the differences between the traditional and the complementary approaches to medicine is essential for a true appreciation of the innovations in Dr. Feldman's practice.

### "The Traditional Approach"

Traditionally trained physicians are very skilled at identifying and treating conditions when they have reached a severe disease state. They are less likely to search out or treat an underactivity, sluggishness, or suboptimal function. Even when such conditions are detected, they are often not considered significant.

The standard therapies for digestive problems include medications such as Tagamet, Zantac or Pepcid for stomach problems or Azulfidine or prednisone for inflammations of the colon. Although these medications may give relief, they tend to suppress the symptoms but do not repair the unhealthy body.

Additional problems may arise from the fact that many traditional physicians are also specialists and tend to be compartmentalized, focusing only on their own area of specialization. For example, they may not make a connection between various diseases and improper digestion. Specialists will tend not to integrate the fact that a joint problem may be related to a digestive problem, because they are looking only for the condition in which they specialize. The typical patient suffering from these two connected problems will end up going to a joint specialist for the first disorder and to a gastroenterologist for the other, and it is likely that the two specialists will remain separate. A connection between the two disorders may never be made.

Finally, traditional medicine generally gives limited attention to diet. For instance, a gastroenterologist will usually consider the role of food only when (1) it is obviously connected to a disease, such as with lactose intolerance, or (2) patients report a direct connection between eating a specific food and a symptom (e.g., when they eat a tomato they get diarrhea). As Dr. Feldman observes, "In this country, the level of suspicion regarding food as irritants is not that high throughout the medical community"

### Dr Feldman's Complementary Medicine

While Dr. Feldman considers himself to be a complementary physician, his approach is unique. Due to differences in philosophy, interests, and experience, each complementary physician develops his or her own concepts and techniques. So although he shares their dedication to the use of alternative methods of diagnosis and treatment, Dr. Feldman, as we will see, has also developed his own individual approach.

How does Dr. Feldman define complementary physicians? In his view, one of their most important characteristics is that they look beyond the disease endstage of severe breakdown of function toward suboptimal or sluggish beginning problems. Rather than wait until a disorder has developed into a full-blown disease state, complementary physicians will tend to identify and treat an organ or a gland that may have only slightly reduced efficiency or function. Their emphasis is on prevention and early detection and treatment, which is significantly different from the traditional approach.

Complementary physicians may also use *special machines* that are not in wide use by traditional physicians, even though these machines are of the highest scientific standards. For example, a complementary physician may use a Heidelberg gastrogram for analysis of stomach acid to verify an opinion regarding stomach acid. Although this machine was scientifically devised at the University of Heidelberg, it has relatively few followers in the American medical community.

Complementary physicians often analyze the body biochemistry via sophisticated blood laboratory testing beyond the usual SMA-24 profile by obtaining blood levels of vitamin and mineral components.

Dr. Feldman may even test beyond the biochemical, by utilizing *electrical* profiles, which comprise an even more sensitive method of determining body function and allow him to test the digestive system in detail. By testing acupuncture meridian-level status, a profile is determined of each part of the digestive apparatus.

Complementary physicians tend to treat via natural substances such as foods or homeopathic preparations. Also, supplements which contain concentrated forms of vitamins and minerals are fundamental elements of body rebalancing.

Complementary physicians tend to be attuned to the concept of mild malabsorption since they frequently see the end product of this condition, namely, deficiencies of nutrients. Thus, they are more likely to focus upon this possibility.

Complementary physicians tend to view body functions in a holistic manner so that they are attuned to the relationship between digestion and vitamin and/or mineral deficiencies related to malfunction of such conditions as arthritis, anemia, and disturbances of the glucose mechanism. For example, Dr. Feldman notes, "The great majority of the people I see with osteoarthritis have a typical profile of deficiencies: low calcium, low magnesium, low vitamin A, low vitamin D, and often low copper. They also frequently have low stomach acid and food allergies." Effective treatment involves dealing with *all* of these problems, which the complementary physician recognizes and practices. Finally, complementary physicians are very interested in the foods eaten, the frequency, the quantity, and whether any specific foods seem to cause irritation or other reactions. Thus they tend to test for food sensitivity as part of a complete analysis of body function.

### How Digestive Problems Occur

The digestive process consists of four main steps, which involve: (1) hydrochloric acid in the stomach; (2) pancreatic enzymes, as food is entering the duodenum; (3) bile, from the liver and gallbladder; and (4) the absorptive processes in the small intestine. If any of the organs involved in digestion are faulty in any way, the efficiency of the absorptive process can diminish and the body will not be receiving the nutrients it needs.

Most digestive problems involve a suboptimal performance by any one or combination of the following four components: the stomach, the pancreas, the bile, and the small intestine. This can occur as follows:

1. *Insufficient or suboptimal production of stomach acid.* This condition, which is not an illness but a sluggish stomach, is the single most common digestive problem, especially in those over the age of 40. In the presence of low stomach acid, food digestion in the stomach is impaired and thus protein and minerals are not digested efficiently. Many persons with this condition of insufficient acid suffer with burping and belching after meals.

As people age, their physical energy tends to weaken, which can

351

affect basic body functions. Because it takes a great deal of energy to make stomach acid, a very strong chemical substance, suboptimal stomach acid production tends to be a common problem as we grow older.

2. *Problems with the pancreas and its digestive enzyme production*. The pancreas is a gland which produces pancreatic enzymes for digesting protein, carbohydrates, and fats. After the stomach does its part, it empties its contents into the duodenum, the first part of the small intestine; this partially digested food, called chyme, is a thick, acidic liquid and the pancreas must first neutralize this acidity and make it alkaline before digestion can proceed further.

Therefore, the first juices from the pancreas are alkalinizing juices to offset the stomach acid. If these pancreatic enzymes are suboptimal or insufficient, or if the interplay between the release of chyme from the stomach (about one teaspoon at a time) and the production of pancreatic enzymes is off balance, difficulties will result. Very often, when a patient complains of digestive problems from two to three hours after eating, the pancreas is the culprit. Many of these problems, which involve carbohydrate and/or protein and/or fat digestion, are a result of faulty pancreatic function. Sluggishness of the pancreas is the second most common digestive disorder seen by Dr. Feldman.

3. *Problems with bile*. The liver produces bile, which is stored in the gallbladder and sent into the small intestine through the bile duct. This alkaline fluid is partly responsible for fat absorption by emulsifying or breaking down fats into smaller particles.

4. *Problems in the small intestine*. When the chyme is released from the stomach into the small intestine, the pancreas produces and releases large quantities of alkaline pancreatic enzymes, which are the next phase of digestion and which also protect the duodenum from the acidic chyme. The digested food then moves further down the small intestine into the jejunum, where food absorption takes place. The nutrients are then carried through the bloodstream to various parts of the body to provide energy and maintain general health.

### Trouble with the Ileocecal Valve

One of the main problems that can take place in this region involves the *ileocecal valve*, which is located between the small and large intestines. Dr. Feldman has found that diarrhea and constipation are often associated with malfunctions of this valve. It is the valve's job to open when the contents of the small intestine are ready to pass through, to let a certain amount through and then to close. However, if the valve stays open too long, or is too tight or closed, problems can occur.

*The open valve*: If the ileocecal valve remains in the open position, it can enhance diarrhea, because everything is flushing through too quickly. Food passes through the digestive apparatus so rapidly that the absorptive process is impaired. In addition to the rapid transit due to the open valve, the movement of food progressing in the normal forward direction may reverse, as the contents of the colon backflush, or move retrograde. The colon is the "garbage disposal" area, whereas the small intestine is the "kitchen" absorptive area. When the waste material back flushes into the small intestine, it may be absorbed into the bloodstream, causing various toxic reactions.

*The closed valve*: If the ileocecal valve is too tight or too *closed*, this can cause constipation. The tight valve, by not facilitating the passage of the small intestine contents into the colon, retards the entire digestive flow, which leads to infrequent bowel movements, or constipation.

Unfortunately, most people are unaware of this valve and its importance in the regulation of proper digestion.

### Symptoms of Digestive Disorders and Related Health Problems

Digestive system disorders can be placed in two main categories: (1) those that are clearly and directly related to digestion and (2) those that are ultimately digestion-related in origin but are a step or two removed from the digestive process, and therefore more difficult to connect with digestion.

Symptoms of digestive system disorders in the first category are more easily recognized.

The most common include burping, belching, flatulence (intestinal gas), a feeling of indigestion, undigested food in the stool or a feeling of food "just sitting there." When such symptoms are present, it is relatively easy to connect the problem to some malfunction in the digestive process.

But other symptoms are not so quickly connected to digestion. These are problems that occur over time and are related to the long-term inefficiency of absorption of nutrients and/or an insufficiency of nutrients in the food to begin with, both of which can lead to deficiencies. Because such problems are not directly connected to digestive difficulties, hardly anyone realizes that they have anything to do with digestion. Such disorders include:

- *Gum problems*: Many problems with receding gums, bleeding gums, and periodontal gum disease have a lot to do with a deficiency of calcium and other nutrients, including vitamin E, GLA (gamma-linolenic acid), bioflavonoids and vitamin C. When he sees these conditions, Dr. Feldman considers the amount of calcium in the diet and also the stomach acid production, because suboptimal production of stomach acid can lead to malabsorption of minerals, especially calcium and iron.
- *Anemias*: Many cases of anemia can be linked to low stomach acid levels, because iron is not absorbed efficiently. Other factors can include blood loss, heavy menstrual cycles, and low iron in the diet.
- *Osteoporosis*: This disease, so common in elderly women, results from a deficiency of calcium and many other minerals, which can be accentuated by digestive malfunctions resulting in malabsorption of calcium.
- *Osteoarthritis*: Insufficient stomach acid production can lead to lack of proper absorption of dietary calcium. Eventually, this results in a deficiency of calcium, where osteoarthritis is a major

component of a long-term deficiency of calcium in the body due to malabsorption, leading to breakdown of the joints.

- *Skin disorders*: Poorly nourished skin is another common result of malabsorption due to digestive problems. The skin may show minor symptoms, such as blemishes, dryness, scaling or a tendency toward irritation. These are often due to dietary deficiencies and/or poor absorption of calcium, zinc, vitamins A and E, and essential fatty acids.
- *Hypoglycemia*: Also called "low blood sugar," this condition is related to nutritional deficiencies, including low zinc, chromium, and manganese, which are associated with uneven levels of glucose in the blood.

### Digestive Mechanism Disorders

In addition to the ailments related to long-term malabsorption, there may also be illnesses of the digestive apparatus. These include:

- *Gastritis*: This condition is an irritation of the stomach, very much like an "internal sunburn," which can cause some of the discomfort of indigestion in the stomach. Some people with gastritis (type B) harbor a bacteria called *helicobacter pylori*. This bacteria is unique in its ability to live in the acid environment of the stomach, where it is able to create a protective coating. Many people with gastritis also have problems with absorption of vitamin B12 and may develop macrocytic anemia as a result.
- *Gastric ulcers*: Up to 70 percent of those with gastric ulcers (of the stomach) have helicobacter pylori in their systems.
- *Duodenal ulcers*: These are severe irritations of the small intestine. Some studies show that up to 90 percent of people with duodenal ulcers also have helicobacter pylori present.

### Diagnosis

As Dr. Feldman explains, malabsorption or the tendency toward even minor malabsorption involves one or more of these four components: (1) production of stomach acid, (2) production of pancreatic

355

enzymes, (3) production of bile juices, and (4) absorption itself that takes place in the mid and lower small intestine. By discovering the precise status of these components, he can then begin to correct or rebalance the specific weak component or components.

Dr. Feldman makes full use of standard medical procedures and tests, including a complete medical history and comprehensive blood laboratory analyses. In addition, he also uses a noninvasive technique, based on acupuncture pressure points, to test the strength of various internal organs and mechanisms.

### Acupuncture as a Diagnostic Technique

One of the most interesting and innovative aspects of Dr. Feldman's approach is his use of acupuncture meridians for diagnosis.

As he explains it, "Acupuncture theory has taught us that there are many energy flows throughout the body. The energy flow is quite specific along anatomical pathways. These pathways were very well worked out for centuries in China. Traditional acupuncture intervenes by inserting needles into special acupuncture points to either improve the flow of electrical energy through that flow channel or meridian, or to reduce the flow. Whereas acupuncture electrical information and its electrical pathways is mainly used as a therapy to rebalance either over- or under-energy flow, the under or deficient electrical flow often reelects an organ weakness. Thus, the liver with an entire acupuncture meridian can be tested by measuring the over or under electrical activity in its meridian. Although acupuncture is thought of almost exclusively as a therapeutic modality, it has equal value as a diagnostic tool."

Because he uses acupuncture theory only for diagnosis and not for treatment, Dr. Feldman has no need for needles. Instead, he has developed his own method of using these meridians to profile the component parts of the digestive apparatus and pinpoint areas that are under active or sub optimal in strength. In this way, he can determine the energy flow or lack of flow and thus assess the body's function.

As he describes it, "Without needles, without any invasion of the body, we can profile the liver's energy, the stomach's energy, the pancreas's energy, the small intestine's energy and the colon's energy. We can see which areas are the weakest, where imbalances are occurring and where the problems are most severe." And all this can be accomplished in minutes.

### Gastroenterology Studies

Once these areas of weakness are identified, Dr. Feldman can then focus on them using other modalities, if needed. At times, the diagnostic input of a gastroenterologist might be required when a specific anatomical or physical determination is needed. The gastroenterologist would decide upon the technical study or studies required, which might include the use of x-rays or visualization with tubes, such as a gastroscope or a colonoscope, allowing the specialist to look directly at the stomach or the colon.

### A New View of Blood Lab Tests

Standard laboratory tests can also yield important data if viewed in a complementary fashion. The tests that are readily available and inexpensive are the SMA-24 blood tests, the complete blood count with differential, the sedimentation rate, an analysis of the urine, and measures of long-term glucose levels and thyroid levels.

Once Dr. Feldman has laboratory results, he can then look for such indicators as elevated levels of various enzymes. For example, the SGOT, an enzyme found in liver cells, can double or triple in the presence of hepatitis. Traditional physicians will generally look for such extremely elevated levels and tend to disregard slightly elevated levels. Dr. Feldman, however, considers that *even a small increase* in the level of this enzyme can indicate that the liver, while not diseased, is off balance and in need of attention. As he explains, "I'm looking for the early evaluation of an imbalanced or a suboptimal liver, not a very diseased liver."

Lab tests can also disclose blood indicators of malabsorption, such as:

(1) the presence of *macrocytic anemia*, an enlarged red blood cell anemia that is associated with vitamin B12 deficiency;

(2) the level of *ferritin*, one of the forms of iron stored in the body, which if relatively low is an early indicator of a low metabolism of iron;

(3) the level of *total protein* in the blood, which when relatively low (especially if there is adequate dietary protein) can indicate malabsorption of protein; and

(4) low body levels of *minerals* such as calcium, magnesium, zinc, manganese, chromium, and selenium, which are very common with malabsorption. Deficiencies of *fat soluble vitamins* such as vitamins A, D and E are also common. The *water soluble vitamins*, including B complex and C, are generally less affected because they are more easily absorbed.

### Infections of the Digestive System

Helicobacter pylori antibody levels in the blood, which may reflect the presence of these bacteria, provide an important clue to duodenal or gastric ulcers. Tests for these bacteria are performed by specialty laboratories.

Parasites, which Dr. Feldman notes "are becoming more and more widespread in the population," are another cause of digestive problems. Traditional testing methods involve taking random stools and looking at them under a microscope to try to find cysts or other parts of the parasites. Now, however, there are more sophisticated methods of finding parasites, including special stains and, more importantly, monoclonal antibodies, which will attach even to small fragments of the parasite or its cysts. The attached antibodies are visualized under the microscope. Thus, these sensitive tests disclose the traces of the parasites, so that it is no longer necessary to literally find the parasites themselves. Giardia, parasites that primarily inhabit the duodenum and upper small intestine, which previously were very difficult to diagnose via their visualization, are now detectable by this test. Also, sophisticated analysis of the stool, with culture of bacteria and other organisms, yields important information regarding the ecology of the flora of the colon.

### Treatment

Once he has identified the areas of weakness of the digestive apparatus, Dr. Feldman can begin to formulate a plan to soothe, replace, repair, and rebuild faulty mechanisms. The treatment chosen depends on diagnostic findings, including (1) the areas of dysfunction—stomach acid, pancreas enzymes, bile, small intestine; (2) whether irritation is present, and where; and (3) whether any pathogens are present, such as parasites or unfriendly, harmful bacteria. To correct any of these problems, Dr. Feldman's treatment relies heavily on natural substances, including vitamins, minerals, herbs, and occasional homeopathic preparations.

The first step in this process is to soothe any parts of the digestive system that are irritated, whether the stomach, the small intestine, or the colon. Various herbal-type preparations, such as marshmallow, slippery elm, and aloe vera may be used for this purpose.

Next, it is important to replace whatever is insufficient or sub optimal. When deficiencies of stomach acid are determined, oral acid tablets may be prescribed in order to optimize the stomach acid phase of digestion. For problems with low production of pancreatic enzymes, oral analogues of pancreas enzymes may be swallowed after the meal to augment this phase of digestion.

### Dr. Feldman's Emphasis on Repair

The most crucial step in Dr. Feldman's treatment is repair. The concept of *repair of suboptimal function* is not a high priority of the American model of medical treatment.

Traditional physicians might consider the use of oral medicine to replace pancreatic enzymes. The main therapies related to the stomach are Tagamet, Zantac, and similar pharmaceuticals which suppress the production of stomach acid. The focus of concern is heavily weighted toward ulcers or other anatomical maladies.

Although the pharmaceuticals that control stomach acid have their place, many natural substances are available that work toward repairing the digestive apparatus. For example, stomach repair might include cabbage juice, licorice preparations, and nutrients including zinc and vitamin A.

### Food Allergy and Digestion

Foods to which a person is allergic or sensitive are considered as invaders or chemicals by the body's immune system. Thus, they irritate and weaken the digestive apparatus. Because of this, it is vital that the patient be educated in terms of diet and food allergies. This is a rather complicated procedure, given our present-day American diets.

For instance, it is quite common to find that persons consume large amounts of foods to which they are, in fact, allergic. Many of our food products contain hidden ingredients that must be recognized and avoided. For example, many products contain corn syrup for sweetening and persons sensitive to corn should avoid them. Wheat is another common allergen that is often hidden in our foods. Thus, learning how to read food labels in this way and choosing food correctly is a critical part of treatment.

### Results of Treating Digestive Problems

Dr. Feldman identifies the most prevalent problem with the digestive system as *mild malabsorption*. "It affects the most people, causing the most trouble, and the vast majority of people don't even know about it." Manifesting itself in gas, indigestion, or stools with undigested food, it is not a true disease in the classical mode.

But whether it is only a slight tendency (off by 10 or 20 percent) or more advanced, malabsorption of food can lead to a multitude of health problems if left untreated, including osteoporosis, gum problems, anemia, osteoarthritis, and skin disorders. This occurs because our bodies are not processing food properly and/or the nutrients we require are not present in the food we are eating. Thus, essential nutrients are not available to the body, which goes into a short supply or a deficiency state. Remember that digestion is designed to break down our food into essential substances that the body absorbs and uses for energy, growth and repair. The importance of its proper function cannot be overemphasized. Dr. Feldman's focus on preventive medicine, the importance of optimal digestion of nutrients, and the necessity for identifying and treating even seemingly minor problems before they develop, separate him from many traditional physicians. By utilizing his unique approach, Dr. Feldman attempts to repair faulty digestion in its very early stages. In this way, many health problems can be mitigated or avoided altogether.

Although the percentage of good results with these natural approaches is quite high, there are occasions when the patient does not respond appropriately. It is in these instances that the diagnostic process must be intensified by consulting with a skilled gastroenterologist, who adds anatomical visualization of the digestive system via those technical studies deemed appropriate.

## A Singular Way to Restore Natural Health

While he has much in common with other physicians practicing complementary medicine, Dr. Feldman has concentrated on the concept of *soothing, replacing, and repairing*. Minimizing the use of traditional drugs, Dr. Feldman has taken an empirical approach to medicine, observing his patients over many years and formulating his therapy, with reliance on natural substances, by finding out what actually works. It cannot be emphasized too strongly that he believes in repairing the body and restoring it to its healthy function.

## Allergies

Food allergies and sensitivities are a major source of digestive trouble. They may be hereditary but may also result from cerebral or gastrointestinal reactions or sensitivities to ingested substances. Wheat, for instance, very commonly incites a cerebral allergy, and a large proportion of the population suffers from gastrointestinal allergies to milk. These kinds of food allergies are responsible for such symptoms as headaches, fatigue, rapid mood swings, heart palpitation, diarrhea, constipation, and shortness of breath. Besides milk and wheat, other common food allergens are corn, eggs, beef, citrus fruits, potatoes, and tomatoes.

Digestive malfunctioning can be the cause of complications when allergens are present. If there is a deficiency of the gastric juices or pancreatic enzymes, for instance, a food will be in the system for a much longer time than it would if there were adequate amounts of acids and enzymes to break it down readily and on schedule. If the food sitting in the system is one to which the body is sensitive, that sensitivity will be heightened by the delayed action of the digestive mechanism. Furthermore, if protein molecules are not broken down into small enough particles because of faulty digestive processes, the larger units entering the bloodstream will be treated like foreign invaders by the body's immune system, and an allergic reaction will ensue.

Children possess less developed gastrointestinal systems than adults, and so they often suffer from obvious food allergies. Later in life, though, as the digestive system becomes more sophisticated, these allergies are manifested in less obvious ways. Even if the symptoms are not the same, the underlying allergy may be. A child who has suffered milk-associated asthma, for instance, may have severe acne as a teenager. The milk allergy is still there, but its symptoms have moved to a different organ system, often misleading the patient and physician into thinking that the original allergy has been outgrown.

Allergies often manifest as disease forms. If a person responds negatively to a food substance so that heart palpitations or gastric distress results, that person may seek and receive treatment from a cardiologist or gastroenterologist. The patient may ultimately be subjected to invasive and taxing drug and/or surgical treatments that have side effects far more debilitating than the original food allergy.

The whole topic of food allergies is the subject of Chapter 7. Refer to it to determine what you can do to avoid or overcome these problems.

High-protein diets pose a special problem with respect to food allergies. People who consume a lot of protein usually tend to have it in their systems around the clock. This is because it takes at least 4 to 7 hours for proteins to be digested, and if the protein is fried, deep-fried, or charcoal-broiled, it can take even longer. If a person starts the day with bacon and eggs and then has a sandwich of cold cuts and cheese at lunch, more meat and maybe milk at dinner, and even a late night snack of milk or ice cream or pizza, that person will have protein in his or her system all the time.

If any substance—in this case, protein—sits in a person's system virtually all the time, two things will occur. First, the person will almost certainly develop an allergy to it because of overexposure. Second, the person will probably not be aware of the allergy because his or her system will never be without the substance long enough for him or her to notice its ill effects when he or she ingests it versus the clearing of those symptoms while he or she is without it. The negative symptoms then become cumulative and chronic and begin to be manifested as disease states. Digestion is usually strained, and the different disorders that appear are generally regarded as signs of poor health, which becomes tolerated as unavoidable or is attributed to genetics or age.

Food rotation is one way to help alleviate this problem or to treat it at home as an adjunct to whatever medical care you are receiving. Don't eat the same foods day after day, because no matter how healthy and nutritious they are, you will not benefit from them if your body rejects or reacts negatively to them. Wheat, for example, is an excellent food, but because it is found in practically every processed food, it is also a very common allergen. Therefore, it must be rotated in the diet with other grains. Eat it no more frequently than every fourth day and in no more than a 4-ounce portion at each meal. Then there is a good chance it can be eaten without causing an allergic reaction.

All foods should be rotated in this manner. Even if your body is not responding negatively in an overt way, you may be having hidden reactions to many different foods. Even if you are not, by overusing a food—eating it too frequently and in oversized portions—you may eventually develop an allergy to it. Try to make a routine of rotating all foods and avoid eating processed foods as much as possible because certain foods, such as corn and wheat, are ingredients in many of them.

### Lactose Intolerance

Lactose intolerance is an almost universal digestive disorder. Probably two-thirds of the world's adults cannot tolerate lactose, which is found in milk and all milk products. This substance is very poorly absorbed in the digestive systems of most adults, with the notable exception of Scandinavians and other northern Europeans. When lactose-sensitive people continue to eat dairy products, they begin to suffer from a wide range of symptoms, which include abdominal cramping and bloating, chronic nasal discharge or post nasal drip, puffiness under the eyes, gas, and diarrhea.

Lactose intolerance is a malabsorption of lactose caused by a deficiency of *lactase*, the enzyme responsible for milk digestion. Lactase breaks down lactose into the readily digestable forms *glucose* and *galactose*. If it is absent or deficient, lactose remains undigested in the system. Some passes through the blood and is excreted in the urine, but most ends up in the large intestine. The lactose molecules draw water out of the tissues and into the intestinal cavity, while the undigested glucose is fermented by intestinal bacteria. Carbon dioxide is given off during this process, and diarrhea, bloating flatulence (gas), and belching may result.

The lactase deficiency can be caused by damage to the intestinal mucosa; this damage may be brought on by acute infectious diarrhea in infants. Malnutrition, cystic fibrosis, and colitis also have been known to cause lactase deficiency. Even in the absence of these traumas, lactase deficiency is very common. The most obvious remedy for lactose intolerance is to stay away from milk and all milk products. Also, keep in mind that lactose is found in many vitamins and most processed foods, and so it is best to avoid processed foods and request from vitamin manufacturers a full disclosure of their exact ingredients. It is important to eliminate lactose from the system completely in order to recover from its ravages. Another option may be to purchase a commercially prepared lactase supplement which boosts your supply of lactase and enables you to better digest the lactose. Some lactase-deficient people, however, can still eat a few fermented milk and dairy products without negative consequences. These items—primarily yogurt, buttermilk, and cottage cheese—must be tested on an individual basis to determine one's reaction to them (see Chapter 7 on allergy testing).

### Gastritis

Gastritis, another very common digestive disorder, involves an inflammation of the mucosa lining the inner wall of the stomach. The inflammation is accompanied by such symptoms as nausea, vomiting, and loss of appetite. In the acute form, gastritis can be caused by infections and/or the ingestion of corrosive agents such as alcohol and aspirin. In the chronic form, gastritis is a serious condition which may be the cornerstone of degenerative diseases such as ulcers. The treatment for gastritis should include the elimination of any substance (an allergen or anything else that is difficult to digest—fried foods, etc.)

known to be causing or aggravating the condition. The diet should include lots of liquids and small amounts of soft foods such as soft-boiled eggs and oatmeal. Vegetables should be steamed to maximize their digestibility and reduce their acidity. A blood chemistry test should be performed to determine what (if any) vitamin deficiencies exist, since they often play an important role in this disorder. Vitamin defciency related to gastritis is responsible for many complications, among which are a prickly sensation in the skin, loss of memory, depression, and general weakness.

### Pressure Diseases

Another group of disorders associated with the digestive system have been termed pressure diseases, because they are caused by a pressure buildup that results from failure to eliminate waste efficiently. They include conditions as diverse as constipation, hiatus hernias, varicose veins, cancer of the colon, diverticulitis, hemorrhoids, and appendicitis.

Diverticular disease is the most troublesome and widespread of these conditions. It occurs when the muscle rings encircling the colon, which move along bulk matter, become clogged. Try clenching your fist and then imagine that mud is stuck in the creases of your hand. The creases can he thought of as diverticula, and the mud in them is the result of food being trapped in the creases of the digestive organs. When bulk and fiber are lacking in the diet, the colon must deal with a mass of food too dry to be pushed along with ease, and so it becomes overworked, overstressed, and overstrained. Its membranes eventually herniate, or rupture, and it is these ruptures that are called diverticula. When there are many diverticula—and there can be hundreds—they tend to become inflamed and cause more acute symptoms. This condition is known as *diverticulitis*. Approximately one in four people with diverticular disease develop these acute symptoms.

Diverticulitis barely existed before the twentieth century, but now is said to affect one-third of all adults middle-aged or older, half the population over 50, and two-thirds of the population over 80. It is the most common digestive disorder of senior citizens.

Research on the genesis and development of diverticular disease has shown that it results from a gross lack of fiber in the diet. The refining of carbohydrates seems to be the main culprit here, since this condition is almost wholly absent in cultures where whole grains, legumes, vegetables, and starches are the mainstays of the diet and where processed foods are not used. Diverticular disease is also limited mostly to the wealthy nations of the west and is rarely seen in underdeveloped areas. In India and Iran, the disease is seen only in the upper classes, whose dietary regimens are not unlike those of the industrial working classes in the west.

The traditional treatment for diverticular disease has been to give the patient stool softeners to help the stool pass through the system and expanders to force it out. Given for about 2 weeks, these agents are typically administered along with antibiotics. Until recently, doctors also put these patients on low-residue, soft food diets. Since it has been shown that this sort of diet exacerbates the condition, the diet has been replaced with a fibrous diet that helps the colon begin processing waste more efficiently and with less strain. Bran is usually prescribed, and patients are often told to avoid milk products and spicy foods since these tend to produce abdominal pain, pressure, and gas.

Alternative treatments for diverticular disease may include the above suggestions but will add to the patient's diet other abdominal and intestinal cleansers taken orally. These include cellulose, hemicellulose, pectin, and noncarbohydrate lignin. Celery, cabbage, brussel sprouts, broccoli, and especially beet juice will also help the condition. Bran should be unprocessed because this type has a shorter intestinal transit time and helps increase stool weight. The diverticula pockets may be cleansed with dietary supplements of chlorophyll, chamomile, garlic, vitamin C, zinc, nondairy acidophilus, pectin, and psyllium. Instead of medicinal antibiotics, good amounts of garlic may be used since garlic is a natural antibiotic.

*Hemorrhoids,* closely associated with constipation, are another pressure disease. Constantly straining to push dry, compacted stools out of the system causes the veins in the rectal and anal passages to become distended and engorged with blood. The veins become weakened, lose their elasticity, and can no longer carry blood properly; they allow the blood to pool instead, creating a ballooning effect.

When the hemorrhoids are internal, they can become obstructive to stool passage. With constant pressure being exerted against them, they may rupture and bleed and, in severe cases, hemorrhage. External hemorrhoids, also called piles, are very sensitive and may grow to the size of golf balls.

It is estimated that half of all Americans over 50 have hemorrhoids and that hemorrhoidal treatment is a $50 million a year industry. Most of the profit comes from sales of suppositories. Suppositories are given to shrink and lubricate hemorrhoids to prevent them from rupturing. Alternative treatments for hemorrhoids center on hygiene, diet, and exercise. If you increase your intake of water, vitamin C, and fiber and exercise regularly, the blood trapped in the hemorrhoidal veins will be reabsorbed into the body and the problem will be cleared up. However, it will recur unless you integrate these changes into a new, more healthful lifestyle.

*Hiatus hernia* is another condition related to constipation and low-fiber dietary regimens. Like the other pressure diseases, it is essentially a modern-day western disorder affecting primarily middle-aged and older people. There are no warning symptoms until it causes a sharp pain just below the breastbone. Caused by the body's straining to evacuate stool, it is a condition in which part of the stomach wall becomes extended and pushes up against the diaphragm and the skeletal system. Obesity may contribute to the condition, which also sometimes develops during pregnancy.

The traditional treatment of hiatus hernia usually includes antacids, a bland diet, and sometimes surgery. These steps are adequate to relieve the pain, and you certainly should follow the suggestions of your physician. The alternative (or even complementary) approach is aimed at going beyond alleviation of the painful symptoms by establishing a dietary regimen that can reverse the condition while ameliorating the source of discomfort. Since constipation due to a low-fiber diet is frequently the cause of this condition, make sure to get plenty of high-fiber bulk foods. In the case of the obese, losing weight may also help. Before resorting to surgery, you may want to explore other alternatives, such as the treatment by Dr. Nathaniel Boyd in New Hope, Pennsylvania, in which a saline agent is injected into the stomach-lining tissue, causing it to tighten and retract from the diaphragm.

Another pressure disease, *appendicitis*, is caused mainly by troublesome elimination. The most common abdominal emergency in the western world, it is brought on by continuous constipation, straining during stool elimination, and anal retention—failing to evacuate solid waste when the body tells you to. By delaying your bowel movements, perhaps because you are too busy to be inconvenienced, you confuse your body. The water from fecal matter begins to be reabsorbed, and the dry, hard stool that is left will pass only with great pain and difficulty. In the meantime, you strain the muscles that must retain this mass and eventually train them to delay normal elimination. Some people learn to have a bowel movement only once a day or even once every 2 or 3 days. You should have two or three bowel movements a day, depending, of course, on what and how often you eat. When there is not enough dietary fiber to move food and waste readily through the digestive system, pressure builds up and blocks the passage of stool. Bacteria accumulates and backs up into the 3- to 6-inch-long appendix which is attached to the large intestine. The appendix becomes inflamed and infected, and an appendectomy must be performed. To see how critical the issue of fiber is here, consider the 6,000 appendectomies performed in the United States each week

compared with only a handful per year in rural Africa, where processed, fiber-depleted food is virtually nonexistent. This again is a
pressure disease that can be avoided or even treated with a high-fiber
diet consisting of complex carbohydrates.

## Ulcers

*Ulcers* are a disorder of the digestive tract, although it is not clear
how closely related the affliction is to the actual digestive process.
Between 10 million and 14 million Americans suffer from ulcers,
including 2 million children. About 1 in 10 men and 1 in 20 women
are afflicted with this malady. The term "ulcer" comes from the Latin
word meaning "sore." Ulcers are sores—lesions—that can be found
anywhere in the body, although the term usually refers to stomach
ulcers. Ulcers were probably alluded to in biblical times by the phrase
"thorn in the flesh." In the late nineteenth century, the peptic or
gastric ulcer was the most common type of ulcer, and the highest-risk
group was young women living in rural America. One hundred years
later, duodenal ulcers are the most common type by far and gastric
ulcers are relatively rare. The high-risk group for duodenal ulcers is
25- to 50-year-old urban males, although children between 6 and 14
years of age recently have emerged as a new high-risk group.

Ulcers result when there is too much digestive acid—usually
pepsin—for the protective mucosal lining of the stomach or duodenum to contain. The only reason these acids devour food but do not
eat through the body is that alkaline buffering cells called mucosal
cells protect the walls of the body's digestive system. However, these
mucosal cells can be overpowered if there is an oversecretion of the
gastric juices, as seems to be the case in most ulcer victims.

It is not clear whether dietary habits actually cause ulcers by
stimulating too much gastric secretion or if they simply aggravate an
existing condition. Stress certainly plays a role in causing the problem,
but not necessarily executive-type stress from overworking and over-
achieving. Life crises such as a death in the family or the loss of a job

(what might more accurately be called *distress*) seem to have a more profound influence. However, studies of air traffic controllers, urban dwellers, and soldiers in basic training have shown that these high-pressure environments are also conducive to the development and aggravation of peptic ulcers.

Ulcers can be sores as simple as slight abrasions of the internal mucosal lining, or they can advance to the stage where they totally perforate the stomach or intestinal wall. The symptoms are primarily pain, which can range from annoying to excruciating. This pain comes most often at night and in the absence of food. In fact, the presence of food stimulates the body's natural buffering action, reducing the effects of acidity and hence pain. Ulcers, which were often confused in diagnosis with the hiatus hernia or gallbladder and pancreatic disease, can sometimes be detected with the x-ray.

Of the two common types of ulcers, the peptic or gastric ulcer affects the stomach, and the duodenal ulcer is usually found in the first few inches of the duodenum, although it may occur elsewhere in the duodenum. The cause of ulcers is either too much hydrochloric acid and pepsin secreted in the stomach or the inability of the intestinal wall to resist the corrosion of digestive juices. Ulcers may reach various stages of development known as perforation, penetration, and obstruction.

In acute perforation, the ulcer eats through the wall of the abdomen. This is the most serious stage and causes the greatest number of deaths. Surgery to close the perforation in the abdomen and contain the highly caustic and damaging gastric juices is virtually unavoidable. Penetration is the stage where the patient usually awakes at night with severe pain to the adjacent organs—the back, liver, and so forth—not just to the stomach. This transfer of affect to other organs makes this type of ulcer diagnostically elusive. Obstruction is the stage in which swelling caused by inflammation affects the stomach and the opening to the small intestine.

The traditional treatment of ulcers was based on a very soft, textureless food diet that included lots of custard and gelatins. Today, most doctors agree that a more nutritious diet—including potatoes, milk, and cottage cheese—is needed and that the patient should avoid things that exacerbate the condition, such as alcohol, nicotine, aspirin, coffee, soft drinks, salt, high-oil nuts, and even raw fruit (except bananas).

Alternative treatments place far greater emphasis on the role of nutrition and fiber in the diet, and much broader lifestyle changes are recommended. Exercise regimens are outlined, and yoga, meditation, and biofeedback are often part of suggested stress-reduction programs. Dietary modification is the most significant part of the treatment. You are urged to seek and eliminate allergens that are not readily digested and therefore overstimulate gastric secretions for long periods. You are encouraged to eat foods that are wholesome, unrefined, and reduced in fat and protein.

The idea behind avoiding certain foods is to minimize gastric secretions. If you eat food that is excessively spicy and difficult to digest, more pepsin will be secreted to deal with it. Thus you don't want to eat a lot of high-protein foods, especially those accompanied with high levels of fat. Animal foods require more gastric involvement and should be avoided if possible. If you do eat meat, at least trim the fat; also, avoid overcooking, deep frying, and charcoal broiling since these processes make the molecules bond more tightly so that more digestive effort is required to break them down. Carbohydrate foods have their own protective buffer in the natural state (brown rice and whole grains and vegetables), but once they are refined (white flour and white rice, cakes and pastries) the buffer is stripped away. Therefore, avoid denatured, processed carbohydrates. Vegetables are usually quite acidic, so avoid those causing gas (turnips, cucumbers, brussels sprouts, broccoli, radishes, and cauliflower), especially in the raw state. Vegetables will be less acidic if you cook them, preferably by steaming since it does not destroy their fibrous structure. Raw cabbage juice has been found to be quite beneficial.

While ulcers require special diets, there are general guidelines for good health. No chapter on digestive disorders could be considered complete without suggesting the sort of dietary modifications that you should undertake to both avoid and overcome these conditions.

## What to Eat

When people talk about what should be eaten and what should not, they invariably compare proteins, fats, and carbohydrates. A common misconception in such comparisons is that diet can be understood in terms of standard weights and measurements. For instance, a hospital dietitian may determine that patients with certain ailments require 35 g of protein a day and then plan a menu with just the right amount of beef, eggs, milk, grain, and beans to reach the day's quota of 35 g. This seems fine, but there are several other factors to consider, including the quality of the protein.

Which proteins are best utilized by the body? A gram of steak is not utilized by the body in the same way or at the same rate as a gram of eggs. Eggs have a much higher net protein utilization rate. When you ingest a gram of each protein, your body will not get to "keep" or utilize each to the same degree or in the same way. Different foods have a different protein quality, fat quality, or carbohydrate quality. Don't become so interested in the quantity of food you are eating that you forget the most critical issue: the quality of what you eat and how it will work with or against your body in promoting tissue growth, maintaining the integrity of the cardiovascular system, optimizing the energy level, and supporting immune and digestive activities. More than the number of calories you are taking in, you need to know what those calories are doing for or against you.

Not many people suggest eating a lot of fats, but there have been many proponents of both high-protein and high-carbohydrate diets in recent years. In fact, many people also eat high-fat diets. Which of these is best?

### The High-Protein Diet

The most popular diet in the United States in the second half of the twentieth century has been one incorporating large amounts of protein. This is one of the main reasons why many people are unwittingly on high-fat diets. The proteins in most diets are derived from animal sources. Beef and pork, cheese and butter, eggs and milk are all common sources of protein. Many people think these foods are essential to their health. However, in the process of trying to get plenty of this kind of protein, you will also be opting for an abundance of fat. All animal products are very high in fat, far higher than plant or vegetable foods. A potato, for instance, has less than 10 percent fat content; cheese, eggs, and even lean steak have well over 50 percent fat. Of course, a potato is a carbohydrate, not a protein, but even plant proteins have far less fat content than do animal proteins. Beans and grains, for example, have as little fat as the potato, and many plant proteins have virtually no fat.

### The Right Diet for You

It is difficult to separate the fats from the proteins from the carbohydrates. You may be eating too much of one to get some of the other, or you may be cutting down on one to reduce the other. Understanding a little about why you do and don't need each one will help you formulate a sensible diet for your particular needs.

Diets should be individual matters. Not everybody requires the same amounts or proportions of proteins, fats, or cabohydrates. Your body chemistry or lifestyle may indicate that you need to slant your diet a little bit toward this or away from that. What's good for your friend may not be the best for you. Men, women, and children have different requirements. Adults at different ages have varying dietary needs. Don't eat what everyone around you is eating or what a book or article suggests. Tailor your diet to your specific needs, which may include your particular health problems. It is best to work with a nutritionist or a physician who is knowledgeable about nutrition in deriving the right program.

Any diet that is right for you must take into consideration certain guidelines. Specifically you must understand and consider the role that fats, proteins, and carbohydrates play in your eating style.

### Protein

Proteins are essential nutrients because they contain the eight amino acids that are not manufactured by the body and so must be obtained through the diet. They help build new tissue and repair damaged tissue. Proteins are important in hormone and enzyme production and play a vital role in the development of skin, bones, and teeth. Despite the fact that the protein is important to your health, you don't have to load up on it, even though the meat and dairy industries may try to convince you otherwise. The typical American gets from 2 to 10 times more protein than is needed. You may reason that if protein is important for your health—which it is—then the more you eat, the better off you will be. Body builders frequently use this line of logic. Since protein helps build new muscle tissue, they figure that the more they ingest, the more muscular they will become. This is like saying that if two aspirins bring a fever down in an hour, a whole bottle should make you completely well in 5 minutes.

The body does not work that way. Most substances do not affect people on a steadily continuing incline or decline but more along the lines of a parabola which rises, peaks within a given range, and then declines. In other words, if you have too little protein, it certainly can affect your well-being adversely, but if you have too much, other problems can occur. Either situation constitutes an imbalance; one will create deficiency problems, while the other will have side effects with symptoms reflecting excess. What you want to do is find the range within which a substance offers optimum results. You may refer to general guidelines as a starting point, but you will have to refine them to meet your individual requirements. When you do, make sure to check the validity of the general guidelines. If they suggest that you need 35 to 40 g of protein, for instance, you should relate that figure more specifically to your overall caloric intake. The World Health

Organization figures that as much as 5 percent of the calories you take in in a 24-hour period should consist of protein. That means 95 percent should come from fats and carbohydrates.

This is a high estimate, and many authorities, such as Dr. John McDougall, M.D., assistant clinical professor of internal medicine at the University of Hawaii and medical director of St. Helena Hospital in Deer Park, California, recommends only 2½ percent protein. He points out that even using the 5 percent figure, you can see how grossly people overconsume protein. For instance, you can convert a daily caloric intake say, 3,000 calories—into actual grams by dividing it by 4—the total calories per gram—and then taking 5 percent of that figure. This gives you 37 to 38 g of protein for 3,000 calories that you would need during the day. To show how easy it is to get that much protein in your diet, if you ate only potatoes, which are composed primarily of carbohydrates, to get the 3,000 calories, you would be getting 80 g of protein. Thus you can double your protein intake without even eating a protein food.

When you overload on protein, you are setting yourself up for many long-range ailments, including chronic food allergies, osteoporosis, kidney stones, kidney disease, digestive disorders, and colon cancer. Most of these problems are associated specifically with animal protein, although too much protein is a problem even if you are eating only vegetable proteins.

Kidney disease, for example, results from the fact that the kidney functions as a filter for proteins and amino acids that are not used by the body. This makes the kidneys overwork and enlarge as pressure builds up inside them. The renal tubules, which are the actual filters, can be irreversibly destroyed by this process, resulting in decreased kidney function. Most elderly people have lost a significant portion of their kidneys, up to 50 percent in many cases. This may not be a major health hazard on its own, because you need only 25 percent of your kidneys to function properly. But if you have other ailments such as diabetes, high blood pressure, or kidney infection, the kidneys may be further destroyed and your health can become perilous.

Excess protein also forces the kidney to excrete large amounts of minerals, including calcium. Calcium joins with uric acid in the urine to form kidney stones. It also washes out of the skeletal system when the kidneys are overloaded with animal protein. This leads to calcium-poor bones, a very common and debilitating condition called *osteoporosis*. In this condition, the bones become dry and brittle and eventually break from mere body weight. Half the women in the United States over the age 75 suffer from osteoporosis, and they are usually told to increase their calcium intake. However, this is not the answer to preventing or overcoming osteoporosis, because the body absorbs very little dietary and supplementary calcium. The only real prevention is to stay away from excessive protein, because that is what causes the calcium to wash out to begin with.

Dr. McDougall says that he controls kidney failure by decreasing protein in the patient's diet. He offers this example:

"The patient was a young girl who had accompanied another family member who was going to be seen by me. The girl's skin was gray, and she seemed to be very sick. After I finished caring for the family member, I asked what was wrong with the girl. I was told she was in kidney failure and was going to have shunts inserted so she could be placed on a kidney machine in a couple of months. I asked if they'd like to try something different and offered to teach the young girl a very low protein diet that contained only vegetable protein and observe what happened. The family agreed. It was 7 years ago that I taught that child this type of diet, and her progressive kidney failure stopped. To this day she is still off the kidney machine. Several other patients of mine have had very similar experiences, all of which are important to the patient because once they are placed on kidney dialysis, life for them will be tough, to say the least."

## Fat

If you, like most Americans, are getting too much protein, primarily animal protein, you are certainly getting too much fat as well. The same meat and dairy products that serve as the traditional source of protein are very high in fat and cholesterol.

Fat is needed for both immediate and reserve energy. It helps round out your physical features and is important in the formation of cell walls, brain tissue, hormones, and enzymes. As with amino acids, some fats are termed essential because they are not manufactured in the body and so must be derived from dietary sources. This may be in the form of either plant fats (polyunsaturated), or animal fat (saturated). Both can cause serious disease states when ingested in excessive amounts.

If you have a diet high in fat, you are likely to be obese, with greasy skin and oily hair. Obesity is a major factor in heart disease, diabetes, and other degenerative conditions. Animal fats are very high in cholesterol. Cholesterol damages the inner walls of the arteries so that blood circulation is impaired and blood platelets may be damaged. This is a precursor to heart and circulatory diseases. Poor circulation can cause damage to virtually any organ, although heart damage is the most obvious and direct result of high-fat diets.

Vegetable fats and oil are not any better, even though people suffering from high cholesterol are frequently advised to switch from animal to plant sources of fat and oil. Plant fats will reduce cholesterol levels, but with serious side effects such as gallbladder disease and gallstones. As vegetable oils—corn oil, safflower oil, peanut oil, olive oil, and others—cause cholesterol to be driven out of the liver, it passes through the gallbladder, where it forms gallstones. When this cholesterol is driven into the colon, it becomes carcinogenic and greatly increases the likelihood of colon cancer and other related problems.

Oils and fats in the diet also interfere with normal blood flow. Blood platelets normally bounce off one another and bend and twist to get through tiny capillaries. Fat and oil in the diet coat the blood cells with a fatty sheathing that makes them heavy, sticky, sluggish, and stiff. They clump and clot and can no longer pass through small capillaries or twist through narrow bends and turns in the vascular system. Oxygen levels in the blood are reduced, and you become tired and lethargic. Eventually you develop chest pains and angina, along with leg cramps and pain that comes and goes with physical exertion (a condition called intermittent claudication). Thus animal or vegetable oils must be severely restricted to avoid these problems. Nearly half the average American diet consists of fat, but only 5 to 10 percent is required for good, balanced nutrition.

## Carbohydrates

If both fats and proteins need to be drastically reduced in the American diet, carbohydrates obviously need to play a more prominent role. High-starch carbohydrates are excellent alternatives to fats and proteins as the main part of a diet. They are low in fat and cholesterol, and they burn slowly and efficiently to provide steady, even energy throughout the day. Because they are high in bulk, they fill you up faster and for a longer period of time than do high-density fats and proteins. At the same time, they are a rich source of naturally balanced vitamins, minerals, and fiber. In fact, they are the only source of fiber in the diet. Fiber is not a nutrient itself but allows for better utilization of nutrients from other sources. It provides bulk so that food moves more easily through the digestive system and is excreted before it can ferment and emit toxins into the system.

There are both simple and complex carbohydrates. The simple ones are simple sugars such as honey, maple syrup, fructose, corn syrup, table sugar, refined flour products, candies, and snack foods. Generally speaking, simple carbohydrates are highly processed junk foods. They are high in calories and virtually devoid of nutrients. By contrast, complex carbohydrates are wholesome, unrefined, unaltered foods. They include such things as whole grains and unprocessed whole-grain cereals, breads and pastas that are unrefined, legumes, vegetables, unaltered nuts and seeds, nut butters, and raw fruit.

Carbohydrates provide the body with fuel. The simple carbohydrates provide a cheap, fast-burning fuel in the form of sugars. These sugars go almost directly into the bloodstream; blood sugar levels rise drastically and suddenly and then drop off just as quickly. You experience a sudden rush of energy, a quick pickup, followed by a big drop off and a crash. The complex carbohydrates provide the most efficient form of fuel. They burn very slowly. All carbohydrates are ultimately broken down into glucose, the only form of sugar that can be utilized on the cellular level. Complex carbohydrates convert only very gradually into glucose so that a high level of energy is sustained for many hours. Moreover, unused energy is converted into *glycogen*, a storable form of sugar that is held in the liver and muscles until it is needed. This is why smart athletes do "carbohydrate loading" the day of or for several days before an athletic event.

It is a common myth that carbohydrates cause weight gain. While this is certainly true in the case of the simple carbohydrates, it is far from the truth in the case of the complex carbohydrates. In fact, complex carbohydrates are rarely converted into fat but are mostly utilized by the body. If you replace fats and proteins in the diet with complex carbohydrates, you are fighting obesity and overweight on two fronts. First, you are getting rid of foods high in fats and cholesterol and triglycerides, which will be stored in your body as fat. Second, the foods you are replacing them with have virtually no fat or cholesterol, will not store as fat but rather as a usable energy in the form of glycogen, and still provide the bulk you need to satisfy your hunger and prevent overeating. This is why you will lose weight if you switch from a high-protein to a high-carbohydrate diet.

Providing energy is the chief but not the sole function of carbohydrates. They are also needed for normal cerebral functioning and play a critical role in maintaining the nervous system. If you don't get enough complex carbohydrates in your diet, your body will convert proteins in the liver to provide energy for the brain and nervous system. But proteins were not meant to do this job, and the conversion process greatly overtaxes the liver. Carbohydrates aid the liver in its ability to detoxify the body. Thus carbohydrates in the diet help you avoid liver complications and possible long-term damage to the brain and nervous system.

### Eating Right to Feel Better

You have seen what you should be eating, but remember that eating is not only a practical enterprise but a uniquely enjoyable one too. Make it an expression of yourself. Take time to enjoy it. Select and prepare your foods carefully and rotate them frequently. Balance your diet by including a wide variety of foods and food types. Make your meals appealing by integrating different textures and colors as well as smells and tastes.

If you develop a digestive disorder, you should have it tended to by a physician who is competent to diagnose and treat it. In the meantime, remember that the first defense against arthritis, food allergies, and many other disorders and complications is a good preventive diet. This diet, along with a solid exercise program, stress management, and lifestyle counseling, forms an excellent adjunct to any medical or noninvasive therapy or treatment. In some cases it may constitute the entire treatment. Before you jump into a serious drug therapy or invasive medical treatment program which is bound to have many negative side effects and may lead to an array of further complications, try altering your lifestyle while you check out some of the less toxic alternative therapies. No matter what may be wrong with you, eating right cannot be wrong.

Current research is focusing on free radical pathology as a cause of disease disorders. In an article entitled "Oxygen derived free radicals and the prevention of duodenal ulcer relapse: a new approach," published in the *American Journal of Medical Sciences* (300(1):1-6, 1990), author Salim says that free radicals have been implicated as a cause of duodenal ulcers. And antioxidant therapy was shown to be superior to cimetidine (Tagamet™) in decreasing ulcer recurrence. Free radicals have also been implicated in the damage caused to the stomach lining by alcohol. And certain nutrients have been found which seem capable of helping to protect the stomach lining (Hollander, Daniel, and Tarnaroski, Andreyej: "The role of nutrient fatty acids in gastric mucocel protection," *Gastric Cytoprotection*, 1990).

Whether you are sick or are eager to avoid sickness and overcome lethargy and malaise—in other words, if you want to improve the quality of your life from this moment on regardless of your current health profile—you must make sure you are eating right. And you must do it now, not tomorrow or the next day. If you want to feel better today, you'll have to start eating right today.

# Conclusion:
# Demystifying the Process

What do you do once you've read the case histories, studied the politics, and become familiar with the alternative therapies? Do you have arthritis, cancer, heart disease, digestive disorders, mental illness, or low back pain? If you choose an alternative approach to treating any of these diseases, your path is unlikely to be smooth. You will probably face opposition from family, friends, and the traditional medical community. They will probably downplay the evidence you present and disparage your choice of alternative therapies.

I suggest you begin by obtaining a traditional diagnosis from the most competent or qualified physician available to you and then get a second opinion and diagnosis, again from a traditional viewpoint, to verify the diagnosis. Many people are mistreated because they are misdiagnosed. Ask if the therapist can guarantee that the treatment being offered is nontoxic and can be proved—based on evidence such as published scientific articles and case histories—to have been effective in helping or curing other patients. If you are given only the physician's personal assurance that the therapy is safe and has a record of success, seek out an alternative therapist.

You should then ask the alternative therapist for proof of success in treating your condition. Ask for five case histories that you can personally investigate through interview or discussion to prove to yourself that the therapy makes sense in your case. Find out whether the patients are alive and well, having had similar diagnoses and having undergone the therapy being presented to you.

It is not always possible to find publications in scientific journals verifying alternative treatments. You will have to give great consideration to the case histories available for your review. Again, if the therapist can guarantee the treatment program only on the basis of a personal perspective, you will have to decide whether to choose the alternative or the traditional therapy or a combination of the two.

You may want to speak to three, four, or five therapists in a given specialty before selecting the therapy that best answers all your questions and meets all your criteria. Do not rush into either a traditional or an alternative therapy simply on the basis of statements by the therapist. Do your research and your homework. The time and attention you give to this could be a matter of life or death. It will also give you something important in the healing of any condition: confidence in the therapy and the therapist. Even after you have selected a treatment and begun a program with the therapist of your choice, do not rule out the possibility of shifting to another therapy if you are disappointed with your progress.

# Glossary

**Angina:** Severe chest pain caused by a blockage of blood flow to the heart; sometimes affects the left arm and shoulder as well; also called angina pectoris

**Arteriosclerosis:** a thickening of the arterial wall accompanied by plaque buildup that impedes blood circulation

**Ascites:** a gross abdominal fluid buildup that often accompanies cancerous tumor growth

**Atherosclerosis:** a type of arteriosclerosis in which the arterial walls are damaged by cholesterol and normal blood flow is blocked

**Autism:** antisocial behavior based on fantasy and withdrawal from friends and reality

**Basal cell carcinoma:** cancerous growth from the epithelium, commonly manifesting in lesions of the face and neck; also called basaloma

**Bursitis:** chronic pain of the joints resulting from inflammation of the bursa, a saclike cavity that keeps the bones and joints from rubbing against each other

**Carcinoma:** a malignant tumor originating in epithelial tissue

**Disinsulinism:** an abnormal amount of insulin secretion

**Diuretic:** a substance used to increase urination and thereby lower body fluid levels and blood pressure levels

**Epithelium:** a thin membrane lining most organs

**Fibroblastic sarcoma:** an extremely fibrous cancer growth

**Hyperglycemia:** a higher than normal blood sugar level, as in diabetics

**Hypoglycemia:** a lower than normal blood sugar level accompanied by a low energy level

**Intermittent claudication:** severe leg cramps and pain during walking and other exercise; the pain subsides when physical exertion ceases

**Lesion:** an open wound or skin ulceration

**Lymphocyte:** a white blood cell that circulates throughout the circulatory system, arresting bacteria and foreign bodies

**Lymphoma:** rapidly spreading disease of the lymphatic system and tissue

**Melanoma:** a rapidly spreading malignant tumor with a dark pigmentation, usually occurring in the skin, genitals, or oral cavity

**Mesothelioma:** a cancer usually caused by asbestos; it most commonly attacks the lungs but may attack the stomach or heart

**Metastasis:** transmission of a disease from its original or primary site to a secondary site.

**Neoplasm:** abnormal new tissue growth

**Osteoarthritis:** an arthritic condition characterized by degeneration of the joints

**Osteoporosis:** a condition in which bones become brittle and dry and can break easily

**Pathological:** refers to diseased and/or dying cells, tissues, and organs

**Prostate:** a gland in males that surrounds the canal through which urine is discharged

**Remission:** cessation nor lessening in intensity of cancerous growth; spontaneous remission occurs for no apparent reason and sometimes endures indefinitely, and temporary remission occurs when a growth stops or slows down but then flares up again

**Rheumatoid arthritis:** chronic and painful stiffness of the joints in which mobility is reduced to varying degrees

**Sarcoma:** a highly malignant tumor formed by connective tissue

**Schizophrenia:** abnormally subjective behavior characterized by complete withdrawal from others

**Scirrhous carcinoma:** a hardened tumor

**Scleroderma:** swelling and hardening of diseased skin

**Seminoma:** a cancer caused by the proliferation of sex cells

**Serum:** yellowish fluid component of blood

**Tumor:** a noninflammatory, abnormal, and nonfunctional growth from existing tissue; malignant tumors continue to grow rapidly and frequently spread too extensively to be completely removed by surgery, and benign tumors are harmless and can be left alone or removed surgically

# Specialists in Alternative Healing Techniques

## AIDS

| NAME | TITLE | PHONE | ADDRESS |
|------|-------|-------|---------|
| Tariq Abdula | MD | (904) 763-7689 | 236 S. Tyndall Parkway, Panama City, FL 32404 |
| Phil Bellman | MD | (212) 645-0161 | 31 West 11 St., Suite 7C, New York, NY 10011 |
| Ahmed Elkadi | MD | (904) 763-7689 | 236 S. Tyndall Parkway, Panama City, FL 32404 |
| Sheila George | MD | (212) 796-5957 | New York, NY |
| Quique Palladino | | (212) 795-6625 | 250 Cabrini Blvd., Apt 5E, New York, NY 10033 |
| Joan Priestly | MD | (212) 957-4210 | 7080 Hollywood Blvd #603, Los Angeles, CA |

## ALLERGY

| NAME | TITLE | PHONE | ADDRESS |
|------|-------|-------|---------|
| John G. Adams | MD M | (214) 938-4363 | 711 E. End Blvd. S, Marshall, TX 75670 |
| Neil D. Adams | MD E | (206) 736-1171 | 123 N. Tower, Centralia, WA 98531 |
| Martin Brody | DDS MD | (305) 822-9035 | 7100 W. 20th Ave., Hialeah, FL 33016 |
| Andrew M. Brown | MD F | (205) 547-4971 | 515 South Third St., Gladsen, AL 35901 |
| Don Bryan | MD PM | (205) 663-5840 | P.O. Box 1857, Alabaster, AL 35007 |
| Rocco D. Cassone | MD M | (803) 536-5511 | 1175 Crook Rd., Suite 230, Orangeburg, SC, 29115 |
| George H. Drumheller Jr. | MD E | (206) 258-4361 | 1515 Pacific Ave., Everet, WA 98201 |
| Francisco J. Figueroa-Roviar | MD PM | (809) 879-0807 | Box 1886, Arecibo, PR 00613 |
| Robert S. Gillcash | MD M | (203) 642-4145 | P.O. Box 37, North Franklin, CT 06254 |
| Donald E. Goehring | MD E | (412) 287-4241 | 503 Union Bank Bldg., Butler, PA 16001 |
| Leland J. Green | MD M | (215) 855-9501 | P.O. Box 508, Lansdale, PA 19466 |
| John A. Green III | MD M | (503) 678-2233 | P.O. Box 99, Aurora, OR 97002 |
| Jerome E. Groll | MD PM | (302) 645-2833 | 421 Savannah Rd., Lewes, DE 19958 |
| Vickey C. Halloran | MD M | (713) 440-0800 | 5629 FM 1960 W #225, Houston, TX 77069 |
| Harris Hosen | MD E | (409) 799-2148 | 2001 Holcomb Blvd., Apt 1301, Houston, TX 77030 |
| G. Hugh Johnson | MD M | (912) 272-8494 | 227 Industrial Blvd., Dublin, GA 31021 |
| Randall A. Langston | MD M | (904) 863-8287 | 1005 Mar Walt Dr., Ft. Walton Beach, FL 32548 |
| Fannie Lou Leney-Hayward | MD E | (918) 299-2661 | 8555 South Lewis, Tulsa, OK 74137 |
| F. Russell Manuel | MD | (907) 562-7070 | 4200 Lake Otis Blvd. #304, Anchorage, AK 99508 |

## ALLERGY continued

| | | | |
|---|---|---|---|
| Jeffrey Marcus | MD M | (904) 726-3131 | 3733 E. Gulf-to-Lake Highway, Inverness, FL 32650 |
| Joseph B. Miller | MD F | (205) 342-8540 | 5901 Airport Blvd., Mobile, AL 36608 |
| Billy Gerald Mills | DO M | (214) 279-6767 | 4725 Gus Thomasson, Mesquite, TX 75150 |
| Herbert I. Moselle | MD M | (305) 472-1212 | 201 N.W. 82 Ave. #103, Plantation, FL 33324 |
| Sunil P. Perera | MD M | (916) 782-7758 | 404 Sunrise Ave., Roseville, CA 95661 |
| Robert B. Richards | MD E | (303) 867-2779 | 727 Park Street, Fort Morgan, CO 80701 |
| Russell R. Roby | MD PM | (512) 451-5484 | 3410 Far West, Suite 110, Austin, TX 78731 |
| Sally J. Rockwell | BS PhD | (206) 547-1814 | 4703 Stone Way N, Seattle, WA 98103 |
| Lillian S. Scala | MA A | (304) 292-7357 | 220 Wilson Ave., Morgantown, WV 26505 |
| David M. Schultz | MD PM | (814) 274-7450 | Cole Medical Center Rt. 6, Cloudersport, PA 16915 |
| George Von Hilsheimer | PhD A | (305) 628-0226 | #14 Maitland Plaza, Maitland, FL 32751 |
| James H. Walker Sr. | MD E | (205) 879-5358 | 3454 Manor Lane, Apt 310, Birmingham, AL 35209 |
| Norman E. Wenger | MD M | (717) 222-9595 | P.O. Box 502, Carbondale, PA 18407 |
| G. A. Woodruff | MD E | (503) 255-4256 | 1110 S. E. Main, Portland, OR 97216 |

## BIO-OXIDATIVE

| NAME | TITLE | PHONE | ADDRESS |
|---|---|---|---|
| Paul V. Beals | MD | (301) 490-9011 | 9101 Cherry Lane Pk. #205, Laurel, MD 20708 |
| Paul V. Beals | MD | (202) 332-0370 | 2639 Conn. Ave. NW #100, Washington, DC 20037 |
| Kenneth A. Bock | MD | (914) 876-7082 | 108 Montgomery St., Rhinebeck, NY 12572 |
| Steve Bock | MD | (914) 876-7082 | 108 Montgomery St., Rhinebeck, NY 12572 |
| John Boxall | MD | (208) 466-3517 | 824–17th Ave. South, Nampa, ID 38651 |
| Prudencio Corro | MD M | (304) 252-0775 | 251 Stanford Rd., Beckley, WV 25801 |
| Martin Dayton | MD DO | (305) 931-8484 | 18600 Collins Ave., N. Miami Beach, FL 33160 |
| Charles H. Farr | MD PhD | (405) 691-1112 | 10101 S. Western, Oklahoma City, OK 73139 |
| T. Hayashida | MD | (213) 323-4090 | 1300 W. 155th St., Suite 204, Gardenia, CA 90247 |
| William L. Hembree | DDS | (904) 387-3535 | 1510 Willow Branch Ave., Jacksonville, FL 32205 |
| H. J. Hoegerman | MD | (805) 963-1824 | 101 W. Arrellaga, Suite D, Santa Barbara, CA 93101 |
| Ronald L. Hoffman | MD | (212) 779-1744 | 40 E 30 St, New York, NY 10016 |
| Gordon H. Josephs | DO | (602) 778-9232 | 315 W. Goodwin St., Prescott, AZ 86301 |
| Mitchell Kurk | MD | (516) 239-5540 | 310 Broadway, Lawrence, NY 11559 |

## BIO-OXIDATIVE continued

| | | | |
|---|---|---|---|
| Roy Kupsinel | MD | (407) 365-6681 | 1325 Shangri-la Lane, Oviedo, FL 32765 |
| Paul Lynn | MD | (415) 566-1000 | 345 W. Portal Ave., San Francisco, CA 94127 |
| Donald Mantell | MD | (412) 776-5610 | 6505 Mars Rd., Evans City, PA 16033 |
| Alfred Massam | MD | (813) 773-6668 | 528 West Main St., Wauchula, FL 33873 |
| Otis Miller | MD | (303) 728-3251 | 408 S. 14th St., Ord, NE 68862 |
| William D. Mitchell | DO | (614) 761-0555 | 3520 Snouffer Rd., Columbus, OH 43234 |
| Kirk Morgan | MD | (502) 228-0156 | 9105 U.S. Highway 42, Louisville, KY 40059 |
| Stanley R. Olszlyn | MD | (602) 954-0811 | 3610 N. 44th St, Suite 210, Phoenix, AZ 85108 |
| Sun F. Pei | DO | (516) 775-5285 | 1 Fairfield Lane, New Hyde Park, NY 11040 |
| James D. Schuler | MD | (707) 487-3405 | 12559 Hwy 101 North, mini-mart, Smith River, CA 95567 |
| Frank Shallenberger | MD | (702) 782-4164 | 1524 Hwy 395, Gardnerville, NV 89410 |
| Robert Sklovsky | ND Pharm | (503) 654-3938 | 6910 SE. Lake Road, Milwaukee, OR 97267 |
| Vincent J. Speckhart | MD | (804) 622-0014 | 902 Graydon Ave., Norfolk, VA 23507 |
| Annette Stoesser | MD | (505) 623-2444 | 112 S. Kentucky, Roswell, NM 88201 |
| Thomas L. Stone | MD M | (312) 934-1100 | 1811 Hicks Rd., Rolling Meadows, IL 60008 |
| Murray Susser | MD | (213) 453-4424 | 2730 Wilshire Blvd, Suite 110, Santa Monica, CA 90403 |
| Melissa Taliaferro | MD | (501) 447-2599 | Cherry St., P.O. Box 400, Leslie, AR 72645 |
| John R. Tambone | MD | (815) 338-2345 | 102 E. South St., Woodstock, IL 60098 |
| John C. Tapp | MD | (502) 781-1483 | 414 Old Morgantown Rd., Bowling Green, KY 42101 |
| Harvey Walker Jr. | MD PhD | (314) 721-7227 | 138 N. Merimec Ave., St. Louis, MO 63105 |

## CHELATION

| NAME | TITLE | PHONE | ADDRESS |
|---|---|---|---|
| Ilona Araham | MD | (818) 345-8721 | 19231 Victoria Blvd., Reseda, CA 91335 |
| Steven B. Acker | MD | (316) 733-4494 | 310 West Central #D, Andover, KS 76002 |
| Vahagan Agbabian | DO | (313) 334-2424 | 28 N. Saginaw St., Suite 1105, Pontiac, MI 48058 |
| Neil Ahner | MD | (407) 729-8581 | 1200 Malabar Road, Palm Bay, FL 32907 |
| Neil Ahner | MD | (407) 744-0077 | 1080 E. Indiantown Rd., Jupiter, FL 33477 |
| Constance Alfano | MD | (201) 444-4622 | 74 Oak St., Ridgewood, NJ 07450 |
| Majid Ali | MD | (201) 586-4111 | 95 E. Main St., Dennville, NJ 07834 |

## CHELATION continued

| | | | |
|---|---|---|---|
| John H. Allshuler | MD | (303) 740-7771 | 7485 E. Peakview Ave., Bldg 1, Englewood, CO 80111 |
| Rathna Alwa | MD | (414) 248-1430 | 717 Geneva St., Lake Geneva, WI 53147 |
| Charles Anderson | MD | (802) 879-6544 | 175 Pearl St., Essex Junction, VT 05452 |
| Leon Anderson | DO | (918) 299-5039 | 121 Second St., Jenks, OK 74037 |
| Scott V. Anderson | MD | (703) 941-3606 | 7023 Little River Tpke. #207, Annandale, VA 22003 |
| Thomas R. Anderson | MD | (317) 564-2777 | 651 Armory Rd., Delphi, IN 46923 |
| Jim P. Archer | DO | (210) 615-8445 | 8434 Fredicksburg Rd., San Antonio, TX 78229 |
| Lloyd D. Armoid | DO | (602) 934-8916 | 4901 W. Bell Rd. Ste 2, Glendale, AZ 85308 |
| Josephine Aronica | MD | (216) 867-7361 | 1867 W. Market St., Akron, OH 44313 |
| Clifton Arrington | MD | (808) 322-9400 | P.O. Box 649, Kealakekua, HI 96750 |
| Robert Atkins | MD | (212) 758-2110 | 152 E 55th St., New York, NY 10022 |
| Norman J. Bacquet | MD | (501) 375-4419 | 115 W. 6th St., Little Rock, AR 72201 |
| Ricardo V. Barbaza | MD | (407) 335-4994 | 1541 S.E. Port St. Lucie Blvd., Port St. Lucie, FL 34952 |
| John M. Baron | DO | (216) 642-0082 | 4807 Rockside, Suite 100, Cleveland, OH 44131 |
| Robert M. Battle | MD | (713) 932-0552 | 9910 Long Point Rd., Houston, TX 77055 |
| Paul V. Beals | MD | (202) 332-0370 | 2639 Conn. Ave NW #100, Washington, DC 20037 |
| Norbert J. Becquet | MD | (501) 375-4419 | 115 W. Sixth St., Little Rock, AK 72201 |
| Laszio Belenyessy | MD | (213) 822-4614 | 12732 Washington Blvd #D, Los Angeles, CA 90066 |
| William M. Bernard | DO | (313) 733-3140 | 1044 Gilbert St., Flint, MI 48532 |
| Murray L. Black | DO F | (509) 966-1780 | 609 S. 48th Ave., Yakima, WA 98908 |
| Neil L. Block | MD | (914) 359-3300 | 14 Prel Plaza, Orangeburg, NY 10962 |
| Horst G. Blume | MD | (712) 252-4386 | 700 Jennings St., Sioux City, IO 51105 |
| Kenneth A. Bock | MD | (914) 876-7082 | 108 Montgomery St., Rhinebeck, NY 12572 |
| Steve Bock | MD | (914) 876-7082 | 108 Montgomery St., Rhinebeck, NY 12572 |
| Grant Born | DO | (616) 455-3550 | 2687–44th St. S.E., Grand Rapids, MI 49512 |
| Jerome L. Borochoff | MD | (713) 461-7517 | 8830 Long Point, Suite 504, Houston, TX 77055 |
| Azael Borromeo | MD | (904) 795-7117 | 206 NE Third Street, Crystal River, FL 32629 |
| Eric Braverman | MD | (609) 921-1842 | 100-102 Tamarack Circle, Skillman, NJ 08558 |
| Brian E. Briggs | MD | (701) 838-6011 | 718 6th St. SW, Minot, ND 58701 |
| W. Douglas Brodie | MD | (702) 832-7001 | 848 Tanager, Incline Village, NV 89450 |
| William Bryce | | (714) 544-3900 | 1254 Irvine Blvd #160, Tustin, CA 92680 |
| Frederick Burton | MD | (215) 844-4660 | 69 West Schoolhouse Lane, Philadelphia, PA 19144 |

## CHELATION continued

| | | | |
|---|---|---|---|
| Harold Buttram | MD | (215) 536-1890 | 5724–Clymer Rd. RFD #3, Quakertown, PA 18951 |
| Harold H. Byer | MD | (215) 348-0443 | 5045 Swamp Rd. #A-101, Fountainville, PA 18923 |
| Andrew Campbell | MD | (713) 497-7904 | 1441 Memorial Dr. #6, Houston, TX 77079 |
| Gary H. Campbell | DO F | (817) 457-8992 | 7421 Meadowbrook Dr., Ft. Worth, TX 76112 |
| Keith J. Carlson | MD | (507) 247-5921 | 210 Highland Court, Tyler, MN 56178 |
| Bob R. Carnett | DO | (314) 729-6225 | P.O. Box 430, Rolli Rd & McArthur St., Salem, MO 65560 |
| Herbert Carr | DO | (512) 787-6668 | P.O. Box 1179, Alamo, TX 78516 |
| Donald J. Carrow | MD | (813) 832-3220 | 3902 Henderson Blvd., Suite 206, Tampa, FL 33629 |
| James P. Carter | MD | (504) 588-5136 | 1430 Tulane Ave., New Orleans, LA 70112 |
| H. Richard Casdorph | MD PhD | (310) 597-8716 | 1703 Termino Ave., Suite 201, Long Beach, CA 95454 |
| Jose Castillo | MD | (215) 567-5845 | 228 South 22nd St., Philadelphia, PA 19103 |
| Robert Cathcart | MD | (415) 949-2822 | 127 Second St. Suite 4, Los Altos, CA 94022 |
| L. Terry Chappell | MD | (419) 358-4627 | 122 Thurman St., Bluffton, OH 45817 |
| Alan Shifman Charles | MD | (510) 937-3331 | 1414 Maria Lane, Walnut Creek, CA 94596 |
| Francis J. Cinelli | DO | (215) 588-4502 | 153 North 11th St., Bango, PA 18013 |
| Alan R. Cohen | MD | (203) 799-7753 | 325 Post Road, Orange, CT 06477 |
| Richard Cohen | MD | (617) 829-9281 | 51 Mill St. #1, Hanover, MA 02339 |
| Elisabeth-Ann Cole | MD | (409) 548-8610 | 303 N. McKinney, Sweeny, TX 77480 |
| Ted Cole | DO | (513) 779-0300 | 9678 Cincinnati Columbus Road, Cincinnati, OH 45241 |
| Jonathan Collin | MD | (206) 820-0547 | 12911–120th Ave, N.E. #A-50, Kirkland, WA |
| Marc Condren | MD | (908) 469-2133 | 15 Cedar Grove Ln. #20, Somerset, NJ 08873 |
| Vicki J. Conrad | MD | (405) 341-5691 | 1616 S. Boulevard, Edmond, OK 73013 |
| Ralph D. Cooper | DO | (417) 624-4323 | 1608 East 20th St., Joplin, MO 64804 |
| Prudencio Corro | MD M | (304) 252-0775 | 251 Stanford Rd., Beckley, WV 25801 |
| Sarafina Corsello | MD | (212) 517-2222 | 200 W. 57 St. #1202, New York, NY 10019 |
| Elmer M. Cranton | MD | (703) 677-3631 | Ripshin Road, Box 44, Trout Dale, VA 24378 |
| Elmer M. Cranton | MD | (206) 894-3548 | 15246 Leona Dr. S.E., Yelm, WA 98597 |
| Paul Cutler | MD | (716) 284-5140 | 652 Elmwood Ave., Niagara Falls, NY 14301 |
| Joseph Cyr | MD | (207) 868-5273 | 62 Main St., Van Buren, ME 04785 |
| Charles K. Dahirgren | MD | (415) 756-2900 | 1800 Sullivan Ave., Suite 604, Daly City, CA 94015 |
| James Dambrogio | DO | (216) 534-9737 | Hubbard Medical Center, 212 N. Main St., Hubbard, OH 44425 |

# CHELATION continued

| | | | |
|---|---|---|---|
| David A. Darbro | MD | (317) 787-7221 | 2142 E. Hanna Ave., Indianapolis, IN 46227 |
| Ronald M. Davis | MD | (713) 470-2930 | 10414 West Main St., La Porte, TX 77571 |
| Martin Dayton | MD DO | (305) 931-8484 | 18600 Collins Ave., N. Miami Beach, FL 33160 |
| James P. De Santis | DO | (206) 244-9619 | 8116 Palm St., Fairchild AFB, WA 99011 |
| Ward Dean | MD | (904) 484-0595 | P.O. Box 11097, Pensacola, FL 32524 |
| Sean Degnan | MD | (619) 320-4292 | 2825 Tahquitz McCallum #200, Palm Springs, CA 92260 |
| Sandra Denton | MD | (907) 563-6200 | 4115 Lake Otis Pkway #200, Anchorage, AK 99508 |
| Stefano DiMauro | MD | (305) 978-6604 | 1333 S. State Rd. 7, Ft. Lauderdale, FL 33068 |
| Stefano DiMauro | MD | (305) 940-6474 | 16666 N.E. 19th Ave. #101, N. Miami Beach, FL 33162 |
| Adonis J. Domingue | MD | (318) 365-2196 | 602 N. Lewis #600, New Iberia, LA 70560 |
| M. Paul Dommers | MD | (815) 544-3112 | 554 S. Main St., Belvidere, IL 61008 |
| Bruce Dooley | MD | (305) 527-9355 | 1493 S.E. 17th St., Ft. Lauderdale, FL 33316 |
| Lawrence E. Dorman | DO | (816) 358-2712 | 9120 E. 35th Street, Independence, MO 64052 |
| Thomas A. Dorman | MD | (805) 781-3388 | 171 N. Santa Rosa St., Suite A, San Louis Obispo, CA 03405 |
| William Campbell Douglass Jr. | MD | (904) 426-8803 | 2111 Ocean Drive, New Smyrna Beach, FL 32169 |
| Michael Doyle | MD | (612) 593-9458 | 10700 Old Ctry. Rd. 15, #350, Minneapolis, MN 55441 |
| Jean R. Eckerly | MD | (612) 593-9458 | 10700 Old Cty. Road 15, #15, Minneapolis, MN 55441 |
| David A. Edwards | MD | (702) 829-2277 | 4600 Kietzke Ln. Ste. M-242, Reno, NV 89509 |
| David J. Edwards | MD | (209) 251-5066 | 360 S. Clovis Ave., Fresno, CA 93727 |
| Mamduh El-Attrache | MD | (412) 547-3576 | 20 East Main St., Mt Pleasant, PA 15666 |
| Naima ABD Elghany | MD | (904) 763-7689 | 710 Venetian Way, Panama City, FL 32405 |
| Stephen K. Elsassar | DO PM | (309) 367-2321 | 205 S. Englewood Dr., Metamora, IL 61548 |
| Carol Englander | MD | (617) 965-7770 | 1340 Centre St., Newton, MA 02159 |
| David Epstein | DO | (404) 525-7333 | 407 Moreland Ave. #100, Atlanta, GA 30307 |
| William J. Faber | DO | (414) 464-7680 | 6529 W. Fond du Lac Ave., Milwaukee, WI 53218 |
| Charles Farinella | MD | (619) 324-0734 | 69–730 Hwy. #106A, Rancho Mirage, CA 92270 |
| Charles H. Farr | MD PhD | (405) 691-1112 | 10101 S. Western, Oklahoma City, OK 73139 |
| Eugene D. Finkle | MD | (707) 984-6151 | P.O. Box 59, Laytonville, CA 95454 |

## CHELATION continued

| | | | |
|---|---|---|---|
| Jerrold N. Finnie | MD | (203) 489-8977 | 333 Kennedy Dr. #204, Torrington, CT 06790 |
| James R. Fish | MD | (719) 471-2273 | 3030 N. Hancock Ave., Colorado Springs, CO 80907 |
| James W. Fitzsimmon Jr. | MD M | (503) 474-2166 | 591 Hidden Valley Rd., Grants Pass, OR 97527 |
| William Irby Fox | MD | (915) 672-7863 | 1227 N. Mockingbird Lane, Abilene, TX 79603 |
| James P. Frackelton | MD | (216) 835-0104 | 24700 Center Ridge Rd., Cleveland, OH 44145 |
| Clifford Fraser | MD | (818) 986-2199 | 4910 Van Nuys Blvd., #110, Sherman Oaks, CA 91403 |
| David C. Freeman | MD | (818) 985-1103 | 11311 Camarillo St. #103, North Hollywood, CA 91602 |
| Milton Fried | MD | (404) 451-4857 | 4426 Tilly Mill Rd., Atlanta, GA 30360 |
| Terry S. Friedmann | MD | (602) 381-0800 | 2701 E. Camelback Rd. #381, Phoenix, AZ 85016 |
| Mura Galperin | MD | (215) 677-2337 | 824 Hendrix St., Philadelphia, PA 19116 |
| John E. Gambee | MD | (503) 686-2536 | 66 Club Rd., Eugene, OR 97401 |
| John Gamble, Jr. | DO | (913) 321-1140 | 1509 Quindaro, Kansas City, KS 66104 |
| Kenneth Ganapini | DO | (313) 733-3140 | 1044 Gilbert St., Flint, MI 48532 |
| Steven Gee | MD | (510) 483-5881 | 595 Estudillo St., San Leandro, CA 94577 |
| Peter C. Gent | DO | (804) 744-3551 | 11900 Hull St., Midlothian, VA 23112 |
| Michael L. Gerber | MD | (702) 826-1900 | 3670 Grant Drive, Reno, NV 89502 |
| Dennis L. Gilbert | DO | (717) 367-1345 | 50 North Market St., Elizabethtown, PA 17022 |
| Joseph G. Godorov | DO | (305) 595-0671 | 9055 S. W. 87th Ave., Suite 307, Miami, FL 33176 |
| Robert Gold | DO MD | (714) 556-4653 | 1220 Hemlock Way Suite 103, Santa Ana, CA 92707 |
| David D. Goldberg | DO | (513) 277-1722 | 100 Forest Park Dr., Dayton, OH 45405 |
| William J. Goldwag | MD | (714) 827-5180 | 7499 Cerritos Ave., Stanton, CA 90680 |
| Carlos F. Gonzalez | MD | (904) 382-8282 | 7991 S. Suncoast Blvd., Homosassa, FL 32646 |
| Harold Goodman | DO | (301) 881-5229 | 8609 Second Ave #405B, Silver Spring, MD 20910 |
| Garry Gordon | MD | (602) 838-2079 | 5535 S. Compass, Tempe, AZ 85283 |
| Ross B. Gordon | MD | (415) 526-3232 | 415 Kains Ave., Albany, CA 94706 |
| Christy Graves | MD | (504) 646-4415 | 1850 Gause Blvd. #205, Slidell, LA 70461 |
| George Graves | DO | (904) 236-2525 | 3501 N. E. Tenth St., Ocala, FL 32670 |
| Allen Green | MD | (310) 493-4526 | 909 Electric Ave., Suite 212, Seal Beach, CA 90740 |
| Howard Greenspan | DO | (914) 358-6800 | Mountainview Medical Bldg., Nyack, NY 10960 |
| Luis E. Guerero | MD | (713) 789-0133 | 2055 S. Gessner, Suite 150, Houston, TX 77063 |
| Tammy Guerkin-Born | DO | (616) 455-3550 | 2687 44th St. S. E., Grand Rapids, MI 49512 |

# CHELATION continued

| | | | |
|---|---|---|---|
| Oliver L. Gunter | MD | (912) 336-7343 | 24 N. Ellis St., Camilla, GA 31730 |
| John L. Gustavus | MD | (301) 758-9350 | 4721 E. Broadway, N. Little Rock, AR 72117 |
| Howard Hagglund | MD M | (405) 329-4457 | 2227 W. Lindsey #1401, Norman, OK 73069 |
| Leonard Haimes | MD | (407) 994-3868 | 7300 N. Federal Hwy., Suite 107, Boca Raton, FL 33487 |
| William W. Halcomb | DO | (602) 832-3014 | 4323 E. Broadway, Suite 109, Mesa, AZ 85206 |
| Dennis Harper | DO PM | (801) 288-8881 | 5263 S. 300 West #203, Murray, UT 84107 |
| Charles Harris | MD | (908) 793-6464 | 1 Ortley Plaza, Ortley Beach, NJ 08751 |
| Burton B. Hart | DO | (509) 927-9922 | East 12104 Main, Spokane, WA 99206 |
| Driss Hassam | MD | (518) 561-2023 | 50 Court St., Plattsburgh, NY 12901 |
| Terrill K. Haws | DO | (708) 577-9451 | 121 S. Wilke Rd., Suite 111, Arlington Heights, IL 60005 |
| Clinton C. Hayes | DO | (314) 583-8911 | 100 West Main, Union, MO 63084 |
| Travis L. Herring | MD | (904) 775-0525 | 106 West Fern Dr., Orange City, FL 32763 |
| Robert R. Hershner | DO | (614) 253-8733 | 1571 East Livingston Ave., Columbus, OH 43255 |
| Thomas Hesselink | MD | (708) 844-0011 | 888 S. Edgelawn Dr., Suite 1735, Aurora, IL 60506 |
| Doyle B. Hill | DO | (417) 926-6643 | 601 North Bush, Mountain Grove, MO 65711 |
| Reino Hill | MD | (716) 665-3505 | 230 West Main St., Falconer, NY 14733 |
| Robert H. Hoagland | MD | (501) 382-4878 | DePaul Health Center, Box 158, Durmas, AZ 71639 |
| H. J. Hoegerman | MD | (805) 963-1824 | 101 W. Arrellaga, Suite D, Santa Barbara, CA 93101 |
| JoAnn Hoffer | MD | (707) 487-3405 | 12559 Hwy. 101 North, mini mart, Smith River, CA 95567 |
| Ronald L. Hoffman | MD | (212) 779-1744 | 40 E 30 St., New York, NY 10016 |
| James W. Hogin | DO | (405) 631-0524 | 937 S.W. 89th St., Suite C, Oklahoma City, OK 73139 |
| Robert Hollingsworth | MD | (601) 398-5106 | Drawer 87, 901 Forrest St., Shelby, MS 38774 |
| Steven Holper | MD | (702) 878-3510 | 3233 W. Charleston #202, Las Vegas, NV 89102 |
| John M. Hope | MD | (602) 778-9510 | 831 Gail Gardner Way, Prescott, AZ 86301 |
| Richard E. Hrdlicka | MD | (312) 232-1900 | 302 Randall Rd., Suite 206, Geneva, IL 60134 |
| Richard P. Huemer | MD | (206) 253-4445 | 406 S. E. 131 Ave., Bldg. C-303, Vancouver, WA 98684 |
| Harold Huffman | MD | (708) 867-5242 | P.O. Box 197, Hinton, VA 22831 |
| Thomas R. Humphrey | MD | (817) 766-4329 | 2400 Rushing, Wichata Falls, TX 76308 |
| Terry Hunsberger | MD | (316) 275-7128 | 602 N. 3rd, P.O. Box 679, Garden City, KS 67846 |

## CHELATION continued

| | | | |
|---|---|---|---|
| Serafin C. Ilagan | MD | (708) 458-0050 | 6252 S. Archer Rd., Summit, IL 60501 |
| Corazon Ilarina | MD | (702) 829-2277 | 4600 Kietzke Ln., Suite M-242, Reno, NV 89502 |
| Bill Illingworth | DO | (814) 623-8414 | 120 West John St., Bedford, PA 15522 |
| Emerson W. Ireland | DO | (816) 776-6933 | 703 Williard Blvd., Richmond, MO 64085 |
| Paul G. Isaak | MD | (907) 262-9341 | Box 219, Soldotna, AK 99669 |
| Richard Izquierdo | MD | (212) 589-4541 | 1070 Southern Blvd., Lower Level, Bronx, NY 10459 |
| M. Jahangirl | MD | (213) 587-3218 | 2156 South Santa Fe, Los Angeles, CA 90058 |
| Eva Jalkotzy | MD | (916) 893-3080 | 158 Eaton Rd., Suite E, Chico, CA 95926 |
| Michael Jansen | MD | (617) 661-6225 | 2557 Mass. Ave., Cambridge, MA 02140 |
| P. Jayalakshmi | MD | (215) 473-4226 | 6366 Sherwood Rd., Philadelphia, PA 19151 |
| Keith E. Johnson | MD | (919) 281-5122 | 188 Quewhiffle, Aberdeen, NC 28315 |
| Gordon H. Josephs | DO | (602) 778-9232 | 315 W. Goodwin St., Prescott, AZ 86301 |
| Gordon H. Josephs | DO | (602) 998-9232 | 7315 E. Evans, Scottsdale, AZ 85260 |
| George J. Juetersonke | DO M | (719) 596-9049 | 5455 N. Union, Suite 200, Colorado Springs, CO 80918 |
| James J. Julian | MD | (213) 467-5555 | 1654 Cahuenga Blvd., Hollywood, CA 90028 |
| Eleazar M. Kadile | MD F | (414) 468-9442 | 1538 Bellveue, Green Bay, WI 54311 |
| Ji-Zhou Joseph Kang | MD | (702) 798-2992 | 5613 S. Eastern, Las Vegas, NV 89119 |
| Svetlana Kaufman | MD | (508) 453-5181 | 24 Merrimack St. #323, Lowell, MA 01852 |
| Roy E. Kerry | MD | (412) 588-2600 | 17 Sixth Ave., Greenville, PA 16125 |
| Robert Kimmel | MD | (206) 734-3250 | 4204 Meridian, Suite 104, Bellingham, WA 98226 |
| Stephen S. Kiteck | MD | (606) 678-5137 | 1301 Pumphouse Rd., Somerset, KY 42501 |
| Arthur L. Koch | DO | (717) 455-4747 | 57 West Juniper St., Hazleton, PA 18201 |
| Michael Kostanko | DO | (304) 253-0591 | 114 East Main St., Buckley, WV 25801 |
| William C. Kubitschek | DO | (619) 744-6991 | 1194 Calle Maria, San Marcos, CA 92069 |
| Richard A. Kunin | MD | (415) 346-2500 | 2698 Pacific Ave., San Francisco, CA 94115 |
| Steve Kuplesky | MD | (504) 751-6965 | 5618 Bayridge, Baton Rouge, LA 70817 |
| Roy Kupsinel | MD | (407) 365-6681 | 1325 Shangri-la Lane, Oviedo, FL 32765 |
| Mitchell Kurk | MD | (516) 239-5540 | 310 Broadway, Lawrence, NY 11559 |
| Michael Kwiker | DO | (916) 489-4400 | 3301 Alta Arden, Suite 3, Sacramento, CA 95825 |
| N. Thomas LaCava | MD | (508) 854-1380 | 360 W. Boylston St., Suite 107, West Boylston, MA 01583 |
| John L. Laird | MD | (704) 683-3101 | Route 1, Box 7, Leicester, NC 28748 |
| Fredrick Lam | MD | (808) 537-3311 | 1270 Queen Emma St. #501, Honolulu, HI 96813 |

## CHELATION continued

| | | | |
|---|---|---|---|
| Charles E. Law Jr. | MD | (818) 761-1661 | 3959 Laurel Canyon Blvd. #1, Studio City, CA 91604 |
| Alan T. Lee | MD | (802) 524-1062 | P.O. Box 306, St. Albans, VT 05478 |
| C. Y. Lee | MD | (201) 738-9220 | 952 Amboy Ave., Edison, NJ 08837 |
| Eugene H. Lee | MD | (813) 251-3089 | 1804 W. Kennedy Blvd., Suite A, Tampa, FL 33606 |
| Richard H. Leigh | MD | (701) 775-5527 | 2314 Library Circle, Grand Forks, ND 58201 |
| Russel A. Lemesh | MD | (415) 731-5907 | 595 Buckingham Way #320, San Francisco, CA 94132 |
| Bernard J. Letourneau | DO | (305) 666-9933 | 6475 SW 40 Street, Miami, FL 33155 |
| Ralph Lev | MD MS | (908) 738-9220 | 952 Amboy Ave., Edison, NJ 08837 |
| Warren M. Levin | MD F | (212) 696-1900 | 444 Park Ave South, 12th Fl., New York, NY 10016 |
| Cathie Anne Lippman | MD | (213) 653-0488 | 8383 Wilshire Blvd., Suite 360, Beverly Hills, CA 90211 |
| Gennaro E. Locurcio | MD | (908) 351-1333 | 610 3rd Ave, Elizabeth, NJ 07202 |
| | MD | (718) 336-2291 | 2386 Ocean Parkway, Brooklyn, NY 11223 |
| Vincent Longobardo | MD | (518) 325-5300 | NY |
| Derrick Lonsdale | MD | (216) 835-0104 | 24700 Center Ridge Rd., Cleveland, OH 44145 |
| Terry W. Love | DO | (309) 764-2900 | 2610-41st St., Moline, IL 61252 |
| Ralph J. Luciani | DO | (505) 888-5995 | 2301 San Pedro N.E., Suite G, Albuquerque, NM 87110 |
| Paul Lynn | MD | (415) 566-1000 | 345 W. Portal Ave., San Francisco, CA 94127 |
| Allan Magazinar | DO | (609) 424-8222 | 1907 Greentree Rd., Cherry Hill, NJ 08003 |
| Denise R. Mark | MD | (415) 566-1000 | 345 W. Portal Ave., San Francisco, CA 94127 |
| Claude Marquette | MD | (415) 964-6700 | 5050 El Carmino Real #110, Los Altos, CA 94022 |
| Linda Martin | DO | (214) 985-1377 | 1524 Independence, Suite C, Plano, TX 75075 |
| Robert E. Martin | MD | (907) 376-5284 | 501 N. Knik, Wasilla, AK 99654 |
| Alfred Massam | MD | (813) 773-6668 | 528 West Main St., Wauchula, FL 33873 |
| William J. Mauer | DO | (708) 255-7030 | 3401 N. Kennicott Ave., Arlington Heights, IL 60004 |
| Conrad G. Maulfair Jr. | DO | (215) 682-2104 | R.R. #2, Box 71 Main St., Mertztown, PA 19539 |
| John Mauriello | MD | (904) 296-0900 | 4063 Salisbury Rd. #206, Jacksonville, FL 32216 |
| K. Peter McCallum | MD | (208) 263-5456 | 2500 Selle Rd., Sandpoint, ID 83864 |
| Ross S. McConnell | MD | (413) 663-3701 | 732 Main St., Williamstown, MA 01267 |
| Edward W. McDonagh | DO | (816) 453-5940 | 2800-A Kendallwood Pkwy, Kansas City, MO 64119 |
| Charles T. McGee | MD F | (208) 664-1478 | 1717 Lincolnway, Suite 108, Cour d'Alene, ID 83814 |
| Thomas McNaughton | MD | (813) 365-6273 | 1521 Dolphin St., Sarasota, FL 34236 |
| Thomas McNaughton | MD | (813) 484-2167 | 540 South Nokomis Ave., Venice, FL 34285 |

## CHELATION continued

| | | | |
|---|---|---|---|
| Eteri Melinikov | MD | (813) 748-7943 | 116 Manatee Ave. East, Bradenton, FL 34208 |
| Richard B. Menashe | DO | (201) 906-8866 | 15 South Main Street, Edison, NJ 08837 |
| S. W. Meyer | DO | (602) 669-8911 | 323 River Front Dr., P.O. Box 1870, Parker, AZ 85344 |
| Anita Millen | MD | (213) 320-1132 | 1010 Crenshaw Blvd., Suite 170, Torrance, CA 90501 |
| Howard J. Miller | MD | (814) 274-7070 | 360 East 2nd St., Coudersport, PA 16915 |
| George C. Miller II | MD M | (717) 524-4405 | Three Hospital Drive, Lewisburg, PA 17837 |
| Robert D. Milne | MD | (702) 385-1393 | 2110 Pinto Ln., Las Vegas, NV 89106 |
| Ralph A. Miranda | MD | (412) 838-7632 | RD. #12, Box 108, Greensburg, PA 15601 |
| George H. Mitchell | MD | (201) 265-4111 | 2639 Conn. Ave. NW, Suite C-100, Washington, DC 20008 |
| Phillip Mitchell | MD | (800) 562-6574 | 407 Bienville St., Natchitoches, LA 71457 |
| William D. Mitchell | DO | (614) 761-0555 | 3520 Snouffer Rd., Columbus, OH 43235 |
| Bernard Mlaver | MD PM | (404) 395-1600 | 4480 N. Shallowford Rd., Atlanta, GA 30338 |
| Leo Modzinski | DO MD | (517) 785-4254 | 100 West State St., Atlanta, MI 49709 |
| Mohammed Moharram | MD | (805) 965-5229 | 101 W. Arrellaga, Suite B, Santa Barbara, CA 93101 |
| Roy M. Montalbano | MD | (504) 626-1985 | 4408 Highway 22, Mandeville, LA 70448 |
| Kirk Morgan | MD | (502) 228-0156 | 9105 U.S. Highway 42, Louisville, KY 40059 |
| Frank Mosler | MD | (818) 785-7425 | 14428 Gilmore St., Van Nuys, CA 91401 |
| Charles Moss | MD | (619) 457-1314 | 8950 Villa La Jolla #2162, La Jolla, CA 92037 |
| Fains Munits | MD | (201) 763-3743 | 51 Pleasant Valley Way, West Orange, NJ 07052 |
| Doly Murphy III | MD | (501) 756-3251 | 812 Dorman, Springdale, AR 72764 |
| Peter H.C. Mutke | MD | (501) 933-2405 | 1808 San Miguel Drive, Walnut Creek, CA 94596 |
| Brij Myer | MD | (214) 248-2488 | 4222 Trinity Mills Rd, Suite 222, Dallas, TX 75287 |
| Roy N. Neil | MD | (913) 628-8341 | 105 West 13th, Hays, KS 67601 |
| Seldon R. Nelson | DO | (517) 349-2458 | 4386 N. Meridian Rd., Williamston, MI 48895 |
| Carlos E. Nossa | MD | (713) 977-3509 | 3800 Tanglewilde #1007, Houston, TX 77063 |
| Eugene C. Oliveto | MD | (402) 392-0233 | 8031 W. Center Rd. #208, Omaha, NE 68124 |
| Stanley R. Olszlyn | MD | (602) 954-0811 | 3610 N. 44th St., Suite 210, Phoenix, AZ 85108 |
| Joseph Ossorio | MD | (813) 921-6338 | 3900 Clark Rd. #5H, Sarasota, FL 34277 |
| Thomas A. Padden | DO | (313) 473-2922 | 39555 W. Ten Mile Rd. #303, Novi, MI 48375 |
| Herbert Pardell | DO | (305) 989-5558 | 210 S. Federal Hwy., Suite 302, Hollywood, FL 33020 |
| Paul A. Parente | DO | (313) 626-7544 | 30275 Thirteen Mile Rd., Farmington Hills, MI 48018 |
| Narinder Singh Parhar | MD | (305) 976-6604 | 7804 Glages Rd. #200, Boca Raton, FL 33487 |

# CHELATION continued

| | | | |
|---|---|---|---|
| Byung Sun Park | MD | (213) 734-6684 | 945 S. Western Ave. #102, Los Angeles, CA 90006 |
| John B. Park | MD | (805) 833-6562 | 6501 Schirra Ct., Suite 205, Bakersfield, CA 93313 |
| John B. Park | MD | (209) 781-6224 | 200 North G St., Porteville, CA 93257 |
| Gerald Parker | DO | (505) 884-3506 | 8206 Montgomery Blvd., NE. #D, Albuquerque, NM 87109 |
| Gerald Parker | DO | (806) 355-8263 | 4714 S. Western, Amarillo, TX 79109 |
| James Parsons | MD | (407) 452-0332 | 5 Minna Main, Merritt Island, FL 32953 |
| Sohini Patel | MD | (703) 941-3606 | 7023 Little River Tpke. #207, Annandale, VA 22003 |
| Paul Peirsel | MD | (814) 443-2521 | R D 4, Box 267-1A, Somerset, PA 15501 |
| Marvin D. Penwell | DO | (313) 735-7809 | 319 S. Bridge St., Linden, MI 48451 |
| Ronald L. Peters | MD | (503) 482-7007 | 1607 Siskiyou Blvd., Ashland, OR 97520 |
| Robert J. Peterson | DO | (215) 579-0330 | 64 Magnolia Dr., Newtown, PA 18940 |
| Terry Pfau | DO | (702) 258-7860 | 2810 West Chelston #55, Las Vegas, NV 89102 |
| James Privitera | MD | (818) 966-1618 | 105 N. Grandview Ave., Corvina, CA 91723 |
| P. Gus J. Prosch Jr. | MD PM | (205) 823-6180 | 759 Valley St., Birmingham, AL 35226 |
| Gary L. Pynckel | DO | (813) 278-3377 | 3940 Metro Parkway #115, Fort Myers, FL 33916 |
| Steven Rachlin | MD | (516) 921-8181 | 8 Greenfield Rd., Syosset, NY 11791 |
| William L. Reed | MD | (303) 241-3631 | 2700 G Road #1-B, Grand Junction, CO 81506 |
| Dan C. Rehem | MD | (305) 977-3700 | 3400 Park Cent. Blvd. N. #3450, Pompano Beach, FL 33064 |
| Donald E. Reiner | MD | (805) 925-0961 | 1414-D South Miller, Santa Maria, CA 93454 |
| Stephen L. Reisman | MD | (615) 383-9030 | 417 E. Iris Dr., Nashville, TN 37204 |
| Razvan Rentea | MD | (312) 583-7793 | 3525 W. Peterson, Suite 611, Chicago, IL 60659 |
| Joan M. Resk | DO | (714) 842-5591 | 18821 Delaware St., Suite 203, Huntington Beach, CA 92648 |
| Sally Anne Rex | DO | (215) 866-0900 | 1343 Easton Ave., Bethlehem, PA 18018 |
| William E. Richardson | MD | (404) 607-0570 | 1718 Peachtree St. NW #552, Atlanta, GA 30309 |
| Vladimir Rizov | MD | (512) 451-8149 | 8311 Shoal Creek Blvd., Austin, TX 78758 |
| Harold Robinson | MD | (813) 644-5088 | 4406 S. Florida Ave., Suite 27, Lakeland, FL 33803 |
| Robert J. Rogers | MD | (407) 679-2811 | 1865 N. Samoran Blvd., Suite 204, Winter Park, FL 32792 |
| Michael Rosenbaum | MD | (415) 927-9450 | 45 San Clemente Dr., Suite B130, Corte Madera, CA 94925 |
| Beverly Rosenfeld | DO | (515) 276-0061 | 7177 Hickman Rd. #10, Des Moines, IO 50322 |

## CHELATION continued

| | | | |
|---|---|---|---|
| Gary S. Ross | MD | (415) 398-0555 | 500 Sutter, Suite 300, San Francisco, CA 94102 |
| Binyamin Rothstein | DO | (410) 484-2121 | 2835 Smith Ave. #209, Baltimore, MD 21209 |
| James Rowland | DO PhD | (816) 361-4077 | 8133 Wornall Rd., Kansas City, MO 64114 |
| Theodore C. Rozema | MD | (800) 992-8350 | 1000 E. Rutherford Rd., Landrum, SC 29356 |
| Charles J. Rudolf | DO | (816) 453-5940 | 2800-A Kendallwood Pkwy, Kansas City, MO 64119 |
| William J. Saccoman | MD | (619) 440-3838 | 505 N. Mollison Ave., Suite 103, El Cajon, CA 92021 |
| Mahmoud Salamatian | MD | (703) 941-3606 | 7023 Little River Tpke, #207. Annandale, VA 22003 |
| K. R. Sampathachar | MD | (215) 473-4226 | 6366 Sherwood Rd., Philadelphia, PA 19151 |
| James H. Sams | MD | (601) 327-8701 | 1120 Lehmburg Rd., Columbus, MS 39702 |
| Michael G. Samuels | DO | (214) 991-3977 | 7616 LBJ Freeway #230, Dallas, TX 75251 |
| Albert J. Scarchili | DO | (313) 626-7544 | 30275 Thirteen Mile Rd., Farmington Hills, MI 48108 |
| Michael A. Schacter | MD | (914) 368-4700 | Two Executive Blvd. #202, Suffern, NY 10901 |
| Robert H. Schmidt | DO | (215) 437-1959 | 1227 Liberty Plaza Bldg. #303, Allentown, PA 18102 |
| Terril J. Schneider | MD | (912) 929-1027 | 205 Dental Dr., Suite 19, Warner Robins, GA 31088 |
| Joya Lynn Schoen | MD DA | (407) 664-2729 | 341 N. Maitland Ave., Suite 210, Maitland, FL 32751 |
| James D. Schuler | MD | (707) 487-3405 | 12559 Hwy 101 North, mini mart, Smith River, CA 95567 |
| John T. Schwent | DO | (314) 937-8688 | 1400 Truman Blvd., Festus, MO 63028 |
| Joseph Sciabbarrasi | MD | (301) 545-8364 | 571-35 Street, Manhattan Beach, CA 90266 |
| Ronald H. Scott | DO | (314) 468-4932 | 131 Meredeth, Sullivan, MO 63080 |
| Shirley B. Scott | MD | (505) 986-9960 | P.O. Box 2670, Santa Fe, NM 87504 |
| Ralph G. Selby | MD | (805) 873-1000 | 1311 Columbus St., Bakersfield, CA 93305 |
| Peter Senatore | DO | (708) 872-8722 | 1911-27th St., Zion, IL 60099 |
| John L. Sessions | DO PM | (409) 423-2166 | 1609 South Margaret, Kirbyville, TX 75956 |
| Carol Shamlin | | (408) 378-7970 | 621 E. Campbell, Suite 11A, Campbell, CA 95008 |
| Robban Sica-Cohen | MD | (203) 799-7733 | 325 Post Road, Orange, CT 06477 |
| Marjorie S. Siebert | DO | (718) 386-2020 | 65-12 Fresh Pond Road, Ridgewood, NY 11385 |
| Chandrika P. Sinha | MD | (412) 349-1414 | 1177 South Sixth St., Indiana, PA 15701 |
| Herbert R. Slavin | MD | (305) 748-4991 | 7200 W. Commercial Blvd. #210, Lauderhill, FL 33319 |
| Jack E. Slingluff | DO | (216) 494-8641 | 5850 Fulton Rd. N W, Canton, OH 44718 |
| Don K. Snyder | MD | (419) 399-2045 | Route 2, Box 1271, Paulding, OH 45879 |
| Donald E. Soll | MD | (702) 786-7101 | 708 North Center St., Reno, NV 89501 |
| Tsilia Sorina | MD | (718) 375-2600 | 2026 Ocean Ave., Brooklyn, NY 11230 |

# CHELATION continued

| | | | |
|---|---|---|---|
| Francisco Soto | MD | (915) 534-0272 | 1420 Geronimo, D2, El Paso, TX 79925 |
| Vincent Spackhart | MD | (804) 622-0014 | 902 Gradon Ave., Norfolk, VA 23507 |
| Harold T. Sparks | DO | (812) 479-8228 | 3001 Washington Ave., Evanston, IN 47714 |
| David A. Steenblock | DO | (714) 770-9616 | 22706 Aspen, Suite 501, Lake Forest, CA 92630 |
| Maurice L. Stephens | MD | (206) 861-2224 | 13820 N. E. 65th St. #550, Redmond, WA 98052 |
| Robert R. Stocker | DO | (414) 258-6282 | 2505 Mayfair Rd., Milwaukee, WI 53226 |
| Annette Stoesser | MD | (505) 623-2444 | 112 S. Kentucky, Roswell, NM 88201 |
| Ron Stogryn | MD | (210) 366-3637 | 7334 Blanco Rd., #100, San Antonio, TX 78216 |
| Walt Stoll | MD | (606) 233-4273 | 6801 Danville Rd., Nicholasville, KY 40356 |
| Cal Streeter | DO | (219) 924-2410 | 9635 Saric Court, Highland, IN 46322 |
| Terri Su | MD | (707) 571-7560 | 1038 4th St., Suite 3, Santa Rosa, CA 95404 |
| Tipu Sultan | MD F | (314) 921-7100 | 11585 W. Florissant, Florissant, MO 63033 |
| Murray Susser | MD | (213) 453-4424 | 2730 Wilshire Blvd., Suite 110, Santa Monica, CA 90403 |
| James E. Swann | DO | (816) 833-3366 | 2116 Sterling, Independence, MO 64052 |
| Rodolfo T. Sy | MD | (908) 738-9220 | 952 Amboy Ave., Edison, NJ 08837 |
| Melissa Taliaferro | MD | (501) 447-2599 | Cherry St., P.O. Box 400, Leslie, AR 72645 |
| John R. Tambone | MD | (815) 338-2345 | 102 E. South St., Woodstock, IL 60098 |
| Saroj T. Tampira | MD | (504) 277-8991 | 812 E. Judge Perez, Chalmette, LA 70043 |
| David H. Tang | MD | (619) 341-2113 | 74133 El Paseo #6, Palm Desert, CA 92260 |
| Yiwen Y. Tang | MD | (702) 826-9500 | 380 Bringby, Reno, NV 89509 |
| Richard E. Tapert | DO | (313) 779-5700 | 23550 Harper, St. Clair Shores, MI 48080 |
| John C. Tapp | MD | (502) 781-1483 | 414 Old Morgantown Rd., Bowling Green, KY 42101 |
| Charles D. Taylor | MD | (405) 525-7751 | 3715 North Classen Blvd., Oklahoma City, OK 73118 |
| John T. Taylor | DO | (505) 884-3506 | 8208 Montgomery Ave NE. #D, Albuquerque, NM 87109 |
| John T. Taylor | DO | (806) 355-8263 | 4714 S. Western, Amarillo, TX 79109 |
| Lawrence Taylor | MD | (619) 296-2952 | 3330 Third Ave. #402, San Diego, CA 92103 |
| Michael Teplitsky | MD | (718) 769-0997 | 415 Oceanview Ave., Brooklyn, NY 11235 |
| Donald Thompson | MD | (615) 581-6367 | P.O. Box 2088, Morristown, TN 37816 |
| Stephen Thornburgh | DO | (208) 466-3517 | 824-17th Ave South, Nampa, ID 83651 |
| Bessie J. Tillman | MD | (916) 246-3022 | 2054 Market St., Redding, CA 96001 |
| John P. Toth | MD | (415) 682-5660 | 2299 Bacon St., Suite 10, Concord, CA 94520 |
| John Parks Towbridge | MD M | (713) 540-2329 | 9816 Memorial Blvd., Suite 205, Humble, TX 77338 |

# CHELATION continued

| | | | |
|---|---|---|---|
| Myrna D. Trowbridge | DO | (219) 462-3377 | 850-C Marsh St., Valparaiso, IN 46383 |
| David E. Turfler | DO | (219) 233-3840 | 336 W. Naverre St., South Bend, IN 46616 |
| Richard J. Ucci | MD | (607) 432-8752 | 521 Main St., Oneonta, NY 13820 |
| Robert Vance | DO | (702) 385-7771 | 801 South Rancho Dr., Suite F2, Las Vegas, NV 89106 |
| James Ventresco Jr. | DO | (216) 792-2349 | 3848 Tippecanoe Rd., Youngstown, OH 44511 |
| Michael G. Vesselago | MD | (206) 367-0760 | 217 North 125th, Seattle, WA 98133 |
| D. Erik Von Kiel | DO | (215) 776-7639 | Liberty Square Med. Ctr. #200, Allentown, PA 18104 |
| James H. Waddell | MD | (601) 875-5505 | 1520 Government St., Ocean Springs, MS 39564 |
| Francis J. Waickman | MD F | (216) 867-3767 | 544 White Pond Dr., Suite B, Akron, OH 44320 |
| Harvey Walker Jr. | MD PhD | (314) 721-7227 | 138 N. Merimec Ave., St. Loius, MO 63105 |
| Robert S. Waters | MD | (708) 790-8100 | 739 Roosevelt Road, Glen Ellyn, IL 60137 |
| Robert S. Waters | MD | (608) 254-7178 | Race & Vine St., Box 357, Wisconsin Dells, WI 53965 |
| William Watson | MD | (904) 623-3836 | 600 Stewart St. N. E., Milton, FL 32570 |
| Douglas Weeks | MD | (216) 835-0104 | 24700 Center Ridge Rd, Cleveland, OH 44145 |
| Ronald R. Wempen | MD F | (714) 546-4325 | 3620 S. Bristol St., Suite 306, Santa Ana, CA 92704 |
| Joseph R. Whitaker | MD | (318) 467-5131 | P.O. Box 458, Newellton, LA 71357 |
| Julian Whitaker | MD | (714) 851-1550 | 4321 Birch St., Suite 103, Newport Beach, CA 92660 |
| Norman E. Whitney | DO | (317) 831-3352 | P.O. Box 173, Mooresville, IN 46158 |
| John L. Wilson | MD | (704) 683-3101 | Route 1, Box 7, Leicester, NC 28748 |
| J. Robert Winslow | DO | (214) 241-4614 | 2745 Valwood Pkwy., Dallas, TX 75234 |
| George Wolverton | MD | (812) 282-4309 | 647 Eastern Blvd., Clarksville, IN 47130 |
| Thomas E. Woodson | MD Retired | | 320 Ward St, Seattle, WA |
| Lon B. Work | MD | (408) 655-0215 | 841 Foam St. #D, Monterey, CA 93940 |
| Jonathan V. Wright | MD PM | (206) 631-8920 | 24030-132nd S. E., Kent, WA 98042 |
| Lance Wright | MD | (215) 387-1200 | 3901 Market St., Philadelphia, PA 19104 |
| William Wright | MD | (501) 624-3312 | 1 Mercy Drive, Suite 211, Hot Springs, AR 71913 |
| Ray C. Wunderlich Jr. | MD M | (813) 822-3612 | 666-6th Street South, St. Petersberg, FL 33701 |
| Jerry N. Yee | DO | (414) 258-6282 | 2505 N. Mayfair Rd., Milwaukee, WI 53226 |
| Terrence Howe Young | MD | (503) 371-1558 | 1205 Wallace Rd. NW, Salem, OR 97304 |
| David Younger | MD | (803) 769-4649 | 383 Grove St., Charleston, SC 29403 |
| Savely Yurkovsky | MD | (516) 333-2929 | 309 Madison St., Westbury, NY 11590 |
| Pavel Yutsis | MD PM | (718) 259-2122 | 1309 W. 7th St., Brooklyn, NY 11204 |
| Steve M. Zekan | MD | (304) 343-7559 | 1208 Kanawha Blvd. E, Charleston, WV 25301 |

## ENVIRONMENTAL MEDICINE

| NAME | TITLE | PHONE | ADDRESS |
|------|-------|-------|---------|
| Laraine C. Abbey | RN | (609) 443-6389 | Warren Plaza W., Rt. 130, East Windsor, NJ 08520 |
| John G. Adams | MD M | (214) 938-4363 | 711 E. End Blvd. S, Marshall, TX 75670 |
| Neil D. Adams | MD E | (206) 736-1171 | 123 N. Tower, Centralia, WA 98531 |
| Hartwig M. Adler | MD | (504) 865-1767 | 4208 Vendome Pl., New Orleans, LA 70125 |
| Jeffry N. Anderson | MD M | (415) 927-7140 | 45 San Clemente Dr., #100B, Corte Madera, CA 94925 |
| Edward M. Arana | DDS SDA | (408) 659-5385 | 107 Quien Sabe, Carmel Valley, CA 93924 |
| Robert M. Armer | MD | (317) 846-7341 | 8803 N. Meridian St., Indianapolis, IN 46260 |
| Richard F. Bahr | MD | (513) 299-8788 | 2353 W. Stroop Rd., Dayton, OH 45439 |
| Sidney M. Baker | MD F | (203) 387-1800 | 60 Washington Ave., Hamden, CT 06518 |
| E. G. Barnet | MD E | (602) 264-7957 | 550 West Thomas Rd. #233-D, Phoenix, AZ 85013 |
| Gerald N. Bart | MD | (314) 842-5082 | 10004 Kennerly Rd. #310, St. Louis, MO 63128 |
| Robert M. Battle | MD | (713) 932-0552 | 9910 Long Point Rd., Houston, TX 77055 |
| Joseph D. Beasley | MD | (516) 789-7031 | 221 Broadway #303, Amityville, NY 11701 |
| Iris R. Bell | MD M | (602) 626-6254 | Dept. of Psych., U of AZ Hlth S, Tucson, AZ 85724 |
| Thomas E. Bensen | MD F | (618) 395-5222 | 1200 N. East St., Olney, IL 62450 |
| Murray L. Black | DO F | (509) 966-1780 | 609 S. 48th Ave., Yakima, WA 98908 |
| Mary Ann Block | DO | (817) 735-2000 | 3500 Camp Bowie Blvd., Ft. Worth, TX 76107 |
| Marvin Boris | MD | (516) 921-9000 | 75 Froelich Farm Blvd., Woodbury, NY 11797 |
| Robert W. Boxer | MD F | (312) 677-0260 | 64 Old Orchard Rd., Skokie, IL 60777 |
| D. Morton Boyette | MD F | (912) 435-7161 | 804 Fourteenth Ave., Albany, GA 31708 |
| John H. Boyles Jr. | MD F | (513) 434-0555 | 7076 Corporate Way, Centerville, OH 45459 |
| Miklos L. Bozcko | MD | (914) 948-8817 | 146 Nelson Rd., Scarsdale, NY 10583 |
| Cicil A. Bradley | MD M | (415) 783-9900 | 27206 Calaroga Ave., Suite 205, Hayward, CA 94545 |
| Nachman Brautbar | MD PM | (213) 662-8866 | 201 S. Alvarado, Suite 402, Los Angeles, CA 90057 |
| Floyd H. Brigham | MD M | (209) 962-7855 | P. O. Box 1228, Groveland, CA 95321 |
| Martin Brody | DDS MD | (305) 822-9035 | 7100 W. 20th Ave., Hialeah, FL 33016 |
| Clifton R. Brooks | MD LME | (405) 329-8437 | 2114 Martingale Dr., Norman, OK 73072 |
| Andrew M. Brown | MD F | (205) 547-4971 | 515 South Third St., Gladsen, AL 35901 |
| David E. Brown | MD F | (513) 223-3691 | 830 Fidelity Building, Dayton, OH 45402 |
| Don Bryan | MD PM | (205) 663-5840 | P. O. Box 1857, Alabaster, AL 35007 |

## ENVIRONMENTAL MEDICINE continued

| | | | |
|---|---|---|---|
| Marian P. Bryan | AB | (314) 961-7424 | 9349 Parkside Drive, St. Louis, MO 63144 |
| Thurman M. Bullock | MD | (919) 654-3143 | 104 East Seventh Ave., Chadbourn, NC 28431 |
| David Buscher | MD F | (206) 453-0288 | 1603-116th N. E., Suite 112, Bellevue, WA 98004 |
| Harry R. Butler | MD | (313) 676-2800 | 1821 King Rd., Trenton, MI 48183 |
| Harold Buttram | MD | (215) 536-1890 | 5724 Clymer Rd., RFD #3, Quakertown, PA 18951 |
| Eugene B. Byron | MD | (701) 780-6000 | 1000 S. Cal Rd., Grand Forks, ND 58201 |
| Dorothy V. Calabrese | MD M | (714) 240-7178 | 655 Camino De Los Mares #126, San Clemente, CA 92672 |
| Christopher Calapai | DO PM | (516) 794-0404 | 1900 Hempstead Tpke., East Meadow, NY 11554 |
| Thomas J. Callender | MD | (318) 233-6022 | 108 Harolyn Pk Dr., Lafayette, LA 70503 |
| Herbert Lee Camp | MD | (517) 631-1254 | 4011 Orchard Dr. #3004, Midland, MI 48641 |
| Gary H. Campbell | DO F | (817) 457-8992 | 7421 Meadowbrook Dr., Ft. Worth, TX 76112 |
| Stanley J. Cannon | MD F | (305) 279-3020 | 9085 Southwest 87th Ave., Miami, FL 33176 |
| Susan Carlson | R.Ph. | (708) 255-1600 | 15 College Dr., Arlington Hgts, IL 60004 |
| Francis M. Carroll | MD F | (919) 654-3143 | 104 Seventh Ave., Chadbourn, NC 28431 |
| Ramon Casanova-Roiq | MD F | (809) 764-5715 | 513 Hostos Ave., Hato Rey, PR 00918 |
| Rocco D. Cassone | MD M | (803) 536-5511 | 1175 Crook Rd., Suite 230, Orangeburg, SC 29115 |
| William J. Cates | MD | (614) 261-0151 | 2885 W. Dublin Granville Rd., Columbus, OH 43235 |
| Stephanie F. Cave | MD | (504) 767-7433 | 7777 Hennessy, Suite 101, Baton Rouge, LA 70808 |
| I-Tsu Chao | MD F | (718) 998-3331 | 1641 E. 18th St., Brooklyn, NY 11229 |
| David F. Charles | MD | (702) 388-7337 | 601 S. Rancho #A-3, Q. Park 2, Las Vegas, NV 89106 |
| Chin Y. Chung | MD M | (814) 445-4429 | 210 E. 2nd St., Erie, PA 16507 |
| Clarence C. Cohrs | MD | (816) 263-1747 | 2 Flower Lane Terrace, Moberly, MO 65270 |
| Robert Coiller | MD F | (919) 654-3143 | 104 Seventh Ave., Chadbourn, NC 28431 |
| Vicki J. Conrad | MD | (405) 341-5691 | 1616 S. Boulevard, Edmond, OK 73013 |
| Carolyn G. Conroy | PhD | (516) 437-1060 | 12 California Ave. #B-408, Albany, NY 12205 |
| Paul R. Cook | MD | (301) 337-2707 | 901 Dulaney Valley Rd., #11, Towson, MD 21204 |
| Prudencio Corro | MD M | (304) 252-0775 | 251 Stanford Rd., Beckley, WV 25801 |
| William G. Crook | MD PC F | (901) 423-5400 | 681 Skyline Dr., Jackson, TN 38301 |
| Linwood W. Custalo | MD PM | (804) 826-0232 | 1832 Todds Lane, Hampton, VA 23666 |
| Aniceto D'Sousa | MD | (815) 344-0090 | 1110H N. Green St., McHenry, IL 60050 |

# ENVIRONMENTAL MEDICINE continued

| | | | |
|---|---|---|---|
| David A. Darbro | MD | (317) 787-7221 | 2142 E. Hanna Ave., Indianapolis, IN 46227 |
| Stoyan P. Daskalov | MD | (216) 823-3219 | 1613 S. Liberty Ave., Alliance, OH 44601 |
| Stuart B. Datt | MD | (216) 261-3040 | 26300 Euclid Ave., Euclid, OH 44132 |
| Paula G. Davey | MD | (313) 662-3384 | 425 East Washington, Ann Arbor, MI 48104 |
| Orville J. Davis | MD E | (714) 283-6033 | 9412 Hilmer Drive, La Mesa, CA 92042 |
| Sandra Denton | MD | (907) 563-6200 | 4115 Lake Otis Pkway #200, Anchorage, AK 99508 |
| Cornelius F. Derrick | MD | (313) 675-0678 | 1821 King Rd., Trenton, MI 48183 |
| F. Keels Dickson | MD | (704) 892-7968 | 485 North Wendover Rd., Charlotte, NC 28211 |
| Alan M. Dishman | AF | (415) 447-7173 | 630 Clyde Court, Mountain View, CA 94043 |
| Crawford S. Duhon | MD F | (303) 223-3970 | 4841 Elorado Springs Dr., Boulder, CO 80303 |
| Paul J. Dunn | MD | (708) 383-3800 | 715 Lake St. #106, Oak Park, IL 60301 |
| Galen Jay Eash | MD | (701) 234-3610 | 1432 N. Forth St., Fargo, ND 58102 |
| Jean R. Eckerly | MD | (612) 593-9458 | 10700 Old Cty. Road 15. #15, Minneapolis, MN 55441 |
| Stephen B. Edelson | MD PM | (404) 981-3550 | 5536 Flat Schoals Parkway, Decatur, GA 30034 |
| W. Robert Eighammer | MD | (217) 446-3259 | 723 N. Logan Ave., Danville, IL 61832 |
| Stephen K. Elsassar | DO PM | (309) 367-2321 | 205 S. Englewood Dr., Metamora, IL 61548 |
| Kenneth J. Emonds | PhD | (617) 465-5009 | 65 Newburyport Turnpike, Newbury, MA 01950 |
| Hobart T. Feldman | MD F | (305) 652-1062 | 16800 N.W. Second Ave., #301, North Miami Beach, FL 33167 |
| Martin Feldman | MD | (212) 744-4413 | 132 East 76th St., New York, NY 10021 |
| Francisco J. Figueroa-Roviar | MD PM | (809) 879-0807 | Box 1886, Arecibo, PR 00613 |
| Dolores M. Finnie | RN A | (203) 489-8977 | 333 Kennedy Dr. #204, Torrington, CT 06790 |
| Jerrold N. Finnie | MD | (203) 489-8977 | 333 Kennedy Dr., #204, Torrington, CT 06790 |
| James R. Fish | MD | (719) 471-2273 | 3030 N. Hancock Ave., Colorado Springs, CO 80907 |
| James W. Fitzsimmon Jr. | MD M | (503) 474-2166 | 591 Hidden Vally Rd., Grants Pass, OR 97527 |
| George R. Fricke | MD E | | 1730 Avenida Del Mundo #105, Coronado, CA 92118 |
| Milton Fried | MD | (404) 451-4857 | 4426 Tilly Mill Rd., Atlanta, GA 30360 |
| Fred M. Furr | MD M | (615) 693-1502 | 9217 Park W. Blvd. Bldg E. #1, Knoxville, TN 37923 |
| Charles G. Gabelman | MD E | (714) 859-9851 | 24953 Paseo de Valencia #16C, Laguna Hills, CA 92653 |

## ENVIRONMENTAL MEDICINE continued

| | | | |
|---|---|---|---|
| Leo Galland | MD PM | (212) 308-6622 | 41 East 60 St., New York, NY 10022 |
| John E. Gambee | MD | (503) 686-2536 | 66 Club Rd., Eugene, OR 97401 |
| Tierry F. Garcia | MD | (317) 783-8830 | 1500 Albany St., Beech Grove, IN 46107 |
| Zane R. Gard | MD TE | (619) 571-0300 | P.O. Box 231309, San Diego, CA 92123 |
| Arthur Gardikes | B | (513) 434-0555 | Homan, Centerville, OH 45459 |
| Esteban Genao | MD | (301) 879-5710 | 4 Vale Road, Belair, MD 21014 |
| Kendall A. Gerdes | MD F | (303) 377-8837 | 1617 Vine St., Denver, CO 80206 |
| Robert S. Gillcash | MD M | (203) 642-4145 | P.O. Box 37, North Franklin, CT 06254 |
| Robert M. Giller | MD | (212) 472-2002 | 960 Park Ave., New York, NY 10028 |
| Thomas S. Glasgow | MD | (601) 234-1791 | 2161 South Lamar, Oxford, MS 38655 |
| Don E. Glines | PhD A | (916) 455-7459 | P.O. Box 2977, Sacramento, CA 95812 |
| Donald E. Goehring | MD E | (412) 287-4241 | 503 Union Bank Bldg., Butler, PA 16001 |
| Sheldon S. Goldberg | MD F | (413) 732-7426 | 2 Medical Center Dr., #110, Springfield, MA 01107 |
| Thomas G. Goodwin | MD | (219) 980-6117 | 6111 Harrison St., #343 MC, Merrillville, IN 46410 |
| Robert J. Gormley | MD | (716) 284-1237 | 638 Ninth Street, Niagara Falls, NY 14302 |
| Leland J. Green | MD M | (215) 855-9501 | P. O. Box 508, Lansdale, PA 19466 |
| John A. Green III | MD M | (503) 678-2233 | P. O. Box 99, Aurora, OR 97002 |
| Allergy Research Group | Af | (415) 639-4572 | 400 Preda St., San Leandro, CA 94577 |
| Fredrick T. Guilford | MD M | (415) 342-8681 | 101 S. San Mateo Dr., Suite 303, San Mateo, CA 94401 |
| P. John Hagan | MD E | (717) 826-1955 | Rd. 1, Box 99, C/O Kreitzberger, Hopbottom, PA 18824 |
| Howard Hagglund | MD M | (405) 329-4457 | 2227 W. Lindsey #1401, Norman, OK 73069 |
| Steven C. Halbert | MD PM | (215) 886-7842 | 1442 Ashbourne Road, Wyncote, PA 19095 |
| Vickey C. Halloran | MD M | (713) 440-0800 | 5629 FM 1960 W #225, Houston, TX 77069 |
| Charles R. Hamel | MD F | (817) 468-7755 | 4412 Matlock Rd. #300, Arlington, TX 76107 |
| Pauline Harding | MD | (708) 653-9900 | 27 W. 281 Geneva Rd., Suite D, Winfield, IL 60190 |
| Dennis Harper | DO PM | (801) 288-8881 | 5263 S. 300 West #203, Murray, UT 84107 |
| Robert E. Hazelwood | MD PM | (512) 458-9286 | 711 W. 38th St. C-4, Austin, TX 78705 |
| Neil C. Henderson | MD F | (407) 368-2915 | 20 S.E. Seventh St., Boca Raton, FL 33432 |
| Richard A. Hendricks | MD M | (805) 434-1836 | 1050 Las Tablas Rd., Templeton, CA 93465 |
| Ralph F. Herro | MD F | (602) 266-2374 | 5115 North Central Ave., Phoenix, AZ 85012 |
| Aaron J. Herschfus | MD F | (617) 784-2082 | 62 South Main St., P.O. Box 336, Sharon, MA 02067 |

## ENVIRONMENTAL MEDICINE continued

| | | | |
|---|---|---|---|
| Norene B. Hess | MD | (708) 446-1923 | 700 Oak, Winnetka, IL 60093 |
| James K. Hill | MD | (317) 846-7341 | 780 Eagle Creek Ct., Zionsville, IN 46077 |
| Charles T.J. Hinshaw Jr. | MD F | (316) 262-0951 | 1133 East Second, Wichita, KS 67214 |
| Ronald L. Hoffman | MD | (212) 779-1744 | 40 East 30 St, New York, NY 10016 |
| W. Kenneth Holbrook | DO | (617) 944-2288 | 276 Woburn St., Reading, MA 01867 |
| Richard B. Homan | MD | (513) 321-7333 | 3444 Mooney Ave., Cincinnati, OH 45208 |
| Kenneth W. Hoover | MD PM | (407) 679-0662 | 5931 Brick Court, Suite 2311, Winter Park, FL 32792 |
| Harris Hosen | MD E | (409) 799-2148 | 2001 Holcomb Blvd., Apt 1301, Houston, TX 77030 |
| Maurice C. Hothem | DO | (207) 797-4148 | 117 Auburn St., Fall Brook Bldg, Portland, ME 04103 |
| Richard E. Hrdlicka | MD | (312) 232-1900 | 302 Randall Rd., Suite 206, Geneva, IL 60134 |
| Jeanne T. Hubbuch | MD | (617) 965-7770 | 1340 Centre St., #203, Newton Centre, MA 02159 |
| Darrel Hunsaker | MD M | (619) 532-9605 | San Diego Naval Hosp., Oto, San Diego, CA 92134 |
| Reed W. Hyde | MD | (702) 731-3117 | 2225 East Flamingo Rd. #301, Las Vegas, NV 89119 |
| Joe A. Izen | MD F | (713) 941-2444 | 3912 Brookhaven, Pasadena, TX 77504 |
| Martin H. Jenzer | MD | (716) 663-5520 | 1589 Ridge Rd. West, Rochester, NY 14615 |
| Alfred R. Johnson | DO F | (214) 368-4132 | 8345 Walnut Hill Lane #205, Dallas, TX 75231 |
| Marjorie Hurt Jones | RN A | (208) 772-8213 | 2615 N. Fourth St., #616, Coeur d'Alene, ID 83814 |
| George J. Juetersonke | DO M | (719) 596-9049 | 5455 N. Union, Suite 200, Colorado Springs, CO 80918 |
| Eleazar M. Kadile | MD F | (414) 468-9442 | 1538 Bellvue, Green Bay, WI 54311 |
| Nyle D. Kauffman | MD | (319) 338-7862 | 2450 Towncrest Dr., Iowa City, IA 52240 |
| John S. Keebler | MD PM | (205) 664-2323 | 6701 Airport Blvd., Suite B123, Mobile, AL 46608 |
| Joseph Patrick Keenan | MD | (413) 568-2304 | 75 Springfield Rd., Westfield, MA 01085 |
| Louise Leney Kennedy | A | (501) 663-1407 | 424 N. University #9, Little Rock, AR 72005 |
| Bruce W. Kenney | DO | (207)774-9668 | 97 India St., Portland, ME 04101 |
| Roy E. Kerry | MD | (412) 588-2600 | 17 Sixth Ave., Greenville, PA 16125 |
| Gerald Keyte | DO | (313) 278-3050 | 388 Inkster Rd., Inkster, MI 48141 |
| Duke D. Kim | MD M | (714) 364-6040 | 27800 Med. Cent. Rd., Suite 116, Mission Vijeo, CA 92691 |
| Howard G. Kimball | MD | (501) 269-4301 | C/O Garst Clinic, Mount View, AR 72560 |
| Daniel A. Kinderlehrer | MD | (508) 465-6077 | 65 Newburyport Turnpike, Newbury, MA 01951 |
| David Kinley Jr. | DM, RPT | (201) 382-2434 | 668 Raritan Rd., Clark, NJ 07028 |
| Wayne H. Konetzki | MD F | (414) 547-3055 | 402 North Grand Ave., Waukesha, WI 53186 |

## ENVIRONMENTAL MEDICINE continued

| | | | |
|---|---|---|---|
| Benjamin P. Kramer | JD A | (303) 759-2227 | 950 S. Cherry St. #915, Denver, CO 80222 |
| Myrtie Jane Kreutzer | RN AF | (303) 493-8933 | 937 Mallard Drive, Fort Collins, CO 80524 |
| Kenneth N. Krischner | MD PhD F | (305) 584-6655 | 910 S.W. 40th Ave., Plantation, FL 33317 |
| Jacqueline Krohn | MD F | (505) 662-9620 | Los Alamos Med. Center #136, Los Alamos, NM 87544 |
| George F. Kroker | MD F | (608) 782-2027 | 615 S. 10th St., P.O. Box 2408, La Crosse, WI 54602 |
| Curt G. Kurtz | MD | (406) 587-5561 | 300 No. Wilson, Bozeman, MT 59715 |
| N. Thomas LaCava | MD | (508) 854-1380 | 360 W. Boylston St., Suite 107, West Boylston, MA 01583 |
| Randall A. Langston | MD M | (904) 863-8287 | 1005 Mar Walt Dr., Ft. Walton Beach, FL 32548 |
| Richard E. Layton | MD | (301) 337-2707 | 901 Dulaney Valley Rd., #602, Towson, MD 21204 |
| Richard H. Leigh | MD | (701) 775-5527 | 2314 Library Circle, Grand Forks, ND 58201 |
| Fannie Lou Leney-Hayward | MD E | (918) 299-2661 | 8555 South Lewis, Tulsa, OK 74137 |
| Alan S. Levin | MD | (415) 677-0829 | 500 Sutter St., Suite 511, San Francisco, CA 94108 |
| Warren M. Levin | MD F | (212) 696-1900 | 444 Park Ave South, 12th Fl., New York, NY 10016 |
| Allan D. Lieberman | MD F | (803) 572-1600 | 7510 Northforest Dr., North Charlston, SC 29420 |
| Cathie Anne Lippman | MD | (213) 653-0488 | 8383 Wilshire Blvd., Suite 360, Beverly Hills, CA 90211 |
| William A. Lockyer | MD M | (415) 921-0833 | 2295 Filbert St., San Francisco, CA 94123 |
| Charles R. Mabray | MD F | (512) 578-5233 | 4204 North Laurent St., Victoria, TX 77901 |
| Allan Magazinar | DO | (609) 424-8222 | 1907 Greentree Rd., Cherry Hill, NJ 08003 |
| Hamid Mahmud | MD | (618) 548-4613 | 1610 N. Broadway, Salem, IL 62881 |
| Malcolm C. Maley | MD F | (214) 793-1153 | 808 Olive St., Suite C, Texarcana, TX 75501 |
| Gopal R. Malladi | MD | (413) 536-2978 | 1221 Main St., C. Horan Med., Holyoke, MA 01040 |
| Marshall Mandell | MD E | (203) 838-4706 | Three Bush St., Norwalk, CT 06850 |
| F. Russell Manuel | MD | (907) 562-7070 | 4200 Lake Otis Blvd. #304, Anchorage, AK 99508 |
| Vincent A. Mark | MD E | (408) 688-8514 | P.O. Box 760, Aptos, CA 95001 |
| George B. Marsh Jr. | MD F | (214) 962-4247 | P.O. Drawer H, Grand Saline, TX 75140 |
| Robert T. Marshall | MD PhD | (312) 446-1923 | 700 Oak, Winnetka, IL 60093 |
| Conrad G. Maulfair Jr. | DO | (215) 682-2104 | R.R. #2, Box 71 Main St., Mertztown, PA 19539 |
| Alan B. McDaniel | MD | (502) 452-6325 | 2019 State St., New Albany, IN 47150 |
| Charles T. McGee | MD F | (208) 664-1478 | 1717 Lincolnway, Suite 108, Cour d'Alene, ID 83814 |
| Martin G. Meindl | DO | (512) 424-0640 | 1190 Briarstone Dr., Mason City, IA 50401 |

## ENVIRONMENTAL MEDICINE continued

| | | | |
|---|---|---|---|
| Donald C. Mettler | MD F | (503) 228-9497 | 2525 N.W. Lovejoy #205, Portland, OR 97210 |
| James M. Miller | MD F | (607) 722-0957 | 50 Front St., Binghamton, NY 13905 |
| Joseph B. Miller | MD F | (205) 342-8540 | 5901 Airport Blvd., Mobile, AL 36608 |
| Lynn Miller | MD | (315) 432-9231 | 605 Franklin Park Dr., East Syracuse, NY 13057 |
| Billy Gerald Mills | DO M | (214) 279-6767 | 4725 Gus Thomasson, Mesquite, TX 75150 |
| George H. Mitchell | MD | (202) 265-4111 | 2639 Conn Ave NW, Suite C-100, Washington, DC 20008 |
| Bernard Mlaver | MD PM | (404) 395-1600 | 4480 N. Shallowford Rd., Atlanta, GA 30338 |
| Michele C. Moore | MD | (603) 357-2180 | 115 Key Road, Keene, NH 03431 |
| Heather Morgan | MD M | (513) 439-1797 | 138 S. Main St., Centerville, OH 45458 |
| Joseph T. Morgan | MD | (503) 269-0333 | 1750 Thompson Rd., Coos Bay, OR 97420 |
| David L. Morris | MD F | (608) 782-2027 | 615 S. 10th St., P.O. Box 2408, LaCrosse, WI 54601 |
| Herbert I. Moselle | MD M | (305) 472-1212 | 201 N.W. 82 Ave. #103, Plantation, FL 33324 |
| Charles Moss | MD | (619) 457-1314 | 8950 Villa La Jolla #2162, La Jolla, CA 92037 |
| Donald S. Nelson | MD | (216) 836-3016 | 544 White Pond #B, Akron, OH 44320 |
| Robert R. Noble | MD M˜ | (214) 458-9944 | 6757 Arapaho Rd. #757, Dallas, TX 75248 |
| John F. O'Brian | MD F | (219) 422-9471 | 3217 Lake Ave., Fort Wayne, IN 46805 |
| James A. O'Shea | MD | (508) 685-7960 | 23 Royal Crest Dr. #8, N. Andover, MA 01845 |
| Gary R. Oberg | MD F | (815) 455-1990 | 31 North Virginia St., Cyrstal Lake, IL 60014 |
| Joseph P. Omelas | MD | (219) 980-6180 | 6111 Harrison St., Merrillville, IN 46410 |
| Henry J. Palalius | MD M | (703) 356-2244 | 1481 Chain Bridge Rd. #101, McLean, VA 22101 |
| Jon B. Pangborn | Ph.D | (708) 231-3649 | P.O. Drawer 400, Lisle, IL 60532 |
| Kalpana D. Patel | MD F | (716) 883-2611 | 191 North St., Buffalo, NY 14201 |
| Sunil P. Perera | MD M | (916) 782-7758 | 404 Sunrise Ave., Roseville, CA 95661 |
| Louis A. Petrucco | MD | (313) 864-7400 | 6001 Outer Drive, Detroit, MI 48235 |
| Guy O. Pfeiffer | MD LM | (217) 234-6441 | R.R. 4 #200 Professional Plaza, Mattoon, IL 61938 |
| William H. Philpott | MD F | (405) 390-3009 | 17171 S.E. 29th St., Choctaw, OK 73020 |
| Charles W. Platt | MD | (513) 526-3271 | 552 S. West St., Versailles, OH 45380 |
| Richard N. Podell | MD | (609) 424-8222 | 29 South St., New Providence, NJ 07974 |
| Robert T. Pottenger Jr. | MD F | (818) 303-2613 | 166 E. Foothill Blvd., Arcadia, CA 91006 |
| Bhaskar D. Power | MD | (919) 535-1411 | P. O. Box 1132, Roanoke Rapids, NC 27870 |
| Raymond J. Psonak | PM | (207) 934-0703 | 27 Date St., Old Orchard Bch., ME 04064 |
| Alston M. Quillin | MD | (614) 436-7188 | 67 E. Wilson Bridge Rd., Worthington, OH 43085 |
| Theron G. Randolf | MD F | (312) 844-9898 | 161 S. Lincolnway #305, North Aurora, IL 60542 |

## ENVIRONMENTAL MEDICINE continued

| | | | |
|---|---|---|---|
| Doris J. Rapp | MD F | (716) 875-5578 | 1421 Colvin Blvd., Buffalo, NY 14223 |
| William J. Rea | MD F | (214) 368-4132 | 8345 Walnut Hill Lane #205, Dallas, TX 75231 |
| John W. Rechsteiner | MD F | (513) 325-0223 | 1116 S. Limestone St., Springfield, OH 45505 |
| Dennis W. Remington | MD M | (801) 373-8500 | 1675 N. Freedom Blvd., Suite 11E, Provo, UT 84604 |
| Charles S. Resseger | DO F | (419) 668-9615 | 853 S. Norwalk Rd., P.O. Box 374, Norwalk, OH 44857 |
| V. Thomas Riley | MD | (319) 234-5582 | Sycamore 501, Suite 611, Waterloo, IA 50703 |
| Russell R. Roby | MD PM | (512) 451-5484 | 3410 Far West, Suite 110, Austin, TX 78731 |
| Sherry A. Rogers | MD F | (315) 488-2856 | 2800 West Genessee St., Syracuse, NY 13219 |
| Raymond S. Rosedale Jr. | MD | (216) 492-2844 | 4150 Belden Village St. N.W., Canton, OH 44718 |
| James Rowland | DO PhD | (816) 361-4077 | 8133 Wornall Rd., Kansas City, MO 64114 |
| Daniel F. Royal | DO | (702) 732-1400 | 3720 Howard Hughes Pkwy., Las Vegas, NV 89109 |
| Charles A. Rush | MD F | (817) 595-0505 | 4351 Booth Calloway Rd. #105, Fort Worth, TX 76180 |
| Vijay K. Sabnis | MD F | (608) 782-2027 | 615 S. 10th St., P.O. Box 2408, La Crosse, WI 54602 |
| Jose E. Sanchez | MD F | (614) 264-1692 | 2615 Sunset Blvd., Steubenville, OH 43952 |
| Bruce A. Sanderson | MD E | (619) 479-5828 | P. O. Box 1166, Bonita, CA 92002 |
| William J. Sayer | MD F | (415) 321-3361 | 145 N. California Ave., Palo Alto, CA 94301 |
| Lillian S. Scala | MA A | (304) 292-7357 | 220 Wilson Ave., Morgantown, WV 26505 |
| Michael A. Schacter | MD | (914) 368-4700 | Two Executive Blvd #202, Suffern, NY 10901 |
| Gene D. Schmutzer | DO M | (602) 795-0292 | 2425 North Alverton Way, Tuscon, AZ 85712 |
| James D. Schuler | MD | (707) 487-3405 | 12559 Hwy 101 North, mini mart, Smith River, CA 95567 |
| Jack A. Seeley | MD | (208) 375-1264 | 10796 W. Overland, Boise, ID 83709 |
| Marja D. Segler | MD M | (407) 278-6008 | 2915 S. Federal Hwy., Dumar Pz., Del Ray Beach, FL 33483 |
| Alan J. Serrins | MD F | (305) 595-1597 | 8400 N. Kendall Dr., Miami, FL 33156 |
| John L. Sessions | DO PM | (409) 423-2166 | 1609 South Margaret, Kirbyville, TX 75956 |
| Escarlito U. Sevilla | MD | (216) 792-1956 | 5437 Mahoning, Youngstown, OH 44515 |
| George E. Shambaugh Jr. | MD F | (312) 887-1130 | 40 South Clay St., Hinsdale, IL 60521 |
| Myra B. Shayevitz | MD | (413) 584-4040 | Veterans Affairs Med. Ctr., Northhampton, MA 01060 |
| Megan G. Shields | MD PM | (213) 655-5928 | 314 N. Harper, Los Angeles, CA 90048 |

## ENVIRONMENTAL MEDICINE continued

Young S. Shin            MD F         (404) 242-0000     3850 Holcomb Bridge Rd, Suite 438, Atlanta/
                                                         Norcross, GA 30092

W. A. Shrader Jr         MD F         (808) 885-6860     Opelo Plaza, Suite. 12, Box 2470, Kamuela, HI 96743

Alan W. Sidel            MD           (219) 484-8545     5110 N. Clinton St., Ft. Wayne, IN 46825

Marjorie S. Siebert      DO           (718) 386-2020     65-12 Fresh Pond Road, Ridgewood, NY 11385

Gordon Siegel            MD           (312) 332-4242     55 E. Washington, Suite 2705, Chicago, IL 60602

Jacob Siegel             MD PA        (713) 973-8832     8300 Waterbury #305, Houston, TX 77055

Frederick H. Simmons     MD           (317) 662-6950     1001 N. Western Ave. #C, Marion, IN 46952

Norman A. Simpson        DO           (303) 675-7310     2171 W. Jefferson Ave. #305, Trenton, MI 48183

Robert J. Sinaiko        MD M         (415) 788-2099     450 Sutter Street, #1124, San Francisco, CA 94108

James A. Smidt           MD M         (602) 266-0660     5225 N. Central Ave. #C, Phoenix, AZ 85012

Ralph Smiley             MD F         (214) 241-0404     8435 Walnut Hill Lane #205, Dallas, TX 75231

Gerald L. Smith          MD M         (307) 632-5589     5320 Education Dr., Cheyenne, WY 82009

Robert Snider            MD           (315) 764-7328     HC 61, Box 43 D, Andrews St., Massena, NY 13662

Robert W. Soll           MD           (515) 247-8750     1044 Forth St., Des Moines, IA 50314

Barbara A. Solomon       MD           (301) 668-5611     8109 Harford Rd., Baltimore, MD 21234

Neil Solomon             MD, Ph.D.    (301) 337-2707     901 Dulaney Valley Rd. #602, Towson, MD 21204

Ralph H. Speken          MD           (212) 601-7208     133 East 73rd St., New York, NY 10021

Marc H. Spencer          MD PM                           400 S. Dixie Hwy., Bldg 2. #210, Boca Raton, FL
                                                         33432

Weldon L. Sportsman      MD LM        (816) 436-7100     7504 North Oak St., Trafficway, Kansas City, MO
                                                         64118

Captain D. E. Sprague    MD MC F      (671) 339-7232     Med. Dept., USS Kittyhawk, CV 63, Phila. Shipyard,
                                                         PA 19112

Gerald F. Staub          MD           (708) 934-1100     1400 Charles, Rolling Meadows, IL 60008

Philip C. Stavish        MD PM        (714) 722-0175     136 Broadway, Costa Mesa, CA 92627

Bruce A. Stayton         MD           (816) 836-5010     1212 W. Truman Rd., Independence, MO 64050

Rheeta M. Stecker        MD M         (501) 767-1144     3205 Albert Pike, Hot Springs, AR 71913

Catherine H. Steele      MD M         (406) 727-4757     2509–7th Ave South, Great Falls, MO 59405

Charles H. Steele        MD F         (406) 727-4757     2509–7th Ave South, Great Falls, MO 59405

Maurice L. Stephens      MD           (206) 861-2224     13820 N.E. 65th St. #550, Redmond, WA 98052

Del Stigler              MD F         (303) 831-7335     2005 Franklin St. #490, Denver, CO 80205

Thomas L. Stone          MD M         (312) 934-1100     1811 Hicks Rd., Rolling Meadows, IL 60008

Tipu Sultan              MD F         (314) 921-7100     11585 W. Florissant, Florissant, MO 63033

## ENVIRONMENTAL MEDICINE continued

| | | | |
|---|---|---|---|
| Joseph F. Tangredi | MD | (702) 382-3421 | 650 Shadow Lane, #12, Las Vegas, NY 89106 |
| Rafael Tarnopolsky | MD | (515) 271-1400 | 3200 Grand Ave., Des Moines, IA 50312 |
| Frances A. Taylor | MA | (505) 662-9620 | P.O. Box 126, Los Alamos, NM 87544 |
| Phillip H. Taylor | MD M | (818) 889-8249 | 325 South Moorpark Rd., Thousand Oaks, CA 91361 |
| Morton M. Teich | MD F | (212) 988-1821 | 930 Park Ave., New York, NY 10028 |
| Wellington S. Tichenor | MD | (212) 517-6611 | 642 Park Avenue, New York, NY 10021 |
| John P. Toth | MD | (415) 682-5660 | 2299 Bacon St., Suite 10, Concord, CA 94520 |
| John Parks Towbridge | MD M | (713) 540-2329 | 9816 Memorial Blvd., Suite 205, Humble, TX 77338 |
| William Louis Traxel | MD | (314) 686-2411 | 666 Lester St., Poplar Bluff, MO 63901 |
| Jeffrey Tulin-Silver | MD | (313) 932-0100 | 6330 Orchard Lake Rd. #10, West Bloomfield, MI 48322 |
| Mechteld C. Van Hardenbroek | MD M | (303) 241-8554 | 205 Country Club Park, Grand Junction, CO 81503 |
| George Von Hilsheimer | PhD A | (305) 628-0226 | #14 Maitland Plaza, Maitland, FL 32751 |
| Francis J. Waickman | MD F | (216) 867-3767 | 544 White Pond Dr., Suite B, Akron, OH 44320 |
| John C. Wakefield | MD F | (408) 732-3037 | 970 W. El Camino Real, Suite 1, Sunnyvale, CA 94087 |
| Jerry A. Walker | DO | (313) 292-5620 | 5681 South Beech Daly Rd., Dearborn Heights, MI 48125 |
| Richard G. Wanderman | MD M | (901) 683-2777 | 5545 Murray, Suite 330, Memphis, TN 38119 |
| Walter A. Ward | MD | (919) 760-0240 | P.O. Box 24039, Winston Salem, NC 27114 |
| Laurence S. Webster | MD | (217) 877-7486 | 3090 N. Main, Decatur, IL 62526 |
| Stanley Weindorf | MD | (516) 921-9000 | 75 Froehlich Farm Blvd., Woodbury, NY 11797 |
| Herbert Weinstein | MD | (309) 686-5900 | 2627 N. Knoxville Ave., Peoria, IL 61604 |
| Ronald R. Wempen | MD F | (714) 546-4325 | 3620 S. Bristol St., Suite 306, Santa Ana, CA 92704 |
| Norman E. Wenger | MD M | (717) 222-9595 | P.O. Box 502, Carbondale, PA 18407 |
| Donald R. Whitaker | DO PM | (714) 855-9746 | 26302 La Paz Road, Suite 207, Mission Viejo, CA 92691 |
| Harold C. Whitcomb Jr. | MD M | (303) 925-5440 | 100 East Main St. #201, Aspen, CO 81600 |
| M. Jeffrey White | MD PM | (813) 876-6117 | 3715 Azeele, Tampa, FL 33609 |

## ENVIRONMENTAL MEDICINE continued

| | | | |
|---|---|---|---|
| James C. Whittingham | MD F | (817) 332-4585 | 1021 Seventh Ave., Fort Worth, TX 76104 |
| Walter L. Wilder | MD | (612) 927-5431 | 6525 Drew Ave S., Minneapolis, MN 55435 |
| Randall E. Wilkinson | MD F | (509) 453-5506 | 302 S. 12th St., Yakima, WA 98902 |
| Richard S. Wilkinson | MD F | (509) 453-5506 | 302 S. 12th St., Yakima, WA 98902 |
| James W. Willoughby | MD F | (816) 781-0902 | 24 S. Main St., P.O. Box 271, Liberty, MO 64068 |
| John L. Wilson Jr. | MD | (612) 679-1313 | 224 7th St., Mora, MN 55051 |
| Joseph S. Wojcik | MD | (914) 793-6161 | 525 Bronxville Rd., Apt. 1G, Bronxville, NY 10708 |
| Otis Jack Woodward Jr. | MD M | (912) 436-9535 | 1304 Whispering Pines Rd., Albany, GA 31707 |
| Aubrey M. Worrell Jr. | MD F | (501) 535-8200 | 3900 Hickory St., Pine Bluff, AR 71603 |
| Jonathan V. Wright | MD PM | (206) 631-8920 | 24030–132nd S.E., Kent, WA 98042 |
| Linda C. Wright | MD M | (303) 678-5891 | 421 21st St., Suite 7, Longmont, CO 80501 |
| Ray C. Wunderlich Jr. | MD M | (813) 822-3612 | 666–6th Street South, St. Petersberg, FL 33701 |
| Robert Y. Yee | MD PM | (707) 544-6891 | 3317 Chante Rd. #2D, Santa Rosa, CA 95404 |
| Richard B. Yules | MD | (617) 791-6305 | 475 Pleasant St., Worcester, MA 01609 |
| Pavel Yutsis | MD PM | (718) 259-2122 | 1309 W. 7th St., Brooklyn, NY 11204 |
| Alfred V. Zamm | MD F | (914) 388-7766 | 111 Maiden Lane, Kingston, NY 12401 |
| Jose R. Zaragoza | MD F | (809) 878-3830 | P.O. Box 1028, Arecibo, PR 00613 |
| John L. Zettelmaier | MD | (219) 926-8525 | 374 Indian Boundary Rd., Chesterton, IN 46304 |
| Erhardt Zinke | MD F | (619) 728-4901 | 2131 Winter Warm Rd., Fallbrook, CA 92028 |

## HOMEOPATHY

| NAME | TITLE | PHONE | ADDRESS |
|---|---|---|---|
| Suzanne Adams | MD | (206) 459-9082 | 3627 Ensign Rd. #B, Olympia, WA 98506 |
| Stephen Albin | ND | (503) 399-1255 | 1880 Lancaster Dr. NE #111, Salem, OR 97305 |
| Kenneth J. Armstrong | PhD, DDS | (505) 275-3167 | 5850 Eubank N.E., #B-38, Albuquerque, NM 87111 |
| Gary A. Bachman | RN, ND | (206) 782-6107 | 7020 13th Ave. N.W., Seattle, WA 98117 |
| Jeff Baker | ND | (808) 878-6660 | HI |
| Donald R. Beans | PhD, CA | (406) 837-5757 | 482 Electric Ave., Big Fork, MT 59911 |
| Peter Bennett | ND | (604) 537-4419 | Canada |
| William Bergman | MD | (212) 684-2290 | 50 Park Ave., New York, NY 10016 |
| Herb Joiner Bey | ND | (808) 988-5301 | 2646 Pamoa Rd., Honolulu, HI 96822 |

## HOMEOPATHY continued

| Peter Borregard | DC | (415) 527-6783 | 1650-D Solano Ave., Albany, CA 94706 |
| Randall Bradley | ND | (402) 381-6714 | 7447 Farnam St., Omaha, NE 68114 |
| Arlene K. Buckett | ND | (206) 523-6591 | 16524 S.E. 145th St., Renton, WA 98056 |
| Michael Carlston | MD DMT | (769) 549-4554 | 1154 Mamguery Dr. #1, Santa Rosa, CA 95405 |
| Peggy Chipkin | BS RN | (415) 849-1925 | 1918 Bonita Ave., HMC, Berkley, CA 94704 |
| Judy Christianson | ND | (206) 329-1237 | 1812 E. Madison #205, Seattle, WA 98122 |
| Christine Clavarella | PA-C | (415) 849-1925 | 1918 Bonita Ave., HMC, Berkley, CA 94704 |
| Karen Cohen | DC | (408) 425-1422 | 556 Ocean View Ave., Santa Cruz, CA 95062 |
| John G. Collins | ND, DHANP | (503) 667-1960 | 500 S.E. 181st Ave., Gresham, OR 97233 |
| Dean Crothers | MD | (206) 542-5595 | 23200 Edmonds Way, Edmonds, WA 98026 |
| Lillian Cunningham | ND | (206) 252-8559 | 4811 Seahurst, Everett, WA 98203 |
| Barbara Dakin | LAc OMD | (916) 272-5046 | 14645 Meadow Drive, Grass Valley, CA 95495 |
| Phyllis Dalzell | RN | (608) 221-7221 | 6320 Monona Dr., Madison WI 53736 |
| Eric J. Dolgin | DO | (213) 452-9591 | 2210 Wilshire Blvd. #281, Santa Monica, CA 90403 |
| Alice Duncan | DC | (503) 392-3779 | P.O. Box 411, Neskowin, OR 97149 |
| Sheila B. Dunn | ND | (206) 822-3716 | 607 Market St., Kirkland, WA 98033 |
| Durr Elmore | DC, ND | (503) 829-7326 | 14653 S. Graves Rd., Mulino, OR 97042 |
| Lila Flagler | ND | (602) 721-8821 | 6737 E. Camino Principal, C, Tucson, AZ 85715 |
| Samuel Flagler | ND | (602) 721-8821 | 6737 E. Camino Principal, C, Tucson, AZ 85715 |
| Mark B. Frank | DC | (813) 788-0496 | 4990 Allen Road, Zephyrhills, FL 33541 |
| Kristy L. Fraser | ND | (603) 427-6800 | 406 The Hill #101, Portsmouth, NH 03801 |
| Suzanne Fromherz | BS RN | (501) 442-7959 | 327 W. Meadow, Fayetteville AR 72701 |
| Jan Gagnon | ND | (206) 632-1978 | 753 N. 35th St. #302, Seattle, WA 98103 |
| Mary Lynn Garner | ND, DHANP | (207) 596-0709 | 17 Masonic St., Rockland, ME 04841 |
| Ellen Goldman | ND | (206) 322-3046 | 2024 S. Dearborn, Seattle, WA 98144 |
| Pearlyn Goodman-Herrick | ND, DHANP | (203) 227-5534 | 21 Trails End Road, Weston, CT 06883 |
| Sally Goodwin | MD | (206) 321-5749 | 616 Edge Clift Dr., Langley, WA 98260 |
| Kevin Gregg | DC | (617) 923-0700 | 294 Belmont St., Watertown, MA 02172 |
| George Guess | MD, DHT | (704) 252-2315 | 340 Mermon Ave., Asheville, NC 28801 |
| Dayton F. Haigney | MD | (603) 427-1370 | 80 Bow St., Portsmouth, NH 03801 |
| Stacy Hartog | RN | (206) 935-1768 | 4117 39th Avenue S.W., Seattle, WA 98116 |

# HOMEOPATHY continued

| | | | |
|---|---|---|---|
| Lisa Harvey | MD | (413) 586-4551 | 16 Center St. #223, Northampton, MA 01060 |
| Amy Haynes | CA ND | (406) 721-2147 | 521 S. Second W., Missoula, MT 59801 |
| Robert E. Hazelwood | MD PM | (512) 458-9286 | 711 W. 38th St. C-4, Austin, TX 78705 |
| Larry Herdener | ND | (503) 434-6170 | 415 E. 3rd St., McMinnville, OR 97128 |
| Connie Hernandez | ND | (808) 965-7887 | P.O. Box 4, Pahoa, HI 96778 |
| Marcel Hernandez | ND | (808) 965-7887 | P.O. Box 4, Pahoa, HI 96778 |
| Nancy Herrick | PA | (415) 849-1925 | 1918 Bonita Ave, HMC, Berkeley, CA 94704 |
| Jane M. Hess | DO | (612) 343-0570 | 1250 Hennepin Ave. S. #202, Minneapolis, MN 55403 |
| Tori Hudson | ND | (503) 255-7355 | 11231 S.E. Market, Portland, OR 97216 |
| Jessica Jackson | LAc | (707) 433-7714 | 513 Center St., Healdsburg, CA 95488 |
| Jennifer Jacobs | MD | (206) 542-5595 | 23200 Edmonds Way, Edmonds, WA 98026 |
| Mark S. James | ND | (602) 884-1880 | 809 N. Humphreys, Flagstaff, AZ 86001 |
| Linda Johnson | MD | (818) 776-8040 | 7549 Louise Ave., Van Nuys, CA 91406 |
| G. William Jones | MD | (612) 735-1377 | 19644 Cleary Rd. N.W., Anoka, MN 55303 |
| Kokayai B. Kamau | MD PC | (212) 545-1958 | 444 Park Ave., New York, NY |
| Gregory Kaufman | MD | (312) 725-6666 | 3029 N. Pulaski Ave., Chicago, IL 60641 |
| Clifford Kearns | DC | (708) 931-7494 | 843 Esmeralda Pl., Elgin, IL 60120 |
| Hollis H. King | DO PhD | (619) 587-1822 | 4150 Regents Park Roy #345, La Jolla, CA 92037 |
| Stephen King | ND, DHANP | (206) 522-0488 | 5502 34th Ave. N.E., Seattle, WA 98105 |
| Kristin A. Kreiger | BS RN | (213) 828-7389 | 903 Centinela Ave., Santa Monica, CA 90403 |
| D. Abba Krieger | DC | (303) 963-2668 | 734 Main St., Carbondale, CO 81623 |
| Adam Ladd | ND | (503) 252-8125 | 320 N.E. 120th Ave., Portland, OR 97220 |
| Eliza Ladyzhensky | MD | (714) 736-8185 | 760 South Washburn #11, Corona, CA 91720 |
| Janet Levatin | MD | (617) 265-5277 | 1993 Dorchester Ave., Boston, MA 02124 |
| Alan S. Levin | MD | (415) 677-0829 | 500 Sutter St., Suite 511, San Francisco, CA 94108 |
| Alan S. Levine | MD | (415) 864-4804 | 20 Eagle St., San Francisco, CA 94114 |
| Blair Lewis | PA-C | (414) 351-2340 | 250 W. Coventry Ct. #111, Milwaukee, WI 53217 |
| Alice Lipscomb | RN, MS | (414) 351-2340 | 250 W. Coventry Ct. #111, Milwaukee, WI 53217 |
| Gennaro F. Locurcio | MD | (908) 351-1333 | 610 3rd Ave., Elizabeth, NJ 07202 |
| Gennaro F. Locurcio | MD | (718) 336-2291 | 2386 Ocean Parkway, Brooklyn, NY 11223 |
| Francine Loeb | ND | (206) 525-4660 | 7201 5th Ave. N.E., Seattle, WA 98115 |
| Anne L. Maguire | RN, ND, | (206) 776-6085 | 23405 84th W., Edmonds, WA 98026 |

# HOMEOPATHY continued

| | | | |
|---|---|---|---|
| Larry Marrich | DC | (505) 889-3333 | 3401 Carlisle N.E., Albuquerque, NM 87110 |
| Ian Marsh | DO | (206) 565-2444 | 2603 Bridgeport Way West, Tacoma, WA 98466 |
| Theodore Matheny | MD | (605) 964-2811 | PHS Indian Hospital, Eagle Butte, SD 57625 |
| Stephen Messer | ND, DHANP | (503) 343-2384 | 1902 Jefferson #2, Eugene, OR 97405 |
| Charles Metzker | DC | (606) 268-4111 | 598 E. High, Lexington, KY 40502 |
| Joseph T. Morgan | MD | (503) 269-0333 | 1750 Thompson Rd., Coos Bay, OR 97420 |
| Roger Morrison | MD | (415) 849-1925 | 1918 Bonita Ave., HMC, Berkeley, CA 94704 |
| Sara C. Murnane | CNM ANP | (907) 235-7268 | Box 15071 FCB, Homer, AK 99603 |
| Harold Ofgang | ND | (212) 684-2290 | 50 Park Ave., New York, NY 10016 |
| Hazel K. Ogawa-Leman | ND | (808) 537-2763 | 1150 S. King St. #404, Honolulu, HI 96814 |
| Laura Paris | OMD LAc | (213) 453-0286 | 2730 Wilshire Blvd. #405, Santa Monica, CA 90403 |
| Philip K. Parsons | DDS | (904) 473-4595 | P.O. Box 266, Keystone Heights, FL 32656 |
| Dhyano Peirson | MD | (802) 862-0836 | 323 Pearl St., Burlington, VT 05401 |
| William Plickerd | DDS | (614) 366-3309 | 974 N. 21st St., Newark, OH 43055 |
| Joan Powelson | MSW | (415) 525-6193 | 570 The Alameda, Berkeley, CA 94707 |
| Nancy A. Rao | ND, RAc | (303) 449-8581 | 2880 Folsom St. #210-A, Boulder, CO 80304 |
| Cathleen M. Rapp | ND | (408) 358-7797 | 451 Los Gatos Blvd., Los Gatos, CA 95032 |
| Rosemary Rau-Levine | MD | (608) 246-9070 | 3602 Atwood Ave., Madison, WI 53704 |
| Judyth Reichenberg | ND, DHANP | (206) 547-9665 | 4072 9th Ave., N.E., Seattle, WA 98015 |
| Horace Reider | MD | (802) 985-8250 | P.O. Box 816, Shelburne, VT 05482 |
| Donald Rich | MD | (408) 423-2078 | 706 Western Drive, Santa Cruz, CA 95060 |
| Mary Richter | MD | (206) 682-0882 | 901 Boren Ave. #1530, Seattle, WA 98104 |
| Philip Robbins | DO | (606) 593-6333 | 238 E. Beachwood Estates, Athens, OH 45701 |
| Karl Robinson | MD | (505) 265-0607 | 122 Dartmouth S.E., Albuquerque, NM 87106 |
| John Roos | MD | (802) 864-7967 | Richardson Pl. #2B, Burlington, VT 05401 |
| Teresa Salvadore | DC | (303) 920-1247 | 605 East Main St. #12, Aspen, CO 81611 |
| Elisabeth Sandler | LAc | (213) 459-1851 | 339 Sycamore Road, Santa Monica, CA 90402 |
| Michael A. Schacter | MD | (914) 368-4700 | Two Executive Blvd #202, Suffern, NY 10901 |
| Joya Lynn Schoen | MD DA | (407) 664-2729 | 341 N. Maitland Ave., Suite 210, Maitland, FL 32751 |

## HOMEOPATHY continued

| | | | |
|---|---|---|---|
| Joya Lynn Schoen | MD, PA | (407) 332-5710 | 701 E. Alamonte Dr. #304, Alamonte Springs, FL 32701 |
| Joseph Sciabbarrasi | MD | (301) 545-8364 | 571–35 Street, Manhattan Beach, CA 90266 |
| Joan Scott | BSN MPH | (205) 871-1288 | 2038 22nd Ct. S, Birmingham, AL 35223 |
| H. A. Seedat | MD | (619) 353-7860 | 1592–1 S. Imperial Ave., El Centro, CA 92243 |
| Jody K. Shevins | ND, DHANP | (303) 449-8581 | 2880 Folsom St. #210-A, Boulder, CO 80304 |
| Jonathan Shore | MD | (415) 461-1981 | 900 S. Eliseo Drive #101, Greenbrae, CA 94904 |
| Irene Simpson | ND | (206) 435-5232 | 104 S. West Ave., Arlington, WA 98223 |
| David L. Stephenson | DDS LAc | (714) 776-7020 | 216 W. Cypress St., Anaheim, CA 92805 |
| Andrea Sullivan | PhD ND | (202) 244-4545 | 4501 Conn. Ave. N.W. #233, Washington, DC 20008 |
| Anthony J. Sweeney | MD | (414) 351-4600 | 8969 N. Port Washington Rd., Milwaukee, WI 53217 |
| Gloria Thoreson | DC | (816) 452-1260 | P.O. Box 28035, Kansas City, MO 64118 |
| Stephen Thornburgh | DO | (208) 466-3517 | 824–17th Ave South, Nampa, ID 83651 |
| Michael Traub | ND | (808) 329-2114 | 75-5759 Kaukini Hwy. #202 Kailua-Kona, HI 96740 |
| Marc Tremoni | OMD | (213) 393-1650 | 1304 Fifth St. #D, Santa Monica, CA 90403 |
| Dennis L. Vossen | MD | (707) 829-0951 | 460 Pitt Ave., Sebastopol, CA 95472 |
| Donald Vradenburg | DC | (503) 754-0325 | 883 N.W. Grant, Corvallis, OR 97330 |
| Dian Wagner | ND | (206) 322-4325 | 1812 E. Madison #206, Seattle, WA 98122 |
| Meris Walton | DC | (408) 479-1700 | 1051 41st Avenue, Santa Cruz, CA 95062 |
| David K. Warkentin | PA–C | (415) 457-0678 | P.O. Box 39, Fairfax, CA 94978 |
| Ronald R. Wempen | MD F | (714) 546-4325 | 3620 S. Bristol St., Suite 306, Santa Ana, CA 92704 |
| Hope Wing | ND | (907) 561-2330 | 520 E. 34th #305, Anchorage, AK 99503 |
| Louise Woehl | RN | (805) 434-1624 | P.O. Box 607, Templeton, CA 93465 |
| Loryne Joyce Young | ND | (202) 832-1029 | 2414 Perry St. N.E., Washington, DC 20018 |
| Anada Zaren | RN | (805) 965-5805 | 28 E. Canon Perdido, Santa Barbara, CA 93101 |

## ORTHOMOLECULAR PSYCHIATRY

| NAME | TITLE | PHONE | ADDRESS |
|---|---|---|---|
| Vahagan Agbabian | DO | (313) 334-2424 | 28 N. Saginaw St., Suite 1105, Pontiac, MI 49058 |
| Sidney M. Baker | MD F | (203) 387-1800 | 60 Washington Ave., Hamden, CT 06518 |
| John M. Baron | DO | (216) 642-0082 | 4087 Rockside, Suite 100, Cleveland, OH 44131 |

## ORTHOMOLECULAR PSYCHIATRY continued

| | | | |
|---|---|---|---|
| Philip J. Berent | MD | (708) 459-1003 | 125 E. Lake-Cook Rd., Buffalo Grove, IL 60089 |
| Brian E. Briggs | MD | (701) 838-6011 | 718 6th St. SW, Minot, ND 56701 |
| Robert Cathcart | MD | (415) 949-2822 | 127 Second St., Suite 4, Los Altos, CA 94022 |
| Sarafina Corsello | MD | (212) 517-2222 | 200 W. 57 St. #1202, New York, NY 10019 |
| Martin Dayton | MD DO | (305) 931-8484 | 18600 Collins Ave., N. Miami Beach, FL 33160 |
| Paul J. Dunn | MD | (708) 383-3800 | 715 Lake St. #106, Oak Park, IL 60301 |
| Stephen Edeison | MD | (404) 841-0088 | 3833 Roswell Rd., Suite 110, Atlanta, GA 30342 |
| Carol Englander | MD | (617) 965-7770 | 1340 Centre St., Newton, MA 02159 |
| Kendall A. Gerdes | MD F | (303) 377-8837 | 1617 Vine St., Denver, CO 80206 |
| Michael Jansen | MD | (617) 661-6225 | 2557 Mass. Ave., Cambridge, MA 02140 |
| James J. Julian | MD | (213) 467-5555 | 1654 Cahuenga Blvd., Hollywood, CA 90028 |
| Howard G. Kimball | MD | (501) 269-4301 | C/O Garst Clinic, Mount View, AR 72560 |
| A. Leonard Klepp | MD | (818) 981-5511 | 16311 Ventura Blvd., Suite 725, Encino, CA 91436 |
| Richard A. Kunin | MD | (415) 346-2500 | 2698 Pacific Ave., San Francisco, CA 94115 |
| Howard J. Lang | DO PM | (817) 268-1171 | 1404 Brown Trail, Beford, TX 76022 |
| Paul Lynn | MD | (415) 566-1000 | 345 W. Portal Ave., San Francisco, CA 94127 |
| Allan Magazinar | DO | (609) 424-8222 | 1907 Greentree Rd., Cherry Hill, NJ 08003 |
| Marshall Mandell | MD E | (203) 838-4706 | Three Bush St., Norwalk, CT 06850 |
| Heather Morgan | MD M | (513) 439-1797 | 138 S. Main St., Centerville, OH 45458 |
| Robert R. Noble | MD M | (214) 458-9944 | 6757 Arapaho Rd. #757, Dallas, TX 75248 |
| Henry J. Palalius | MD M | (703) 356-2244 | 1481 Chain Bridge Rd. #101, McLean, VA 22101 |
| William H. Philpott | MD F | (405) 390-3009 | 17171 S.E. 29th St., Choctaw, OK 73020 |
| William J. Rea | MD F | (214) 368-4132 | 8345 Walnut Hill Lane #205, Dallas, TX 75231 |
| Dennis W. Remington | MD M | (801) 373-8500 | 1675 N. Freedom Blvd., Suite 11E, Provo, UT 84604 |
| Albert F. Robbins | DO MSPH | (407) 395-3282 | 400 S. Dixie Hway., Bldg. 2, #210, FL |
| William J. Sayer | MD F | (415) 321-3361 | 145 N. California Ave., Palo Alto, CA 94301 |
| Thomas L. Stone | MD M | (312) 934-1100 | 1811 Hicks Rd., Rolling Meadows, IL 60008 |
| Richardo Tan | MD | (915) 445-9090 | 423 South Palm, Pecos, TX 79772 |
| John Parks Towbridge | MD M | (713) 540-2329 | 9816 Memorial Blvd., Suite 205, Humble, TX 77338 |
| James T. Walker | D Min | (815) 477-7977 | 475 W. Terra Cotta Ave., Crystal Lake, IL 60014 |
| Otis Jack Woodward Jr. | MD M | (912) 436-9535 | 1304 Whispering Pines Rd., Albany, GA 31707 |
| Aubrey M. Worrell Jr. | MD F | (501) 535-8200 | 3900 Hickory St., Pine Bluff, AR 71603 |
| Robert Y. Yee | MD PM | (707) 544-6891 | 3317 Chante Rd., #2D, Santa Rosa, CA 95404 |

# OTOLARYNGOLOGY

| NAME | TITLE | PHONE | ADDRESS |
|---|---|---|---|
| Neil D. Adams | MD E | (206) 736-1171 | 123 N. Tower, Centralia, WA 98521 |
| Jack B. Anon | MD PM | (814) 456-7866 | 225 W. 25 St., Med Arts #207, Erie, PA 16502 |
| Robert Arbon | MD M | (801) 375-4433 | 777 N. 500 W. #105, Provo, UT 84601 |
| Martin Brody | DDS MD | (305) 822-9035 | 7100 W. 20th Ave., Hialeah, FL 33016 |
| Andrew M. Brown | MD F | (205) 547-4971 | 515 South Third St., Gladsen, AL 35901 |
| Rocco D. Cassone | MD M | (803) 536-5511 | 1175 Crook Rd., Suite 230, Orangeburg, SC 29115 |
| Charles R. Chung | MD M | (817) 267-1521 | 1850 Central Dr., Bedford, TX 76021 |
| Linwood W. Custalo | MD PM | (804) 826-2032 | 1832 Todds Lane, Hampton, VA 23666 |
| John Lee Davis III | MD M | (405) 843-6619 | 333 N.W. 56th, Suite 602, Oklahoma City, OK 73112 |
| Richard B. Dawson | MD M | (405) 528-2051 | 707 NW 13th, Oklahoma City, OK 73103 |
| Donald M. Dushay | DO M | (918) 744-0228 | 4444 S. Harvard Ave. #100, Tulsa, OK 74135 |
| Dean E. Goblirsch | DO PM | (414) 475-1711 | 9900 West Bluemound Rd, Milwaukee, WI 53266 |
| Donald E. Goehring | MD E | (412) 287-4241 | 503 Union Bank Bldg., Butler, PA 16001 |
| P. John Hagan | MD E | (717) 826-1955 | Rd. 1, Box 99, C/O Kreitzberger, Hopbottom, PA 18824 |
| David J. Harbrecht | MD PM | (801) 292-8303 | 425 Medical Drive #107, Bountiful, UT 84010 |
| Anthony E. Harris | MD M | (803) 648-7897 | 154 Waterloo St., Aiken, SC 29802 |
| Darrel Hunsaker | MD M | (619) 532-9605 | San Diego Naval Hosp., Oto, San Diego, CA 92134 |
| J. R.B. Hutchinson | MD M | (404) 939-1090 | 1462 Montreal Rd., Tucker, GA 30084 |
| Constantine A. Kotsanis | MD PM | (817) 481-6342 | 1600 W. College Street, Grapevine, TX 76051 |
| Howard J. Lang | DO PM | (817) 268-1171 | 1404 Brown Trail, Bedford, TX 76022 |
| Randall A. Langston | MD M | (904) 863-8287 | 1005 Mar Walt Dr., Ft. Walton Beach, FL 32548 |
| Sidney P. Lipman | MD PM | (814) 452-2405 | 225 W. 25th. St. #207, Erie, PA 16502 |
| Jeffrey Marcus | MD M | (904) 726-3131 | 3733 E. Gulf-to-Lake Highway, Inverness, FL 32650 |
| John F. Moyer Jr. | MD PM | (412) 741-2123 | 701 Broad Street, Sewickley, PA 15143 |
| Roger D. Neal | MD M | (703) 628-9547 | P.O. Box 1328, Abington, VA 24210 |
| Gerald L. Smith | MD M | (307) 632-5589 | 5320 Education Dr., Cheyenne, WY 82009 |
| Marvine Weatherby | MD E | (817) 594-4256 | P.O. Box 670325, Dallas, TX 75367 |

# AANP Regular Members

*Alphabetical Order—as of January 15, 1993*

## A

| NAME | | ADDRESS | PHONE |
|---|---|---|---|
| Aagenes ND | Nancy | 1820 Harrison, Butte, MI 59701 | (406) 723-6609 |
| Abshier ND | Thomas Lee | 2615 SE 111th, #4, Portland, OR 97266 | (503) 761-8495 |
| Adams ND | Suzanne | 3627 Ensign Road, Suite B, Olympia, WA 98506 | (206) 459-9082 |
| Adams ND | Marie R. | 3931 Bridge Way North, Seattle, WA 98103 | (206) 634-1600 |
| Adele ND | Ruth | 1625 W Uintah St., Suite I, Colorado Springs, CO 80904 | (719) 636-0098 |
| Aesoph ND | Lauri M. | 1415 West 31st St., Sioux Falls, SD 57105 | (605) 339-3645 |
| Alexander ND | Jonna | 635 NE 78th, Portland, OR 97213 | (503) 252-1599 |
| Alstat ND | Edward K. | 14385 SE Lusted Road, Sandy, OR 97055-9549 | (503) 256-4330 |
| Alvarado ND | Gilbert | 1829 E. Franklin Street, Chapel Hill, NC 27514 | (919) 933-7373 |
| Ancharski ND | Michael R. | 2472 Donegal Ct., West Linn, OR 97068-3907 | (503) 252-8125 |
| Anderson ND | David Royce | 9015 NW Holman Road, Suite #2, Seattle, WA 98117 | (206) 782-2363 |
| Arthurs ND | Kevon | 223 SE 114th, Portland, OR 97216 | (503) 225-0085 |
| Arvidson, ND | Steven | 1421 Arabian Ct., Newberg, OR 97132 | (503) 538-2342 |
| Austin ND | Stephen P. | 3207 SE 25th, Portland, OR 97202 | (503) 232-2142 |
| Axelrod ND | Leslie | 8030 Yavapai Rd., Prescott Valley, AZ 86314-8442 | (602) 772-6516 |

## B

| NAME | | ADDRESS | PHONE |
|---|---|---|---|
| Bachman ND | Gary | 1910 Riverside Drive (#5), Mt. Vernon, WA 98273 | (206) 424-3460 |
| Badillo-Cochran ND | Jorge | 607 Market St., Kirkland, WA 98033 | (206) 822-3716 |
| Bar-Shalom ND | Ruth | 222 Front St., Fairbanks, AK 99701 | (907) 451-7100 |
| Barnow ND | Felice H. | 2705 East Madison, Seattle, WA 98112 | (206) 328-7929 |
| Barrett ND | Richard | 6132 SE Yamhill St., Portland, OR 97215-2830 | (503) 239-6595 |
| Barrett ND | Deborah Peters | 6132 SE Yamhill St., Portland, OR 97215-2830 | (503)239-6595 |
| Barrie ND | Stephen A. | 18/A Regent Park Blvd., Asheville, NC 28806 | (704) 253-0621 |

| Barton ND LicAc | Shiva L. | 1152 Beacon St., Brookline, MA 01246 | (617) 277-4150 |
| Baruffi ND | Paula | 9236 SE Shoreland Dr., Bellevue, WA 98004 | (206) 453-5050 |
| Bastyr ND | John B. | 735 10th Av. E, Seattle, WA 98102 | (206) 323-4336 |
| Bauer ND | John M. | 1020 North US Hwy 41, Dunnellon, FL 34432 | (904) 489-5540 |
| Baungartner Dale ND | Ellen W. | 25170 Montana Drive W, Golden, CO 80401 | (303) 526-0217 |
| Bayard ND | Bernie | 1722 NE Schuyler, Portland, OR 97212 | (503) 288-9793 |
| Beaston ND | Littlebrave | 430 NE Ravenna Blvd., Apt. 101, Seattle, WA 98115 | (206) 527-2176 |
| Beaty ND | Janet K. | 6 Smith Ave., Lexington, MA 02173 | (617) 863-0598 |
| Beck ND | Cindy | 107 N. Tower, Suite 5, Centralia, WA 98531 | (206) 330-0562 |
| Beeson ND | Margaret R. | 328 Grand Ave., Billings, MT 59101-5923 | (406) 259-5096 |
| Berg-Johannessen ND | Robert P. | 335 Quechee W. Hartford Rd., White River Jct., VT 05001 | (802) 296-7503 |
| Bergkamp ND | Michael | 516 Fuller Ave., Helena, MT 59601 | (406) 442-2091 |
| Best ND | Janet | 3017 NW 60th St., Seattle, WA 98107 | (206) 783-2924 |
| Betcone-Jolley ND | Barbara | 748 SE 181st, Portland, OR 97233 | (503) 661-2137 |
| Bettenburg ND | Rita | 730 NE 93rd Ave., Portland, OR 97220-4540 | (503) 650-2452 |
| Bettner ND | Donald R. | 1127 W McDowell Rd., Phoenix, AZ 85007 | (602) 433-1872 |
| Beyrle ND | Stanley W. | 2708 East Central, Wichita, KS 67214 | (316) 687-0035 |
| Binder ND | Timothy A. | 173 Blodgett Camp Rd., Hamilton, MI 59840 | (406) 363-4041 |
| Birdsall ND | Tim | 7005 Selle Rd., Sand Point, ID 83864 | (208) 265-5208 |
| Black ND | Andrea | P.O. Box 1053, Okanogan, WA 98840 | (509) 422-5700 |
| Blackman ND | Kenneth S. | 3002 E Florence Dr., Tucson, AZ 85716 | (602) 325-3001 |
| Bloom ND | Rena | 161 Madison, Denver, CO 80206 | (303) 355-4547 |
| Booker ND | Jennifer | 203 E 4th, Suite 305-306, Olympia, WA 98501 | (206) 754-0104 |
| Borg-Comaduran ND | Adrienne | 74 East 18th Ave., Suite 12, Eugene, OR 97401 | (503) 686-3330 |
| Bove ND | Mary Louise | 3110 NE 125th, Seattle, WA 98125 | (206) 524-8016 |
| Boyle ND | Wade | 623 Neely Manor Blvd., East Palestine, OH 44413 | (216) 426-2600 |
| Bradbury ND | Thomas | 2051 S. Dobson #17-183, Mesa, AZ 85202 | (602) 649-8453 |
| Bradley ND DHANP | Randall S. | 7447 Farnam St., Omaha, NE 68114 | (402) 391-6714 |
| Brayce ND | Collon | 1129 E Main St., Suite 107, Wailuku, HI 96793 | (808) 242-6787 |
| Brett ND | Jennifer | 998 Nichols Ave., Stratford, CT 06497 | (203) 377-1525 |
| Brewer BA DC NMD | Dr. John L. | 5002 W Glendale Ave., Suite 101, Glendale, AZ 85301-2791 | (602) 937-4576 |
| Brinker ND | Francis J. | 6417 E Hayne St., Tucson, AZ 85710-4638 | (602) 747-1898 |

| Brinkman ND | Richard M. | 4320 Calaroga Dr., West Linn, OR 97068-1008 | (503) 635-4145 |
| Broadwell ND | Prudence A. | 18837 Brookhurst St., Suite 205, Fountain Valley, CA 92708 | (714) 965-9266 |
| Brooks ND | Fran | P.O. Box 1921, Vashon Island, WA 98070 | (206) 463-5611 |
| Brown ND | Don | 3644 Bagley Ave., North, Seattle, WA 98103 | (206) 632-8620 |
| Buratovich ND | Nick D. | 2435 E Southern Ave., #9, Tempe, AZ 85282 | (602) 831-0717 |
| Burke ND DHANP | Jack L. | 615 Piikoi St., Penthouse #3, Honolulu, HI 96814 | (808) 537-4345 |
| Buttler ND | Brian B. | P.O. Box 227 (300 E Main St), Molalla, OR 97038 | (503) 829-2297 |
| Byron ND | James A. | 15 Oakwood Ave., West Hartford, CT 06119 | (203) 523-0741 |

# C

| NAME | | ADDRESS | PHONE |
| --- | --- | --- | --- |
| Calabrese ND | Carlo | JBC/144 NE 54th, Seattle, WA 98105 | (206) 523-9585 |
| Calpeno DC ND CAc HANP | Anthony | 4111 A Bridgeport Way West, Tacoma, WA 98466 | (206) 565-2444 |
| Campbell ND | Clarence W. | P.O. Box 744, Canyonville, OR 97417 | (503) 839-4421 |
| Campbell ND | Andy | 1217 Burnside #701, Gresham, OR 97030 | (503) 665-4977 |
| Canavan ND | Donald M. | 555 Pierce St. #724C, Albany, CA 94706 | (510) 524-8652 |
| Canvasser ND | Bruce L. | 805 SE Sherman, Portland, OR 97214 | (503) 232-5710 |
| Capon ND | Lyndon C. | 16504 6th Ave. W, Lynwood, WA 98037-8102 | (206) 743-9355 |
| Caprio ND | Lawrence J. | 830 Post Rd. E, Westport, CT 06880 | (203) 226-4167 |
| Carianna ND | Ember | 1211 Prosperity Farms, Suite 223, Palm Beach Gdns, FL 33410 | (407) 622-4334 |
| Carson ND | Jacqueline | P.O. Box 725, Hilo, HI 96721 | (808) 934-3233 |
| Carter ND | Kathleen E. | 900 South Finley Point Rd., Polson, MI 59860 | (406) 887-2902 |
| Caselli ND | Mary F. | 2348 NW Lovejoy, Portland, OR 97210 | (503) 224-7224 |
| Chan ND | Jim | #101–3380 Maquinna Drive, Vancouver, BC V55 4C6 | (604) 435-3786 |
| Chester ND | Rick | 825 E. Orange Drive, Phoenix, AZ 85014-3253 | (503) 257-8507 |
| Chodosh ND | Lowell | 17068 SE McLoughlin Blvd., Milwaukie, OR 97267 | (503) 659-5029 |
| Christianson ND | Judy L. | 1812 E Madison, Suite 205, Seattle, WA 98122 | (206) 329-1237 |
| Clapp ND | Debra | 3828 Meridian Ave. N, Seattle, WA 98103 | (206) 632-1011 |
| Clark, ND | Lunda A. | 11611 SE Market St., Portland, OR 97216 | (503) 256-7837 |

| Coletto ND | Joseph J. | 10525 SE Cherry Blossom Dr. 107, Portland, OR 97216 | (503) 640-3760 |
|---|---|---|---|
| Collins ND | Drew | 8030 Yavapai Road, Prescott Valley, AZ 86314 | (602) 772-6516 |
| Collins ND DHANP | John G. | 800 SE 181st Ave., Gresham, OR 97233 | (503) 667-1961 |
| Costarella ND | Linda | 3110 NE 125th St., Seattle, WA 98125 | (206) 367-3400 |
| Crinnion ND | Walter J. | 13401 NE Bel-Red Rd. #A4, Bellevue, WA 98005 | (206) 747-9200 |
| Cronin ND | Michael J. | 2530 E Indian School Rd., Phoenix AZ 85016 | (602) 954-0227 |
| Cronin ND | Kyle H. | 2530 E Indian School Rd., Phoenix, AZ 85016 | (602) 954-0227 |
| Cropley ND | Charles M. | 2885 E. Aurora, Suite 19, Boulder, CO 80303 | (303) 449-1295 |

# D

| NAME | | ADDRESS | PHONE |
|---|---|---|---|
| D'Adamo | Dr. James L. | 186 St. George St., Toronto, ON M5R 2N3 | (416) 968-0496 |
| D'Adamo ND | Peter J. | 54 Lafayette Pl., Greenwich, CT 06830 | (203) 661-7375 |
| Dahl ND | Ilene L. | 868 Gravenstein Hwy N, Sebastopol, CA 95472 | (707) 823-4511 |
| Daugherty ND | Jack D. | 12195 SW Allen Blvd., Beaverton, OR 97005 | (503) 646-0697 |
| Davis ND | Teri L. | 6342 Calle Luna, Tucson, AZ 85710 | (602) 790-4231 |
| Davis ND | Steven W. | 6708A 144th St. NW, Gig Harbor, WA 98335-8738 | (206) 857-5544 |
| Davison ND | Kevin | 21198 Vineyard Ave., Wailuku, HI 96793 | (808) 252-6000 |
| De Kadt ND | Sharon | 1427 Chapel St., New Haven, CT 06511 | (203) 785-1154 |
| DeLaney ND | Susan R. | 103 Weaver South, Carrboro, NC 27510 | (919) 929-1132 |
| DeLoe ND | Paul | 6161 E. Speedway, Tucson, AZ 85712 | (602) 290-8665 |
| Demanski ND | Rosanne | 34 East Main, Avon, CT 06001 | (203) 676-BABY |
| Demeaux ND | Jenny | 3520 Sunset Beach Dr. NW, Olympia, WA 98502 | (206) 866-4328 |
| Dev ND | Prem | 15925 SE Stark, Portland, OR 97233 | (503) 254-3051 |
| DiPalma ND | Michael | 58 E. Oakland Ave., Doylestown, PA 18901-4651 | (215) 345-0731 |
| Dickens ND | Michael J. | P.O. Box 307, Lahaina, HI 96767-0307 | (808) 242-7031 |
| Dickson ND DHANP | Bruce A. | 1900 N Hwy. 99 W, Suite A, McMinnville, OR 97128 | (503) 434-6515 |
| Donovan ND | Colleen | 706 1/2 E. Denny Way, Seattle, WA 98122 | (206) 328-2703 |
| Donovan ND | Patrick M. | 207 NW 73rd, Seattle, WA 98117 | (206) 782-0448 |
| Downey ND | Catherine M. | 3093 Akahi St., Lihue, HI 96766 | (808) 245-2277 |
| Dubey ND | Steven G. | 3093 Akahi St., Lihue, HI 96766 | (808) 245-2277 |

| Dunn ND | Sheila B. | 607 Market St., Kirkland, WA 98033 | (206) 822-3716 |
| Dunn ND | Jon | 9863 Bowline Ct. NW, Olympia, WA 98502-9702 | (206) 632-0354 |
| Dunne ND | Nancy | 218 E Front St., Suite 303, Missoula, MT 59802 | (406) 728-8544 |
| Durgin ND | Pamela | 612 Santa Monica Blvd., Santa Monica, CA 90401 | (310) 576-6176 |
| Durward ND | Dorothea | 343 N. 103rd St., Seattle, WA 98133-9124 | (206) 789-4887 |

# E

| NAME | | ADDRESS | PHONE |
| --- | --- | --- | --- |
| Eaton ND | David E. | 2891 53rd St. N, St. Petersburg, FL 33710 | (813) 321-4286 |
| Edmisten, ND, LAc | Karen Elizabeth | 344 SW 7th, Newport, OR 97365 | (503) 234-5623 |
| Edwards ND | Louise N. | 929 East 3rd Ave., Durango, CO 81301 | (303) 247-2043 |
| Ellis Jr ND | Edward R. | 6 Courthouse Land (#9), Chelmsford, MA 01824 | (508) 453-3035 |
| Elmore ND DHANP | Durr | 14653 South Graves Rd., Mulino, OR 97042 | (503) 829-7326 |
| Epstein ND | Paul G. | #9 Berkeley St., Norwalk, CT 06850 | (203) 853-6800 |

# F

| NAME | | ADDRESS | PHONE |
| --- | --- | --- | --- |
| Faith ND | Hope | 8315–5th NE #A, Seattle, WA 98115C | (206) 527-1366 |
| Farberow ND | Hilary | 1330 SE 39th Ave., Portland, OR 97214 | (503) 232-1100 |
| Fassler ND | Kristy | 406 The Hill, Suite 101, Portsmouth, NH 03801-3736 | (603) 427-6800 |
| Feingold ND | Jeffrey H. | 5743 East Thomas Rd., Suite 1, Scottsdale, AZ 85251 | (602) 945-8773 |
| Field ND | David R. | 1820 Sonoma Ave./Doctors Pk #46, Santa Rosa, CA 95405 | (707) 576-7388 |
| Filkoff ND | B. David | 760 Farmington Ave., West Hartford, CT 06119 | (203) 523-8462 |
| Fine ND DHANP | Howard G. | 468 Main St. North, Westport, CT 06880 | (203) 221-0216 |
| Flagler ND DHANP | Samuel | 6737 E Camino Principal #C, Tucson, AZ 85715 | (602) 721-8821 |
| Flagler ND DHANP | Lila | 6737 E Camino Principal #C, Tucson, AZ 85715 | (602) 721-8821 |
| Flanagan, ND | Cathryn M. | 12 Roosevelt Ave., Mystic, CT 06355 | (206) 525-2675 |
| Fleming ND | Molly C. | 323 Pearl St., Burlington, VT 05401 | (802) 862-0836 |
| Forwell, ND | Joanna Theresa | 4800 Phinney Ave. No. #6, Seattle, WA 98103 | (206) 548-1567 |

| Freeman ND | Elizabeth | 10603 NE 14th St., Bellevue, WA 98004 | (206) 454-0908 |
| Freeman ND | Brian | 975 York Rd., Dillsburg, PA 17019 | (717) 432-8755 |

# G

| NAME | | ADDRESS | PHONE |
| --- | --- | --- | --- |
| Garcia ND | Gregory P. | 9830 SW McKenzie, Tigard, OR 97223 | (503) 624-1321 |
| Garner ND DHANP | Mary Lynn | 4 Milk St., Portland, ME 04101 | (207) 772-5227 |
| Garrison ND | Robert L. | 143 Park Lane, Kirkland, WA 98033 | (206) 827-4467 |
| Gear Jr NMD, DC | Robert L. | 3543 N 7th St., Phoenix, AZ 85014 | (602) 263-8484 |
| Geller ND | Edward M. | 1744 E McAndrews Rd., Suite A, Medford, OR 97504 | (503) 772-2787 |
| Germain | Jacqueline E. | 87 Bernie O'Rourke Drive, Middletown, CT 06457 | (203) 347-8600 |
| Germain ND | Kathleen | 545 First Street, Lake Oswego, OR 97034 | (503) 635-6643 |
| Gibson ND | Debra A. | 1900 S. Ocean Blvd. #9-G, Pompano Beach, FL 33062 | (305) 783-0544 |
| Gibson ND | Norman T. | 104 SW 5th St., Suite 2, Belle Glade, FL 33430 | (415) 996-7105 |
| Gignac ND | Mark | 5802–224th Pl. SW, Mountlake Terr, WA 98043 | (206) 774-3232 |
| Gilbert ND | Mirian | P.O. Box 882, Patagonia, AZ 85624 | (602) 394-2670 |
| Goldman ND DHANP | Ellen L. | 2024 South Dearborn, Seattle, WA 98144 | (206) 332-0199 |
| Goodman-Herrick ND | Pearlyn | 21 Trails End Rd., Weston, CT 06883 | (203) 227-5534 |
| Gotzl ND | Joseph A. | 16528 N Florida Ave., Lutz, FL 33549 | (813) 949-4982 |
| Green ND | Julie Claire | 850 Third St., Suite C, Santa Rosa, CA 95401 | (707) 527-7525 |
| Greenberg ND | Miles | P.O. Box 3188, Lihue, HI 96766 | (808) 245-2277 |
| Greenspan ND | David A. | 11818 SW King James Place, Tigard, OR 97224 | (503) 684-1875 |
| Griffith ND | Lester E. | 19514 64th Ave. West, Lynwood, WA 98036 | (206) 771-9000 |
| Griffith ND | Mary | 6708 A 144th St. NW, Gig Harbor, WA 98335 | (206) 549-2580 |
| Gross ND | Barbara E. | 6020 34th Ave. NE, Seattle, WA 98115C | (206) 524-8122 |
| Grotzinger DC ND | Jerold B. | 1190 Olive St., Eugene, OR 97401 | (503) 485-4548 |
| Groven ND | Mark D. | 1307 N. 45th St., Suite 200, Seattle, WA 98103 | (206) 632-0354 |
| Guiltinan ND | M. Jane | 1307 N. 45th, Suite 200, Seattle, WA 98103 | (206) 632-0354 |
| Gutowski ND | Louise D. | 1033 E Sutton Drive, Scottsdale, AZ 85260 | (602) 451-5300 |

# H

| NAME | | ADDRESS | PHONE |
|------|------|---------|-------|
| Hagney ND | Tim | 315 SE 20th, Portland, OR 97214 | (503) 236-6848 |
| Hall ND | Ursula | 8303–97th St. SW, Tacoma, WA 98498 | (206) 581-0408 |
| Hangee-Bauer ND | Carl S. | 862 Folsom St., Suite 300, San Francisco, CA 94107 | (415) 974-5596 |
| Hansen ND | Clark H. | 10615 N Hayden, Suite 100, Scottsdale, AZ 85260 | (602) 991-5092 |
| Harmon ND | Kenneth F. | 1835 SW 152 St., Seattle, WA 98166 | (206) 243-5252 |
| Harris ND | Roland K. | 975 W Ridge Drive, Jackson, MS 39209 | (601) 922-3967 |
| Hasan ND | Ananias | 717 Blue Hills Ave., Bloomfield, CT 06002 | (203) 243-5055 |
| Hastings ND | Patricia L. | 4324 Martin Way, Suite B, Olympia, WA 98506 | (800) 438-2882 |
| Haynes ND | Amy | 521 S 2nd W, Missoula, MT 59801 | (406) 721-2147 |
| Head ND | Kathleen A. | 2496 E St., Suite 300, San Diego, CA 92102-2024 | (619) 236-8285 |
| Healy ND | Helen C. | 1365 Englewood Ave., Suite 12, St. Paul, MN 55104 | (612) 644-4436 |
| Hecht ND | Leon | 406 The Hill, Suite 101, Portsmouth, NH 03801-3736 | (603) 427-6800 |
| Herdener ND | Larry J. | 415 E 3rd St., McMinnville, OR 97128-4612 | (503) 434-6170 |
| Hernandez ND | Connie | P.O. Box 192, Brattleboro, VT 05302-0192 | (802) 254-9332 |
| Hernandez ND | Marcel | P.O. Box 192, Brattleboro, VT 05302-0192 | (802) 254-9332 |
| Heron ND | Silena | P.O. Box 1438, Sedona, AZ 86336 | (602) 282-7136 |
| Herrick ND | Linda | 586 Glenwood Dr., Ashland, OR 97520 | (503) 482-0409 |
| Herring ND | Pamela | 46 South Main St., Concord, NJ 03301 | (603) 228-0407 |
| Herscu ND DHANP | Paul | 115 Elm St., Suite 210, Enfield, CT 06082 | (203) 763-1225 |
| Hibbs ND | John G. | 1523 E Madison St., Seattle, WA 98122-4013 | (206) 322-4416 |
| Hinton ND | David A. | 3074 Lancaster Drive NE #205, Salem, OR 97305 | (503) 390-8401 |
| Hobbs ND | H. Ron | 14015 55th Ave., West, Edmonds, WA 98026 | (206) 745-5049 |
| Hoey ND | Glenn R. | 310 S Mission Ave., Wenatchee, WA 98801-3044 | (509) 662-1302 |
| Holder ND | Autumn | 1001 North Swan Rd., Tucson, AZ 85711 | (602) 323-7133 |
| Hudson ND | Victoria | 3722 NE 20th Ave., Portland, OR 97212-1417 | (503) 255-7355 |
| Huntoon ND | Jenefer S. | 1329 N 45th St., Seattle, WA 98103 | (206) 632-8804 |
| Hutton ND | James M. | Box 69027 Hwy. 47, Mist, OR 97016 | (503) 755-2440 |

# I

| NAME | | ADDRESS | PHONE |
|------|------|---------|-------|
| Immel ND DHANP | Wm. Mark | 537 NW Wall, Suite E, Bend, OR 97701 | (503) 385-8174 |

# J

| NAME | | ADDRESS | PHONE |
|---|---|---|---|
| Jacobs ND | Michael | P.O. Box 497, Wilsonville, OR 97070 | (503) 682-8871 |
| James ND | Mary | 94 Center Rd., Woodbridge, CT 06525 | (203) 397-8890 |
| James ND | Mark S. | 809 N Humphrey's, Flagstaff, AZ 86001 | (602) 774-1770 |
| Jamison ND | Scott L. | 369 S Franklin #300, Juneau, AK 99801 | (907) 586-6810 |
| Jangaard ND | Robert E. | P.O. Box 130, Freeland, WA 98249 | (206) 321-6470 |
| Jardin ND | Kyrie | S 1403 Grand Blvd., Suite 204-So, Spokane, WA 99203 | (509) 838-5413 |
| Jasper ND | Cary | 924 W Fireweed Lane, Anchorage, AK 99503 | (907) 276-4611 |
| Jasper-Litov ND | LaraLee | 804 N. 43rd St. #5 Seattle, WA 98103 | (206) 548-0377 |
| Jeffries ND | John H. | 4280 Southwest 110th, Beaverton, OR 97005 | (503) 626-0709 |
| Jenkins ND | Hugh A. | 2148 W. 95th St., Chicago, IL 60643-1120 | (312) 445-6800 |
| Jenner ND | Jo | 1837 SE 35th Place, Portland, OR 97214 | (503) 234-0142 |
| Johnson ND | Dorothy Laura | 16504 6th Ave. W, Lynwood, WA 98037-8102 | (206) 743-9355 |
| Jones ND | Eric S. | 1307 N 45th St., Suite 200 Seattle, WA 98103-6704 | (206) 632-0354 |

# K

| NAME | | ADDRESS | PHONE |
|---|---|---|---|
| Kail ND | Konrad | 13832 N 32nd St., Suite C2-4, Phoenix, AZ 85032 | (602) 493-2273 |
| Kallenborn ND | Gabriele | 54 Lafayette Place, Greenwich, CT 06830 | (203) 454-5989 |
| Karcheski ND CC | Dorothy | 2622 Pacific Ave., Suite C, Olympia, WA 98501 | (206) 357-6448 |
| Keaton ND | Dana | 5702 N. 4th Place, Phoenix, AZ 85012 | (602) 265-9121 |
| Kell ND | Ernest E. | 1420 S 20th Ave., Hollywood, FL 33020 | (305) 922-5627 |
| Kelly ND | Kimberly | 6729 180th SE, Snohomish, WA 98290 | (206) 281-9047 |
| Kimata ND | Lori G. | 181 South Kukui, Suite 207, Honolulu, HI 96813 | (808) 545-2093 |
| Kimball ND | Jeana D. | 1911 11th East, Seattle, WA 98102 | (206) 860-1226 |
| King ND DHANP | Stephen J. | 5502 35th Ave. NE, Seattle, WA 98105 | (206) 522-0488 |
| Kipnis ND DHANP | Sheryl R. | 5502 34th Ave. NE, Seattle, WA 98105 | (206) 522-0488 |
| Kirk, ND | Joan | P.O. Box 1661, Taos, NM 87571 | (505) 758-9704 |
| Kirschner ND | Richard M. | P.O. Box 896, Ashland, OR 97520 | (503) 488-2992 |
| Kitaeff ND | Richard J. | 23700 Edmonds Way, Edmonds, WA 98026 | (206) 784-3371 |

| Klass ND | Jeffrey J. | 625 E Main St., Branford, CT 06405 | (203) 481-5219 |
| Kos, ND | Cheryl A. | 3216 NE 45th Place, Suite 304, Seattle, WA 98105 | (206) 525-6030 |
| Krassner ND | Devra | 402 State St., Portsmouth, NH 03801 | (603) 433-3212 |
| Kreitzberg ND | Susan | 1404 1/2 Second St., Santa Fe, NM 87501 | (505) 986-0919 |
| Kroes ND | Susan | 1563 Jefferson St., Muskegon, MI 49441-2456 | (616) 722-0398 |
| Kruzel ND | Thomas A. | 800 SE 181st Ave., Gresham, OR 97233 | (503) 667-1961 |
| Kunkler ND | Karen M. | 2002 Atwood Ave. #209, Madison, WI 53704 | (608) 241-1911 |
| Kuprowsky ND | Stephan | 104-2786 W 16th Ave., Vancouver, BC V6K 3C4 | (604) 738-2111 |
| Kuramoto ND | Doug | 55 Victoria Road, Suite 202, Nanaimo, BC V9R 5N9 | (604) 753-0280 |

# L

| NAME | | ADDRESS | PHONE |
| --- | --- | --- | --- |
| LaMont ND LAC | Sally | 560 First St., Suite 204, Lake Oswego, OR 97034 | (503) 636-2734 |
| Lamar ND | Daniel | 819 Locust Ct., Ft. Collins, CO 80524 | (303) 490-4400 |
| Lamden ND | Mark J. | 6204 8th Ave. NW, Seattle, WA 98107 | (206) 782-3080 |
| Lamson ND | Davis Williams | 24030 132nd Ave. S.E., Kent, WA 98042 | (206) 631-8920 |
| Lane ND | Sarah | P.O. Box 375, St. Ignatius, MT 59865 | (406) 726-3000 |
| Lang, ND | Michael | 1657 Riverside Drive, Laramie, WY 82070-6627 | (302) 742-0787 |
| Larmer ND | Jack | 34 Bussell Court, Dumont, NJ 07628 | (201) 385-7106 |
| Laurance ND | Joan | 209 Oak St., Hood River, OR 97013 | (503) 386-4844 |
| Laux ND | Marcus | 32410 Civic Ctr. Way, Suite E-5, Malibu, CA 90265 | (310) 456-1972 |
| Lee ND | Thomas | 10211 N 32nd St., Suite C-3, Phoenix, AZ 85028 | (602) 953-2213 |
| Lee-Engel ND | Christy | 9410–44th Place NE, Seattle, WA 98115 | (206) 525-3935 |
| Lemkin ND | James M. | 7 Cole Rd., Haydenville, MA 01039 | (413) 268-3500 |
| Lewis ND | Doug | 9111 Roosevelt Way NE, Seattle, WA 98115 | (206) 525-8078 |
| Lind ND | Amy | 4141 California Ave. SW, Seattle, WA 98116 | (206) 938-1393 |
| Linton ND | Molly A. | 313 W McGraw, Seattle, WA 98119 | (206) 281-9047 |
| Lipelt DDS ND | Michael | 8201 W Dry Creek Rd., Healdsburg, CA 95448 | (707) 433-8250 |
| Liva ND | Enrico P. | 87 Bernie O'Rourke Dr., Middletown, CT 06547 | (203) 347-8600 |
| Lommen-Hayes ND | Erin | 19365 SW 65th Ave. #211, Tualatin, OR 97062 | (503) 691-9886 |
| Long ND | Valerie | P.O. Box 17101, Anaheim Hills, CA 92817-7101 | (714) 777-5609 |

| | | | |
|---|---|---|---|
| Lucchesi-Cook ND | Teresa | 5437 Scotts Valley Drive, Scotts Valley, CA 95066 | (408) 438-7300 |
| Lucking ND | Andrew J. | 3546 Grand Ave., South, Minneapolis, MN 55408 | (612) 924-8112 |
| Lukats, ND | Alexander | 7350 S.U.S. 191 Hwy., Safford, AZ 85546 | (602) 428-2881 |
| Lynch ND | Pamela J. | 800 SE 181st, Gresham, OR 97233 | (503) 667-1961 |

# M

| NAME | | ADDRESS | PHONE |
|---|---|---|---|
| MacIntosh PhD ND | Anna | 545 First St., Lake Oswego, OR 97034 | (503) 255-4860 |
| Macallan ND | David | P.O. Box 16224, Portland, OR 97216 | (503) 232-1100 |
| Maguire RN ND DHANP | Annie | 23405–84th Ave., West, Edmonds, WA 98026 | (206) 776-6085 |
| Mally ND | James R. | 112 Douglas Blvd., Roseville, CA 95678 | (916) 782-1275 |
| Marinelli ND Dipl Ac | Rick | 2445 SW Cedar Hills Blvd., Beaverton, CA 97005 | (503) 644-4446 |
| Marschall ND | Richard A. | 162 S. Barr Rd., Port Angeles, WA 98362 | (206) 457-1515 |
| Marsh ND C,NM | Bonnie | 511 First St., Suite 217, Encinitas, CA 92024 | (619) 436-3455 |
| Martin ND | Morgan | 2705 East Madison, Seattle, WA 98112 | (206) 328-7929 |
| Martin-Belleville ND | Debra L. | 1185 Arthur St., Eugene, OR 97402 | (503) 683-4071 |
| Martinez ND | Robert M. | 903 5th Ave. Suite 103A, Kirkland, WA 98033-6316 | (206) 827-3870 |
| Marz ND | Russell B. | 2002 SE 50th Ave., Portland, OR 97215 | (503) 233-0585 |
| Massey ND | James B. | 3285 SW 78th Ave., Portland, OR 97225-3007 | (503) 292-1724 |
| Mather ND | Patricia | P.O. Box 477, Lsupshoehoe, HI 96764-0477 | (808) 982-5808 |
| Mather ND | Jonathan C. | P.O. Box 6923, Kamuela, HI 96743 | (808) 885-7711 |
| Mathieu ND | Brent | 4130 Plum Street ND, Boise, ID 83703-4417 | (208) 338-5590 |
| Maxwell ND | Catherine | 7114 Roosevelt Way NE, Seattle, WA 98115 | (206) 524-6123 |
| May ND | Marilyn A. | 211 King St. W, Dundas, ON L9H 1V6 | (416) 627-9434 |
| May ND | Robert | 4020 48th Ave. South, Seattle, WA 98118C | (206) 723-1469 |
| Mazur ND | Nancy A. | P.O. Box 1644, Avon, CT 06001 | (203) 676-2240 |
| McKee ND | James C. | 2020 W Fairbanks Ave., Winter Park, FL 32789 | (407) 628-2603 |
| McMahon ND | John | 157 Old Ridgefield Rd., Wilton, CT 06897 | (203) 761-9638 |
| Medeiros ND | Faizi | 335 Quenches W. Hartford Rd., White River Jct, VT 05001 | (802) 296-7503 |
| Melead ND | Donna Leia | 1405 NE Broadway, Upper Suite, Portland, OR 97232 | (503) 282-1224 |

| Mercer ND | Nancy | 7114 Roosevelt Way NE, Seattle, WA 98103 | (206) 547-8393 |
| Merrill ND | Mary L. | P.O. Box 1862, Santa Fe, NM 87504 | (505) 989-4309 |
| Merritt MD ND PhD | Henry N. | 6037 Longchamp Dr, Jacksonville, FL 32244 | (904) 771-8934 |
| Meseroie ND | Lisa | 4836–38th NE, Seattle, WA 98105 | (206) 526-1339 |
| Messer ND DHANP | Stephen A. | 1902 Jefferson St. #2, Eugene, OR 97405 | (503) 343-2384 |
| Miles, ND | Michael | 515 Cedar St., Marysville, WA 98270 | (206) 659-2605 |
| Miller ND | Irvin H. | 1640 Barr Rd. Ext., Port Angeles, WA 98362 | (206) 681-2230 |
| Miller ND | Owen W. | 2611 N Stevens, Tacoma, WA 98407 | (206) 752-2558 |
| Miller ND | Alan L. | East 3154–29th Ave., Spokane, WA 99223 | (509) 535-9135 |
| Milliman ND | W. Bruce | 5312 Roosevelt Way NE, Seattle, WA 98105 | (206) 525-8015 |
| Milner ND | Martin | 1330 SE 39th Ave., Portland, OR 97214 | (503) 232-1100 |
| Minor ND | Mary A. | 520 East 34th, Suite 305, Anchorage, AK 99503 | (907) 561-2330 |
| Mische ND | Magda | P.O. Box 22, Orcas Island, WA 98279 | (206) 376-5454 |
| Mitchell ND | M. Anne | 2558 Whitney Ave., Hamden, CT 06518 | (203) 230-2200 |
| Mitchell ND | William A. | 518 1st Ave. N, Suite 28/29, Seattle, WA 98109 | (206) 284-6040 |
| Mittman ND | Paul | 12 Roosevelt Ave., Packer Bldg, Mystic, CT 06355 | (203) 572-9566 |
| Moore ND | Willow T.M. | P.O. Box 192, Bozeman, MT 59771 | (406) 586-9413 |
| Moore ND | Robin E. | 3627 Ensign Rd., Suite 8, Olympia, WA 98506 | (206) 459-9082 |
| Morris ND | Lance J. | 1001 N Swan Rd., Tucson, AZ 85711 | (602) 323-7133 |
| Morrissey ND | Robert | 516 North Humphreys, Flagstaff, AZ 86001 | (602) 779-1016 |
| Morstein ND DHANP | Mona | 518 9th St. SE, Great Falls, MT 59405 | (406) 727-6680 |
| Murphy ND | Robert M. | 118 Migeon Ave., Torrington, CT 06790 | (203) 482-4730 |
| Murphy ND LAc | Patricia A. | 4511 SE Hawthorne, Suite 112, Portland, OR 97215 | (503) 238-1032 |
| Murray ND | Michael T. | 15401 SE 54th, Bellevue, WA 98006 | (206) 747-9925 |
| Mussman ND | Ian | 1234 N. Ogden Drive, W. Hollyood, CA 90046-4707 | (213) 650-1382 |
| Myatt ND | Dana | 4018 N 40th St., Phoenix, AZ 85018 | (602) 955-0551 |
| Myers ND | Robert M. | 805 Miller Valley Rd., Prescott, AZ 86301-1815 | (602) 445-1999 |
| Myers ND | Sheila | 1850 NE 6th St., Bend, OR 97701-4004 | (503) 385-6249 |

# N

| NAME | | ADDRESS | PHONE |
| Newman ND | Diane | 509 S. Clayton St., Wilmington, DE 19805 | (302) 655-7841 |
| Nunn ND | William Allen | 1071 S 9th E, Salt Lake City, UT 84105-1349 | (801) 363-6616 |

# O

| NAME | | ADDRESS | PHONE |
|------|------|---------|-------|
| O'Connor ND | Deirdre J. | 12 Roosevelt Ave., Packer Bldg., Mystic, CT 06355 | (203) 572-9566 |
| Ofgang ND | Harold M. | 57 North St., Suite 323, Danbury, CT 06810 | (203) 798-0533 |
| Ogawa-Lerman ND | Hazel | 1150 South King St., Suite 404, Honolulu, HI 96813 | (808) 537-2763 |
| Osik ND | Loretta | 1 Maplewood Drive, Danbury, CT 06811 | (203) 792-3187 |
| Ostroff ND | Diana Joy | 1750 Kalakaua St., Suite 2107, Honolulu, HI 96826 | (808) 947-1315 |

# P

| NAME | | ADDRESS | PHONE |
|------|------|---------|-------|
| Paetzhold ND | Pamela | 4616 SW Vermont, Portland, OR 97219 | (503) 293-1404 |
| Pais, ND | Gregory | 2920 A SE 109, Portland, OR 97266 | (503) 761-0474 |
| Parry ND LM | Tayna A. | 515 Cedar Ave., Marysvlle, WA 98270 | (206) 659-2605 |
| Peabody ND | Judy E. | Rt. 1 Box 197-11, Banks, OR 97106 | (503) 324-7672 |
| Penrod ND | Sigrid | 6738 13th Ave. NE #620, Redmond, WA 98052-9563 | (206) 882-2089 |
| Perry ND | Andrew M. | 410-B Lancaster Dr. NE, Salem, OR 97301 | (503) 364-1441 |
| Petersen ND | Judith L. | 12195 SW Allen Blvd., Beaverton, OR 97005 | (503) 646-0697 |
| Peterson ND | Noel S. | 560 First St., Suite 204, Lake Oswego, OR 97034 | (503) 636-2734 |
| Petherbridge ND | Carol J. | 1603 E Barnett Rd., Medford, OR 97504 | (503) 846-7507 |
| Pettijohn ND | Patton D. | P.O. Box 878894, Wasilla, AK 99687 | (907) 276-5077 |
| Phillips ND | Cynthia | 343 103rd North, Seattle, WA 98133 | (206) 784-0993 |
| Pizzorno Jr ND | Joseph E. | 144 NE 54th St., Seattle, WA 98105 | (206) 523-9585 |
| Pomeroy ND | Katherine D. | P.O. Box 2744, Kanuela, HI 96743 | (808) 885-9661 |
| Pontius ND | D. Eugene | 393 Kinchant St., Quesnel, BC V2J2R5 | (604) 992-5712 |
| Poore ND | Mary C. | 809 N Humphreys, Flagstaff, AZ 86001 | (602) 774-1770 |
| Posmantur Jr. ND | Richard A. | 2705 E. Madison, Seattle, WA 98112 | (206) 328-7929 |
| Poss ND | Margot J. | 1155 N. State St., Bellingham, WA 98225 | (206) 324-7798 |
| Potthoff DC ND | Ellen | 4400 Park Green Court, Sacramento, CA 95821 | (916) 481-9020 |
| Pouliot ND | Michelle J. | 118 Migeon Ave., Torrington, CT 06790 | (203) 482-4730 |

# R

| NAME | | ADDRESS | PHONE |
|---|---|---|---|
| Raistrick ND | Jonathan | 65 Cables #23, Waterbury, CT 06488 | (203) 262-6755 |
| Rao ND | Nancy | 2880 Folsom St., Suite 210A, Boulder, CO 80304 | (303) 449-8581 |
| Rapp ND | Cathleen | 451 Los Gatos Blvd., Suite 204, Los Gatos, CA 95032 | (408) 358-7797 |
| Reece ND | Michael | 1065 W Main St., New Holland, PA 17557 | (717) 656-4256 |
| Reichenberg-Ullman ND | Judyth L. | 4072 9th Ave. NE, Seattle, WA 98105 | (206) 547-9665 |
| Reilly ND | Paul E. | 5702 N 26th St., Suite C, Tacoma, WA 98407 | (206) 752-4544 |
| Reilly ND | JoHannah | 2660–13th St., Boulder, CO 80304 | (303) 541-9600 |
| Reingold ND | Howard J. | 365 NE Greenwood, Suite 3, Bend, OR 97701 | (503) 389-6935 |
| Reisinger ND | Gerald | 6 Gersnom Place, Kingston, PA 18704 | (717) 283-5194 |
| Resnick ND | Corey | 2204-8 NW Birdsdale, Gresnam, OR 97030 | (503) 661-5401 |
| Rifkin ND | Kenneth H. | 338 SW 2nd St., Lake Oswego, OR 97034 | (503) 636-2975 |
| Riley ND | Kathleen M. | 80 Dodgingtown, Bethel, CT 06801 | (203) 790-6889 |
| Ringdahl ND | Sarah Catherine | 501 Franklin Ave., Santa Fe, NM 87501 | (505) 989-8470 |
| Ritterman ND | Robin | 2558 Whitney Ave., Hamden, CT 06518 | (203) 230-2200 |
| Rivers ND | Kaiten | 811 West Yakima Ave., Suite 105, Yakima, WA 98902 | (509) 576-0811 |
| Robbins ND | Patti | 1653 E 31st, Tacoma, WA 98404 | (206) 581-2188 |
| Roberts ND | Susan M. | 4444 SW Corbett Ave., Portland, OR 97201-4207 | (503) 224-4003 |
| Robertson ND | Marley | 315 W. Goodwin, Prescott, AZ 86303 | (602) 778-6169 |
| Rodriguez Malave ND | Efrain | Calle Lodi 571, Urb Luarco, Rio Piedras, PR 00924 | (809) 751-4862 |
| Rogers ND | Cathy A. | 900 Madison St., Seattle, WA 98104 | (206) 464-0757 |
| Rollo ND LAc | Peggy M. | 833 SW 11th, Suite 612, Portland, OR 97205 | (503) 223-7067 |
| Rose ND | David | 117 W 6th St., Jacksonville, FL 32206 | (904) 356-5080 |
| Rothenberg ND DHANP | Amy B. | 356 Middle St., Amherst, MA 01002 | (413) 584-2997 |
| Rovin ND | Richard G. | 1090 Elkader St., Ashland, OR 97520-3405 | (808) 941-0528 |
| Rubman ND | Andrew L. | 800 Main St. S, Southbury, CT 06488-2217 | (203) 262-6755 |
| Rudd ND | Terry | 3701 E. Olsen, Amarillo, TX 79109 | (806) 359-1003 |

# S

| NAME | | ADDRESS | PHONE |
|---|---|---|---|
| Sahni ND | Ravinder S. | 9570 SW Beaverton Hillsdale Hwy., Beaverton, OR 97005-3309 | (503) 641-8503 |
| Sandberg-Lewis ND | Steven I. | P.O. Box 493, East Sound, WA 98245-0493 | (206) 376-4002 |
| Saunders ND | Paul R. | 211 King St. W, Dundas, ONT L9H1V6 | (416) 627-9434 |
| Schlapfer ND | Todd A. | 1000 W Hubbard, Suite 120, Coeur d'Alene, ID 83814 | (208) 664-1644 |
| Schor ND | Jacob | 161 Madison St., Denver, CO 80206 | (303) 355-4547 |
| Schwartz ND | Robert J. | 1237 State St., Hood River, OR 97031 | (503) 386-4489 |
| Schweitzer ND | Marvin P. | 71 E Ave. Suite F, Norwalk, CT, 06851 | (203) 853-6285 |
| Scopes ND | Suzanne | 316 NE 28th, Portland, CT 97232 | (503) 230-0812 |
| Scott ND | Mary | 2100 NE Broadway, Suite 3-B, Portland, OR 97332 | (503) 284-4311 |
| Scott ND | Leo M. | N 122 Argonee #3, Spokane, WA 99212 | (509) 928-8701 |
| Scott ND | Patricia | 29761-128th Ave. SW, Vashon, WA 98070-8805 | (206) 352-7880 |
| Seipt ND | Ann | 242 Stanford Ave., Berkeley, CA 94708 | (510) 524-1429 |
| Seliski ND | Lawrence | 1187 Johnston Road, White Rock, BC V4B 3Y7 | (604) 531-0252 |
| Sensenig ND | James S. | 2558 Whitney Ave., Hamden, CT 06518 | (203) 230-2200 |
| Serkalow ND | Alex O. | 665–12th St. SE, Salem, OR 97301 | (503) 588-2333 |
| Seymour ND | Sylvia M. | 65 W. Kagy, Suite B, Bozeman, MT 59715 | (406) 586-6464 |
| Shears ND | Barbara | 1023 N. Weber St., Colorado Springs, CO 80903-2421 | (719) 630-1108 |
| Shefrin ND | David K. | 12525 SW Third St., Beaverton, OR 97005 | (503) 644-7800 |
| Shelton ND | Laura A. | 1321 King St., Suite 1, Bellingham, WA 98226 | (206) 734-1560 |
| Shevins ND DHANP | Jody K. | 2880 Folsom St., #210A, Boulder, CO 80304 | (303) 449-8581 |
| Silbert DC ND | Barbara | 4 Federal St., Newburyport, MA 01950 | (508) 465-0929 |
| Simpson ND | Irene D. | 104 South West Ave., Arlington, WA 98223 | (206) 435-5232 |
| Small ND | Marian | 1523 East Madison, Seattle, WA 98122 | (206) 789-0188 |
| Smith ND | Lucy Maria | 1307 N 45th St., Suite 200, Seattle, WA 98103 | (206) 632-0354 |
| Smith ND | Andrea | 1614 SE 38th Ave., Portland, OR 97214 | (503) 255-4860 |
| Sodhi ND | Virender | 10025 NE 4th, Bellevue, WA 98004 | (206) 453-8022 |
| Soileau ND | John D. | 222 Front St., Fairbanks, AK 99701 | (907) 451-7100 |
| Sporn ND | Stephen | P.O. Box 9946, Berkeley, CA 94709 | (510) 524-5477 |
| Squillanty ND | Daniel W. | 4526–40th St., Long Island City, NY 11104 | (718) 729-1417 |

| | | | |
|---|---|---|---|
| Standish PhD ND | Leanna | 801–34th Ave., Seattle, WA 98122 | (206) 523-9585 |
| Stansbury ND | Jill | 506 E Main St., Battle Ground, WA 98604 | (206) 687-2799 |
| Starbuck JD ND | Jamison | Tillbury Bldg., 1123 SW Yamhill, Portland, OR 97205 | (503) 223-8909 |
| Stargrove ND | Mitchell B. | 4720 SW Watson Ave., Beaverton, OR 97005 | (503) 526-0397 |
| Stargrove ND | Lori Beth | 4720 SW Watson, Beaverton, OR 97005 | (503) 526-0397 |
| Stauber ND | Catherine | 1517 Bellevue Ave. #F, Seattle, WA 98122 | (206) 856-0603 |
| Steinberg ND | Mark W. | 1919 Broadway #206, Bellingham, WA 98225-3239 | (206) 738-3230 |
| Stern ND | Peter | 70 W. Coast Rd., Box 769, Redway, CA 95560 | (707) 923-2783 |
| Story ND | Stephanie D. | 244 West 12th Ave., Eugene, OR 97401-3434 | (503) 484-7272 |
| Stowell ND | Thomas W. | 1365 Englewood Ave., Suite 102, St. Paul, MN 55104 | (612) 644-4436 |
| Sullivan PhD ND | Andrea D. | 4601 Connecticut Ave. NW #6, Washington, DC 20008 | (202) 244-4545 |
| Summerland ND | Rhonda G. | P.O. Box 115, Index, WA 98266-0115 | (206) 793-1033 |
| Sumpter Phd ND | G. Roy | Iowa Wesleyan College, Mt. Pleasant, IA 52641 | (319) 385-6339 |
| Swan ND | Farra | 2435 E Southern, Suite 8, Tempe, AZ 85282 | (602) 820-0911 |
| Swope III, ND | Harry F. | 12522 Moorpark, Suite 108, Studio City, CA 91604 | (818) 508-4505 |

# T

| NAME | | ADDRESS | PHONE |
|---|---|---|---|
| Tallman ND | Nora J. | 10360 NE Wasco St., Portland, OR 97220 | (503) 252-8125 |
| Taub ND | Frederick J. | 6034 4th Ave., NW, Seattle, WA 98107-2108 | (206) 882-8080 |
| Taylor ND | Barry S. | 1505 Commonwealth Ave., Boston, MA 02135 | (617) 254-7700 |
| Thom DDS ND | Dickson | 4720 SW Watson Ave., Beaverton, OR 97005 | (503) 526-0397 |
| Tilgner ND | Sharol Marie | 3427 NE 72, Portland, OR 97213 | (503) 233-1174 |
| Timberlake ND | Patricia | 2625 SE Hawthorne Blvd., Portland, OR 97214 | (503) 238-9788 |
| Tonskamper ND | Gudrun | #304 1493 Johnston Rd., White Rock, BC V4B 3Z4 | (604) 536-1400 |
| Traub ND DHANP | Michael L. | 75-5759 Kuakini Hwy. #202, Kailua-Kona, HI 96740 | (808) 329-2114 |
| Tsoulas, ND | Katherine | 245 Highway 1, Carmel Valley, CA 93923 | (408) 629-6079 |
| Turner ND | Chris | 459 William Ave., Winnepeg, MB R38 0J5 | (204) 956-1555 |
| Turska ND | William A. | Highway 47, Box 69027, Mist, OR 97016 | (503) 755-2440 |

# U

| NAME | | ADDRESS | PHONE |
|---|---|---|---|
| Ullman ND DHANP | Robert W. | 17027 37th Ave. NE, Seattle, WA 98155-5426 | (206) 547-9665 |
| Upchurch ND | Robert C. | 1055 Ruth St., Suite 6, Prescott, AZ 86301 | (602) 778-4711 |
| Urbaniak, ND | Eva | 4262 Whitman Ave. North, Seattle, WA 98103 | (206) 632-7515 |
| Ure ND | Audrey | 105 Vancouver Ave., Penticton, BC V0H 1K0 | (604) 493-6060 |

# V

| NAME | | ADDRESS | PHONE |
|---|---|---|---|
| Varon ND | Michael B. | 11842 B 31st Place NE, Seattle, WA 98125 | (206) 367-7522 |
| Vickers ND | Edythe | 2348 NW Lovejoy St., Portland, OR 97210-3022 | (503) 233-1324 |
| Vishvanath ND | K. Pramila | 299 Green Farms Rd., Westport, CT 06880 | (203) 227-5534 |
| Vodicka, ND | H.G. | 2975 Overland, Burley, ID 83318 | (208) 678-8666 |

# W

| NAME | | ADDRESS | PHONE |
|---|---|---|---|
| Wagstaff ND | S Craig | #110 1890 Cooper Rd., Kelowna, BC V1Y 8B7 | (604) 763-3566 |
| Walden ND | Watson A. | P.O. Box 1940, Fort Myers, FL 33902-1940 | (813) 332-1611 |
| Walker ND | Donald C. | 3619 SE Division, Portland, OR 97202 | (503) 235-0333 |
| Wallace ND | Ed | P.O. Box 8918, Iowa City, IA 52245 | (503) 692-4096 |
| Waltz ND Dipl Ac | Ann | 322 2nd Avenue West, Suite B, Kalispell, MT 59901 | (406) 756-0308 |
| Warnock ND | William E. | 2 Harbor Rd., Shelburne, VT 05482 | (802) 985-8250 |
| Watrous ND | Letitia | W 1137 Garland Ave., Spokane, WA 99205 | (509) 327-5143 |
| Weintraub ND | Skye | 1628 Lawrence St., Eugene, OR 97401-3875 | (503) 345-0747 |
| Weiss ND | Ralph R. | 121 Genessee, Medford, OR 97504 | (503) 772-9713 |
| Weiss ND | Shandor | 238 E. Main St., Suite A, Asland, OR 97520-2857 | (907) 586-4325 |
| Williams ND | Deirdre | 157 Old Ridgefield Rd., Wilton, CT 06897 | (203) 761-9638 |
| Wilson ND | Kevin C. | 1049 SW Baseline, Suite 310, Hillsboro, OR 97123 | (503) 648-0484 |
| Wilson ND | Ralph W. | 23700 Edmonds Way Rd., Suite 102, Edmonds, WA 98026-8978 | (206) 776-5353 |
| Wilson ND | Rex | 8383 Wilshire Blvd., Suite 360, Beverly Hills, CA 90211 | (213) 653-8713 |

| Wing ND | L. Hope | 520 E 34th Ave. Suite 305, Anchorage, AK 99503-4116 | (907) 561-2330 |
| Wood ND | Cheryl L. | 7614–195th St. SW, Edmonds, WA 98020 | (206) 778-5673 |
| Wood ND | David B. | 7614–195th St. SW, Edmonds, WA 98026 | (206) 778-5673 |
| Woods ND | Heather | 5919–148th St. SW, Edmonds, WA 98026 | (206) 742-5598 |
| Wu ND | Sara | 4444 SW Corbett Ave., Portland, OR 97201-4207 | (503) 244-4003 |
| Wulsin ND MA Dipl Ac | William F. | 753 North 35th St., Suite 302, Seattle, WA 98103 | (206) 632-0411 |
| Wynsome ND | Rebecca | 3931 Bridge Way North, Seattle, WA 98103 | (206) 634-1600 |

# Y

| NAME | | ADDRESS | PHONE |
| --- | --- | --- | --- |
| Yaeger Jr ND | Carl Elliot | 1177 Martin Luther King Blvd., Miami, FL 33150 | (305) 759-6689 |
| Young ND | Thomas J. | 8909 Gravelly Lake Dr. SW, Tacoma, WA 98499-3109 | (206) 584-0341 |
| Young ND | Daniel | 21328 SE Alder Ct., Gresham, OR 97030 | (503) 667-6357 |

# Z

| NAME | | ADDRESS | PHONE |
| --- | --- | --- | --- |
| Zampieron ND | Eugene R. | 900 Straits Trnpk. Middlebury, CT 06762 | (203) 598-0400 |
| Zeff ND | Jared L. | 18540 NW Baker Creek Rd., McMinnville, OR 97128 | (503) 255-4860 |
| Zupa ND | Victoria | 179 Berkeley Place, Brooklyn, NY 11217c | (718) 622-7800 |